The man who created Hitler

The man who created Hitler

Joseph Goebbels

BY

VIKTOR REIMANN

Translated from the German by

Stephen Wendt

WILLIAM KIMBER · LONDON

Published in Great Britain in 1977 by
WILLIAM KIMBER & CO. LIMITED
Godolphin House, 22a Queen Anne's Gate
London SW1H 9AE

Dr Joseph Goebbels, published in Germany
by Fritz Molden Verlag,
copyright © 1971 by Verlag Fritz Molden
Translation copyright © 1976 by Doubleday & Company, Inc.

ISBN 0 7183 0155 2

Reproduced and printed by photolithography and bound
in Great Britain at The Pitman Press, Bath

Contents

List of Illustrations

All photographs courtesy of UPI.

Introduction

Hitler and Goebbels

Hitler was the product of an atmosphere of doom: God was dead or dying, and the West was about to perish. The authoritarian structures of the German Empire were gone, and new ones had not yet been formed: Chaos seemed about to descend. The individual became a mere cog in the wheel of the new industrialized society, a part of the enormous machinery that drove a faceless technocratic world with no will of its own. The individual's relationship to society, his responsibility to the community, were destroyed.

This atmosphere of doom led to panic. In this period of apocalyptic dusks and dawns, Hitler made his appearance, and Goebbels transformed him into a *Lohengrin* figure. The German people, deceived by the victorious nations, oppressed, abused, their national pride offended, had come to believe that despite their hard work in the face of growing economic difficulties, only radical solutions could save them. Since, however, the majority were conservative, they chose not communism but National Socialism, which protected established status symbols from the destructive zeal of certain intellectuals, yet offered something new: the legend of the Reich. This was only possible because Hitler was an Austrian; and the Austrians, especially since the founding of the Reich by Bismarck, had always had quite a different conception of the Reich from those who actually lived in it. The Austrians had always dreamed of a Reich that was as difficult to realize and as remote as the Kingdom of Heaven. They began to love even their own Reich, the monarchy, only after it had disintegrated. Little did the Germans suspect what they were inflicting on themselves when they adopted the Austrian, Hitler.

The Third Reich did not perish through political terror but

through an ignorance of historical reality. It is idle to speculate on how history would have judged Hitler if he had won the Second World War or kept the peace. Bismarck's words about Napoleon—"His good fortune in war made him aggressive and presumptuous"—apply even more to Hitler. Other points Hitler had in common with Napoleon were an appetite for military adventure, the desire to gain world political importance, and a megalomaniac ambition to become a second Alexander the Great or Julius Caesar. Hitler's substitution of a world of fantasy for the real world, and his denial of historical reality, caused his downfall; and to Hitler's undoing Goebbels made a decisive contribution. From the primitive, dark, instinctual elements in Hitler, Goebbels created a myth: the man of destiny, the new savior.

Hitler and Goebbels had much in common despite their differences of character. Both were disappointed and unacknowledged "artists" who sought to compensate for their frustration indirectly, through politics. In this field they became experts in terror. "Either the enemy walks over our dead bodies, or we over his," Hitler declared on June 27, 1925, in the Munich *Bürgerbräu* cellar. In their political actions both Hitler and Goebbels were guided almost exclusively by irrational factors; for them the real world had practically ceased to exist. Yet it was their differences rather than their similarities that enabled them to further each other's progress. Hitler was intuitive rather than intelligent. Goebbels was intelligent, but he was a born intellectual outsider, and this had a decisive influence on the development of his character.

Goebbels also had a tragic side, which singled him out among the other National Socialist leaders. Unlike Hitler, who was trying to change the political balance of power, Goebbels wished to change the social structure. While enjoying the amenities of the bourgeois world, Goebbels hated it and wanted revolution. Hitler made use of revolutionary slogans, but he was really a reactionary who declared the revolution over the moment he came to power. Goebbels dreamed of a national socialism; Hitler dreamed of Germany as a world extending from the Atlantic to the Urals.

The Hitler/Goebbels combination is perhaps unique in world history. Nietzsche maintained that schizophrenia, an exception among individuals, was the rule among nations. Only in the Third Reich did two highly schizophrenic individuals obtain unlimited power over a nation which, under pressure of catastrophic events, had itself become schizophrenic.

Without Hitler, Goebbels would probably have become a successful journalist or a parliamentary orator. Without Goebbels, Hitler would never have gained total power. By creating his Hitler myth, Goebbels offered the masses the savior for whom they yearned, endowed with the grace of God and led by providence safely through all perils. And it was Goebbels' Fuehrer myth that quelled Hitler's last doubts about his vocation for greatness. But perhaps the most astonishing factor of all is that Goebbels himself became a victim of the myth he himself had created. Toward the end of the war neither could exist without the other. They comforted and strengthened each other, they were both, perhaps unconsciously, consumed by the same death wish. In the last months of their lives death formed part of the setting of a grand finale that they tried to delay, not from fear of annihilation, but for fear that they would end on the rubbish heap of history.

The Hitler Movement

It was Goebbels who established the equation NSDAP = Adolf Hitler. Before Goebbels was appointed NSDAP head of propaganda, various ideas were current within the party as to how the state should be organized once they came to power. This changed when Goebbels introduced the name "Fuehrer" and made its use compulsory.[1] The word evoked a number of associations. It was borrowed from fascism. Mussolini was called Duce, the Italian equivalent of Fuehrer. In content, however, the two terms differed. The Duce was the head of the movement, but the Great Fascist Council had certain rights. In his function as Prime Minister, Mussolini was responsible to the King. The Italians might shout with typical southern abandon "Duce! Duce!," but it did not occur to them to see Mussolini as a kind of deity. For that they looked toward St. Peter's.

It was different in Germany. In the first years of the movement, Hitler's followers called him "Meister" (Master), which meant at once more and less than "Fuehrer." It had an artistic connotation to Wagner and his admirers. The element implying some sort of quasireligious order—and the elite of the NSDAP were in a sense an order—may already have been present, but as yet it did not play an important part.

Hilter had been leading the party since July 1921, when he was appointed chairman with unlimited powers. The term "Fuehrer" was only agreed upon at the end of 1931; it was at Goebbels' insistence that it became compulsory for the party, and later for the state. From the outset "Fuehrer" had a wider connotation than "Duce." It implied the fealty of the medieval vassal to his lord. Disloyalty to the

Fuehrer was considered a treasonable act and, after Hitler's seizure of power, the worst of crimes. Goebbels also gave the term a pseudoreligious content. He introduced the greeting "Heil Hitler" —thereby arousing the protest of several party bigwigs. "Heil" sounded more like an exorcism or magic formula than a greeting. It was designed to replace the customary *"Grüss Gott"* or *"Guten Tag"* ["Good Day"]. The personal Judaeo-Christian, Western God was dead, as Nietzsche proclaimed. But a people without a god could hardly be expected to make sacrifices that went against their own material well-being. A new god, a god for the masses, was needed to spur them on to greater efforts. Goebbels had read Le Bon's *Psychology of the Masses*. He knew that what the masses needed was a god and human sacrifice. For a god he gave them Hitler; as sacrificial victims he offered them first the "system" and later the Jews.

Goebbels was the first ever to succeed in deliberately building up a Fuehrer figure, a process regarded today by all parties as perfectly normal. At first he had to build up Hitler in the face of opposition from the press and radio; later, when he had the radio at his disposal, Goebbels was the first to make full use of its potential as an instrument of political propaganda.

True, Goebbels had in Hitler the ideal type to inspire a population yearning for a material and spiritual savior. Hitler was a gift for a propagandist who had learned all the tricks of the trade and invented quite a few of his own. All characteristics of the masses were combined in Hitler. He was moody, brutal, with an insatiable appetite for victory. He was unjust, unpredictable, hysterical, cruel, and barbaric. But he was also sentimental and capable of self-sacrifice, and therefore better than anyone else, even Goebbels, at seducing and intoxicating the crowd. He was part of them, he virtually merged with them physically; the masses could practically feel they were being saved; *Sieg Heil!* for the savior, Adolf Hitler, whom God has sent us.

But Hitler was not only *of* the masses, he was also above them, focusing in himself all their individual, and without him ineffectual, wills. Hitler's own will power was extraordinary, demoniacal; no one who had anything to do with him, friend or foe, ever denied it. He often imposed his will on others in spite of themselves. Many confessed to a feeling of paralysis in his presence. But there was little need to impose his will the hard way on his associates and, through them, on the German people. He preferred to use his powers of seduction, to let the irrational tip the scales in his favor. He wanted people to think: "It is senseless to oppose the Fuehrer, because he will turn out to be right in the end. He talks so convincingly. He is a man of destiny." Such an attitude implied a conscious or unconscious acceptance of the Fuehrer myth, Joseph Goebbels' most inspired, and most disastrous, creation.

The Fuehrer myth surpassed by far the Communist "personality cult." There, too, untiringly repetitive propaganda succeeded in transforming a tyrant into "Little Father Stalin." But Stalin's entourage submitted reluctantly and only because they were frightened men. The tyrant's cruelty did not, in fact, remain hidden from the masses. They followed the trials, they knew about the executions and the countless victims in Siberian labor camps. But, ignorant of the real reasons for the deportations and murders, they were not particularly troubled. Violent and cruel as Stalin may have been, his fellow Communists considered him as only a temporary figure, whose presence or absence could not impede the inexorable historical movement toward world revolution, world peace, a classless state, and ultimately a stateless society. For a true Communist, the party was all that mattered. Faith in the party transcended all moral considerations, all doubts.

For the true National Socialist, the party was Hitler, and Hitler was the party. Later on, Goebbels coined the slogan "Adolf Hitler is Germany, and Germany is Adolf Hitler." Though his entourage may have unconsciously feared Hitler, the main source of their devotion to him was not fear, but conviction. The party was Hitler's creation; its members were Hitler's creatures. It was not the party that was supreme, as communism was, but the Fuehrer. His person was taboo. Right up to the very end, Hitler's entourage put the blame for anything that went wrong on themselves, on the army, on industry, or on the Church, but never, even when it was obvious that Hitler himself had blundered, on the Fuehrer himself.

To the people Goebbels presented not only Hitler the mystic, but also Hitler the good and generous, sacrificing himself for the people, and, last but not least, Hitler the artist. Goebbels went to great lengths to cover up Hitler's cruelty. Goebbels frequently spoke of the bloodless revolution. He called the murder of Roehm and his comrades a necessary action to save the state from monsters prepared to drown Germany in a sea of blood. The additional murders of people who had nothing to do with Roehm's "conspiracy" were dealt with by a whisper campaign directed against Goering and Himmler, some of which, as it happens, was based on fact. But what mattered to Goebbels was not the truth, but rather, keeping Hitler's name spotlessly clean. As for the *Reichskristallnacht* (Reich Crystal Night), Goebbels took credit for it, even though the idea had been Hitler's. Hitler's name was never connected with the cruelties that were later committed—and they surpass all imagination. Those in the know spoke of "harsh necessity." The others blamed Himmler and the SS for whatever leaked out. "If only the Fuehrer knew" became a byword in the Third Reich. Its originator was very likely none other than Joseph Goebbels.

Hitler was rarely suspected of having anything to do with the disorganization, injustice, lawlessness, cruelty, and barbarity that occurred in Germany and in the occupied territories. Even many of Hitler's enemies hated Himmler, Goebbels, or Bormann more than they hated the Fuehrer himself. Everything possible was done to maintain the image of Hitler as the savior who would rescue Germany from the shackles of the November regime, ward off the danger of the Roehm "rebellion," cleanse Germany of the shame of the *Versailles Diktat* [Versailles Peace Treaty], and rescue the homeland from the clutches of Jewish world conspiracy. Hitler's character had to be kept above reproach, though he himself had shown few scruples on that account in *Mein Kampf*. But the man in the street never read books—a fact Goebbels counted on when he built up the Hitler image.

Goebbels forbade jokes about Hitler, laid a smoke screen over many of Hitler's personal weaknesses, and even got back Hitler's drawings and watercolors from dealers. Goebbels even banned the use of quotations from *Mein Kampf* or from Hitler's speeches without the permission of the Propaganda Ministry. Only certain selected private photographs were released for circulation: Hitler surrounded by children; Hitler with his dog in the mountains—the friend of children and animals, the lover of nature. Otherwise Hitler was seen only in full regalia as chief of state, the Fuehrer of the NSDAP, and in wartime as the supreme commander—every pose showing him as the greatest of his kind. There he stood among the field marshals and generals, wearing a simple military tunic without insignia, yet towering above them all.

The conclusions to be drawn were obvious. They were the aim of Goebbels' propaganda: Hitler towers over everything and everybody, he is the soul of everything. The harbinger of all glory, chosen by destiny.

The nature of the Nazi movement also helped Goebbels build up the Hitler myth. The NSDAP was not a party in the ordinary sense. It had a program, but the twenty-five points drawn up by Anton Drexler, Gottfried Feder, and Hitler could also be found in the programs of other parties. What was new was the demand that all department stores be nationalized and leased to small shopkeepers at low rents, thereby creating an "economically healthy middle class." All the other points had been made in the past by other parties: the unification of all Germans; the abolition of unearned incomes; the participation of the state in industry; and the abolition of ground rent. Even the demands for the abrogation of the peace treaties, as well as the demand for a strong, centralized state government, were hardly new. What was novel, and sometimes shocking, was the way some of the points were formulated: for example, the death penalty was no longer to be confined to treason, as it had been previously, but was henceforth also to apply to crimes of usury and financial malpractice. Another innovation: Jews were to be banned from working in government offices or in the press; they were also to be deprived of the right to apply for naturalization.

The spectacular rise of National Socialism was due not to its party program, but mainly to the spiritual unrest of the times; to the catastrophic economic situation, especially after the Wall Street crash on October 24, 1929; and to Goebbels' systematic buildup of the Hitler myth, which finally persuaded not only the masses but also industrialists, bankers, and financiers to see in Hitler the man of destiny.

The spiritual unrest in Germany became virulent after her defeat in the First World War. There had already been a malaise before the war as a consequence of growing mechanization and the accompanying decline of spiritual values. The de-Christianization of morals, together with a simultaneous growth of imperialist ideas, particularly in the economic field, nourished at one and the same time both chauvinism and antinationalist tendencies. This development was worldwide and not only confined to Germany. So it is understandable that the catastrophe of 1918 shook the German people deeply, particularly those who had fought in the war, made sacrifices, and endured hardships, only to find themselves cheated of everything. Those who had regarded war as senseless turned to the socialist parties, which preached a message of eternal peace and blamed the war on the Kaiser, the industrialists, the big landowners, and the bourgeoisie.

Others, unable to assimilate the idea of defeat, searched for its cause and the deeper meaning of the war.

The idealists found an answer in Ernst Jüngers' book, *In Stahlgewittern* (In Storms of Steel), published in 1920, in which the author claimed that war fostered a mental attitude of heroic realism. This "heroic attitude" became the slogan of a whole generation. It demanded a new nonbourgeois man and opposed liberalism as a political creation typical of the bourgeoisie. It was also against parliamentary government and the multiparty state.

Valuable support was also drawn from the works of Oswald Spengler, a follower of Nietzsche who rejected a civilization that had become materialistic. Spengler saw the great civilizations as organic entities possessing a life cycle of birth, maturity, and decline, ending with death. Once you had recognized this, you faced the future—your irrevocable destiny—with dignity and fortitude. Spengler's vision of the decline of Western civilization declared war on the dream of establishing justice and peace on earth. According to Spengler, man was a "zoological being," and the fate of the world was decided not by dreams of progress but by the will of the strongest and by the racial instinct.

Spengler saw the 1914–18 war as merely the beginning of an era of world wars. This meant that, in the future, armies and "Caesarian" forms of government would take over from parliament and multiparty systems. Spengler called the revolution of 1918 "dirty."

Such were the spiritual bases of the antiparliamentarian and antiliberal attitudes of a section of the middle-class intelligentsia. They, as well as their counterpart on the left, the Communists, developed a strong social conscience, condemning not only liberalism, but also shameless profiteering. In their search for an ideal, they thought they had found in Prussianism the desired combination of warrior and worker. Spengler wrote a book called *Preussentum und Sozialismus* (Prussianism and Socialism). Soon afterward he set down his historical view of antiquity, with the accent on Sparta rather than on Athens.

National socialism was eclectic: It took from everywhere whatever could be made to serve its purpose. It refused Spengler's vision of decline, but accepted his prophecy of a "Caesarian era" and made use of his condemnation of the "dirty" revolution of 1918 and the parliamentarian system. In *Mein Kampf,* Hitler reduced Spengler's evaluation of man as a "zoological being" to the simple formula of "eat or be eaten." Goebbels, too, borrowed Spengler's and Jünger's ideas for his propaganda, but quite deliberately robbed them of their spiritual content. He, too, dragged valuable ideas into the political mud. After reading Moeller van den Bruck's *Das Dritte Reich* (The Third Reich), Goebbels wrote in his diary: "Beware of intellectualizing the most vital things in life, politics or history. We are sick of political aesthetics; we don't want to know about it." Goebbels had adopted this attitude well before he became a supporter of Hitler. The heroic attitude, the warrior, the worker, Prussianism, socialism, antiliberalism, antiparliamentarianism, the dirty November revolution, the beginning of an era of wars, the will of the stronger, racial instinct, the coming Caesar, the Third Reich—all these terms can be found in some excellent books, created quite independently by their respective authors. But national socialism, and especially Goebbels, took them up conveniently, altered them, and disseminated them as their own original thoughts, so simplified that the meanest intellect could grasp them. Many people recognized, even in this simplified form, passages they had read in Nietzsche, Jünger, Spengler, Moeller van den Bruck, and even Ottmar Spann, but they only concluded that national socialism had the needs of the younger generation close to its heart.

National socialism failed to produce one single great work. There are two would-be important books—Hitler's *Mein Kampf* and Rosenberg's *Mythus des zwanzigsten Jahrhunderts'* (Myth of the Twentieth Century)—but both authors failed to produce any original thoughts. They borrowed from Nietzsche, Houston Stewart Chamberlain, as well as Spengler. As for Hitler, it was not even clear if he had actually read these authors, or had received the gist of their ideas from Rosenberg and Dietrich Eckart. In any case, Hitler found in Nietzsche and Chamberlain two basic arguments in support of his belief that he had been chosen by destiny. He also found in Nietzsche's *Geneologie der Moral* (Genealogy of Morality) and in Chamberlain's works the prophecy of a German *Herrenvolk* to come. From Nietzsche stem terms such as "the conscience of the beast of prey" and "the joyful monster" for whom murder, rape, arson, and torture represent merely a "student's prank." The *Herr* has nothing in common with the morality of the average man. He is above it. He is "beyond good and evil." Hegel had already rejected morality as an arbiter of historical action, and he indirectly influenced Karl Marx's evaluation of the historical actions of Communist revolutionaries.

Hitler appropriated Nietzsche's thoughts and acted accordingly, a fact Goebbels' propaganda did its best to conceal. Houston Stewart Chamberlain, who expanded the racialist theories in Gobineau's *Essai sur l'inégalité des races humaines,* stated in *The Foundations of the Nineteenth Century* that the German was the soul of civilization and that only two pure races were left: the Germans and the Jews. The rest were a chaotic racial mixture. The future belonged to the Germans as the coming *Herrenrasse.* They alone were the guardians of the heritage of Antiquity, of Greek art and philosophy, of Roman law, of the person of Christ, and would overcome the prevailing spirit of materialism to bring forth a grand new era for the whole world.

With such ideas Hitler could certainly do a thing or two. They sup-

ported his anti-Semitism, which he had in fact already adopted from
far more obscure sources during his early days in Vienna. These
ideas confirmed his faith in the Germans as a chosen people, and
since Chamberlain regarded Christ as an Aryan, exempted Hitler
from an open fight against Christianity, which might have proved
dangerous for the movement. Chamberlain's positive views—for example, the notion that the Jews were not inferior to, but merely different from, the Germans—Hitler chose to ignore. Seeing himself as
a Siegfried, he needed a dragon to slay. It was Richard Wagner's
works that had made the strongest impression on him. Wagner's
operas had enthralled Hitler in his student days, and that admiration
lasted to his dying day. In Wagner Hitler found the most perfect expression of the Germanic *Weltanschauung*. Wagner built up the
heroic crescendo to the powerful climax Hitler needed; the mystic
music allowed him to whip up or calm down the demoniacal forces
seething inside himself. When the end came, Wagner's music was
perhaps for Hitler a kind of opiate in his last bout of self-intoxication
—this time with death.

Hitler's *Mein Kampf,* though not read by many National Socialists,
acquired the importance of a political program for the movement,
while Rosenberg's *Myth of the Twentieth Century* succeeded, at
least in the years following its publication, in diverting the hostile
attention of national socialism's ideological enemies, both Jewish
and Christian, away from Hitler onto Rosenberg. The Rosenberg
book, which appeared in autumn 1930—too late to become a "text-
book" of the National Socialist *Weltanschauung*—was also based
largely on Nietzsche's and Chamberlain's ideas as well as on some
others taken from Jacob Burckhardt, Gibbon, Bachofen, Frobenius,
Spengler, Paul de Lagarde, and particularly from Hanns F. K.
Günthers' three books *Rassenkunde des Deutschen Volkes* (Raciology of the German People), *Rassenkunde Europa's* (Raciology of
Europe), and *Rassenkunde des Jüdischen Volkes* (Raciology of the
Jewish People).

Countless books provided Rosenberg with the theory that the Jews
were neither a race nor a religious community, but a people of mixed
races who presented a great danger for the cultural life of Europeans
and North Americans. The idea that the disappearance of Nordic
blood would seal the end of the Aryan race altogether was most
clearly formulated in Günthers' books.

Rosenberg's book is practically unreadable and often very confused. In any case, Rosenberg's ideas did not carry much weight
within the National Socialist state. Rosenberg wanted the party to
become an order. This in itself showed how far removed he was from

political reality. He did not realize to what extent Hitler cared for
power alone, only making use of a mass movement to secure it.
Goebbels' idea of creating a general staff consisting of first-rate men
was far more realistic and to the point than Rosenberg's blueprint for
founding an order (a notion which, incidentally, had been knocking
around in Himmler's head for some time, though perhaps in a different form).

Perhaps the fact that national socialism was a hodgepodge of all
sorts of borrowed ideas was one of the main causes of its success.
The same applies to its economic and social policy, which, again, explains the undeniable success of such measures as the organization of
labor, and the building of houses and roads. Economic conditions actually improved after 1933 for the great majority of the
German people, and this may explain why they accepted, at least in
the first two years, the loss of freedom of speech and press, and high-
handed, even illegal, acts.

Later, when the decline of freedom and law emerged in all its
brutality, the power of the German people to resist was paralyzed,
especially since the shortsightedness of the rest of the world had enabled Hitler to carry off considerable successes in his foreign policy.

Goebbels was well aware of the advantages of not giving national
socialism a reasoned and coherent basis. In a sea of borrowed concepts it was easier to swim in all directions. He therefore did his utmost to prevent Rosenberg's ideas from being accepted officially and
to stop them from spreading beyond a small circle.

But since the party program neglected social policy, Goebbels had
to find some substitute to inspire the masses, some idol whose prophecies they would listen to. He created this idol in Adolf Hitler. Hitler
was the symbol of the party. Through Hitler alone the party was held
together. His word was law, and once his voice had died, the life-
line of the party snapped.

1

From National Bolshevik to Hitlerite

Background and Youth

Paul Joseph Goebbels was born on the Odenkirchnerstrasse in the industrial town of Rheydt, on the left bank of the Rhine, on October 29, 1897. When he was three months old the family moved to a terrace house they had bought at 156 Dahlenerstrasse. Joseph's father, Friedrich Goebbels, worked in the local wick factory, W. H. Lennartz, and rose from office boy to manager.

His family described Friedrich Goebbels as an ambitious and serious man, but not without a sense of humor. Despite their straitened economic circumstances, there was laughter around the family table. The children benefited from their father's diligence and thrift. Friedrich Goebbels gave his sons a good, sound education, hoping they might achieve what he had missed himself, and rise from the *petite bourgeoisie* to the middle class.

Joseph's mother, Maria Katarina, was the daughter of a blacksmith, Johann Michael Odenhausen, and of his wife, Johanna Maria Coevers, who came from a working-class family. Maria Katarina was much loved by all her children, and particularly by Joseph. She was a simple, pious woman, who would not change her mode of living when her son's career soared upward, perhaps too steeply for her to grasp its full significance. If she ever trembled for the safety of her favorite son, she certainly never showed it, and she bore his death with the same dignity and calm with which she had accepted his triumphs.

Joseph had two brothers, Hans and Konrad, both older than he, and a sister, Maria, who was twelve years his junior. His second sister, Elisabeth, died in 1915, when he was eighteen.

Despite their simple background and modest means, the life of the Goebbels family seems to have been harmonious. The parents loved their children and did everything to give them a better chance in life than they had had themselves.

Joseph was particularly close to his mother, who always stood by him, even when the young Dr. Goebbels went in a direction that must have been disquieting for a pious person. For his father Joseph felt great respect, but the son's hostility toward the Catholic Church and his reluctance to pursue a "proper" profession brought about an estrangement. Goebbels later called his father a nice, well-meaning *petit bourgeois*.[1] Friedrich Goebbels died in 1929. He had lived to see his son rise to become the "Superbandit of Berlin"—and that could hardly have filled Friedrich with joy.

Joseph Goebbels' ancestors were peasants. His grandfather, Konrad Goebbels, was an estate manager from the district of Jülich.[2] The Goebbels family appeared in the village Titz for a hundred years under the name of Ackerer. Konrad Goebbels married Gertrud Margarete Rosskamp, who came from a peasant family in Beckrath, near Düsseldorf, and they moved to Rheydt, where Friedrich, father of Joseph Goebbels, was born. The rumor spread by Goebbels' enemies in the late twenties—that the Gauleiter of Berlin was a Jew whose real name was Göbbeles—was without any foundation. This rumor, incidentally, also penetrated to Nazi circles.

Goebbels' youth was not blessed by fortune. He had a limp, which was due to a clubfoot; his left leg was in irons. The true story of this malformation is not known; several versions exist. One is that he contracted polio at the age of four and was left with one leg shorter than the other. Another account[3] speaks of inflammation of the bone, which necessitated an operation on his left thigh when he was seven years old. Goebbels himself told a conference of Berlin party officials on June 10, 1927, that his clubfoot was the result of an accident in his childhood.[4] It is significant that all versions attempt to explain the malformation as the result of illness or accident. A man actually born with a clubfoot would not have been acceptable to the NSDAP. Since there is no known case of malformation in Goebbels' family history, one may perhaps assume that his was in fact not congenital; yet it cannot be entirely ruled out. It wouldn't matter one way or another had Goebbels not been the chief propagandist of a party that created a cult of physical beauty and regarded inherited malformation—like belonging to the Jewish race—as a kind

of capital crime. In any event, no one could fail to notice the irony
of the limping Goebbels preaching the National Socialist ideal of
Nordic beauty.

The boy's physical misfortune meant that he was excluded from
many normal activities—playing, running, fighting, and, later on,
dancing and sports. This probably created a certain number of complexes in him. He may have overcome them later by his intelligence,
but some of Goebbels' characteristics—his cynicism and his contempt
for mankind—probably took root then. This factor might also explain
his desire to "show them," to humble or dominate the physically
strong by means of his superior intellect, and by taking roughnecks
as his henchmen, and beautiful women as his bed partners. Since
Fate had marked him as inferior, he would return the compliment
by humbling those whom Fate had favored.

Quite apart from his physical malformation, Joseph was a rather
ugly child, with an enormous head set on a weedy little body. But
he was very bright and precocious—"Little Joe," as they called him
at home. He read books while the other children played. There were
not many books at home, but there were the two volumes of Meyer's
Encyclopedia, Mommsen's *History of Rome,* and a few volumes of
poetry—enough to expand his knowledge and stimulate his imagination. When he entered the *Gymnasium** his father gave him a piano.
Although during the winter months Joseph was obliged to practice
in an unheated parlor, he thoroughly enjoyed it, and he continued
to play when he had become a minister.

Although Joseph's brothers had also attended the *Gymnasium,*
only Joseph was allowed to stay on until he graduated. He was a
good pupil, and also showed some acting talent. His schoolfellows
nicknamed him "Ulex," short for Ulixes, after the wily Greek hero
of the Trojan wars. Goebbels later used the nickname as a pseudonym in his early journalistic efforts. When World War I broke out,
Goebbels volunteered and was duly rejected, upon which he retired
to his room. He refused nourishment for several days, though he
must have known that he had no real chance of being accepted for
military service. How much he was genuinely grieved, and how much
he was only play-acting, is open to conjecture.

Goebbels now had the advantage of being able to take an exam-
ination that was much simplified because of the war. As writer of the
best German essay, he was asked to give the graduation speech for
his class.

In his book *Vom Kaiserhof zur Reichskanzlei* (From Hotel

* The *Gymnasium* is equivalent to high school [translator's note].

Kaiserhof to the Reich Chancellery), Goebbels quotes the words of
his headmaster on that occasion: "Good speech, Goebbels, very good
speech! The content was excellent even—but you will never make a
good orator."[5]

His parents wanted Joseph to become a priest. Finance must have
played an important part in their deliberations, for there were no
financial worries attached to a theological career, and this was an
important factor in those hard times. Fortunately, material considerations conformed to their innermost wish. What could be more
beautiful than for their favorite son, physically underprivileged but
spiritually so talented, to stand at the altar, dominating the congregation, saying Mass and preaching to an attentive crowd? After all,
the Goebbels lived in the Rhineland, one of the most powerful Catholic centers in Germany. Here some of the splendor and glory of the
prince-electors of the past still survived. Joseph Goebbels, having a
highly developed theatrical sense and a strong desire for the lime-
light, was not entirely opposed to fulfilling his parents' wish. The
influence of the Catholic Church provides yet another similarity between Hitler and Goebbels. Hitler also went to a monastic school,
in Lambach in Upper Austria, and was marked by similar early impressions. The Catholic Church, with its incomparable organization,
its disciplined education, its effective propaganda, its splendor, and
its soul-catching technique, served Hitler and Goebbels alike as an
example in many an enterprise.

It is not known what finally decided Goebbels to disregard his
parents' wish. He registered as a student in the Faculty of Philosophy
of the University of Bonn for the summer semester of 1917. First
he read classical philology, but soon he changed to German literature.
In June 1917 he was called up by the Army for clerical work, but was
soon released. He intended to take up his studies again but was faced
with the old problem: How was he going to pay his way? During the
last semester he had somehow managed to balance his budget by
giving lessons. But that was too uncertain and took too much of his
time. He decided to seek other sources of income and turned to the
Catholic Church.[6] He chose the Albertus Magnus Society, a Catholic
institution, which among its other activities gave help to penurious
Catholic students. Goebbels had been one of the most brilliant students in religious instruction, as his teacher, Johannes Mollen, who
later became a bishop, readily confirmed. The priest of St. Maria's
in Rheydt knew the Goebbels as a pious family who had always done
their Christian duty. What was really decisive, however, in winning
Goebbels a grant was his membership in the Catholic Students' Association, Unitas, which he joined upon entering the university.

Members of this association—they did not wear specific colors, like most other student associations—undertook to go to church regularly and to advance Catholic thinking. Their adversaries nicknamed them the "Rosary Brothers." But their influence was considerable. It took Goebbels only one year to be promoted to *Fuchsmajor*† in the summer of 1918, with the task of instructing younger candidates, the "foxes." Yet the following winter Goebbels left the association. The Albertus Magnus Society lent Goebbels 180 marks free of interest for four successive semesters, including the winter semester 1919–20—for a total of 960 marks. Though he had undertaken to furnish the society with regular progress reports, he did not bother to do so once he had received the last installment.

Two years after he graduated, Goebbels transferred 10,000 marks to the society in repayment of its loan. This was in May 1923, at the height of the inflation that had already engulfed Germany. The 10,000 marks were now equivalent to 109 pfennigs in gold, or a little more than a single gold mark. The word "gratitude" never had been, and never would be, part of Goebbels' vocabulary.

As soon as the currency was stabilized, the Albertus Magnus Society credited to Goebbels' account two reichsmarks repaid, and in December 1925 they sent him a bill for 516 reichsmarks still owing. Goebbels refused to pay. The society obtained judgments in various courts, and finally, in 1929, compelled Goebbels to pay four installments of 100 marks each, the last to be paid in February 1930.[7]

Goebbels continued his studies from the summer of 1917 to the spring of 1921, at the universities of Bonn, Freiburg, Würzburg, then once again at Freiburg, and at Munich. During the winter semester 1920–21 he was at Heidelberg University, where he received his Ph.D. In addition to his loan from the society, Goebbels received 50 marks a month from his father. His mother mailed him regular food parcels, and occasionally sent him money she had saved up secretly. In Heidelberg, when he was no longer receiving payments from the Albertus Magnus Society, he was obliged to give lessons and do occasional clerical work. Though he was undeniably short of money during his university studies, he never had to go hungry—no more than Adolf Hitler had had to in his early years in Vienna.

In Freiburg, during the summer of 1918, Goebbels met his first great love, Anka Stahlherm, a pretty blond student from Recklinghausen who came from a good family. The astonishing thing was that Anka fell in love with Goebbels: He was small and weedy,

† "Fox major" was equal to an officer rank [translator's note].

narrow-shouldered, weighed around 100 pounds, and walked with a limp. But although he was no Adonis, he had his points—long, transparent hands, a baritone voice, and deep brown eyes. He liked to play with his hands and draw attention to them with big grand sweeping gestures; his voice was sensual. Lida Baarova, a famous and beautiful film actress of Czech origin, tells how his voice electrified her and sent shivers down her spine. Goebbels' eyes had a strange magic. "He seemed all eyes," says Else Janke,[8] his second great love. And he certainly had great charm. The first impression was perhaps of an ugly charm, but it improved when he spoke. And he could be overwhelmingly amiable, particularly with beautiful women. He seemed to prove that spirit could triumph over body. According to a note in his diary dated April 16, 1926, his love affair with Anka ended in the winter of 1919. It had lasted about six months. Shortly thereafter Anka married a lawyer. She later divorced him and went to see her ex-lover, who in the meantime had become a minister, to ask for a job. He found her a post in the weekly paper *Die Dame*. Perhaps Anka had a sense of humor or liked to boast—but in any case, she showed her colleagues a volume of Heinrich Heine's *Buch der Lieder* [Book of Songs] that Goebbels had given her in the faraway days of their love affair, with a duly passionate inscription.[9] Naturally, the story got around and was rather embarrassing. The same man who had had all racially impure literature consigned to the flames had himself once admired Heine, the Jew, poet of all lovers.

The Prodigal Son

The time Goebbels spent studying in Munich in the autumn of 1919 was decisive for his spiritual development. He became acquainted with the literature of the left. The world of Marx, Engels, and Lenin, as well as the thoughts of Rathenau, touched him more than the National Socialist *Weltanschauung* in Rosenberg's *Myth of the Twentieth Century,* a book he probably did not read very thoroughly. This leftist literature was given to him by his friend Richard Flisges, whom he had already known in Rheydt. Goebbels was attracted by Flisges, who possessed all that nature had withheld from Goebbels himself. Richard Flisges had a splendid appearance; he was a "hero." He had been decorated several times in the war and had been wounded several times. After a serious injury to one of his arms, he was discharged in 1917. He found it difficult to integrate himself into civilian life again. He tried to get a university degree and failed, but instead of blaming himself, he blamed the antiquated educational system. The demobilized hero turned to pacifism. He began to hate the bourgeois society. He and others like him—the young, frustrated generation—held the bourgeoisie responsible for everything that had gone wrong before and after the war, including the abortive attempts at revolution in 1918–19. Deep in his heart Flisges was an anarchist, though his political arguments had a Marxist veneer. He thought he had found a substitute for the lost faith of his childhood in Dostoevsky's religious mysticism.

Goebbels' passion for Flisges was understandable. This man, outwardly perfectly formed by nature, was inwardly feeble. He could not derive any clear conclusions from his study of Marxist works, let alone sufficient stimulation for an active political life. Nor had he received any real religious impulses from Dostoevsky's writings. Flisges' nihilism was not the result of painful thinking, not a harsh but courageous *Weltanschauung*. It was the expression of his own disillusionment, his own pessimism and disgust with the world. He found in Goebbels an understanding comrade-in-arms. Joseph, too, was disappointed, felt cheated by Fate, and looked upon the political and social scene with profound pessimism. Under Flisges' influence, and influenced by the books Flisges had given him to read, Goebbels began to turn away from the faith in which he had been born and raised. We learn this from letters exchanged between Goebbels and his father.[10] In a letter, Joseph informed his father that he no longer believed in the Catholic faith, at the same time begging his father not to curse the "prodigal son" who had left his parents and lost his way in the wilderness. In his letter to Joseph his father put only two questions: "Have you written, or do you intend to write, books that do not conform to the Catholic faith?" and "Do you intend to take up a profession that would not befit a Catholic?" He assures Joseph that his Catholic faith forbids him to curse his son. On the contrary: "I am praying for you, as I have done often before."

But Goebbels' inner decision was not followed up by action. He never actually left the Catholic Church. Torn as he was between different loyalties, the loss of his faith was, no doubt, an important experience for Goebbels. But in order to escape the narrow confines of the parental home and his own nature, still not free of bourgeois tendencies, he had to attack the bourgeoisie at its strongest root, the Christian religion. This had been the classic method of all revolutionaries before him, for there can be no revolution without breaking down the barriers set up by Christianity to human passions and earthly desires for salvation—barriers the bourgeoisie will always uphold, notwithstanding their own sins and perversions. And Goebbels began to feel himself a true revolutionary, even if for the time being only in mind. Before long he would be an active political revolutionary. But later, after Goebbels had made his spiritual genuflection to Hitler, all that was left of the great revolutionary were his attacks on the "bourgeoisie" and the "ambitious power politics of the Church." The revolutionary Goebbels had reverted to his faith, with the sole difference that Adolf Hitler had been substituted for the Christian God.

But even while he was still a revolutionary, Goebbels was of a different kind from the great revolutionaries of the left. Lenin, when he broke with the Russian Orthodox faith at the age of sixteen under the influence of his pious father's death, had exorcised all religious feeling in himself; Goebbels, on the other hand, went on intoxicating himself with religious emotion. The figure of Christ remained for him the guiding star of humanity. Nearly all the productions of Goebbels' literary period returned in one form or another to the theme of Christ. Goebbels had only turned away from the organized Church. "The confessional," he wrote in *Michael*, "has failed abysmally. It is no longer in the forefront, but has been pushed into the background, and from there it still terrorizes the emergence of a new religious will. Millions wait for this, but their yearning remains unfulfilled. . . . But the day will come when we shall have a magnificent religious awakening too."[11]

In the autumn of 1920 Goebbels arrived in Heidelberg full of Marxist revolutionary notions, Rathenau's plans for world improvement, and Dostoevsky's ideas for saving mankind. Here he met a professor who introduced him to a rather different conception of the world, Friedrich Gundolf, whose original Jewish name was Gundelfinger. Gundolf was one of the foremost literary academics of his time, with the special aura surrounding all the privileged persons forming the intimate circle around Stefan George. George's personality had an astonishing influence on the science of his time. Gottfried Benn[12] finds an explanation for this in the fact that at the time of Stefan George's first publication—a volume of poems, which appeared in 1898—scientists were searching for the firm foothold they had lost through the rapid development of the natural sciences and which philosophy and theology could no longer provide. "But George," says Benn, "was the nucleus around which revolved Spengler, Curtius, Troeltch, Frobenius, Scheler, Worringer, Keyserling, Bertram, and Schuler." Benn should have also mentioned Gundolf; he probably omitted to do so because at the time that Benn's book *Art and Power* appeared (1934), Gundolf's name was already on the blacklist.

Gundolf's works, his Goethe and George biographies, his books *Caesar, the Story of Fame* and *Shakespeare and the German Spirit,* and his ten volumes of Shakespeare translations all breathed the spirit of George. They all expressed a reverence for form, which for George was not just an aesthetic problem but a faith, well-nigh a creation in itself since, according to George, creation passed through form. George's attitude was antiliberal: For him the age of liberalism was "covered with the spittle of the lowest kind of fawning," as he wrote in his last work, *The New Reich,* published in 1919. In this we find the vision of the future Fuehrer who possesses "the chaste, clear barbaric eye" and who says about himself "I am sent with torch and steel to harden you." The world of Stefan George was, indeed, diametrically opposed to that of the left, but Goebbels found in it a poetical reaffirmation of the message he had read in the political, social, and economic writings of the left, announcing that the age of liberalism was gone forever. In all walks of life, in the economic field, in art, religion, and in politics, the senile bourgeois era was tottering toward its end. Something new had to come.

The spiritual and political life of this era was filled with prognostications and prophecies. Had the savior actually been found in Lenin, and the way by which mankind would be saved in Russian communism? Or had one still to search for an answer? These questions occupied Goebbels, as they did so many others of his generation who had seen a war lost and a revolution miscarried, and whose disappointment had turned to hatred against the intolerable world in which they lived. It was only after great heartsearchings and many disappointments that Goebbels became a cynic and signed a pact with the devil.

For the subject of his dissertation, Goebbels chose, on Gundolf's advice, "The dramatist Wilhelm von Schütz. A contribution to the history of the Romanticist drama." Wilhelm von Schütz, a little-known dramatist of the romantic period, had embraced Catholicism, as had so many of his colleagues who belonged to the same circle. Goebbels called von Schütz's renegade zeal "tendentiously Catholic."[13] Goebbels' alienation from the Catholic Church had begun to manifest itself.

Goebbels graduated on April 21, 1921, as doctor of philosophy. His joy was slightly marred by worry about his professional future. As has already been mentioned, he had been obliged to give lessons while studying at Heidelberg. He had also written articles and essays, and submitted them to the *Berliner Tageblatt,* of which he was a regular reader; he particularly admired the Monday lead editorial, written by the editor-in-chief, Theodor Wolff.

Goebbels' articles were rejected, and when he applied for a permanent position on the editorial staff of the *Berliner Tageblatt,* he was turned down. Further refusals followed his applications for jobs as reader and *Theater Dramaturg* [resident literary adviser. Translator's note] and to complete his misery, the Ullstein publishing house returned the script of his novel *Michael.*

After all these failures, Goebbels went home to Rheydt to an unenthusiastic reception from his father and two brothers, who looked with some suspicion upon their learned brother, the *Herr Doktor,* who had once again become a burden. While continuing with his writing, Goebbels managed to earn some money by giving lessons and doing occasional jobs. He spent his nights writing poems, plays, and articles, and, last but not least, his novel *Michael.*

He had found a new love, Else Janke, and they frequently met his old school friend Prang and Prang's girl friend Alma. Goebbels, Prang, and the two girls, both teachers who also happened to be friends, would often make up a foursome and have heated discussions. At the beginning they were joined by Richard Flisges. They would all gather around a bottle of wine in an apartment belonging to Prang's father, a Freemason and factory owner. However, neither love, writing, nor discussions could gloss over the depressing fact that Goebbels had no definite occupation. He noticed the questioning looks of his father and his brothers. Though insolent by nature —and later he learned only too well how to exploit this facility ruthlessly—Joseph Goebbels could not help feeling mortified when he read in the expressions on his father's and brothers' faces that he was a failure. The two years following his graduation were probably the most humiliating in Goebbels' life. He spoke of suicide, and appointed one of his brothers his literary executor.[14] At the same time he escaped into his literary outpourings, and the pity he lavished on his heroes was, in fact, the pity he felt for himself.

Michael: a German Fate

Goebbels' literary output from 1921–24 included several plays, most of them unfinished: one about Christ, *Judas Iscariot;* another, *Heinrich Kämpfert;* and plays called *The Sowing* and *The Wanderer.* *The Wanderer* was produced on November 6, 1927, by the National Socialist experimental stage company in a matinee performance of a memorial service at the Wallner Theater in Berlin. This play, consisting of a prologue, fourteen scenes, and an epilogue, borrows its form from Dante's *Divine Comedy.* Just as Virgil leads the Italian poet through Inferno, so the wanderer leads the despairing author "over the heights and through the valleys of German history." A repeat performance given five days later was to be the last.[15]

Early in the twenties Goebbels was obsessed by the idea of his literary vocation. In *Michael* he described his powerful creative impulse:

"July 15: I am lying in bed sleepless, wrestling with the powers that press upon me.

"There is in me rebellion, indignation, revolution. An idea grows inside me to grandiose proportions. Danse macabre and resurrection."

"July 18: I feel as if I no longer belong to this world. I rave in a state of intoxication, in a dream, in anger.

"I divine new worlds.

"Farawayness grows in me.

"Give me the strength, Lord, to say what I suffer."

At first his novel *Michael*—a mere 160 pages—was not published. It was written in the form of a diary and described the spiritual evolution of a young German searching for the meaning of life, for God, for the sense of mankind's true task and calling. Since the German universities with their antiquated system failed to give him an answer, he turns to the common people, becomes a miner, and dies down in the mine, mortally wounded by a falling rock. The story is frequently interrupted by reflections on every kind of topic. These aphorisms are neither particularly original nor well formulated. Most of them are stylistically reminiscent of Nietzsche, though they are sadly lacking in Nietzsche's language and wealth of thought.

There are four main figures in this novel: Michael; Herta Holk, his girl friend; Iwan Wienurowsky, a Russian student; and Michael's school friend, Richard. Michael has much of Goebbels' mental outlook, but Michael's appearance is that of his friend, Richard Flisges, to whom the novel was dedicated. (Flisges had actually died in an accident in a mine in Bavaria in July 1923.)

This composite figure of Goebbels and Flisges is hardly convincing. A Michael who thinks like Goebbels can never be a glorious hero but only pose as such:

"June 20: I put my helmet on, draw my sword and declaim Liliencron.

"Sometimes I am overcome by a yearning to be a soldier, to stand guard.

"One must be a soldier always.

"A soldier serving the revolution of one's people."

On the other hand, a Michael who looks like Flisges cannot think like Goebbels. He will be by nature much more straight, more simple, even if he indulges in his own pessimism, as Flisges used to. Goebbels' failure to present a convincing hero came from his inability to create a living figure rather than a projection of his own wish fulfillment.

While Michael expresses the thoughts of Goebbels, Iwan Wienurowsky presumably represents those of Flisges. But Iwan, too, lacks a clear outline. He remains a cliché—a Russian as Goebbels would imagine him after reading too much Dostoevsky. But compared with Dostoevsky's deep psychological insight and the profound and tortured revelation of his hero's guilt, Goebbels' attempt looks like scraps picked up from the floor of the master's workshop.

Michael liberates himself—as any good German would—from Iwan's influence. And Wienurowsky's last letter to Michael strikes the note of things to come:

"July 8: I wish Russia had created a new world. Rome has come to an end. The new Rome: Russia . . . for me you represent the German youth about to liberate itself, you are strong, but we will be stronger!

Michael: Yes, we will cross swords. The German and the Russian man. Germans and Slavs!"

Michael's school friend, for whom Fritz Prang served as a model, plays only a minor part. He becomes a bourgeois, so Michael loses all interest in him.

"July 2: The political bourgeoisie has no significance and does not wish to have any. All they want is to live, and live in a primitive way. That is why they will perish. I hate the bourgeois because he is a coward and no longer prepared to fight. He is just an animal in a zoo, that is all."

In Michael's view the bourgeoisie should be thrown on the rubbish dump of world history and be replaced by the working class. After his attack on the bourgeoisie, Michael writes:

"July 2: The working class has a mission to fulfill, particularly in Germany. It has to liberate the German people within Germany, as well as in her relationship with the outside world. This is a mission of universal importance. If Germany perishes, then the light of the whole world will go out.

"Soldiers, students, and workers will build the new Reich. I was a soldier, I was a student, I want to be a worker. I must pass through all three stages to show the way. . . . The new man will be born in the workshops and not in books."

Alas, Goebbels missed the first and the third stages. He had never been a soldier nor a worker. He was excluded from the former by his physical shortcomings; and as for the latter, it soon would have spoiled his well-groomed hands.

Michael was probably written at the end of 1923 and the beginning of 1924. Its original title was: *Michael Voormann: The Diary
of a Man's Fate*. It was published only in 1928, not, as Goebbels had
wished, by Ullstein, but by the National Socialist party's official publishers. Both title and content had undergone changes. In the title
the name Voormann was dropped and *a Man's Fate* had become
the Fate of a German. The differences between the original (1923)
and the published version (1928) were probably due to the fact that
Goebbels had met with Hitler and had meanwhile risen to a high
position in the party. The numerous anti-Semitic outbursts in the
published version could hardly have been included in the original
submitted for publication to the Jewish Ullstein publishing house.
In many places one can trace the influence of Hitler's *Mein Kampf,*
which was still unpublished when Goebbels wrote the original
Michael. In the original Goebbels had addressed himself to mankind. In the published version mankind in general was replaced by
the Germans in particular. The wings of the idealist have been
clipped. Before us stands a meekly conforming member of the
party.

Michael is the work of a beginner, with all the corresponding
weaknesses. It was Goebbels' first attempt at creating a hero. But
Goebbels absolutely lacked any true feeling for nature and any real
curiosity about the intricacies of the human soul. *Michael* is no more
than a collection of slogans, not even particularly well presented.
But while Goebbels strained to create the book of a true writer, he
was neglecting the talent that later made him into the greatest
propagandist of all time. Goebbels' new religion was a concoction
of Faust, Christ, and Zarathustra. Three books are found in Michael's
drawer after his death: Goethe's *Faust,* the Bible, and Nietzsche's
Zarathustra. The Bible was always an important element in Goebbels'
strange *Weltanschauung*. And it is perhaps significant that he left this
sentence, "I took with me two books, the Bible and *Faust,*" in the
published version. The Bible has first place, and *Zarathustra* isn't
even mentioned. It is surprising that no critic has ever remarked on
the dominant part the image of Christ plays in Goebbels' *Michael*.

"August 12: . . . in the evening I sit in my room and read the
Bible. From afar I can hear the pounding of the sea.

"I lie awake for a long time and think of the quiet pale man of
Nazareth."

The figure of Christ remained powerfully present in Goebbels'
imagination to the very end. Even quite late he was still planning a
book about Christ: "I cannot think of a more fascinating personality
in history than Christ. . . . I know no more powerful speech than
the Sermon on the Mount. Every propagandist ought to study it."[16]

The Resistance Movement in the Ruhr

Different versions exist of Goebbels' activities in 1923. The German
Fuehrer Dictionary of 1934–35 writes: "[Goebbels] first fights in the
student movement, then under an assumed name, forms the first
local groups in the Rhineland and in the Ruhr right under the noses
of the occupation forces. The little town of Hattingen in the Ruhr
was their headquarters. In 1924 he was expelled by the Occupying
Power." This version was strictly adhered to by all biographers writing in the Third Reich.

In January 1923 French and Belgian forces entered the Ruhr. The
reason given was that the Germans had fallen behind with the delivery of goods stipulated in the so-called London ultimatum of May
4, 1921. This agreement permitted Germany to pay a part of her war
reparations, which amounted to 123 billion goldmarks, in goods, up
to 26 per cent of her yearly exports. When Germany fell behind,
France denounced this as an act of sabotage. The legal foundation for
France's action was extremely weak. For the Germans, the French
entry into the Ruhr was nothing less than a brutal act of war perpetrated in peacetime. France's own allies, the United States, the
United Kingdom, and Italy, reacted to the Franco-Belgian interven-
tion with little sympathy. It brought about the first, though still rather
mild, change of mood in world opinion toward postwar Germany.

The then Reich Chancellor, Wilhelm Cuno, acting in agreement
with the trade unions, ordered passive resistance, which led to inflation and the collapse of the German currency. Cuno's successor,
Gustav Stresemann, was therefore compelled to give up resistance.
Active resistance groups had been formed in the occupied territories.
Several acts of sabotage had occurred on supply lines, as well as attacks in the rear of the French and Belgian troops. Among the resistance fighters, one figure stood out on account of his brilliance and
bravery. His name was Albert Leo Schlageter. He was captured by
the French after a few months, condemned to death, and executed
on May 26, 1923, in the Golzheimer Heide near Düsseldorf.

Most Germans, no matter what party they belonged to, saw
Schlageter as a martyr paying for the resistance of a defenseless
people against a victorious oppressor. Goebbels made Schlageter into
a National Socialist, although Schlageter was never a member of the
NSDAP. There is no proof whatever of the posthumous claim that
Schlageter had been a member of the Berlin NSDAP. It was probably just one of Joseph Goebbels' inventions. But Goebbels could
scarcely have picked a better man than Schlageter for the party hero.

Schlageter was not a casualty in the internal political battle with Marxists, as some SA men were. He was not a victim of a bloody quarrel among Germans, which was viewed with little sympathy by most of the population. Schlageter died in the fight for the freedom of his people and his country against high-handedness and oppression by Germany's archenemy, France. Yet Goebbels served Schlageter ill with his exalted propaganda, which only darkened, in many German hearts, the memory of a true patriot.

In short, it is highly unlikely that Goebbels took any active part in the resistance in the Ruhr. A man made conspicuous by deformity was hardly suitable for a resistance fighter. He had no military or athletic training, no knowledge of sabotage. He would only, in fact, have been a burden on all the others.

The German Fuehrer Dictionary says that Goebbels acted under an assumed name. But this pseudonym is nowhere mentioned. And surely, Goebbels would have seen to it that it was mentioned in the history books of the Third Reich if there had been any legends, let alone deeds, attached to it. We can even exclude the possibility that Goebbels and Schlageter ever met. In fact, Else Janke and Fritz Prang[17] tell us quite another story: Goebbels, they say, had been employed in the Cologne branch of the Dresdener Bank at the time of the resistance in the Ruhr. When after eight months Goebbels tired of his position, Prang actually got him a job, he tells us, at the stock exchange in Cologne. But this statement should be taken with a certain amount of caution.

Fritz Prang[18] claimed to have guided Goebbels toward politics. Himself a member of the NSDAP since 1922, Prang brought his friend Joseph National Socialist newspapers and pamphlets to read. The National Socialist party program, with its twenty-five "theses"— Hitler borrowed the term from Luther when expounding them for the first time on February 24, 1920, in the Festsaal of the Münchener Hofräuhaus—could have hardly surprised Goebbels who, after all, had read Marx and Lenin. He must have been moved, however, by its nationalist appeal, to which he would readily respond, particularly after the events in the Ruhr.

The failure and sudden end of the Ruhr resistance contributed to a certain extent to the development of the NSDAP, leading indirectly to the so-called national rising that General Ludendorff and Hitler carried out according to a plan drawn up by Lieutenant Colonel Kriebel, marching together to the Feldherrnhalle in Munich on November 9, 1923. There it all ended in a complete fiasco. No words of abuse were ever strong enough for Hitler and Goebbels for all the German revolutions that had taken place in 1918. Yet the national revolution of Hitler and Ludendorff was the most miserable of the lot.

It is not such a rare occurrence in history to see failure transformed
into success. Hitler's 1923 Munich putsch ended miserably, yet he
personally emerged in court as the victor. The putschmaker Hitler
had been beaten; the agitator Hitler had won an important battle. As
if mesmerized, the judges and the public listened to a man who
simply inverted the roles, displaying an overriding arrogance as he
stood there, the accuser and not the accused. "The judges of this
state," his voice rang through the courtroom, "may condemn us for
what we have done. History, the goddess of a higher truth and a
better law, will one day smile and tear up its verdict, and pronounce
us free of all guilt."[19] The public and even the majority of nationalistic Germans had condemned the putsch, but Hitler won back many
sympathizers and, indeed, added new ones by his speech in court.
He also won the authority he needed to become head of the party,
once he was set free. Goebbels, who must have read the speech,
must have been struck not only by its nationalist verve but even
more by its remarkable psychological assessment of the nationalist
and bourgeois mentality. In fact, Hitler's performance on this occasion served Goebbels as a model, later, for his own performances in
court where he even managed to surpass his master. Hitler had at
least respected the dignity of the court, but Goebbels transformed
German courts into rallies where the accused would turn accuser
and attack the "system," supported by shouting and laughter from
the unruly crowd. Hitler's highly dramatic performance was turned
into farce, with Joseph Goebbels as the star performer.

As a consequence of the Munich putsch in November of 1923,
the NSDAP was dissolved and declared illegal. Goebbels could no
longer hope to work for the party. Hitler could be of no help—he was
confined to the Landsberg fortress. There he wrote the National
Socialist gospel, *Mein Kampf.*

Joining the Völkische‡

On January 23, 1924[20] Goebbels applied for the post of editor
of the *Berliner Tageblatt,* an indication that he was, at that time,
still politically open-minded. He was prepared to work on the
"Jewish" *Berliner Tageblatt,* which identified itself with the Weimar
Republic. Yet he seemed no less keen to join the national opposition,
which had declared war on the same Weimar Republic. Had it not
been for the fact that the gentlemen of the *Berliner Tageblatt* re-

‡ Völkische was a special name for the right-wing nationalist groups [trans-
lator's note].

turned Goebbels' article, probably unread, Goebbels might possibly have become editor of the *Berliner Tageblatt* and would probably have made a very able journalist, a typical left intellectual who would have fought Adolf Hitler and the National Socialists, including their anti-Semitism, with a brilliant and poisonous pen. There were, after all, quite a few talented young journalists trying to place articles in Berlin at that time, many of them more deserving than the beginner from Rheydt. The gentlemen of the *Berliner Tageblatt* would have been surprised to learn that a mere ten years later their fate would be in the hands of that same beginner.

Since the *Berliner Tageblatt* denied Goebbels the chance of becoming a journalist, why should he not try to get that same chance from the political right? Fritz Prang[21] tells us how in mid-August 1924 he took Goebbels with him to Weimar, where various nationalist groups met to form a common block for the impending Reichstag elections. Three personalities stood out at this conference. First, General Erich Ludendorff, former chief of staff to Hindenburg, and after 1916 first quartermaster general of the Supreme Command, responsible for German military conduct in the First World War. Although it was he who, on September 29, 1918, had urged the German government to ask the Western powers for an armistice, he employed at this conference in 1924 the same language as Corporal Hitler. He spoke of the "November criminals," of the stab in the back inflicted by treacherous politicians on an undefeated army.

The second important personality was Albrecht Graefe-Goldebec, who had also taken part in the putsch and the march on the Feldherrnhalle. He had, together with some other members of the Reichstag, left the *Deutschnationale Volkspartei* (German National People's party) and founded the *Deutschvölkische Freiheitspartei* (German *Völkisch* Freedom party). He must have regretted this step later; his party was reduced to complete insignificance, while Hugenberg's German National People's party rose at the 1924 elections from 44 to 103 members, to remain the second-biggest party in the Reichstag until 1930.

The third nationalist leader at this conference was Gregor Strasser, who emerged more and more during Hitler's imprisonment as the spokesman of the NSDAP, which although illegal was still very much in evidence.

Before his transfer to Landsberg, Hitler wrote to Alfred Rosenberg asking him to lead the party.[22] He knew very well that he had picked the weakest organizer among the National Socialist leaders, incapable of carrying out the job even in far more favorable circumstances. Hitler quite deliberately avoided giving the leadership of the

party into the hands of a man whose personality might prove strong
enough for him to remain in charge after his own release from Landsberg. Yet Rosenberg was weak even as a stand-in, and this facilitated the rise of Gregor Strasser. Strasser, a member of the Bavarian
Landtag and a chemist by profession, had also taken part in the
November putsch, but had gotten off scot-free, because of his parliamentary immunity. Before long Gregor Strasser became the most important figure in the National Socialist movement. In order to give
themselves some kind of political legality, he and Rosenberg founded
the *N.S.—Deutsche Freiheitsbewegung* (N.S. German Freedom Movement), with Erich Ludendorff's blessing, benefiting from the general's
national popularity. The three "Fuehrers" of these various nationalist
groups united at the conference in Weimar to form one block (the
Völkische block) at the impending elections. All three had taken
part in the march on the Feldherrnhalle. All three were involved in
the putsch, which did not prevent at least two of them from claiming
the parliamentary immunity extended to them by the democratic constitution of Weimar, which they were combating so fiercely. And,
Ludendorff (who became a member of the Reichstag only in December 1924) owed it to the Germans and to the great reverence
they felt for the former Army leader, even though he had lost the
war, that he still walked the streets a free man instead of sitting in a
cell next to Corporal Hitler.

Goebbels did not manage to meet any of the three leaders
personally. But he made contact with Franz von Wiegershaus, a member of the Prussian Landtag and Gaufuehrer, Rheinland Nord of the
Deutschvölkische Freiheitspartei. By profession a commercial representative, and in his spare time a writer and dramatist, von Wiegershaus had edited since mid-March 1924 the *Rheinisch-Westfälische
Kampfblatt für ein Völkisch-soziales Grossdeutschland* (The Rhine
and Westphalian Fighting Journal for a *Völkisch*-socialist Greater
Germany) and a weekly *Völkische Freiheit* (*Völkisch* Freedom).
Goebbels became Wiegershaus's secretary and a contributor to his
publications.

In September 1924 Goebbels moved to Elberfeld and stepped into
the political arena, which he was never to leave again. He was said
to have been paid 100 marks per month,[23] a sum barely commen-
surate with the amount of work he did.

Goebbels' first article appeared on September 30, 1924. The heading *National und Social* describes precisely the theme of the article:
Goebbels submits that the social question cannot be solved on an
international but only on a national basis. The same issue also contained the first installment in a series by Goebbels called "Political
Diary," in which he recounts events in Germany's foreign and

domestic politics. Goebbels used exactly the same style as the intellectual know-it-alls Hitler so ardently detested. Each issue included a column called "Roving spotlights" that was signed "Ulex," the nickname Goebbels had used as a student. It presented twenty short news items, together with brief but pungent comments. For the first time, it is possible to recognize Goebbels' devastating, acid tongue. The emotionally intoxicated poet has given way to the journalist, and to a brilliant journalist at that. Goebbels had not gotten rid of all his mannerisms, but what he wrote now was highly readable and stimulating, and each article offered some surprising turn of thought.

If we remember that Goebbels edited this weekly practically single-handed, yet without neglecting his duties as secretary and orator, we can easily imagine the zeal and diligence with which he attacked his newly won position. At last he had arrived; he had become a professional writer, albeit on a somewhat humbler level than he had hoped. Everything he had stored up in himself, his thoughts, his anger, his hopes, he now coined into words. He demonstrated his considerable journalistic power, and for the first time he hit at the Jews.

The world had failed to recognize his talent, his genius. It had forced him to waste it on this insignificant little paper instead of using it in a powerful Berlin daily, where he would have discussed important matters with intelligent editors instead of wasting time on mediocrities. The warped development of a man oversensitive by nature and frustrated by circumstance was bound to lead to anti-Semitism. "The Jews" had deeply hurt his honor and, what was worse, his vanity.

Goebbels Becomes a National Socialist

Hitler was released from the Landsberg fortress and started rebuilding the party again as soon as the order prohibiting it was rescinded. That meant the dissolution of the "German *Völkisch* Freedom Movement," which had secretly hoped to step into the shoes of the National Socialist Movement in West and North Germany. Wiegershaus discontinued publication of the *Völkische Freiheit*. The last issue appeared on January 17, 1925. Three days later he wrote a letter to Goebbels, breaking with him. Wiegershaus considered Goebbels a traitor, and not without reason. Goebbels had devoted an article, published on January 1, 1925, in the *Völkische Freiheit,* to an enthusiastic welcome for Hitler. Goebbels spoke of the "herald of the renaissance of German faith," and he called Hitler the "incarnation of our faith and our ideas." Goebbels offered Hitler his services: "The German youth has found their Fuehrer. We are awaiting his orders," writes the young Joseph Goebbels. At first he waited in vain for Hitler's answer: The Fuehrer had other things to do than read an insignificant little paper (although linguistically he might have profited from Goebbels' article).

Having failed to get into direct contact with Hitler, Goebbels tried the indirect approach. In the late autumn of 1924, during the election campaign for the Reichstag, Goebbels made the acquaintance of the National Socialist leader of Elberfeld, Karl Kaufmann.[24] Goebbels offered Kaufmann his services, was accepted and, at a meeting of the leaders of the newly formed Gau Rhineland North, was elected member of the standing committee of the *Gau* (province). This meeting took place in February 1925. Alfred Lutze, later chief of staff of the SA, also sat on the committee, as did Erich Koch, one of the most sinister figures among the Nazi leaders, who later became *Gauleiter* (head of the district) of East Prussia and Reich commissioner of the Ukraine. Koch had started in civilian life as a railway official. Rosenberg called him a *"petit bourgeois* run berserk" and "the most unbalanced brute among Hitler's satraps in the occupied East."[25] Koch eventually became one of Goebbels' archenemies. The only one who failed to make a career in the party was journalist Axel Ripke, whom the committee had elected gauleiter.

Kaufmann and Goebbels got rid of Ripke in the summer of the same year, accusing him of having embezzled party funds. A triumvirate consisting of Kaufmann, Lutze, and Goebbels took over the leadership of the Gau.

In September 1925 the Gau Rhineland-North was united with the Gau Westphalia. Kaufmann became the leader of the Gau —he was gaufuehrer—while Goebbels only had the title of gauleiter. A new triumvirate was formed, including the Westphalian Franz von Pfeffer, who later became OSAF (Obarstar SA Fuehrer) West.

Karl Kaufmann was the first important party leader with whom Goebbels collaborated. Kaufmann was a member of the Freecorp Brigade Erhardt and belonged to the most active anti-Semitic fighting group, the Alldeutsche Schutz- und Trutz-bund (Pan German Fighting Association). Kaufmann's infamous hate propaganda against Rathenau was considered largely responsible for Rathenau's assassination, which led to the dissolution of the Schutz- und Trutz-bund. Compared with such "national" merits, Goebbels was but an innocent, a beginner.

At first Kaufmann and Goebbels got on famously. The diligent Goebbels, working to full capacity, tried hard to establish a friendly relationship with Kaufmann, who was three years younger than he. They soon addressed each other by the intimate *Du.* It is interesting to note that Kaufmann remained the only party leader with whom

Goebbels was on intimate terms. It points up Goebbels' spiritual and human isolation within the party hierarchy. According to Kaufmann, Goebbels proved in the first few months a very hard-working collaborator and a charming and amiable colleague, whose only failing seemed to be his open jealousy when Kaufmann consulted someone else on the staff more often than the little doctor. The relationship between these two changed only after Goebbels left Strasser and joined Hitler. Kaufmann, who in the Third Reich was appointed gauleiter of Hamburg, felt a growing dislike for Goebbels. Dislike of Goebbels was rampant among gauleiters—most of them hated him for his arrogance and conceit, and particularly for having wormed himself into Hitler's special favor. Speer reports in his memoirs[26] that at the end of the war, Kaufmann even planned to assassinate Goebbels.

Indeed, Goebbels was not a friend you could trust. Unable to be anyone's friend, he never had a friend himself. His diary shows his growing alienation from Kaufmann, though Goebbels does not realize it is he himself who has brought it about. Goebbels was smarting from being unjustly pushed into the background, all the more as he felt himself immensely superior to Kaufmann.

Goebbels' first reference to Kaufmann in his diary was still in a major key: "Kaufmann is a good fellow. I want to be his friend." (August 17, 1925). But already by the end of December 1925, at the Gau conference when Kaufmann was appointed leader, Goebbels, though he refused to admit it to himself, obviously felt humiliated. "I can feel a shadow of rancor in my heart against Kaufmann. I am doing the work and he 'leads.' But it will pass. The 'Cause,' that is all that matters." (December 28, 1925).

When saying goodbye to Pfeffer and Kaufmann after their stay in Munich, where Goebbels had made his definite choice and accepted Hitler as his Fuehrer, Goebbels noticed a certain cooling off on the part of his colleagues. "Something has come between us." (April 13, 1926). Back in Elberfeld, Goebbels perceived that an intrigue was afoot against him: "There is a bad spirit abroad in our Gau and it has sunk its claws into Kaufmann. Say what you like, politics corrupt the character. Or rather: politics show us how corrupt the character of men is." (June 7, 1926).

Five days later, Goebbels writes: "Owing to Kaufmann's negligence the gau has become a pigsty." And on June 19, 1926, Goebbels concludes: "It has come to a sort of break between me and Kaufmann. He is not honest." It obviously did not occur to Goebbels that it could be his own honesty that was wanting; or if it did, he suppressed the thought so effectively that not even his diary was entrusted with the confession. Goebbels wanted to build up a career for himself at all costs. That was why he wooed first Kaufmann and then Strasser.

But as soon as he saw an even greater career beckoning at Hitler's side, his friendship with those two was no longer of any interest. Again and again Goebbels would present himself a victim whom others had betrayed through sheer envy. Yet it was he who had sacrificed the old gods on the altar of a new one, his last and supreme god—Adolf Hitler.

With the exception of Hitler, Goebbels had no stronger political bond with anyone than he had with Gregor Strasser. He met the two Strasser brothers through Kaufmann at the end of 1925. Ex-Lieutenant Gregor Strasser, a chemist in civilian life, had joined the NSDAP in 1920. He first became SA leader in Landshut and, shortly afterward, district leader in Lower Bavaria. In the year 1924, during Hitler's incarceration in the Landsberg fortress, Strasser came to the forefront. He was favored by his parliamentary immunity, which allowed him to hold public meetings and still be protected from prosecution, and this enabled him to keep the outlawed party and its supporters together. The people liked him. He was not a good speaker, but he was a popular orator who would speak his mind, and knew how to address the man in the street. Buttressed by his brother, Otto, his social conscience was stronger than that of Hitler. Otto Strasser had come from the Social Democrats. Gregor Strasser, who had figured on the list of candidates representing the *Völkisch* Block, was duly elected and became a member of the Reichstag. Gregor sold his chemist's shop and founded, with his brother, a publishing house called the *Kampf-Verlag*.

At the mass meeting in Munich on February 27, 1925, Hitler spoke for the first time after his release from Landsberg. Strasser's absence was taken by many as a gesture of personal censure against Hitler. Yet soon afterward, Hitler invited Strasser to meet him. An agreement was reached, leaving Strasser a free hand to organize North Germany. This was a great concession on Hitler's part, as it was his principle rather to centralize his power. And Strasser used his license to the full. He organized—organizing was his great talent—appointed several gauleiters and created a smooth-running party machine entirely devoted to him. He published the *National Sozialischehe Briefe* (National Socialist Letters) in Berlin, with Goebbels as its most prominent contributor. Finally, Strasser established a close link with the organization in the Rhineland and in the Ruhr. He founded the *Arbeitsgemeinschaft Nordwest der NSDAP* (Work Co-operative Northwest of the NSDAP). This, too, was against the statutes of the party. But Hitler magnanimously chose to disregard these incidents. He needed Strasser as organizer, knew that he was popular, and, as so often, let matters drift while waiting for the right moment to pounce. And soon enough it came. The Strasser brothers, together with Goebbels, had drawn up a revised version of the party program and sent it to various party friends for their re-actions. The two most important points were, first, the nationaliza-tion of heavy industries and the large estates, and second, the es-tablishment of a *Ständekammer* (Corporative Chamber) built on the Fascist pattern and designed to supplant the Reichstag. In Hitler's eyes a revised version of the party program was tantamount to rebellion. Although Hitler had, generally speaking, a poor opinion of the value of any party program, he adhered to the principle that the National Socialist Party program was "a political declaration of faith" and should therefore remain untouched even if it were possible to im-prove the formulation of some of its points. "Such attempts are bound to end disastrously. They lay open to discussion something meant to be unshakably firm." Hitler cites the Catholic Church as a shining example, ". . . although its educational structure comes into collision —incidentally sometimes quite unnecessarily—with exact science and research, the Church is not prepared to alter even one syllable of its dogma."[27] Hitler at once felt the danger that might arise if he were to tolerate a new version of the program, which might divide the party into a right wing and a left wing.

The situation came to a head when Strasser called a meeting of the gau leaders of North Germany, the Rhineland, and the Ruhr, in Hanover. There were many heated discussions, in some of which even Hitler was not spared. Most historians, as well as Goebbels' biog-raphers, give the date of this meeting as November 22, 1925.

In fact it took place on January 24, 1926, in the apartment of the gauleiter of Hanover, Bernhard Rust. There was in fact another meet-ing on November 22, 1925, at which the Northwest Committee was founded. This included Rhineland North, Rhineland South, Westphalia, Hanover, Hanover South, Hessen-Nassau, Lüneburg, Schleswig-Holstein, Greater Hamburg, Greater Berlin, and Pomerania. The decisions made at this meeting were reported in No. 5 of the *National Socialist Letters* of December 1, 1925:

"Para. 5: The business of the Northwest Committee . . . will be conducted by the party members, Gregor Strasser and Dr. Goebbels." This officially confirmed Goebbels in his important position.

"Para. 6: The Northwest Committee has its own fortnightly publi-cation called *National Socialist Letters* published by Strasser and edited by party member Dr. Goebbels." This made Goebbels not only a contributor but editor-in-chief.

"Para. 7: The Northwest Committee and the *National Socialist Letters* are officially sanctioned by Hitler."

This explains Goebbels' note in his diary, dated October 26, 1925: "We are in the clear with Hitler." This sentence stands by itself and surprises the reader who only a few days earlier learned from the same diary how impossible it was to make contact with Hitler.

The meeting of January 24, 1926, was attended by more than twenty gauleiters and one party leader, including the brothers Strasser, Goebbels, Kaufmann, Erich Koch, Hans Kerrl, and Robert Ley. According to Otto Strasser[28] a heated discussion arose about whether Hitler's emissary, Gottfried Feder, should be admitted. Goebbels shouted, "We do not want any spies!" In the end Feder was admitted with the majority of one vote.

Along with the proposed new version of the party program, another vital point was heatedly discussed: a bill brought in by the Social Democrats and Communists that envisaged the dispossession without indemnity of all estates and other property owned by the former German princes. A referendum was to be held on this question. The Strasser group was in favor of supporting the campaign of the left. Hitler opposed in principle the socialist proposal, rejecting any intrusion into the lawful right of private property whichever group of persons it concerned, aristocratic or otherwise. But Hitler's attitude was at least as much determined by political considerations as by his concern for upholding the law. He had no intention of spoiling his pitch with the aristocracy and their circles, or with the big industrialists, often connected with the aristocracy by marriage. His instinct of self-preservation also worked against supporting the socialist proposal. Later, when he came to power, Hitler did not allow himself to be encumbered by considerations of law and principle when he gave the Gestapo a free hand to confiscate private property of all kinds— Church and monastic property, the property of parties, of trade unions, of Jewish organizations, and of private individuals.

The debate concerning the dispossession of the princes became very heated. Everyone except Dr. Ley voted in favor of the socialist proposal. Ley, gauleiter of Cologne, opposed the motion and demanded that the decision be left to Hitler. At that moment (still according to Otto Strasser)[29] Goebbels—red in the face—climbed on a chair and shouted, "I propose that the *petit bourgeois* Adolf Hitler be expelled from the NSDAP."

Many hard words must have been used against Hitler's policy at that conference, opinions for which their authors would, no doubt, have paid with their lives after Hitler had come to power, let alone during wartime. But Germany was then still a democracy and not at war. According to some reports—and we cannot be sure that they are reliable—Goebbels was the most radical of all present, and the one who shouted the loudest.

But he surely never spoke those words demanding Hitler's expulsion from the party; these, incidentally, were ascribed by Kaufmann and Otto Strasser to Gauleiter Rust who, very likely, did not say them either.[30] Goebbels was not stupid. And it was highly unlikely that he, in fact the most intelligent of the lot, would openly insult the Fuehrer at the risk of being expelled from the party by Hitler at the next opportunity; and this would have probably been the case if Goebbels had actually pronounced that ominous sentence.

It is obvious why such a story should have been circulated. Goebbels' numerous enemies, including the whole party hierarchy, sought to compromise the little doctor; they tried to paint an image of a double-dealing, underhanded, disloyal creature who was not only physically but also mentally deformed—in fact, the devil incarnate. They hoped to blacken Goebbels by rumors and slander, not only in the eyes of Hitler and the party, but also in the eyes of the people. Otto Strasser, the originator of this story, was particularly bent on destroying Goebbels, and not without good reason.

We may safely assume that Goebbels had not demanded Hitler's expulsion. Goebbels was probably one of the most radical speakers at the conference, and as such may have pronounced another sentence ascribed to him: "Hitler has betrayed socialism." This was in keeping with the radical socialist views Goebbels held at the time, and it is perfectly conceivable that in his state of excitement he actually could not restrain himself from saying it, though it was once again one of Goebbels' enemies, later to become his chief adversary, Alfred Rosenberg, who recorded it in his diary on March 1, 1939. Rosenberg added: "I know a gauleiter who still possesses in black and white the original record containing these words."[31]

Hitler would never have forgiven anybody for having demanded his expulsion from the party; it was, however, another matter to be accused of having betrayed socialism; that did not bother Hitler too much. The sinner might be forgiven.

Goebbels and Strasser

What was the bond uniting Joseph Goebbels and Gregor Strasser? First and foremost, their social radicalism. Both Strasser brothers had, by their radical pronouncements and their intellectual ability to infiltrate their socialist ideas into the lower reaches of the party, secured a powerful position within the party.

Their creation, the *National Socialist Letters,* with Goebbels as editor, was the best National Socialist periodical. With the help of the organization Gregor had built up in North and West Germany,

and of the *National Socialist Letters,* it was in their power to establish
a strong wing within the party which, by its radical socialism, might
have constituted a viable opposition to the NSDAP led from Munich.
However, they might have found it difficult to wean the workers away
from the well-organized Social Democrats and Communists who had
the necessary material resources and their roots firmly planted in the
trade unions. A Strasser party would have been short of money, of
daily newspapers, and of Fuehrer personalities necessary to at-
tract the masses. Parties with a claim to bringing salvation to the
masses need hard men, prepared to go to any lengths—to commit
crimes, if need be; men like Lenin, Trotsky, and Stalin, like Mussolini,
Hitler, and Tito. Gregor Strasser was not such a personality. He was
far too much of a tame bourgeois to commit a crime; and no other
strong personality from among the group was available. Goebbels was
ruled out if only because of his physical malformation.

Up to the time of the conference in Bamberg, Goebbels was much
closer to Strasser than to Hitler, both humanly and politically. And
yet one can clearly perceive in Goebbels' diary, written at the time
when he still adhered to the Strasser group, the difference he made
in his assessment of these two personalities. Goebbels admired
Strasser, too, no doubt, but there is nowhere in his notes any indication that Strasser exerted the magic on him that Hitler obviously did.
Strasser was the boss—an amiable, helpful boss—who luckily saw eye
to eye with him in most matters, but he was just a boss who might,
for all it mattered, be replaced by another tomorrow. But Hitler was,
from the first moment on, the Fuehrer whom Goebbels looked up
to and whose favors he coveted.

Goebbels' first note about Strasser reads: ". . . a magnificent fellow, Bavarian, massive, wonderful sense of humor. Has a lot of sad
stories to tell about the Munich setup. That slovenly pigsty there at
headquarters. Hitler is surrounded by false bodies. . . . The 'West
Block' publishes the *National Socialist Letters.* This is a fighting instrument in our hands against the sclerotic big shots in Munich. We
will get Hitler on our side in the end. Strasser has a lot of initiative.
One can work with him. And what a wonderful character. . . ."
(August 21, 1925).

Let us remember: "that slovenly pigsty there at headquarters";
"sclerotic big shots." Eight days later Goebbels wrote in his diary:
". . . I have been reading Hitler's book in the evenings. Wonderful. What political instinct! I am full of admiration." And on September 12, 1925, Goebbels writes: "Hitler is coming! What joy that
will be!"

And about Gregor Strasser, Goebbels writes again on September

25, 1925, ". . . Colossal meeting in Hattingen. Strasser made a smart and clever speech. Strasser is a nice fellow. He has still got a lot to learn and, no doubt, he will. But he is ready for the radicalization of the cause. He is our battering ram against the Munich bosses. The battle may be imminent."

And two days later: "Several conferences with Strasser. We are in perfect agreement. I now also feel very close to him as a man. . . . Strasser is far from being as bourgeois as I thought. He is certainly very ambitious, although he keeps on repeating that he is not. Hence his hatred for Esser and the Munich set around Hitler who stand in his way. I think he tends to see things rather gloomily. When our combined forces are big enough we will pass to the general attack. . . ."

The entry in his diary dated October 12, 1925, is particularly interesting—Strasser apparently attempted to get Goebbels up against Hitler, but Goebbels directed his anger not against Hitler but against Hitler's entourage.

Hitler's mistrust caused Goebbels great pain and anxiety.

". . . Telegram from Mannheim asking me to make an election speech. Kiss my arse. A letter from Strasser. Hitler mistrusts me. He has talked badly about me. How it pains me. If he reproaches me on October 25 in Hamm I will leave. I could not bear it on top of everything else. To sacrifice everything, and then get a load of reproaches from Hitler personally. Scoundrels are busy in Munich. Idiots who will not tolerate a good brain for fear that it could show up their own stupidity. That is the reason for their fight against Strasser and me. . . . I will have to go to Munich one day. Strasser sounds quite desperate in his letter. I expect very much from the meeting in Hamm. If I could only be alone with Hitler for a couple of hours it would clear up everything, but he is surrounded by his minions like an old monarch. Perhaps I will be able to get at him in Hamm after all. Things must be cleared up, I want to know exactly for what I am ruining myself."

Goebbels was hurt by Hitler's lack of trust and felt desperate. He would have had all reason to be angry with Hitler; but two days later, Goebbels wrote in his diary: "I am coming to the end of Hitler's book with growing excitement! Who is this man? Half plebeian, half God! Christ or John? . . ."

But the meeting in Hamm brought no solution.

"October 19: Hitler will be in Hamm and Dortmund on Saturday and Sunday. Strasser is with him as a protective screen. That damned idiot Hermann Esser.[32] I will not take part any longer in this Byzantinism. We have to get at Hitler. The question is not only Hermann Esser. The program, the spiritual and economic issues—all that still remains unclear—not to me, all the more to the others. That is not the way to make revolution. Most among us need a shot in the arm."

The meeting with Hitler must have taken place after all, because Goebbels notes on October 26:

"We are in the clear with Hitler. He, too, is prepared to move closer to us. They offered me the post of editor of the *Beobachter* [*Der Völkische Beobachter*]. Should I accept? But then what will happen here in the West? I am not at all sure what to do. Together with Strasser in Elberfeld. We spent a happy evening together. He is a loyal, fine fellow. . . ."

Goebbels' understanding with Hitler—it soon enough turned out to be one—filled Joseph with optimism. His note of November 6, 1925, shows that Hitler is the center of all his thoughts. Everything else has become insignificant; the program, Strasser, the party in the South, the West, and the North of the Reich, compared with the one and only to whom he raises his moist eyes, like the disciple to his master, feeling his heart pounding:

". . . We go by car to see Hitler.* He is at table. He jumps up, there he stands before us, presses my hand like that of an old friend. And those large blue eyes, like stars. . . . I am overwhelmed with happiness. . . . On my way to the meeting. My speech lasts two hours. Great applause. Then shouts of 'Heil' and clapping. He has arrived. He shakes my hand. He is still tired out from his long speech. [Hitler had on that day, November 3, already spoken twice.] Yet he holds another speech here lasting half an hour, full of wit, irony, humor, sarcasm, gravity, and glowing passion. This man has everything to be King. The born people's Tribune. The coming Dictator."

On November 23—that is, one day after Goebbels demanded Hitler's exclusion from the party (according to some historians)— Goebbels wrote:

". . . A minor meeting, Hitler asked me to speak first. He speaks after me. How small I feel! He gives me his photograph. . . . I want to have Hitler as my friend. His photograph stands on my table. I could not bear ever to despair of him."

Goebbels, who felt he was by far mentally superior to all the others, including Strasser, and who would call most members of the party hierarchy "arse drummers," became humble and quite modest when talking about Hitler. He felt honored like a schoolboy when Hitler shook his hand. He behaved like someone in love who would blush when the loved one gave him a deep, meaningful look. His whole

* [A conference of the gaus took place at Braunschweig. Translator's note]

behavior would appear ridiculous if it did not testify to a state of pathological dependence, with all its implications. It had the compulsive nature of a fateful involvement that deprived Goebbels of his will power and rendered him defenseless when faced with Hitler. The relationship between Goebbels and Strasser, which had begun so well and ended in deadly enmity, has been the subject of controversy ever since. And Goebbels gets the worst of it every time. The National Socialist leaders agree with the historians and biographers who accuse Goebbels of brazen ingratitude to Strasser, whom in the end he betrayed. There is certainly a great deal of truth in this, but it does not touch upon the deeper problem. Goebbels simply went over to Hitler because Hitler was the stronger, and the man to whom the future belonged. Strasser was, in fact, the more pleasant, the more sympathetic "Fuehrer," but he lacked Hitler's personality and magic. Goebbels felt Hitler's enormous will power and fell under the spell of Hitler's magnetic personality from the very first moment. Even Goebbels' initial doubts, noted in his diary, can be explained only by his uncertainty as to whether Hitler would want him.

Goebbels sees Hitler as an artist of politics. Both stranded artists, they discover politics as their great field of action. So much for the points they had in common. But what about Goebbels' socialist programs? The little doctor was, as all agreed, the most radical, the most "Red" among the Brownshirts. But Hitler's interest in social and economic questions was limited to their usefulness in his political plans, which were to unite Germany, make it strong—and, above all, get into power.

The first condition of a united Germany was the *Volksgemeinschaft* [a conscious adherence to the German community comprising the German race and the German people. Translator's note]. Hitler planned to bring this about by means of a national dictatorship. *Volksgemeinschaft* was, after all, a wide term. It could well mean nationalization of natural resources, establishment of just wages, participation of the workers, and equal chances for all, irrespective of their social and economic position. All these points were in fact included in the program drawn up by Goebbels and Strasser. But *Volksgemeinschaft* could also mean total oppression of a regimented people with the view to realizing the dream of an obsessed mind for world power. The latter was Hitler's concept.

But was not Goebbels' change-over to Hitler—the brothers Strasser and other members of the work co-operative called it "Damascus"—a betrayal of his convictions? Goebbels and the Strassers knew how to realize socialism within National Socialism. The others did not. And it was the Strassers' very ignorance, their way of using big words that had no meaning, that had caused Goebbels to be always rather pessimistic about the future realization of the Strassers' ideas. Goebbels had come to be convinced that Hitler alone was capable of carrying through what he had begun. Goebbels therefore wrote an open letter, addressed to his former friends and published in the *National Socialist Letters* on September 15, 1926, with the headline "Revolution for Its Own Sake":

"For once do not talk of 'conviction' but of reality. We have 'convictions' galore, the other side too incidentally, and, God knows, it is nothing we need be particularly proud of. Yet when I sat together with you, we regularly got stuck at 'convictions' and did not get much further . . . and the shattering thing about it is that every group still nurtures yet another conviction, each claiming to be exclusive: It is enough to make you laugh and cry at the same time. . . . But there is one thing I am still waiting to hear from you: What do you really want. You let the others make fools of themselves. . . . But you remain silent and enthroned in Olympian inaccessibility at golden tables through never-ending feasts."

Nobody has ever better characterized the mental attitude of the National Socialism of that period than Goebbels in this letter. Germany's "saviors" did not know what they wanted. They did not know how far they should venture in their socialism, their nationalism, in their religious, and respectively antireligious attitudes. It was only Adolf Hitler who simplified this unholy mixture of ideas and reduced it to a few simple aims: We want power, we want to destroy Marxism, we want to chase the Jews out of Germany, and we want to make the Reich great. Goebbels inclined before these simple maxims: "We will have to be revolutionaries first, if we want to become statesmen."

These words foretold the historical events that followed. For Hitler —as well as for Goebbels—revolution was no more than a means for coming to power, and lasted only as long as their struggle for power lasted. Hitler actually announced in 1933 the official end of the revolution, which led to plans of rebellion by those who saw themselves robbed; while still deliberating, they were brutally liquidated in June 1934.

Goebbels had become an unconditional disciple of power. Pure power was not only "right," as Hitler thought, but was also a means to everything, including socialism, which Goebbels persuaded himself he was still fostering. But although socialism had a certain task, it was "not an ideology created by brain artists and tired acrobats of the human soul. At stake is Germany and Germany alone."

Since the ex-"brain artist" and ex-"acrobat of the soul" had finally cast his vote for power, he could now say in his best voice that "if we stand united behind the Fuehrer it is not a Damascus: We do not submit to him out of byzantine coercion, only because he ordered us and we had to obey. We incline ourselves with the venerated pride of men before the thrones of Kings, with a secure feeling that he is more than you and I, and the calm certainty that he needs men, and lets men be men. And that he, too, is but an instrument of the divine will which shapes history. . . ."

All men of power are revolutionaries in action. Goebbels recognized that Adolf Hitler was the only one who could transform this gigantic, confused, nationalist hive into an instrument of power. And Hitler left Goebbels in the belief that the worker would be the main actor in the national revolution. Perhaps Hitler believed it himself up to a point. In any case, Goebbels based all his activity in Berlin on this assumption. He acted the bogey of the bourgeoisie, he wooed the workers: "It is the historical task of the German worker to liberate Germany. We shall imbue him with the necessary strength by making Germany his very own," Goebbels wrote when taking leave of his friends in the Rhineland and the Ruhr on the eve of his move to Berlin.[33]

"As only Hitler could accomplish the national revolution, and not Strasser, you had better work through Hitler to bring about a social revolution." And Goebbels still believed that the national and social revolution were interdependent, thereby persuading himself that he had remained true to his convictions. The first thing was to get into power with Hitler, and all else would follow naturally.

Goebbels had signed himself over to the National Socialist movement and to its Fuehrer who, clearly, was not Gregor Strasser but Adolf Hitler. Goebbels lost no time and tried to draw the Fuehrer's attention to himself, aiming at penetrating the party hierarchy—no simple task, as he represented exactly what National Socialism rejected: He was an intellectual. Later on he often attacked intellectuals, in a sense throwing mud at himself. With his clubfoot and shriveled body he was, according to their racial theory, a misfit. He would have to show his personal courage, which he did time and again, in fights at political meetings; when beer mugs, table legs, and chairs were thrown around, and leather belts and knuckle dusters flew through the air, when blood dripped from daggers; there he would stand calm and unruffled like a bronze statue, no trace of fear on his face. And his bodyguards, stimulated by his posture, would go into battle for this little man with a limp, their gauleiter, who showed so much courage. True, he would not be declaiming Liliencron with a sword in his hand, like Michael in his novel, but there he would stand with his arms crossed on his chest, overlooking the battlefield like a warlord, unmoved by the belting of friend and foe alike. Goebbels was one of the most courageous among Hitler's close associates. At the Fuehrer's side Goebbels was supreme. The little cripple equaled any of the Nordic blond giants; he even surpassed them by virtue of his intelligence, which enabled him to put them in his pocket, complete with their blue-eyed, empty, blond heads.

Hitler looked through Goebbels, but he also recognized his potential and saw how useful he could become. This must have decided him to try to wean the little man away from Strasser, who, with Goebbels at his side, might have become a real danger, if allowed to pursue his socialist course.

Hitler also saw that Goebbels could be bought once he was shown the opportunities open to him at the Fuehrer's side. Hitler lost no time. He started wooing Goebbels at once. He brought his whole charm and art of seduction to bear, and soon had Goebbels in a state of intoxicated enthusiasm. From then on Goebbels was utterly dependent on Hitler and remained faithful to him to the end—to Hitler, not to the party. Whether Goebbels had actually taken part in any rebellion against Hitler before remains a mere supposition. But from then on he was certainly not even tempted to betray his master.

Goebbels was not the only one who was virtually possessed by Hitler. In a certain measure this was also true of Goering, Himmler, and Speer, to name only some of the more important; Strasser, too, felt paralyzed in Hitler's presence, unable to marshal sufficient will power to resist him. Even when they parted company he did not mobilize his battalions. Strasser, in fact, never dared mount a revolt against Hitler: "I have fought as Hitler's man and I will be buried as such," were his words.[34] He was a "nice fellow," but no born Fuehrer.

Russia—the Natural Ally

The *National Socialist Letters,* published on the first and fifteenth of each month, contained either four or eight pages. Goebbels' articles, in the form of open letters, set the paper's style. They were, journalistically, vastly superior to anything the NSDAP had produced until then. Goebbels called the paper "his favorite problem child." He expected a lot from it. "It will perhaps one day play an enormous role in our movement."[35]

The articles were excellent; they were spiritual and sarcastic, tackling every political problem with courage and determination. Goebbels did not hesitate to attack views of old standing with open brutality; he intended to shock—and not only the nationalistic bourgeoisie but also his own party headquarters in Munich. Never again was Goebbels to give his views so freely and uncompromisingly. The NSDAP was, in these first years, not yet a firmly structured party. Spiritual discussions were still possible; Hitler was not yet Fuehrer by the grace of God whose word was law, as it later became. Goebbels was as much to blame for this as anyone else. Having at first been the main driving force in keeping up the spiritual controversy within the party, he was later contented to be Hitler's megaphone.

In the fourth issue of the *National Socialist Letters* of November 15, 1925, Goebbels dealt with the "Russian problem" in an open letter addressed to Iwan Wienurowsky, the Russian character we met in his novel *Michael*. Thoughts and phrases from this work are often made use of in Goebbels' articles and speeches.

". . . Once Russia has awakened, the world will witness a miracle. . . . It is our task to do everything to be able to match this miracle as equal partners or allies. . . . Great things are happening in your Russia. Not with a lot of noise, not with the sound of fanfares as bourgeois ignoramuses imagine. Quietly, awesomely still, the future is being born there in your country. . . . Once Russia wakes up it will be more terrible than war. This awakening will create the socialist national state."

It must have been bitter for Goebbels to realize, at the end of his life, that it was Hitler who had caused the rise of a socialist national Russia with imperialistic, expansionist tendencies, the beginnings of which went back as far as the thirties, when Stalin deported the true world revolutionaries to Siberia, executed them, or had them assassinated.

Socialism meant for Goebbels a rejection of materialism and the capitalist mammon worshiped by the West, not so much as an ideology but as an ethical concept. It was the love of possessions and the desire to increase them that he rejected:

"That is why we look toward Russia, because she is the most likely to show us the way to socialism. She is our most natural ally against the diabolical temptations and corruption of the West. With bitter pain we must look on while so-called German statesmen destroy bridge after bridge between us and Russia; and we are pained, not so much because we love Bolshevism and its Jewish architects, but because we can see in the building of a truly national and socialist Russia the beginnings of our own national and socialist existence." In the seventh *Letter,* of January 1, 1926, Goebbels returned to his theme: orientation toward the West or the East:

". . . The present constellation . . . demands that Germany's policy be orientated, in the foreseeable future, toward the East. We have to choose between the diseased neighbor in the West, and the other in the East abounding with creative health. Today, in the era of Stresemann, we are dependent on the money of world capitalism. But in our last desperate fight only one thing will save us: the bread and the strength of the East. The only danger that could threaten our logical orientation toward the East is our own disunity and impotence."

"It is madness," says Goebbels, "to seek protection against Bolshevism in the capitalist West," and he submits "that we have far more in common with Eastern Bolshevism than with Western capitalism."

The closing passages of Goebbels' article are so utterly opposed to Hitler's political concept that reading through it we are, even today, shocked to see to what extent a man can betray his convictions and abdicate his inner self and spiritual liberty, once he has crossed the Rubicon and stepped onto the other bank, where spiritual terror and serfdom reign. Before crossing over, Goebbels had used a language worthy of Walter Ulbricht:

"Do not let us deceive ourselves; a destruction of Russia as a future national center of power would also mean the final bankruptcy of what is left of a national will in Germany; it would mean Germany's resignation from her position as an independent state and a leading nation of European culture. With the collapse of Russia we would have to bury forever our dream of a National Socialist Germany."

The following quotation throws an interesting light on Goebbels' character and his political gambler's instinct. It reflects Goebbels' gravest error of thinking: his assumption that you can sign a pact with the devil without paying with your soul; it was not long before he and his beloved Germany had to pay the price for this miscalculation.

"A National Socialist Germany can even sign a pact with the devil without harming its soul. The democratic Germany, allied to an inferior partner, will always be the loser. . . . Love and sympathy play no part in history. History, that is politics—which, in fact, is history in the making—is shaped by iron necessity . . . whether Russia will break its Soviet rule or not, is her own business. . . . Alone we are powerless. Therefore we must force open the gates to the East. . . .

"Russia's needs shall be our needs, and vice versa. We feel bound to Russia by a common fate. Russia's freedom shall be our freedom, and vice versa. We stand at Russia's side as equal partners in the fight for freedom, which means everything to us."

Already on October 25, 1925, he had noted in his diary: "We shall merely be the mercenaries hired against Russia on the battlefields of capitalism, however much they may try to twist the truth. They have already sold us over the counter. But if it comes to the last stand, then better go down with Bolshevism than become eternal slaves of capitalism. . . ."

Simultaneously, Goebbels' views on interior policy also moved radically toward the left. His National Socialism became hardly distinguishable from what we call today national communism. In the sixth *Letter,* of December 15, 1925, he settled his account with the *Völkische* who, only a year earlier, he had supported in speeches and articles he wrote for their paper. This particular article shows that Goebbels had never felt very happy in the company of the *Völkische.* But was he actually very happy with the National Socialists? Or was he not rather a deeply frustrated man all his life?

He called this "letter" *The Radicalization of Socialism* and addressed it to a Mr. Vanguard *(Herr Vorkämpfer).* Goebbels found that Marxism had falsified socialism just as much as nationalist parties and associations had falsified nationalism. Marxism and the bourgeoisie had, therefore, lost their right to oppose the "system," both having taken part in it for their own advantage. The bourgeoisie had fallen victim to capitalism. They had rejected joining in the fight of the National Socialists who, by necessity, had to turn "to recruiting their fighters from among the so-called proletariat for the liberation of Germany from capitalist bondage."

The nationalist groups and associations believed that anti-Semitism provided the best proof for their nationalistic attitude. Goebbels commented:

"They are right: Anti-Semitism has first place in our concept, but it is not everything. It is no more than a beginning, and has already become second nature to us. But they get stuck with it, rave in the most primitive way against the Jews and their associates, and often choose to overlook the guilt of their own countrymen."

We can see that Goebbels' anti-Semitism was at that point slightly embarrassed and mainly produced to prevent his party colleagues from accusing him of wishing to exclude anti-Semitism from the National Socialist program; they regarded anti-Semitism as one of the cardinal points. All the same, Goebbels' main attack then was directed against the bourgeoisie. Even today's intellectuals could not improve on Goebbels' characterization of the bourgeoisie: He accused them of "remaining nationalists only for as long as the nationalist concept guarantees them their possessions, peace, and order." The bourgeoisie sees in Bolshevism, Goebbels continues, "not so much the destroyer of the national will and *Völkisch* instinct than the despoilers of their possessions, uncomfortably threatening their peace and order."

But such an attitude is of no value whatever to National Socialists. "We are socialists," Goebbels states, underlining the difference between the National Socialists on the one hand and the nationalist bourgeoisie, as well as the *Völkische,* on the other hand.

National Socialism must not under any circumstances, warned Goebbels, become "a black-white-red [the colors of the Weimar Republic. Translator's note]. Police force for the protection of the bourgeoisie, bourgeois profit, and bourgeois peace and order." At the end Goebbels fired a last frightening salvo: "and they will get a shock once they have seen the radicalism of our demands."

Lenin or Hitler

Goebbels the orator made history. But, then, his career as an orator had only just begun. He hurried busily from place to place to propagate the thesis of the national left, but was still far from being the brilliant orator he later became.

Yet his speech "Lenin or Hitler" clearly shows his outstanding talent in this field. No other National Socialist speaker can compare. It is masterly in content, and linguistically on a level rarely attained by orators of the Weimar Republic. The headline alone revealed a propagandist of genius. It showed Goebbels' natural gift for putting things in the right perspective. Whereas Lenin, dead since January 21, 1924, had already thrown his giant's shadow over the world's historical events, Adolf Hitler stood only at the beginning. For the great majority of Germans he was nothing more than a wild adventurer who had unsuccessfully dabbled in revolution, hoping as others before him to usurp power by staging a putsch, and hardly anybody would have seen in him a future maker of world history. But reading his name suddenly on posters next to Lenin's, offered as an alternative choice, made many begin to wonder if this Hitler was not, after all, somebody to be reckoned with.

The name of a German politician as an alternative to Lenin was something new. But this was not the only point Goebbels scored. By reducing the complex political situation to these two names, he practically excluded all other parties. There was only one alternative: communism or National Socialism—the two powerful wings that would encircle Germany's political center in a pincer movement and crush it. The German youth, to whom the future belonged, could sensibly vote only for one of these two parties. The center was old and tired and would be blown away by the storm of revolution.

Obviously, the problem was not a purely German one. German communism drew its force not from Germany but from Russia. Hence the alternative "cannot be Thälmann or Hitler." Thälmann was only a Russian stand-in; communism was equal to Russia. But Communist Russia was the historical work of Lenin, and only an equally great German revolutionary could be put up as an alternative choice. And there was only one man of this stature in Germany: Hitler. And just as Lenin had realized the gigantic Communist revolution, so would Hitler accomplish the gigantic national revolution, making world history, too.

Hitler, himself a propagandist of genius, did not take long to size up the situation. He invited Goebbels to repeat his speech at Munich, despite the fact that he disagreed with it basically. Hitler must have made up his mind then and there to charge Goebbels with more important tasks; he had picked him, Joseph Goebbels, from among the provincial bosses and placed him right up in front at the side of politicians of world importance.

Goebbels' speech was published as a pamphlet in 1926.[36] It mentions that he made that speech for the first time on February 19, 1926, at the opera house in Koenigsberg. This is not correct, according to his own diary. Goebbels wrote on October 9, 1925:

"Düsseldorf: Enormous red posters all over the town 'Lenin or Hitler.' Meeting packed. All Communists. They try to interfere. I soon have them spellbound and do not let go for two whole hours."

Goebbels' study of Marxist literature provided the basis for his speech. It gave him an advantage over other party speakers. His assessment of the development in the Soviet Union was in many ways incorrect; yet it should be remembered that Goebbels composed the speech in 1925, only one year after Lenin's death. But more important was that he assessed correctly the world historical significance of the Russian revolution, unlike most politicians of that period—bourgeois or Social Democrats, inside and outside Germany. And even more remarkable is Goebbels' sympathetic attitude toward the revolution, his realization that it meant a gigantic step forward in the history of mankind. There was no one in the party who shared this view; the brothers Strasser had closely followed the Russian development without showing any particular antagonism, and went even so far as to warn against viewing it with the prejudicial eyes of the Russian emigrés. But Goebbels went farther: He was a passionate advocate of common action with Russia. Only an alliance with Communist Russia could secure a national future for Germany. And only with Russia's help could the social revolution be accomplished. Goebbels was virtually obsessed with the idea of a German/Russian alliance.

"I am deeply pondering the problems of our foreign policy. Russia cannot be circumvented. Russia is the beginning and end of any imaginative German foreign policy."[37]

Goebbels idealized Lenin and was deeply impressed by his greatness—in fact, much more than any German Social Democrat. In his speech he dealt far more with Lenin than with Hitler. To give historical justice to the Communist revolution, and particularly to Lenin, was certainly most unusual for a Nazi speaker; it testifies to Goebbels' historical sense. "Lenin or Hitler"—Goebbels clearly foresaw the world historical importance of both. In his view only three important political movements existed in Germany: in the center "all parties defending tradition, reactionary tendencies, the conservative block with its roots in the 'system.' " It encompassed the whole range, from the Social Democrats on the left to the German Nationals on the right.

". . . Because they all agree to protect the 'system': democracy, liberalism, capitalism, which they all regard as sacred and untouchable."

On both sides of the center stood the revolutionary movements, Communists and National Socialists, who "have realized that reform will not suffice to build the future state; nothing less is needed than a decisive revolution. The system of the liberal-capitalistic democracy is so far gone at the core that there is nothing left to mend or reform. It must be basically destroyed, spiritually and politically annihilated. . . ."

Goebbels blamed for this breakdown the growing materialism, the expanding industrialization, and the fatal estrangement from the state and the nation of the proletariat who had left the countryside and immigrated into the towns, an ideal chance for that "systematic destroyer of every genuine workers' movement, the Marxist Jew, to shepherd the yearning masses into the wrong direction." The "tragic guilt of the bourgeois-nationalistic intelligentsia" lies in their failure to see this development, and having left it to the "Jewish intelligentsia . . . to take the lead of the workers fighting for their existence," instead of taking the lead themselves. Germany after 1870 was so satiated that it had no more political desires. All political wisdom this "liberal slowly disintegrating bourgeoisie with their mercenary spirit and their greed for profit" had left was wishing to conquer the world in peaceful competition. And the nationalist bourgeoisie with all its nationalist intelligentsia, looked on, while the working population was bleeding to death "from the gaping wound of social distress." In 1914 the people had pulled themselves together once again, and stood for four long years "unshaken in storms of steel only to collapse more miserably in the end than any other people in history." Goebbels did not omit to say that the men of 1918, "the November criminals," who "promised freedom, peace, and bread, and destroyed everything," were guilty men. "But history demanded that those, too, should expiate their guilt who, dwelling in the so-called nationalist camp, blind with egoism, had helped to lay the historical foundations for November 9, 1918, by expelling millions from their midst."

Goebbels considered November 9, 1918, as a day of treason, committed by both sides. The nationalist leaders sitting in the "mouse-holes" had failed, but the Marxists had failed too, "by letting themselves be taken into tow by international Jewish-capitalistic vested interests. This was no revolution! This was mutiny, this was a poor, miserable, cowardly stock-exchange rebellion. . . . November 9, 1918, might have had historical significance if the Marxist leaders had called upon the people like their apostles exhorting them to fight for their right to build a socialist state, instead of destroying their arms, their will, and their fanaticism; they systematically crippled their will to act and their instinct to resist. Why? Because they did not really want revolution, not in the true sense—they never wanted socialism."

All that followed, the long "chain of national humiliations," stemmed from that. An "enslaved people has neither the right nor the time for socialism. It has to work for its taskmasters." The final decision about the structure of the future state would, according to Goebbels, be fought out between Communists and National Socialists. But this explanation between them should take place in "all earnestness, objectivity, without demagogic trickery, or too much worrying over the present." Goebbels implored his audience: "We must come to an understanding—you from the left and we, because basically we both want the same . . . we want freedom!" And the only question is: "How shall we achieve this freedom and what will it look like? It is impossible that National Socialism and communism can be equally right. But we are both right in rejecting capitalism."

Goebbels continued by saying that Marxism, "the ally of the Jewish scoundrels of the Stock Exchange," cannot bring a solution. Only

National Socialism can, which sees its main task in finding a solution
to the social question:

"We consider the solution of the social question to be the main
problem of our time. Not in the sense of less work and more pay,
but as a possibility for, and the ability of, our compatriots to understand each other. Germany shall be free the moment the thirty million of the left and the thirty million of the right have understood each
other. Neither the bourgeois parties nor Marxism are capable of
bringing this about.

"There is no other movement that can accomplish this." National
Socialism embodied in its Fuehrer, Adolf Hitler.

"We no longer believe that Germany can be liberated with a
hurrah-and-beer patriotism. When faced with a proletarian who
stands before us saying: 'I have no fatherland,' we must know that
his accusation is profoundly justified. I cannot ask anybody to love
what he cannot respect, or to respect what he does not even know.
The German proletarian does not love his fatherland because he has
no share in it. We are going to give him his share. We demand
participation in ownership of property, in management of property,
participation in the management of the state."

It is therefore the main task of National Socialism to overcome the
bourgeois and proletarian way of thinking. But it will need a revolution to accomplish this, a national and social revolution.

"We have realized that we cannot make any headway without him
[the proletarian. Author's note] . . . But we do not approach him
with bourgeois mollycoddling and social commiseration, but with a
profound recognition that he is part of Germany, if not Germany
itself. . . . The social question is not a question of bourgeois
commiseration, but of socialistic state necessity. . . . We know that
the means we shall have to employ are not the ballot paper but those
of upheaval and revolution. We want the social revolution to make
Germany free, and the national revolution to make the social revolution secure for all time.

"History has always chosen a minority that knew its aims, inspired by a radical will for freedom and renovation. You may laugh
about the young ones who turn against their elders. We are proud to
see the youth in our ranks. We do not give a tinker's damn for the
experience and the distilled wisdom of our elders."

Youth against their elders; sons against their fathers; the per-
ennial fight between the generations—Goebbels, too, took part in it.
He, too, felt superior because he was young—wisdom and experience did not count. Only when everything had fallen apart, the elders
would be graciously permitted to pick up the pieces.

The Defeat—Bamberg

After the stormy meeting in Hanover which, no doubt, Hitler's emissary Gottfried Feder, as well as Robert Ley, reported to him, the Fuehrer called another meeting of the party leaders in Bamberg on February 14, 1926. The anti-Munich faction obviously hoped that Hitler would show himself amenable to making certain concessions. Goebbels' note of February 11 points to this: "I talked to Strasser on the telephone. He saw Wolf [a code name for Hitler used by party leaders at that time] on Saturday. Wolf has moved nearer to us. I, too, must go to Bamberg . . . we will play the coy beauty there and lure Hitler into our parlor. I noticed to my great joy that everywhere our spirit, that is the spirit of socialism, is on the march. No one believes any longer in the Munich setup. Elberfeld must become the Mecca of German socialism."

But Hitler showed in his speech no spirit of rapprochement with the Strasser group. He gave the beauty no chance to play coy. On the contrary, Hitler dealt pitilessly with everything that was important to the Strasser group: their socialism, their ideas on foreign policy, their plan to dispossess the princes without indemnity. The second volume of *Mein Kampf* had not yet been published. But Hitler's concept of foreign policy had already been drawn up: an understanding with England and Italy in exchange for a free hand against Russia. There in the East lay Germany's future. There was the land that would, once and for all, solve the German tragedy of being a people without *Lebensraum*. Gottfried Feder spoke in support of Hitler, criticizing in his arrogantly ironical manner the economic and social program of the Strasser group. A discussion followed, apparently limited to half an hour.

The first to reply was Strasser. But he was practically speechless. Was this Hitler's rapprochement? His brutal rejection of all ideas the Strasser group had drawn up left no door open for any compromise. Strasser's words came slowly, hesitantly, without conviction or will to resist. There was only one man who could, after Strasser's pitiful performance, save the situation: Joseph Goebbels. The members of the Strasser group looked at him expectantly. But Goebbels remained silent. Why?

Goebbels' entry in his diary of February 15 may explain it: ". . . Hitler speaks. Two hours. I feel obliterated. What a Hitler! A reactionary? Magnificently clumsy and uncertain. The Russian question: a complete miss. Italy and England natural allies. Fright-

ful! Our task is to smash Bolshevism. Bolshevism is a Jewish brew!
We must inherit Russia! 180 millions!!! Indemnify the dispossessed
princes. Right must remain right. That includes the princes. Do not
touch private property. Horrifying! The party program suffices as it
is. . . . He is satisfied with it. Feder nods. Ley nods. Streicher nods.
Esser nods. It hurts my innermost soul to see you in this company!!!

"Short discussion. Strasser speaks hesitantly, tremblingly, clumsily,
the brave, honest Strasser. God, how badly we measure up to those
swine down there. Half an hour discussion after four hours of
speeches. [Having mentioned two hours for Hitler's speech, Goebbels apparently added Feder's ramblings.] Stupidity you have won!
I am unable to utter a word. I feel as if someone hit me on the head.
By car to the station. Strasser is beside himself. Waving and Heil. I
feel pain in my heart. Goodbye to Strasser. We shall meet again in
Berlin the day after tomorrow. I want to cry. On my way home. Sad
fatherland . . . a frightful night. One of the greatest disappointments
of my life. I cannot any more fully believe in Hitler. The terrible
thing is I feel no longer secure in myself. Only half of me is left.
Gray dawn of the morning. Elberfeld. A few hours' sleep. Kaufmann.
I feel like embracing him. We speak what is on our minds. . . .
The conclusion: We are socialists, and we do not want to see our
socialism come to nothing. Telegram to Lohse, Strasser, Vaalen. No
unnecessary haste, let us have a frank discussion in Göttingen tomorrow. Then, on Wednesday, to Strasser. Proposal: Kaufmann,
Strasser, and I should go to Hitler to try to convince him. He must
not allow himself to be tied up in knots by those scoundrels down
there."

Goebbels was shocked, no question. Hitler had not convinced
him. Hitler was a reactionary in the social field. Goebbels called
Hitler's concept of foreign policy "frightful!" Why, then, did Goebbels not speak up? Goebbels tried to plead his case to himself. "Half
an hour's discussion after four hours of speeches," he moaned, but it
was a rather weak excuse. If he had answered Hitler with brilliant
arguments, surely nobody would have cut him short.

"[Gregor] Strasser speaks hesitantly, tremblingly, clumsily . . ."
This sounds more convincing. After all, Strasser was the chief of the
group. As such he should have stood firm. He was head of the party
organization and transacted the daily party business. He was greatly
respected in the widest party circles and was a member of the
Reichstag. He had been a first lieutenant in the war and had been
decorated, like Hitler, with the IKN (Iron Cross First Class). He
had money, a publishing house, and newspapers. He was the only
one among them who could really afford to stand up to Hitler, even
rebel against him. But Strasser withdrew. After the conference he said

to Rosenberg: "I should now leave the party, but that would mean that several gauleiters would follow me. I, therefore, cannot do it."[38]

But if Strasser, the only powerful figure in the party next to Hitler, failed to put up resistance and capitulated, why should Goebbels play the strong man? His earnings were so meager despite all his hard work that he often could not afford to invite a friend to a meal, and he still received money from his mother occasionally to help him out.

"How badly we measure up to those swine down there—this means they have all the money, and are therefore stronger than we are. They can crush us if they like." If that happens, what is Dr. Goebbels to do? Join the Communists? Become an editor at some newspaper? What newspaper would still want him, after he had shown himself to be an anti-Semite and confirmed Nazi? He was twenty-nine years old. There were not so many possibilities for a career open to him.

"You win!" This remark was not meant only for Hitler's victory with regard to the party program and the dispossession of the princes, it was also meant for Hitler's victory over Joseph Goebbels. He is "struck dumb" and "feels as if someone hit me on the head," and all he wants is to get away as quickly as possible, because he is ashamed. In his innermost soul Goebbels knows that he has capitulated. Lenin or Hitler? The answer is Hitler. He is there and alive, and all-powerful, even if only within the party—as yet.

In Bamberg all Strasser's and Goebbels' grand ideas about the party's economic, social, and foreign policy were shoved into a big coffin and buried forever. From then on, radical socialism, or a foreign policy orientated toward friendship with the Soviet Union, was eradicated from National Socialism once and for all. Only the radical shouting would persist. And only the more piercingly, as a transformation of society toward greater social justice had been definitely dropped from the program.

The Disciple Recognizes the Master

Goebbels felt that the moment had come to abandon the road he had mapped out for himself. From now on he would take only one direction—that of Adolf Hitler. Not only the poet but also the independent thinker, Goebbels was going to be left behind forever. He noted in his diary on March 27, in Weimar: "Only a scoundrel will write poems today and forget that his people are in mortal danger." Adorno wrote something similar after 1945: "After Auschwitz, poetry is no longer possible."

For one long moment Joseph Goebbels found himself falling between two stools, when, at last, Hitler came to his rescue. Goebbels noted in his diary on March 25 that Hitler had invited him by letter to speak in Munich on April 8. Goebbels was picked up by Hitler's chauffeur. There is an account in Goebbels' diary dated April 13 of what happened on that memorable day:

"We drove to the Hotel. What noble reception." Later Hitler appeared. "Tall, fit, full of life. I like him. He is embarrassingly kind to us [with Goebbels are Kaufmann and von Pfeffer] . . . in the evening at eight o'clock by car to the Bürgerbräu. Hitler is there already. I can feel my heart beating to the bursting point. We enter the enormous restaurant hall. Tumultuous reception. It is jammed full, a sea of heads, Streicher opens the meeting. Then it is my turn. I speak for two and a half hours. I give all I have. They rave, they shout. In the end Hitler embraces me. Tears are in his eyes. I feel something like true happiness. . . . Hitler is waiting for me in the hotel alone. We have dinner together. He is my host. And even in that, what greatness!"

Then and there the enchantment is accomplished. One might apply the political version of Goethe's *Halb zog sie ihn/Halb sank er hin* (Half did she drag him/Half he gave himself to her). Goebbels was lost. A new grand landscape opened up before his eyes: Leave Strasser join Hitler! This meant skipping several steps in status. And it all seemed so easy. Obviously, Hitler was a man of genius, worthy of unconditional submission. Goebbels had found a replacement for the God he had lost. And Hitler would reward him by presenting him with paradise on earth—all the more readily accepted, since Goebbels had lost his faith in the other kingdom long ago.

The next day a discussion took place among Hitler, von Pfeffer, Kaufmann, and Goebbels. Kaufmann was rebuked for a rude letter he had written to Philipp Bouhler, Reich administrator of the NSDAP. Kaufmann was struck dumb. We encounter this phenomenon again and again; when Hitler attacks, everybody present is paralyzed. Having finished with Kaufmann, Hitler turned to Goebbels. Yet compared with Kaufmann, Goebbels was let off lightly. Having gotten it off his chest, the Fuehrer forgave, and the air was cleared: "In the end perfect unity was established. Hitler is great. He warmly shakes hands with us. The slate is wiped clean."

During the second meeting more fundamental questions were discussed: "Policy toward the East. Social questions. The arguments used in Bamberg. He spoke for three hours brilliantly. This man can really shake you. Italy and England are our natural allies, Russia will devour us. All this is written in his pamphlet, and in the second volume of his *Kampf,* which is about to appear. We move closer toward one another. We put our questions. He answers brilliantly. I love him. . . . The social question. Completely new vistas. He has thought of everything. His ideal: a mixture of collectivism and individualism. The land for the people and all that is on it and in it. Limited individual production to remain private, big combines, trusts, transport, etc., to be nationalized. That is certainly a basis for discussion. Everything seems secure in his hands. He is a man, taken all in all. Such a hotheaded fellow my Fuehrer can be! I incline before the greater, before the political genius. A warmhearted farewell. We all three get firm confirmation [in their posts of fuehrers of the Gau Ruhr. Author's note]. And may henceforth peace reign among us. We take leave and sit down to a meal together, and get ourselves drunk, bubbling over with enthusiasm."

It was probably the only time that Goebbels got really drunk.

Hitler entirely won over his future chief of propaganda during that dinner on April 8. Goebbels was completely enchanted, carried away by Hitler's amiability and charm. It was, in a sense, their wedding night. The next day the dowry was discussed. Hitler started by reproaching the members of the work co-operative with their disobedience. How did they dare to do this to their Fuehrer? Goebbels felt it was mainly addressed to him. But Hitler pulled his punches; the loved one sulks a little on account of the partner's escapades, but in the end everything is forgiven and forgotten. And the dowry? Maybe Hitler was right in saying the Russian Communists wanted "to devour Germany." He spoke so convincingly. And all Goebbels had to say to this cardinal point that would determine the whole future foreign policy on which he and Hitler had held diametrically opposed views before, was: "I love him." That surely is the end of all discussion and argument. After all, people in love are crazy—and no longer capable of cold logic.

The social question was somewhat less important to Hitler, and he made quite a few concessions. His economic program was still vague and, in fact, remained so throughout. It vacillated between free and planned economy until Hjalmar Schacht, and the captains of industry and banks, exerted a decisive influence on Hitler's economic policy. At least in this field Goebbels could save some of his political dowry and was only compelled to capitulate up to a point.

After their visit to Munich, an estrangement between Goebbels and his former colleagues set in. They had gotten themselves drunk together after meeting Hitler, "bubbling over with enthusiasm," but Goebbels' lyrical adoration of Hitler was apparently too much, even for them, and they parted with a distant goodbye: "Something has come between us," Goebbels recorded.

After Munich, Goebbels accompanied Hitler and Hess to Stuttgart, where Goebbels delivered another speech. Again Hitler embraced him enthusiastically at the end. The master celebrated his thirty-seventh birthday with them, and Goebbels wrote in his diary emotionally punch drunk: "Adolf Hitler, I love you, because you are great and simple at the same time. You are what's called a genius." (April 19, 1926).

Back home Goebbels felt the estrangement between him and his former colleagues; but it did not bother him unduly. Still under the spell of his Hitler experience, he wrote an open letter to the Fuehrer of the party, published on May 15, 1926, in the sixteenth issue of the *National Socialist Letters:*

"Dear and most revered Herr Hitler! We are a movement of the future, still struggling to find our definite form, both spiritually and politically. Everything with us is still fermenting, it pushes and pulls, roars and splutters. It must be mastered and directed. . . . A selection must be made with discipline and severity. Only the best, the most courageous, the most ready for sacrifice among us must be chosen. Applying a puritanical cruelty against yourself, you must steel your heart for the day when more will be demanded of us than just our convictions: namely brutality, firm action, unfailing judgment, a clear view. Our future leaders . . .

"We have closed our ranks around you, in whom we see the embodiment of the Idea, the man who binds us by thoughts and formative force to the ineffable end. The Legion of the Future, determined to go through despair and pain, the terrible way right to the finish. There may come a day when all around us breaks apart. We shall not break. The hour may come when the mob around you will slaver and scream 'crucify him.' Then we shall stand firm, men of iron, we shall exclaim and sing: 'Hosanna!' Then you will see round you the phalanx of the last guard, who will not know despair, not even in death. That guard of men made of iron who will not want to live when Germany dies."

A prophetic letter, indeed. But it was not so great about that iron guard refusing to live when Germany died. Most of them even preferred to be hanged by their necks to sharing their Fuehrer's death with him.

The purpose of Goebbels' open letter was obvious: Goebbels wanted to leave Elberfeld, where he felt more and more isolated. He strained to get into Hitler's inner circle and become his favorite disciple. This strange desire to be loved never leaves him. It is a cripple's constant yearning for love and recognition.

In the middle of June, Hitler visited the Rhine and Ruhr districts. Goebbels accompanied him to Cologne, Düsseldorf, and Essen. Hitler was still banned from speaking in public and, therefore, spoke in Essen before an invited audience of about three thousand people. Goebbels was now entirely convinced that Hitler's social policy was right, because Hitler "found the final form of German socialism. Such a man can change a whole world. Last night was a great, great experience. Hitler will lead us out of this misery one day." (June 17, 1926). The last sentence, which echoes the words of a hymn, is an early indication of Goebbels' future deification of Hitler.

As a parting gift, Goebbels received Hitler's invitation to come to Berchtesgaden. On June 21, Goebbels wrote in his diary: "Hitler has just left, and a long spell of complete repose lies before me." It gave Goebbels time to wrap himself up more and more into his Hitler experience. He had to wait until July to see his hero again at the party conference in Weimar. Goebbels noted on July 6, 1926: "Hitler speaks . . . profoundly and mystically. It is almost like the Gospel. Shudders of awe. At his side you pass the abysses of life; the final word is spoken. I am grateful to destiny to have given us this man." A further stage of deification is reached: mysticism, gospel, shuddering with awe, the abysses of life, the final word. The disciple has finally recognized the savior.

The three weeks Goebbels spent in Berchtesgaden were a feast of joy for him. Only his foot gave him pain, and he was tormented by his longing for a female body, tormented "to the marrow." But as soon as he was in Hitler's company the dark desires of his body calmed down. His sexual need was transformed into admiration, amazement, and adoration for the great man:

"Hitler recounts and revels in his fantasies. He is a pure man—a child. . . . He spoils me like a child. The kindly friend and master.

"We walk down the mountainside, only the two of us, and he talks to me like a father to his child, and always drawing life with large strokes. This master of life." (July 25 and 26, 1926).

Master and disciple woo each other. Each wants to be loved by the other. Hitler shows himself humanly from his best side. But he also empties his soul of all he stored up, and which he is about to write down for the whole world to read in the second volume of *Mein Kampf.* And Goebbels makes a superb audience. He listens devoutly and absorbs every word of the master. He receives it as though it were the Gospel. He undergoes a process like hundreds of

others before him and after him: They were mesmerized by Hitler's
torrent of words, and took the most banal thoughts, including obvious errors of thinking, for revelations; whether they were pronouncements concerning social questions, the state, race, or architecture, Goebbels had surely read better stuff than Hitler was telling
him. Even Goebbels himself had said and written much more in-
telligently on all these topics. But he listened, mouth open, in
wonderment:

"The social question: thoughts that he had already developed in
Munich, but again new and compelling, illustrated by irrefutable examples. Indeed this is a man worthy to be served, this, doubtless, is
the creator of the Third Reich." (July 23, 1926).

"The Chief speaks about racial questions, it is almost impossible
to render it. You had to be present. He is a genius. The independent
creative instrument of a divine will. I stand before him deeply shaken.
That is how he is: like a child, dear, good, full of compassion. Like a
cat, sly, clever, and smart, like a lion roaring, powerful and overpowering. A real fellow, a man. He speaks about the state . . . of
the structure of the state and the sense of political revolution.
Thoughts that I had myself but never pronounced. . . . I feel overcome by something like true happiness! This life is worth living:
'My head will not fall before my mission is fulfilled.' These were his
parting words to me. That is how he is! Yes, that is how he is! I lie
sleepless for a long time." (July 24, 1926).

Goebbels has his National Socialist novitiate behind him, and his
mentor was Hitler, the master, as his entourage still called him then,
seeing in him the great political revolutionary as, before him, Richard
Wagner had been the great musical revolutionary.

For Goebbels the way was now clear: "These days have shown
me the way and the direction I have to take! In darkest distress a
star has appeared! I feel bound to him to my last breath. My last
doubts have vanished. Germany will live. Heil Hitler!" (July 25,
1926).

Hitler knew that he had won a victory over a man—not just any
man, but the most intelligent among the party leaders. Hitler always
had to have victory, be it over individuals, masses, parties, or peoples. He was insatiable for victories. But this particular one was very
important for him. Not that it had been so very difficult; the little
cripple had brought him his heart on a platter even before the master
could work his magic. Unlike Goebbels, Hitler understood human
beings, at least their weaknesses. And those of Goebbels' were only
too obvious: a high degree of exaltation as a consequence of continuous suppression of his complexes; bitterness about a lack of

recognition of his abilities; and last but not least, an almost hysterical desire to be needed and loved.

Hitler had it in his power to relieve Goebbels of all his needs. And the brilliant little man would be grateful to him until death, would give him everything he had, all his brainpower, and repay Hitler's magnanimity with a still greater gift, making him in his lifetime into a myth for the German people.

Hitler knew that in taking Goebbels away from the Strasser group he had eliminated their most dangerous member. The history of Hitler's rise, and Goebbels' contribution to it, shows how providently Hitler acted then. If the revolt of the Strasser faction had succeeded at the conference in Bamberg, the Hitler movement would never have become as strong as it did, and Goebbels might have just as easily damned the "Fuehrer" as the devil incarnate, as he later elevated him to a god. He who knew no loyalty to women or ideas, displayed a loyalty to Hitler that lasted unto death. Goebbels loved Hitler in a sublimated homoerotic sense; he loved him as an idol. There is no other interpretation possible of the adolescent confessions of love that he confided to his diary, nor of his later eulogies when he had become minister.

And what about Hitler? While abusing Goebbels' love he developed a strange attachment to him. He, in fact, never let Goebbels down, even when others demanded his head. Despite their basic difference of character, there existed a deep affinity between them, a deep-rooted sympathy that created an intimate spiritual partnership. They served each other the right cues like a couple of tennis players their services. They stimulated each other in deriding others. From time to time, Hitler would humiliate his favorite disciple, which only drove the other to greater efforts to please his "Fuehrer." Right up to the very end, Goebbels courted Hitler's favor. And not so much for fear of the other leaders who would have destroyed him if Hitler had not protected him, but out of genuine loyalty and devotion. The brutal Hitler was far from Goebbels' former ideal of a hero. Goebbels sold his soul to him in Munich, fulfilling Luther's demand to blind and kill his reason; with the difference that Goebbels did this not, as Luther demanded, for God, but for Hitler.

The Diary

Of all the Goebbels' papers in our possession his diary, covering the period from August 12, 1925, to the end of October 1926, helps us most to understand his character. The diary was found in the

courtyard of the Ministry of Propaganda. It came into the possession of former United States President Herbert Hoover, who donated
it to Stanford University. Helmut Heiber published it in 1960 in the
Quarterly Review of Contemporary History. Some of the pages
were damaged by water and fire, partly blackened and difficult to
decipher, partly totally indecipherable. Heiber, who did his work
with scientific exactitude, assesses Goebbels not as a demoniacal
figure but rather as a *petit bourgeois* deserving utter condemnation.
But Heiber bypasses essential points of the diary.

Heiber admits that the Goebbels diary is the only genuine writing
of Goebbels and therefore a key document enabling us to understand Goebbels' personality. But he calls it bombastic nonsense and
the sloppy romanticism of a schoolboy. Heiber adds that the whole
thing has the standard of a dime novel, and particularly draws attention to the high standard of Goebbels' articles in the *National Socialist Letters* written during the same period.

But in making this comparison, Heiber points up the weakness of
his judgment. Diaries are no material for literary evaluation. They
rather serve to throw light on the author's character, revealing his
inner tensions and vacillations, showing the influence of his environment on him. In fact, the less literary a diary is, the more
valuable it is for the historian. Goebbels himself demonstrated in
his book *From Hotel Kaiserhof to the Reich Chancellery* how to use
a diary. Equally wrong as Heiber's literary evaluation of the diaries
is his judgment of Goebbels' character. He accuses Goebbels of having "built himself up" as he later built up Hitler and other personalities.

According to Heiber this melodrama is full of scoundrels, and
has only one impeccable hero—Joseph Goebbels. Goebbels does not
behave as if he were twenty-eight, but only eighteen, which might
be expected after all that highfalutin nonsense and adolescent exal-
tations. Heiber arrives at the conclusion—also expressed in his Goebbels biography—that Goebbels was not a demon but an ambitious
little man, an intriguer, willing to sell himself to the highest bidder.
Much ado just for the price of believing obediently what the other
wished him to believe. Heiber's deduction that Goebbels, often and
rightly called the biggest liar, was the victim of his own lies in his
diary, does not appear to be logical. Either Goebbels was the victim
of his own lies, or he was a corrupt opportunist. The two things do
not seem to go together. These diaries obviously reflect events and
experiences spontaneously recorded. They still mirror emotional re-
actions and moods, and therefore should not be taken as a literary
autobiography, not even as "self expression," as Heiber does; to be

that they lack introspection, the inner dialogue between accuser and accused.

Goebbels wrote without inhibition, without self-control. His judgment about people vacillates, which only shows how spontaneous his notes were. The "nice fellow" Kaufmann later becomes a man who is "not quite honest."

The same Gregor Strasser who is determined to radicalize everything, becomes someone who finds it difficult to be a revolutionary. These changes of opinion follow changes of circumstances.

In his diary Goebbels attacks neither Strasser nor Kaufmann with real venom. He only moves away from them, trying to prove to himself that he made an error in the first place, when assessing their capabilities—and history proved him right.

When calling Ley a "pig," Esser an "idiot" and "pretty boy," and Rust and Streicher "arse drummers," Goebbels was not so far from the truth. Admittedly, all this sounds vulgar, but Goebbels just wrote down what others thought or said among themselves. Heiber is irritated by the carelessness with which this eternal adolescent pronounced his judgments in the exaltation of the moment only to discard them the next day, if need be. But this eternal adolescent had entered politics and worked for a radical party. His language could no longer be the same he had employed at the university. The frustrated poet and star journalist Goebbels had to adjust himself to his new environment, unless he wanted to become even more of an outsider, as he already was with his clubfoot and superior intelligence.

Goebbels raged against Fate, which had made him underprivileged, and created an ideal image in Michael, the splendid hero endowed with Goebbels' intelligence, a true genius of the kind he imagined himself to be, and not the one he actually was—a great agitator. Outwardly he tried to be charming and amiable. He wanted to be loved, win over everybody who recognized him and helped him in his career. Time and again he would attempt to establish a bond between himself and the others, both on a professional basis and on a personal basis. He wished Kaufmann to be his friend, as well as Gregor Strasser; and he wished Hitler to be his friend. But he was never to have a friend, and only one patron: Adolf Hitler. At the beginning of his political career, too exalted in his Hitler adoration, too obviously ambitious, later on too vicious, Goebbels was in the end completely isolated.

Goebbels' struggle against his own nature, against the burden of his fate, appears to me to be the real problem enclosed in his diary.

Hitler, as we have seen, occupied a special position from the beginning. Goebbels' attacks in his diary are strictly directed against Hitler's entourage, against the "pigsty" at Munich, but never against Hitler personally. The isolated two passages that are critical of Hitler concern his ideas on foreign and social policy. The person of Hitler remains taboo throughout. Gregor Strasser is viewed with benevolence, even with a kind of friendship, but for Hitler there is pure admiration from the beginning. The reader of the diary has the uncanny feeling that, even before Goebbels met Hitler for the first time through Kaufmann, in September 1925, the magician sitting in Munich was sending his magnetic rays to Elberfeld. Goebbels' biographers tended to overlook these important points when analyzing the diary; their attention was, possibly, too much focused on Goebbels' abuse of other politicians, and particularly his references to his love affairs. Goebbels felt that Fate had treated him shabbily. From his grievance against Fate he derived the right to be an egoist in order to catch up with the others, employing his intelligence and his ruthless ambition, and allowing neither friendship nor love to stand in his way. All this should be seen as a consequence of his frustration. And when, as it sometimes happened, he suddenly recognized the shoddiness of his behavior, he would not accuse himself, but blame others, or life itself:

"And a limitless contempt for this beast man. Vomit!" He wrote in his diary on October 14, 1925.

Clearly, he realized that he, too, belonged to this despicable species, but it needed a really heavy blow, such as falling into disfavor with Hitler, or the end of a love affair, to make him admit it to himself. When he finally knew he would have to separate from Else because she was half Jewish, he did not accuse himself directly of being a scoundrel, he rather chose to say it in a roundabout way. "Torment outside and inside. If only Hitler would call me to Munich now, then at least I would get out of all this muck. Now all depends on his decision. Does he want me? Once I am there my motto will be, work and keep away from mankind. They are all brutes, including myself." (June 12, 1926).

Once Hitler had chosen him, Goebbels had to cut this last tie that might have impeded his career. Hitler might accept the clubfoot (as long as it was due to an accident or illness), but a half-Jewish fiancée would have been pure sacrilege. Goebbels had sacrificed all his ideals to his career. Why not a girl too? In his love life Goebbels was also unbalanced: in part sentimental dreamer, in part uninhibited sensualist. He himself provided the best description of his relationship to women: "Every female excites me to the marrow. I rave around like a hungry wolf. At the same time I am timid like a child. I sometimes do not understand myself. I should marry and become a bourgeois. And hang myself after eight days." (July 15, 1926).

Goebbels' desire for women was essentially physical. No giant by nature, nor in a position to demonstrate his virility as a soldier or parade it successfully in the party uniform, he became a sexual show-off, intrinsically unfaithful. He had only to see a pretty woman to be after her. As a guest he would assess his host's wife or daughter as to their respective bedworthyness. In his fantasies he dragged every beautiful woman into bed. His political aggressiveness may have partly been the expression of his suppressed libido. Once he was minister and had as many women as he wanted, his alertness and political activity flagged, and it needed a great shock to make him pull himself up again to his old form.

Many notes in his diary are about Else Janke. Else came from a good middle-class family. Her mother was Jewish. She was the teacher of Goebbels' sister Maria, and that was probably how they met. Another version suggests that Alma, the friend of Fritz Prang, introduced Goebbels to Else. The two couples spent a lot of time together. Else and Joseph got engaged. She called him Ulex, or by his pet name "Stropp." After she had obtained a position for him at the Kölner (Cologne) Bank, they wrote each other long letters every few days. Occasionally they spent their holidays together.[39] Else was vivacious, intelligent, pretty, and full of natural charm. Their relationship lasted from the end of 1921 to autumn 1926, interrupted by painful separations, followed by passionate reunions.

During the year in which the notes concerning Else were written, Goebbels lived in Elberfeld, separated from her. Constantly in the company of self-important politicians, or mixing at political meetings with people who reeked of beer, tobacco, and sweat, he would return to his poorly furnished room, and there he would sit all alone, longing for a woman, actually not so much concerned about who she might be, as long as she was a woman. He was longing for Else, he was longing for Alma, he was longing for Anka. He was longing for all three at the same time:

"I think often of Anka. Why just now? Because it is a good time to travel. How wonderful it would be to travel together with her! What a wonderful female! I feel a longing for Elslein! When will I hold you in my arms again . . . ? Alma, you easy little dear! Anka, I will never forget you! And how lonely I am now . . . !" (August 15, 1925).

Time and again his political remarks are interrupted by sentences like: "When will I see Elslein again? I am longing for her" or "I am

standing on the Rhine waiting for you, come, oh come, you kind
dear soul and bless me." When he was too much tortured by his
loneliness and plagued by his sexual urges, he started complaining:
"Else's love lacks a spirit of sacrifice, she loves as long as it is good
for her health. A truly great love—I could, and would, give my life
for it. Hopeless, poor and miserable world." (August 29, 1925).

All these are big words and should be taken with a grain of salt,
but they are moods that Goebbels recorded for himself and not for
the world, and it is not impossible that they were true, at least while
he was writing them.

Goebbels' political activity was bound to erode the love of these
two. The end came when Hitler invited him to Munich.

Else wrote him a "brief, matter-of-fact" goodbye letter. They met
once again at the end of September in Rheydt—and the meeting was
"short and sweet." Goebbels returned home in pain to sleep, but felt
so miserable the next day that his sister took pity on him: "I am
suffering. In the end Maria went to fetch Else. She arrives. She has
been crying. She accompanies me to the station."

Their last scene is reported in typical journalese: "We are waiting for the train for what seems to be an eternity. Autumn has come.
The train roars in. The luggage coach. A pitiless voice shouts 'luggage
all in.' The signal goes up! The train starts moving. Else turns away
crying. The window goes down. The rain pelts down on the roof. I
have said goodbye to another's life. Heartbroken." (September 26,
1926).

On October 20, his diary mentions his abandoned fiancée for the
last time: "I sometimes think of Else." His heart may be broken, but
when receiving Hitler's letter appointing him gauleiter of Berlin, he
writes: "Berlin is in the bag. Hurrah!"

The love story between Joseph and Else was merely an episode,
but not insignificant, as it happened when Goebbels matured into
manhood. His romantic phase was behind him, he had resigned himself to his fate. He no longer resented that he was not a tall, handsome hero. He had also accepted that he was not a poet. But he had
come to recognize his capabilities. Hitler, too, had recognized them
and gave him a chance. Goebbels took it and used it as no other
politician could have done. He conquered Berlin, "the reddest city
in the world after Moscow," for Adolf Hitler, with the aid of but a
few hundred party members. This remains his greatest achievement.

2

The Conquest of Berlin

Goebbels Arrives in Berlin

Berlin in the 1920s was Germany's spiritual center, and one of the most open-minded capitals in the world. Everybody who nurtured new ideas came to Berlin, where he might become famous overnight. Only the very latest could pass as new enough. Progress at any price was the motto.

Berlin was the "reddest city after Moscow." It was the headquarters of the best-organized Social Democratic party in the world. It also had a strong and efficiently organized Communist party. The greater part of the intelligentsia was in the ideological left—from Heinrich Mann and Bertol Brecht to Kurt Tucholsky who, at that time, edited the *Weltbühne,* the mouthpiece of the intellectual left, before Carl von Ossietsky took over from him six months later. Even Gerhart Hauptmann was a fellow traveler.

The political struggle found perhaps less definite expression in music, but here, too, all new creative attempts were supported by the left. Arnold Schoenberg taught at the Prussian Academy of Arts; Franz Schrecker, Kurt Weill, Paul Hindemith, Hans-Heinz Stuckenschmidt, and Ernst Krenek had made Berlin their home. Berlin was the focal point of all modern movements in the arts: Dadaism, futurism, and cubism—Ernst Nolde, Max Pechstein, Ernst Ludwig Kirchner, Otto Dix, Karl-Schmidt-Rottluff, Käthe Kollwitz; the architects, Bruno Paul and Mies van der Rohe; the sculptors, Ernst Barlach as well as Ludwig Gies—all were working in Berlin.

The Jews had a considerable share in Berlin's spiritual life in the late twenties. Some of the artists mentioned above were Jews— Tucholsky, Schoenberg, Weill, and Bruno Paul. There were several

Jewish writers, such as Arnold Zweig, Alfred Döblin, and Bruno Frank; such theater people as the theater wizard, Max Reinhardt; musicians and conductors, such as Bruno Walter, Otto Klemperer, and Bronislaw Hubermann; critics such as Alfred Kerr; scientists such as Albert Einstein; Berlin's cultural life would have been unthinkable without them. There were several reasons for this development. The breakdown of the German Empire greatly stimulated the development of Germany's Jewry. The remnants of a feudal society seemed to have disappeared, and the Jews, now freed from all fetters, almost exploded with stored-up intelligence. Hundreds of years of ghetto life had made them resistant and tough, leaving them, at the same time, spiritually unspent. The Jewish intelligentsia was progressive. They had suffered so long under religious prejudice, blind hatred, political reaction, and narrow conservatism that now they advocated almost everything that served spiritual and material progress, that was antimilitarist, or that combated chauvinism and advanced the idea of world citizenship. That alone sufficed to challenge antagonistic forces. Already Spengler had put forward the thesis whereby all world citizens pursued "ideals of serfs" which, if successful, would bring about the "historical resignation of the nation, not in favor of permanent peace, but of other, namely younger or less spent nations."

But there was another reason for the progressive attitude of the Jewish intelligentsia. Judaism is the only religion, apart from Buddhism in its pure form, that refuses to call upon the happiness of another world to help overcome the misery of the one we live in. Moses forbade his people to make themselves an image of God and paradise. The promised land, flowing with milk and honey, lay here on earth and was only attained by great hardship and sacrifice. Marxism with its promise of happiness on earth necessarily fascinated the Jewish intelligentsia. Many members of the intelligentsia reached responsible positions in socialist parties, many smashed idols of the past that barred the way to progress, to the gates of a human paradise on earth. If they sometimes overdid it, the blame, surely, rested with the stolid toughness of the idols they tried to overthrow and their own pugnacity, peculiar to fighters for progress.

Goebbels stepped into this kind of world on a gloomy November day in 1926. All he had was a suitcase containing his belongings, a little money, and Hitler's letter appointing him gauleiter of Greater Berlin, with full powers: power over a party that had hardly a thousand members, fighting one another in bitter disunity. And Goebbels' task was to conquer Berlin for Adolf Hitler. The mere idea seemed ludicrous. But Goebbels possessed, like Hitler, the will power to make the impossible possible. Thus this little man nobody would have noticed especially, had it not been for his slight limp, walked down the platform at Friedrichstrasse Station, and whatever his thoughts may have been, he could never have imagined that he would actually conquer the city of Berlin so that the Fuehrer could transform it one day into a gigantic pile of ruins. Yet the important thing was that he took over a task, though not an easy one, that allowed him to be his own master. Here, in Berlin, he had no superior, no Gregor Strasser over him. He was directly responsible to Hitler, reigning as Hitler's appointed governor under the pompous title of "gauleiter of Greater Berlin" over a gau that only existed in pure fantasy. Even in the weakest district of Berlin, the Communists counted more members than the NSDAP did in the entire city. Adolf Hitler's party was the smallest in Berlin, a minute party, actually no party at all, but rather a querulous crowd fighting among themselves.

In his book *The Struggle for Berlin,* mainly based on his diary, and suitably streamlined for publication, Goebbels described the position of his party in Berlin at that time. Quarrels among the leaders had shaken the organization, if it deserved that name. Two groups faced each other with bitter hostility, and experience had shown that it was impossible to give one of the two precedence. It was an excited, confused hive of a few hundred people, who had adopted National Socialist ideas. Each of them had his own version of National Socialism. Actual fights among them were a daily occurrence.[1]

The party headquarters was situated in a back building at 109 Potsdamerstrasse, "a kind of dirty cellar, we called it the opium den. It seemed to be a most fitting name for it. It had artificial light only. On entering one was hit by the thick air of cigar, cigarette, and pipe smoke. It was unthinkable to do solid and systematic work there. Unholy confusion reigned. Any real organization was practically non-existent. The financial position was hopeless."[2]

Goebbels did not exaggerate. His first task was to bring order into the party. Within a few days of his arrival he called a general meeting at Spandau of all members. Spandau was the strong point of the party. Here the party had received 137 votes at the local elections on October 25, 1925—137 NSDAP votes against 604,696 SDP and 347,381 KPD votes—a mouse faced with two elephants.

At the meeting Goebbels first let the people talk. The two groups, who usually fought each other, combined in attacking Goebbels. He listened for a while, then stood up and said: "We shall forget the past and make a new start. Anybody who does not agree will be expelled from the party. . . ."[3] After this first meeting the Berlin party lost, according to Goebbels, a fifth of its membership, approximately 200 members.

Goebbels' radical measures were backed by the powers he had been given by Hitler, which included the right to "purge," without giving those he had expelled the right to submit their case to the Arbitration Committee. Goebbels got rid of the "mischiefmakers," and at the same time made an alliance with the head of the Berlin SA, Kurt Daluege, who later became chief and general of the Ordnungspolizei (Order Police). Goebbels joined up with the stronger element knowing he needed radical, ruthless fighters to realize his plans.

An SA man was worth more than three ordinary party members. And under Goebbels' special powers the SA in Berlin was also under his orders. They formed his fighting core. It became the most notorious SA group in the land.

But Goebbels also knew that a party member will only give his heart fully if called upon to make sacrifices. Members who were not prepared to vote for their own party were useless. Unlike Hitler, Goebbels maintained that "a revolutionary fighting party that aims at smashing international capitalism should never use capitalist money for their own buildup."[4]

He therefore called a meeting of party members for November 5 —their day of atonement—at Wilmersdorf. Six hundred people attended. Goebbels appealed to their spirit of sacrifice essential for building up the Berlin organization. He must have sounded convincing, since every member promised to make a monthly contribution of 1,500 marks. The active party members—those who declared themselves prepared to contribute as much as 10 per cent of their income —Goebbels formed into a tightly disciplined organization, the Freiheitsbund (Freedom Association), and immediately began to carry out a precise plan for building up the party and the propaganda machine. He started with smaller meetings at which he discussed mainly points of the party program. He fixed a monthly gau day (Gautag) when all leaders and the SA would meet together. On these occasions, Goebbels discussed fundamental issues of propaganda, organization, and political tactics. All these measures were designed to establish a closer contact among the active members of the party. And once they felt a strong leading hand, they began to conform.

By January 1, 1927, when the party moved into new quarters at 44 Luetzowstrasse, Goebbels had accomplished the first phase of his plan. In merely six weeks he had welded together a small but active fighting group and had created a command center. He wrote: "We have climbed from the cellar to the first floor. The smoky debating den has been transformed into a political center." Goebbels hired the necessary staff, against the opposition of some party members, "who had become so much accustomed to the old rut that they considered it indispensable, and tended to take improvements as a sign of capitalist boasting and megalomania." Goebbels therefore carried out a second purge among those "whose attitude was more worthy of a patriotic skittle club than a revolutionary movement."[5] Another 200 party members were expelled.

Goebbels proceeded with the second phase of his plan in the new year. The NSDAP was still the smallest party in Berlin, if such a minor group had a right to call itself a "party," and would so remain unless something was done to draw the people's attention to the movement. But in the first few weeks, which he needed to build up the organization, Goebbels rather welcomed the fact that no one in Berlin noticed the NSDAP and their new gauleiter much: "That Marxism and the Jewish gutter press did not take us seriously then was our good luck. If, for instance, the KPD in Berlin had guessed who we really were and what we wanted, they, no doubt, would have pitilessly and brutally drowned the beginnings of our efforts in a bloodbath."[6]

The Battle in the Pharus-Säle

Soon Goebbels considered that the time had come for the first attack against the Red fortress Berlin: "They took us for harmless madmen who were best not interfered with, or hurt in any way." This contemptuous attitude would only stimulate Goebbels: "One day our enemies will laugh at us no longer,"[7] he rightly predicted.

He knew very well how feeble his organization still was—"We were a ludicrous little band"—but he knew how to bluff. Accordingly, the second phase of his plan consisted of mass meetings, provocations, battles at meetings, and political manifestations. The aim was to draw the enemy, provoke scandals, and arouse public interest.

Goebbels had been in Berlin only eight weeks, but he already knew: "Berlin needs a sensation like a fish needs water. This city lives on it, and any political propaganda that does not take this into account is bound to fail." Another thing he had learned was that "the pitilessness of this town has found expression in its people. The motto here in Berlin is: 'Eat up, bird, or starve!' (*'Vogel friss oder stirb!'*), and who has not learned how to use his elbows will go down."[8]

Thus Goebbels is prepared to offer Berlin a sensation and to use his elbows.

The first public meeting was fixed for January 25, 1927. It was meant to be a kind of general rehearsal, and took place in Spandau, where the party was relatively strong. Goebbels lured the Marxists into the meeting by choosing the theme "The German worker and socialism." According to Goebbels, 500 Red Front fighters were present. After opening the meeting, the gauleiter declared he was prepared for "any open discussion with any honest compatriot," and would grant "every party sufficient speaking time," but "the business of this meeting would be determined by us who, after all, are the hosts, and whoever refused to conform will be expelled by the SA without mercy."[9]

Goebbels comments in his book that that language "had, so far, been only used at Marxist meetings in Berlin," as "the Red parties were only too sure of their power." It was essential, in his view, to speak the language "that the Marxist understands."

Goebbels' address in the Spandau Seitz-Festsäle lasted over two hours: "Five hundred men who had been sent to use their hard proletarian fists on us, became more and more attentive."[10] This description—it is his own—may have been somewhat exaggerated, but his remarkable gift of oratory must have impressed his adversaries too.

Goebbels had promised that a discussion would follow his address, yet hardly had the opposing speaker begun when Goebbels interrupted him. The gauleiter declared that he had just learned that two of his party members who had left the meeting early had been set upon by a Red commando squad and been beaten up and stabbed. The NSDAP considered it therefore "beneath its dignity to permit the representative of a party to continue speaking . . . whose followers had tried to substitute cowardly, in the darkness of the night, the use of the truncheon and dagger for what they apparently lacked in spiritual argument."

Upon this declaration, the opposing Communist speaker, strongly protesting, was pulled down from the platform and passed from hand to hand over the heads of Goebbels' stalwarts to the exit, where he was expelled: "The meeting," Goebbels triumphantly concluded his report, "ended with total victory. The Red special commandos slunk away with their tails between their legs, while our own party members had, for the first time, the grand feeling that, at last, the movement in Berlin had broken its fetters, and ceased to be merely a party political sect; it had openly declared war, which will now flare up along the whole front. There was no stopping now. We had challenged the

enemy, and we all knew they would not leave our challenge unanswered."[11]

Goebbels' plan had worked. He had lured the followers of the
socialist parties to his meeting, and had them listen with interest to
his address. The attack on the party comrades that had triggered off
the fight had come in handy; possibly it was Goebbels' own inven-
tion. The risk he took could not have been all that great, considering
that the majority of the audience consisted of National Socialists,
among them a great number of storm troopers.

The second yet more significant result was the strong reaction of
the left: "The Nazis converted their meeting in Spandau into a
bloodbath. The alarm has sounded for all revolutionary workers of
the Reich capital," wrote the *Rote Fahne* (Red Flag), the party
organ of the KPD, the next day. This was exactly what Goebbels
wanted. In his speech "Lenin or Hitler" he had succeeded in pictur-
ing Hitler as the only alternative to the most famous Russian revolutionary; and now he had induced the Berlin left to depict the NSDAP,
in actual fact Berlin's smallest party, as Berlin's greatest menace.
His own men had won heart; the enemy had been alerted. And now
after this first victorious skirmish, the time had come for a carefully
planned, strategically masterminded general attack on the enemy's
stronghold. Its success or failure would show if the NSDAP could
gain a foothold in the capital.

Goebbels lost no time. A few days later, Berlin was flooded with
enormous red posters:

"The bourgeois state is tottering toward its end! And rightly so!
Since it is no longer capable of liberating Germany. We must create
a new Germany, no longer a bourgeois, no longer a class society, a
Germany of work and discipline! For this task history has chosen
you worker of the brain and of the fist! In your hands lies the fate of
the German people. Remember that and act! Friday February 11,
eight o'clock in the evening, in the Pharus-Säle, Berlin, No. 12
Müllerstrasse Pg., Dr. Goebbels will be speaking about "the collapse
of the bourgeois class society."

The red color of the posters, with their challenging text, was not
Goebbels' idea, but Hitler's; the propagandist directives always came
from Hitler. But significant was the masterly skill with which Goebbels used them, varied them, deprovincialized them—at that time
Hitler's ideas still had a strong provincial tint.

The red posters, and still more their content, were challenging for
Berlin's socialists. A reactionary party openly dared to claim the
workers for their fight against the bourgeoisie. But worse still was

the locality they had picked for the meeting. The Pharus-Säle, situated in the heart of Red Wedding (a predominantly Communist suburb of Berlin), had, ever since 1918, been the meeting place of the Communists. The KPD foamed at the mouth. Their paper, the *Red Flag,* called the Goebbels meeting an "unbearable provocation." The walls of the houses surrounding the Pharus-Säle were covered with stickers: "Red Wedding for the Red proletariat. Whoever dares to put his foot into the Pharus-Säle will be beaten to a pulp."[12]

Goebbels' action was extremely daring, impudent, and challenging, but it showed courage. He gave a description of what he felt on his way to the meeting: "About 8 P.M. we left the city center in an old ramshackle car and drove to Wedding. A cold, gray drizzle fell from a starless sky. I could feel my heart beating to the bursting point, tense with impatience and expectation."[13]

There was a dense crowd waiting in front of the Pharus-Säle in the Müllerstrasse: by six-thirty the meeting hall was packed, and doors had to be shut. The leader of the Schutzstaffel (SS) reported to Goebbels that "Two thirds of the audience are Red Front fighters." Goebbels comments in his book: "This was exactly what we wanted. The hour of decision had struck, whatever the outcome. And we were prepared to put every ounce behind it."

The account the other side gave reads rather differently. According to their reports, the audience consisted of four fifths Nazis and only one fifth left party supporters. It can be assumed that Goebbels, who always planned everything well in advance, had arranged for his own partisans to occupy the greater part of the meeting hall long before he arrived. Whatever the actual position, there was enough of the enemy to cause a fight. On Goebbels' entry a hostile chorus greeted him with cries of "butcher" and "murderer of the workers." But they couldn't outshout the triumphant welcome his Nazis gave him. "Passionate battle cries" were heard coming from the platform occupied by the National Socialists.

All National Socialist meetings in Berlin were presided over by an SA leader, thereby emphasizing its fighting character; at this particular meeting the presider was Daluege, the then supreme SA leader of Berlin. He stood "strong as an oak" on the platform, according to Goebbels' court biographer, Wilfried Bader.[14]

Goebbels himself toned it down somewhat: "As tall as a tree he stood there at the footlights in all his grandeur, his arms raised bidding them to be silent." Easier said than done. Derisive laughter was the answer. Tumult, shouts . . . it was quite impossible to get the crowd to quiet down."[15]

No one doubted any longer that an explosion would occur, even before Goebbels started his speech. Below, in front of the platform, stood approximately twenty uniformed SA and SS men. On the platform, behind the speaker, was an even more awe-inspiring row of stalwarts. At the back of the hall on the right sat the Communists in a "bunch." The laughter and shouting had come from there, when Daluege had made an attempt to open the meeting, and ever so often a "sinister individual" would jump up and shout in a "shrill" voice, "point of order," his demand taken up by a wild chorus, answered by Daluege, who shouted: "There will be a discussion after the address. But it's we who decide the business of the day." He might just as well have gone on shouting until he was hoarse without making the slightest impression. Now Goebbels, obviously acting according to a carefully laid plan, stepped forward and nodded to the leader of the Schutzstaffel, who forthwith dispatched his men to those points in the audience where the disturbance had come from. And before the Communists knew it, the SA and SS men had seized the provocateur and dragged him to the platform. Then, Goebbels reports, a beer mug came flying through the air and shattered on the floor at Goebbels' feet. The sudden removal of the heckler from the midst of his comrades, and the flying beer mug, set off the explosion:

"A battle raged for about ten minutes. Glasses, bottles, table- and chair legs flew through the air. An ear-splitting tumult set in. The Red beast had got loose and demanded its victims. At first it looked as though all of us were lost. The Communist attack had come so suddenly that it took us by surprise, although we had expected it."[16]

According to Goebbels, the National Socialists mounted a counterattack and beat the life out of the enemy, expelling them from the premises. This proved, Goebbels adds ironically, "that the Communist party may well have the masses behind them, but that the same masses turn into cowards and run like hares if they meet a disciplined and stouthearted opponent."

Goebbels listed ten National Socialist casualties without mentioning any among his opponents, which the papers put as high as seventy-five.

But the real show was still to come. In order to make quite sure that the fighting would bring home to the enemy the superior strength of the NSDAP, and afford his own followers the triumph of a victory, Goebbels decided to add something special, catering to the lower range of their emotions. The propagandist in him knew only too well how close bestiality and sentimentality lay together. Accordingly, he produced for the rest of the audience, still in a state

of extreme excitement, a real tearjerker. The wounds of the SA men
were dressed and bandaged, and the men were put on stretchers and
placed on the platform. Kurt Daluege resumed his place at the
speaker's stand and said with perfect calm, as though nothing had
happened, "I declare the meeting in session, the speaker has the
floor."

"In these circumstances it was quite impossible," Goebbels continues, "to give a coherent speech. I had hardly begun when our
ambulance squad entered and picked up a seriously wounded SA
man from the platform and carried him outside on the swaying
stretcher. One of the ambulance men, showered with obscene abuse
of the lowest kind by those bestial apostles of mankind, called out
for me in his despair, and loud enough to be heard on the platform.
I interrupted my speech, crossed the audience still sprinkled with a
few enemy shock troops, looking rather cowed after the unexpected
treatment meted out to their comrades, and took leave of the wounded
SA man. At the end of my speech I coined for the first time the
phrase, "unknown SA man."[17]

During the war Goebbels is said to have recounted in his intimate
circle how the provocative shouts, and the whole battle, had been
carefully prepared in advance, and that none of the men on the
stretchers had actually been casualties: also that notes for "his
spontaneous speech" about the unknown SA man had been lying on
his desk days before the meeting took place.[18]

There can be no doubt that Goebbels had planned the whole battle. The proof lies in the turn it took. It is, however, highly improb-
able that in a fight where over seventy Communists were wounded,
not a single SA or SS man should have come to grief. On the other
hand, Goebbels' remark, at the end of his speech, about the unknown SA man was probably the only spontaneous moment of the
whole evening.

This inversion of the truth is a good example of the attempts
Goebbels made later to build himself up as the unmatched genius of
propaganda. His entourage should never cease to be astounded at
this "astonishing man," whose subtle game had deceived friend and
foe alike.

With the battle in the Pharus-Säle Goebbels achieved practically
everything he had planned. Almost the whole Berlin press gave it
front-page coverage. Goebbels personally had a bad press, which
mattered little to him. His aim was to be talked about in the papers
and get the people talking, and it was perfectly irrelevant whether
the comments were favorable or not. He had given the Berliners

their sensation, and the press was full of it. Goebbels and the NSDAP were the talk of the town.

His main enemy, the KPD, had received a hard knock. It showed in the report published the next day in the *Red Flag,* with the headline "National Socialists assail workers. Carefully prepared attack in the Pharus-Säle."

This article was significant. It obviously described the events from a different angle, but it admitted that the Communists had intended by their repeated interruptions, shouts of "point of order," and demands for discussion, to prevent Goebbels from speaking. Another interesting fact emerging from this article was that the National Socialists, marching away after the meeting was over, had to be protected from the Communists by the police.

Before Goebbels' arrival in Berlin, the NSDAP had been a ridiculous little organization. This was perhaps the reason why Berlin's Communists and Social Democrats had failed to draw their lesson from what had happened to their comrades in Munich. They had already been faced for some time with a dilemma mentioned by Hitler in *Mein Kampf:* either they stayed away from National Socialist meetings and left the streets to the brown battalions without a fight, or they attended them, in which case they were almost invariably beaten up. Most of the SS and SA men were veterans of the Freikorps (Free Corps Fighters). They were true mercenary roughnecks, who knew how to fight to the last.

The party leaders of the left had also overlooked the fact that the NSDAP speakers, particularly Goebbels, had adopted an aggressive and revolutionary style, similar to if not even more radical than their own. Goebbels knew exactly how to get at the workers. He was able to convince them of the sincerity of his affection for the working classes and of his faith in the future Reich, in which the worker would be one of the main pillars. No Communist speaker equaled Goebbels in malice and irony when depicting the bourgeoisie, or in the acid satire and contempt he would pour on the left party bosses; and no one else could paint such a beautiful paradise for the worker: the coming Reich of social justice. Goebbels' speeches succeeded in weakening the fighting strength of the workers. They became uncertain of themselves, enough to paralyze their aggressive spirit. Here, they felt, was someone fighting for their soul, offering them his heart.

Goebbels' conquest of Berlin began with the battle in the Pharus-Säle. He had become known, he had gathered the activist party members around him, he had strengthened their fighting morale and whetted their aggressive appetites. They had tasted blood.

The New Aristocrats

Goebbels' definition of the unknown SA man as the new aristocrat of politics now needed, in his view, a further affirmation by a test of bloodletting. On May 20, 1927 he concentrated the SA in Trebbin (Teltow District).

Against the decor of a gigantic burning woodpile erected near a mill, the SA took the oath of allegiance. They returned by train to Berlin on the following day. They would disembark at the station Lichterfelde-Ost and, for the first time in their history, march together to West Berlin. A few groups of Red Front fighters, also returning from a demonstration, happened to be traveling on the same train. Soon fights had started, and when the train arrived at Lichterfelde-Ost, the Red Front fighters, continuing to the Anhalter Station, fired some shots, as the train began to move out, at the SA men who had already left the train. Thereupon—still according to Goebbels—one of the SA men jumped on the train and pulled the emergency brake. A regular battle ensued in which the SA, far superior in numbers, beat up the Red fighters mercilessly. Fifteen among the Red fighters were seriously injured. There also were a number of light casualties on both sides. Flushed with victory, the SA marched across Lichterfelde, Steglitz, and Wilmersdorf up to the Kurfürstendamm, where the marching columns dispersed. And to crown the day, some SA men beat up Jewish passersby and penetrated into the Romanische Kaffee [a famous Berlin cafe, meeting place of intellectuals and artists] near the Gedächtniskirche, where they again molested and manhandled Jewish clients. The *Berliner Tageblatt* spoke of pogrom. The rest of the press also severely condemned the SA, appealing to the government and the police to stop these shameless actions, likening National Socialism to organized crime.

Goebbels' simple comments on the brutalities of his SA men were: "Late in the evening we meted out to some impudent Hebrews who apparently couldn't keep their unwashed mouths shut, a few good hard slaps in the face. This presented the Jewish gutter press with a welcome oppportunity to let loose a vindictive campaign of hate the next day."[19]

For the first time the SA ruled the streets in Berlin; for the first time Jewish passersby were attacked physically. The man who had presented his first lady-love with Heine's poems, *Buch der Lieder,* as the most perfect expression of his own feelings, rehearsed with his hired toughs the first act of the greatest pogrom in German history, the *Reichskristallnacht* (Reich Crystal Night). And this was the same SA, the "new aristocracy," of whom Goebbels said:

"We mean the type of political soldier who through the National Socialist movement represents the new Germany for the first time. The SA man cannot, in any way, be compared with a member of any other military organization. [Hitler had already stated this—author's note]. Military associations were essentially non-political or, at best, generally patriotic. . . . But patriotism is something we have to overcome."[20]

The last sentence is significant: It once again shows Goebbels' radicalist tendency to cut all bonds with the past and the basically patriotic bourgeoisie. The following remark is even clearer: "It has never been, and is not, his [the SA man's. Author's note] task to act on the fringe of politics, as a tout for the big capitalist powers, or as security police guarding bourgeois money safes."

Like Adolf Hitler, Goebbels believed in terror, taking Marxism for a worthy example to emulate:

"Marxism, it is well known, became great by using terror. It has conquered the street by terror. The bourgeois circles considered it rather vulgar and unrefined to go on the street and demonstrate for their ideals, or fight for them.

"But the street belongs to modern politics. Whoever is able to conquer the street will be able to conquer the masses, and whoever has conquered the masses will conquer the state. The man in the street is only truly impressed by a show of force and discipline."[21]

And who was more equal to the task of conquering the street than the SA man? Only he, in Goebbels' view, had enough force to stake his life for the cause. Goebbels' opponents held a different view, and saw in the SA man a paid assassin or mercenary who gave his loyalty to whoever provided him with the best spoils and paid him the most. Goebbels admitted that the majority of the SA were recruited from among the unemployed. But he saw in this an advantage:

"It is inherent in the worker not only to believe in a political idea but also to fight for it. The worker has no possessions. And he who has nothing will always be prepared to give everything for a cause. Indeed, he has nothing to lose but his chains."[22]

Goebbels saw in the working-class background of the SA man a guarantee against his being blown off course "into the stagnant waters of bourgeois concessions. The proletarian element, especially the SA, would give the movement a renewed stimulus of revolutionary elan." The SA man is, therefore, for Goebbels, the backbone of the movement.

With his hymn of praise of the unknown SA man, Goebbels also introduced his talent for turning ideas upside down. Jüngers' non-bourgeois man, worker, and soldier in one person, who takes a heroic attitude toward inescapable fate, had become Goebbels' unknown SA man, the new aristocrat who beats up his political opponents and slaps Jews in the face.

The Berlin NSDAP Is Banned

With the fight at the station and the pogromlike actions of the SA on the Kurfürstendamm, Goebbels had created another sensation, but knew that he risked trying the patience of the authorities beyond endurance: "The fate of the movement hung on a fine thread. . . . We knew we were moving fast toward being banned."[23] But Goebbels had his reward: He was on every Berliner's lips. He could even afford to ask Hitler to visit the capital. Hitler was still banned from speaking publicly, which obliged Goebbels to call a meeting of party members that would be regarded as a closed circle. It was the first time that Hitler spoke in Berlin at a large gathering.

Goebbels' left tendency once again came to the fore when he invited Hitler to speak on May 1, the workers' official holiday, won for them by the Social Democrats after a hard fight. Hitler delivered his speech in the Clou, an old amusement hall in the center of Berlin. The hall was packed with five thousand people. But Berlin's press did not take much notice, and the few papers that did, gave it a bad writeup. Goebbels was furious.

He called a mass meeting in the House of the Soldiers' Association. His speech turned into a poisonous harangue against the "Jewish press" whose offices he called "rotation synagogues"; but he also attacked the liberal, Catholic, and nationalist papers, particularly the latter, because they had denigrated Hitler's speech in giving it a brief and unfavorable mention. Suddenly, in the middle of his attack, an interjection was heard, obviously addressed to him personally. "You yourself don't look all that special." For a moment there was silence. Goebbels, taken aback, stared at the man. Then, pulling himself together, he said: "You're trying to disturb the meeting. Do you wish us to make use of our right as hosts, and throw you out?"

There are two versions of what followed. Goebbels recounts: "Since the individual in question refused to sit down but tried to continue his provocation in a loud voice, a few stalwart SA men approached him and slapped his face heartily. They gripped him by his neck and backside and propelled him outside."[24]

Very different is the report in the *Deutsche Allgemeine Zeitung* of May 6, 1927: "Goebbels began his speech by reading out press comments of Hitler's speech of May 1, 1927, calling the responsible editors 'Jew pigs and swines.' The Vicar Stucke of the Reformed Church (Reformgemeinde) made his interjection, whereupon Nazis sitting near him jumped up simultaneously, as though obeying an order, and belabored the man, clearly identifiable by his suit as a vicar, with beer mugs. Covered in blood, the Reverend Stucke staggered outside, accompanied by shouts and abuse."

This description, even if journalistically a little inflated, is probably far nearer to the truth, although it omits a most significant point, namely that Stucke's interjection attacked Goebbels personally. Even in his book Goebbels' chagrin still rankles.

"And in the ensuing breathless silence, the individual repeated ostentatiously, quite obviously in order to provoke and entice the audience to unwise actions, his personal abuse against me, which at first I had failed to grasp. This was all the more outrageous as I had not given anybody any reason whatever for such uncouth behavior."[25]

Abusive expressions such as "Jew pigs and swines" apparently belonged in Goebbels' view to perfect behavior. But woe to whoever dared pass remarks about the gauleiter's physical deformation.

Goebbels had done it all right: He had produced his sensation. But it looked as though it might prove rather costly this time. The whole press took up the case, most papers on their front pages, but they all demanded, as with one voice, that all measures be taken to put an end to the brown terror. The fact that the victim was an elderly vicar—the official Church statement that Stucke had actually no legal right to call himself vicar, had not yet become known[26]—was just what the papers, irrespective of their political complexion, needed. The case, once torn from its purely political context, could be simply treated as a common crime. In any case, Goebbels realized that disaster was around the corner.

He managed just in time to rescue the postal account of the party, and the most important documents. In the evening of the following day, May 5, a policeman, dispatched by police headquarters, appeared at the party offices with an official letter to be signed for. Goebbels refused to accept it, upon which the policeman proceeded to affix the letter to the door. An SA man removed it, drove in uniform to police headquarters, forced his way to the office of the head of police, opened the door brusquely, and insolently threw the letter inside, shouting, "The National Socialists refuse to recognize the ban of our party."[27]

Yet the police action had inflicted a damaging blow on the party.
The number of party members had grown in these few months to over
three thousand, and the number of SA men had trebled. Only six
months earlier the party, divided among themselves, and looked
down upon as no better than a political skittle club, had now become
a sort of political sensation. Their quarrels appeared to have been settled and their activity had reached a new high. Hitler was still in
Berlin at the time of the ban, and it worried him. He could not deny
that Goebbels had achieved in Berlin within a few months more than
anybody else in the party. On the other hand, some leaders, among
them the brothers Strasser, pointed out that it was Goebbels' radicalism that had provoked the police into banning the party. Rumors were
rife that disputes had arisen between Hitler and Goebbels. There was
talk of Goebbels' imminent arrest. When in the beginning of June
Goebbels left for Stuttgart to attend a party gathering, part of the
press reproached him with having left his party colleagues in Berlin
in the lurch. They were proved wrong two days later by the dense
crowd waiting at the Anhalter Station to welcome Goebbels back.
Scorning the police and their ban, the masses demonstrated and
shouted the little doctor's battle cry, "Despite the ban not dead."
(*Trotz Verbot nicht tot.*)

In the Beginning Was the Word

In the Brown House [the name given to Nazi headquarters all over
Germany, translator's note] hung a painting by H. O. Hoyer, a
painter from Oberstdorf. It depicted Hitler talking to a gathering of
solemnly listening men. Underneath was written "In the Beginning
Was the Word."

Hitler was the greatest magician among all orators of his time; he
was, so to speak, an oratorical wonder. How else could a man
whose technical abilities of oratory were, at the best, mediocre, fascinate millions of all ages and classes?

There can be no doubt that National Socialism became what it was
because of its orators, and particularly its two most important orators, Hitler and Goebbels. This points to a vital difference between
National Socialism and Marxism. Marxism is a doctrine built on
scientific premises and by scientific methods. It contains visions of the
future. Communism too bases its visions of the future on a scientific
foundation, and declares the dogma unalterable. National Socialism,
on the other hand, was never a doctrine built on scientific premises; it
had a primitive party program that offered solutions of actual or

imagined problems, such as the racial problem, but only in slogans. Unlike Marxism, National Socialism left the details of how to execute its program open. All such a movement needed were orators to feed the people with these sloganized solutions.

If we compare Hitler's and Goebbels' recorded speeches we find Goebbels easily the far better orator. He had everything needed to make a good speaker. There was a warm undertone to his pleasant baritone voice, which would rise, when required, to a perfectly mastered high register. His voice would express humor, irony, sarcasm, hysteria, each color clearly defined. Nothing was left diffuse. Sadness, sentiment, pathos, menace, and rebellion—all were well within his range. One looks in vain for such technical perfection in Hitler's speeches. His voice was raucous, guttural, and hoarse, getting sharper and shriller with advancing years. Today Hitler's speeches seem uninteresting in content and form. They strike one as so many empty phrases.

Goebbels was able to create moods and emotions with the precision of a measuring instrument. He could foresee the reaction of the public—the laughs; the boos; the applause; outbursts of indignation, of hysteria, and of enthusiasm. He was a master organ player who knew how to play his instrument. Hitler, too, prepared his speeches most thoroughly, inserting the necessary hiatus wherever he expected applause or boos of indignation. But it could happen that he miscalculated, or forgot to give the necessary cue to his audience.

The same applied to the visual performance the two offered. Both Goebbels and Hitler were good actors; both used to rehearse their mimicry, gestures, and poses in front of a mirror. (This, incidentally, was also true of another great orator, Winston Churchill.) Among such well-rehearsed expressions was, for instance, Goebbels' twisting and tightening of his lips as a sign of contempt. Or he would turn on his charm, put his hands in his trouser pockets, and smile; and the audience would smile with him. Before going into attack he would stand arms akimbo. Then he would start hacking into the enemy with words and hands, so that his audience would involuntarily back away. Once he was finished with his opponent, he would, with one rapid movement of his hand, wipe him off the face of the earth. When speaking about the Fuehrer and the Reich, he would raise his hands in a gesture of entreaty.

Hitler, too, often employed pious gestures. But his aggressive expression was more marked than Goebbels'. He would clench his fist and drum the desk, hitting it with a degree of violence that seemed to depend on the size of the enemy, whereby his famous lock of hair would fall deep over his forehead. Goebbels' gestures appeared more artificial, Hitler's more ungainly, more brutal. Goebbels had the gracefulness of a fencer, Hitler the uncouth force of a lumberjack.

And yet as an orator Hitler was superior to Goebbels. Goebbels could exhaust his audience, stimulate them, whip them up to real hatred, at best enthuse them to the point of ecstasy; but Hitler would mesmerize them, put them into a trance, embracing them with the spirit of salvation. The atmosphere at Goebbels' meetings was tense; at Hitler's, sultry. Sociologists and psychologists speak of a kind of sexual interdependency between Hitler and his audience, some even of a religious communion between Hitler and the masses. Whatever these formulations mean to imply, Hitler no doubt obtained by his speeches a sort of salvation effect—salvation for himself and for his congregation.

What Goebbels had to say was usually evil and unfair, but always brilliant, hitting straight at the solar plexus. Even his most primitive phrases had a smooth finish and a certain sparkle.

These qualities stand out in Goebbels' speeches, irrespective of whether they are recited or read. What Hitler had to say was often confused and never a feast of great oratory. Reading a Hitler speech today is pretty hard going and sometimes even painful. Yet the immediate effect of his speeches, the magic he exerted on his audience keeping it spellbound, was, at the time, apparently irresistible. Here they would find everything to release them from the narrowness of their existence. Sultryness, closeness, inarticulate sounds, twilight, intoxication, dreams, ecstasies, salvation—Adolf Hitler's speeches were the LSD and hashish of his time.

Goebbels' development as an orator was the result of his diligence and inexhaustible energy. He discovered his talent soon after having entered politics, and from then on he never ceased improving on it. He read newspapers, especially the Marxist press, and studied the lead editorial, analyzing them as though they were short written speeches. Gradually he created his own style which, at the beginning, tended to be somewhat solemn, almost ecclesiastical. The rhythm of Nietzsche's *Zarathustra,* which had so deeply influenced Goebbels' *Michael,* is still much in evidence in his early speeches. But later as his intellect took over more and more, his speeches became clearer and more systematic. His erudition enhanced his vocabulary, further enriched by his great gift for creating new words, particularly when he poured contempt and ridicule on his enemies. He had soon learned how to present these new word creations with fitting intonations of voice, facial expression, and gestures. His mastership in combining word, rhythm, and gesture was unequaled by any other speaker of his time.

Goebbels prepared every speech conscientiously, working at it like an artist. Every new speech was written down carefully, looking like the working copy of a theatrical producer, with different signs in various colors for anticipated laughs, applause, boos, outbreaks of enthusiasm, indications for certain intonations and manner of delivery, pauses, and effective last-curtain phrases. But he was also perfectly capable of speaking extempore, always uncannily assessing the mood of his audience. But then again he might deviate from his carefully prepared speech when he felt that a certain mood of his audience demanded stronger stuff or, as the case may be, toning it down. He would start his speeches cautiously, slowly feeling his way. He would address the audience simply, perhaps too simply—almost primitively. Gradually, the audience would relax. This was the moment for him to increase the tempo more and more until he had them exactly where he wanted them. He would give them the full treatment until they were shouting at the top of their voices, quite beyond themselves. Like a wizard he would conjure up for them a whole string of emotions. Not unlike Hitler, Goebbels spent himself physically until he stood there covered in sweat, while remaining as cool as a cucumber inside himself. He could not cast Hitler's magic spell over his audience, but he would bewitch them. He did not fuse together with his audience like the master, but knew how to pull the right strings and make them dance as though they were puppets. He did not show them the gates of salvation but set them on fire all the same. Remaining outside, he did not take part in the Black Mass; he only directed it.

There was yet another difference between Goebbels' and Hitler's oratory. Goebbels' technique was superior and the effect on his audience was actually greater, once he set out to put his enemies in the pillory, to crush them, obliterate them by sheer words. But when it came to resurrecting their faith, Hitler would leave Goebbels far behind. Goebbels spoke of destiny; but Hitler was the man of destiny. Yet the man responsible for the resurrection of the atavistic twilight of faith, for the medicine man's abracadabra that took deep roots in the masses, was the man who created the Hitler myth: Joseph Goebbels.

Adolf Hitler believed in himself and his mission. When he started doubting his mission, he was no longer able to speak with the same effect. In his last years Hitler became increasingly reluctant to address the people, knowing he had lost his magic faculty for putting his audience into a state of trance by his oratory. And whenever he actually spoke in those last years, usually prodded by his Minister of Propaganda, he did so unwillingly and not without suffering. Those

speeches sounded empty and weak, notwithstanding their often mar-
tial content. Did he actually feel that Providence, in which he firmly
believed, had withdrawn her hand?

Not so Goebbels, whose oratory sparkled brilliantly right up to the
bitter end. He had, ironically enough, become in those grim last years
of the war the harbinger of consolation in times of need—the only
voice the people would still listen to. He played them a merry tune
to their last dance. Goebbels' adversaries called him a devil, likening
him to Lucifer, who might have brought light to the world instead of
throwing it into darkness by his lies. He truly competed with Hitler
in lying to the people—only that Hitler was a born liar, while Goebbels
rather lied against his nature. Goebbels committed the one un-
forgivable sin that according to the Bible knows no forgiveness, the
sin against the spirit.

Der Angriff

During the ban of the party, lasting from May 5, 1927, to March 31,
1928, an important event took place: the foundation of a newspaper.
It was Goebbels' idea, and he called the paper *Der Angriff*. It appeared once a week, every Monday. Goebbels wrote the lead editorial,
which soon became famous and notorious. Goebbels was driven to
this enterprise by the serious deterioration of the whole position,
particularly of party finance. The banning of the party made a regular
collection of contributions from party members impossible. And only
the sacrificial spirit of the party activists, banded together in the
Freedom Association, produced enough money to pay the staff of the
illegal party bureau working under the disguise of a secretariat of
some Nazi members of the Reichstag. The employees on the staff
had agreed to halve their salaries, and even that was paid out to them
in dribs and drabs. Another important financial source had been the
entrance fees taken at political meetings. They no longer came in.
But the party organization had suffered no less than party finances.
The ordinary members dispersed, and only the SA succeeded in main-
taining their organization somehow. They founded various associations or clubs. As soon as the police had banned one, a new one came
into being. The names of these disguised Nazi organizations often
contained an ironical allusion to the police. Skittle clubs were called
All Nine Pins (Alle Neune) and Good Wood (Gut Holz); swimming
clubs, High Wave (Hohe Welle), The Quiet Lake (Zum ruhigem See),
and Wet Right Through (Gut Nass); the fishing association, Moldy
Crab (Der Moder Krebs [the word *Krebs* means both crab and cancer

in German]); walking clubs, Walking Club (Wanderverein), Near
Berlin (Bei Berlin), To The Pretty Acorn (Zur schönen Eichel), and
Wandering Birds 1927 (Wandervogel 1927); saving clubs, such as
Lolly Lolly (Pinke Pinke) and To the Golden Dinner (Zum Goldenen
Sechser).

That way you kept the activists close to the party, yet left the
party itself ostensibly outside politics. The Berlin press and the other
parties ignored the NSDAP as though it didn't exist. Goebbels
searched desperately for a way out of this impasse. No longer permitted to speak publicly, he founded a "School for Politics," where
he lectured at evening classes, using the incoming monthly fees to fill
the empty party coffers. Some of the Nazi members of the Reichstag
would call election meetings where followers and members of the
NSDAP could gather. But these meetings did not always turn out as
Goebbels would have wished, since a good many Reichstag members,
particularly Gregor Strasser, opposed Goebbels' policy, in which
they saw the reason for the ban. More successful was another tactic
Goebbels used: He would arrive at meetings of other political parties
accompanied by a large number of his activists, would soon call for a
point of order, and succeed in changing proceedings by the sheer
number of his supporters. Having achieved this, he would dominate
the discussion by his own speeches, often lasting as long as two
hours. Goebbels also organized groups of SA who would take turns
paying an evening visit to the Kurfürstendamm to molest and beat up
Jews.

As early as May 30, 1927, the *B.Z. am Mittag* demanded that the
authorities make an end to the Kurfürstendamm outrages: ". . . it
cannot be admitted that the brutalities of the Nazis perpetrated on
Kurfürstendamm become the daily amusement of those young hooli-
gans." But after a time the complaints in the press discontinued.
They considered silence more effective, and left it to the police to arrest the worst evildoers, who actually received prison sentences of up
to six months. And indeed, this silence of the press drove Goebbels
nearly out of his mind. Internal party difficulties added to his plight—
intrigues of the brothers Strasser and their group.

This was the position when Goebbels decided to publish a weekly
paper. This audacious decision, taken against odds, was typical of his
gambler's nature. He had, as it was, great pain in finding enough
money to keep the illegal party apparatus turning over, yet he would
throw himself into the adventure of founding a newspaper without
sufficient financial means and with a dearth of collaborators. But had
he not always been tempted by the impossible? He personally borrowed 2,000 marks from party friends, and appointed his party

colleague, Dr. Julius Lippert, editor-in-chief. Lippert organized a staff of spare-time journalists, found a paper supplier who accepted IOUs, and persuaded the proprietor of a small printing press to print the paper on credit.

The launching of the paper on July 4, 1927, was a miserable failure. The Berlin press ignored the new arrival completely, and Goebbels' own party attacked it violently, particularly the brothers Strasser. They had been publishing *Die Berliner Arbeiterzeitung* since March 1926. Goebbels had no time to lose if he wanted to break the resistance in his own party. He immediately called a "gau day" at Potsdam. There he beseeched his audience not to let him down, since this would mean "the end of the National Socialist movement in Berlin and the loss of everything they had conquered so far."[28] Goebbels' speech impressed. His Berlin party colleagues granted him a suspension of sentence, and Goebbels used it to the full. In a short time he had succeeded in giving the paper its own character, and after Lippert's completion of the prison sentence he had received for breaking the press laws, the layout of the paper was also completely changed.

Der Angriff, emulating the Marxist fighting press, had printed above the paper's name its motto: "For the oppressed, against the oppressors." The paper did not even attempt to give general information, but picked only news that served its combative mission. The front page had five columns, the last of which was reserved for the editorial, the very heart of the issue, signed "Dr. G." Goebbels used the lead editorial technique of papers, as he had done before in his speeches. The style was outstandingly vivid and, if not always the product of a master hand, full of elan and attack. Goebbels' creation of new words was inexhaustible when it came to depicting his enemies. They were impudent and meant to hurt; and they did.

"The political lead editorial in our paper was just like a written poster or, better still, like a written speech delivered in the street. It was brief, to the point, soundly constructed, and propagandistically effective."[29]

There were two important items, apart from the lead editorial: "The political diary" and the cartoon. "The political diary" served to launch vehement attacks against the Weimar Republic and its institutions. Here the "system" was pilloried and covered with ridicule, irony, contempt, and venom. The cartoon, together with the lead editorial, became the most notorious journalistic weapon of the *Angriff.* Goebbels discovered among his party colleagues the designer, Hans Schweitzer, who worked under the pseudonym Mjoelnir. Schweitzer did not bother with any particular subtlety of drawing or

1. Goebbels leaving court in 1931.

2. Adolf Hitler relaxes from a strenuous campaign at the home of Berlin Gauleiter Dr. Goebbels.

3. Adolf Hitler acted as best man at Goebbels' wedding to Frau Magda Quandt (formerly Fräulein Magda Ritschel). Above, the bride and groom are followed by Hitler after the ceremony. December 29, 1931.

spiritual irony. His cartoons were meant to serve the political struggle and nothing else; they were coarse, even brutal, using a primitive black-and-white technique. Thus Mjoelnir created the prototype of the SA man: blond, athletic, with the face of a fighter; and his counterparts: the prototype of the boss, bulging with fat, a blown-up reactionary in a cutaway and sash, or the repellent Jew with enormous nose, cauliflower sticking-out ears, bowlegs, and flat feet. Mjoelnir's cartoons appealed to the reader's primitive instincts. The victim was mercilessly dragged to the block.

"What the law forbade us to say in so many words, we expressed in the cartoon, which was legally difficult to pin down. In every issue we attacked the main opponents of our movement in Berlin, singling out the police vice president, Dr. Weiss. This was done so astutely and with so much insolent audacity as to make it almost impossible for the attacked Dr. Weiss to invoke the law—unless, of course, he wanted to be taken for a spoilsport and humorless ninny. The reading public very soon got used to this type of aggression by means of cartoons, and was virtually waiting for each new issue to see what the *Angriff* would do next with the high and mighty president of the Alexanderplatz [police headquarters. Author's note]."[30]

In the *Angriff* Goebbels had succeeded in creating an effective fighting paper for the Berlin party. The edition, at first small (it started with two thousand), increased steadily, and reached sixty thousand by the time the Nazis took over. But what mattered was that the Berlin party members read the paper and thus got at first a weekly; then, from October 1, 1929, onward, twice weekly; and from November 1, 1930, a daily shot of political poison. The paper was dangerous because of its subtle simplicity, its use of hypocritical indignation based on the inherent enjoyment of another's misfortune. It pandered to the evil instincts dormant in so many.

The Break with the Brothers Strasser

The foundation of the *Angriff* was also a direct consequence of Goebbels' break with the brothers Strasser. The Berlin gauleiter wanted his own paper so as to be independent of the Strassers and their *Berliner Arbeiterzeitung,* and, in some degree, of Rosenberg, who was editor-in-chief of the *Völkische Beobachter.* Goebbels' relationship to the brothers Strasser had deteriorated since Easter 1926, when he suddenly joined up with Hitler, forsaking Strasser and his other party friends in the West and North of the Reich.

Admittedly, Gregor Strasser had consented to Goebbels' appointment as gauleiter of Berlin. He probably had even worked for it behind the scenes, if only to prevent Goebbels from being called to Munich by Hitler. Strasser also hoped Goebbels would fail in his task in Berlin. But only too soon he had to recognize that he had underestimated Goebbels' will power, energy, and strength of personality. Goebbels advocated a radicalism and a left ideology superior to any the National Socialists had hitherto dared to propagate. He certainly surpassed therein Gregor Strasser who, after all, fancied himself as the leader of the party's left wing.

Just to spite Goebbels, Strasser's *Berliner Arbeiterzeitung* of April 23, 1927, published an essay on the "Consequences of racial mixture." The article was written in the usual vein of the National Socialist racial theory, and attempted to prove that a mixture of races tended to produce bad characteristics. The article would probably not have aroused any special attention if it had not included Talleyrand, emphasizing the connection between the man's character and his clubfoot. The intention was obvious. The article singled out Talleyrand but meant Goebbels. Goebbels, understandably enough, was outraged. In a five-page letter addressed to Hitler, he wrote: "This infamous action carried out with cowardly and obvious calculation having the one and only aim of destroying me in the movement, beats anything I have ever experienced before in my whole political life. I have to confess that I have never been attacked in such an infamous and base manner, either by Jews or Marxists. . . . Personally I refuse to fight with similar methods, and faced with such infamous cowardly aggression, I must confess that this is for me an 'either-or' situation. I will never doubt the National Socialist German Workers' party, and even less the chief of this party. But the moment may be near when I might be ashamed of the men at my side, or behind me, in the struggle for German freedom. This moment is nearer than one might think. . . . "When seeing how the whole Jewish press is conducting their campaign—in an underhand manner, of course—no longer against the NSDAP but against my *person,* and how suddenly everywhere, as though complying with a secret order, there is talk of a dispute between you and me—I am not naïve enough to believe that there are not men in the movement who feed the Jewish press with this kind of material. . . .

"Can you really tolerate any longer that party members use such methods against other party members? Can you advise me to say meekly 'yes and amen' to this latest infamy? If you can, then *I am of course prepared to submit to absolute party discipline . . . in case, however, that party discipline should compel me to submit silently,*

I beg you to relieve me of my post of gaufuehrer of Berlin-Brandenburg. . . ."[31]

This letter is further proof of Goebbels' oversensitivity to any allusions to his physical deformation. Such attacks had become particularly grievous for him since he was occupying a leading position in the party. These pagan zealots of race religion regarded a clubfoot as a challenge. Goebbels was not far from the truth when complaining that even his political opponents treated him more fairly than his own party colleagues, since for his political opponents a clubfoot was just an ordinary accident and not a racially reprehensible deficiency. Goebbels resented any personal attack bitterly, seeing in it exclusively the intrigues of those who envied him his success. One might wonder at so much self-delusion, but this assessment was part of Goebbels' defense mechanism. His mind and heart told him that he was treated with bitter injustice. Nobody could deny the many sacrifices he had brought. He had worked from dawn until deep into the night, beset by worries about finance and organization of the party, as though they were his own. For himself he allowed very little; his mode of living was Spartan. He had staked everything on one card. Naturally, he felt rather anxious about the way the game was being played. Goebbels wanted to be the top disciple of Adolf Hitler, and took all attacks as shabby attempts to blacken him with his master. Not only did he make sacrifices, but he also felt he was being sacrificed. Truth and self-delusion merged here, in strange confusion, into a virtual tragicomedy.

Hitler looked with equanimity upon the quarrels between the Berlin factions. When Rosenberg reported Goebbels for having voiced the suspicion that Strasser's mother was a Jewess—sufficient reason for him, Rosenberg, to suggest that Goebbels should be relieved of his Berlin post—Hitler's reply was that the gentlemen would have to learn to work together.[32] Then Gregor Strasser, in turn, complained in a letter addressed to Rudolf Hess that Goebbels had reproached him with "being descended from Jews" and "with being dependent on the big capitalists," and this would oblige him, Strasser, to "ask Herr Hitler to decide in this matter."[33]

This is an interesting phenomenon: Rosenberg and other veteran party members in Munich who did not object to seeing Goebbels attacked for his physical deformation, were outraged when Goebbels was reported to have suspected Strasser's mother of being a Jewess. The true anti-Semites among the party leaders took up position against Goebbels' only because Goebbels' anti-Semitism was selling better—and this perhaps because it was not a product of his inner conviction but of cold calculation and political tactics.

Goebbels always failed to establish a genuine relationship with the old guard. He had only Hitler. The old guard would always regard him as an outsider and intruder. The only one who did not take the slightest exception to Goebbels' physical appearance was Hitler himself. Therein lies one of the deeper reasons for the strong bond Goebbels established with Hitler, for the profound affection and gratitude he felt for the Fuehrer. The controversy between Goebbels and Strasser that to all appearances ended without decision, had actually brought Goebbels a victory. Both parties were asked to end their quarrel and wipe the slate clean. On July 20 and 21, 1927, a meeting took place among Goebbels, Hitler, Hess, and General Heineman, chairman of the Committee of Enquiry and Settlement of Party Disputes (Untersuchungs und Schlichtungsausschuss), the result of which can be found in a letter dated July 21, 1927, which the general addressed to the two parties concerned:[34]

"1. Herr Hitler will deal with the case personally in the presence of as many representatives as possible of the two parties concerned, when all claims for obtaining satisfaction will be considered.
 2. A statement by Hitler shortly to be published in the *Völkische Beobachter* denying the lying contentions published in Marxist papers referring to a disagreement between Hitler and Goebbels.
 3. The integration of the newspaper *Der Angriff* into the publishing house Eder und Nachfolger."

With point No. 3 Strasser had lost his press battle. In his letter of June 15, addressed to Hess, he had pointed out a contradiction between Hitler's assurance that Goebbels' paper would have a neutral character and Goebbels' actual position as Hitler's deputy in Berlin. The decision to put the *Angriff* under the wing of the party publishers practically destroyed any chance of the *Berliner Arbeiterzeitung* becoming the main organ of the NSDAP in Berlin. The hate-filled struggle between Goebbels and the brothers Strasser was destructive to both and led to bitter enmity between the warring parties, which found its expression even on the streets, when occasionally SA vendors of the *Angriff* beat up their colleagues selling the *Berliner Arbeiterzeitung*.

Hitler's promised statement was published in the *Völkische Beobachter* on June 25, 1927. "I declare that all those reports [concerning the dispute Hitler/Goebbels, author's note] are pure inventions of the Jewish gutter press, construed for obvious reasons. My relationship to Herr Dr. Goebbels has not changed in any way. He enjoys, as before, my fullest confidence."

This declaration meant Goebbels' complete rehabilitation—not only in the eyes of the general public, who had actually never taken these NSDAP feuds very seriously, but, what was more important, also within the party itself. Hitler had expressed his complete confidence in him. From then on, some whispered allusions to Mephisto Goebbels' clubfoot might still be heard in National Socialist circles, but no one would dare refer to it openly. And Goebbels, now under Hitler's official protection, would use his superior brainpower to get the better of the less-endowed NSDAP leaders. His urge to prove he was better than anybody else, one of Goebbels' main traits, would finally spell disaster, not alone for himself but for the whole German people. If Goebbels had had a normally built body, who knows, the history of National Socialism might have been different.

The Book Isidor

The "system," the Jews, and "Isidor" were the three principal objects of Goebbels' campaign. His attacks owed their success to a combination of brutality, pitilessness, and gleeful enjoyment of others' misfortune.

The man deserving our pity perhaps more than any other—he was completely helpless despite his position of power—was Dr. Bernhard Weiss, vice president of the Berlin police. Goebbels called him the "Vipopra." This highly successful word creation was soon common usage. Even the enemies of National Socialism would thoughtlessly speak of the "Vipopra" when referring to Dr. Weiss. But worse still was the other name Goebbels found for him, or at least propagated so effectively that it was soon on all Berliners' lips: "Isidor."

Dr. Bernhard Weiss was known as a good official, proud of his past as a *Korpstudent* [member of a student association. Translator's note] ex-soldier, and officer of the Reserve. Dr. Weiss, no doubt, possessed a number of virtues, but the one he lacked was humor. Instead of ignoring Goebbels' personal attacks against him while at the same time using his connections with the press to pay him back in kind, Weiss rose to the bait, reacting with grim anger. He cited the gauleiter before a court and obtained judgment and an injunction forbidding Goebbels to use the name "Isidor" in connection with the vice president of the police. Yet these court actions provided Goebbels with just the forum he needed for popularizing the name Isidor, and he did not pull his punches. As usual, Goebbels proceeded most astutely applying his courage, stubbornness, and insolence: "Who has got the police headquarters in Berlin, has got Prussia, and who has got Prussia has got the Reich."[35]

The NSDAP's brutal introduction of serious political unrest into the life of the capital, resulting in bloodshed and street battles, necessitated the use of usual police methods for the protection of democracy and its institutions, such as the infiltration of agents and stool-pigeons into the Nazi movement (these were called in Berlin slang tuppenny boys [*Achtgroschen Jungen*]). The police closely watched all National Socialist demonstrations, marches, and meetings. Goebbels searched for a scapegoat he could put into the pillory for all the world to see.

"We decided to single out the vice president Dr. Bernhard Weiss personally for our attack. He would emulate the Social Democrats, who before the outbreak of the war [the First World War—translator's note], attacked not only a system but also a tangible, vulnerable representative of the system . . . this meant including in our aggressive strategy not only the Alexanderplatz [police headquarters] but also the vice president of the police personally. We could have hardly found a more ideal target.

"Dr. Weiss possesses for his position much that does not, and little that normally belongs to it. He is a descendant of the Jewish race, which ipso facto made him suspect in our eyes. Heaven knows how he came to be called Isidor. Only later did we realize that 'Isidor' had been foisted on to him, and that he actually possessed the innocent name of Bernhard.

"However, I have to admit that the name Isidor, if not originally his, was most ably invented. . . ."[36]

Goebbels did not admit having invented the name, although all his biographers after 1935 say that he had. This is actually irrelevant. What matters was his perfidious way of using it. Goebbels once more methodically built up a figure—as he had done with Hitler, Horst Wessel, and certain war heroes before—only this time in the negative sense. His aim was the destruction of a conscientious and irreproachable government official, whom he made into a figure of fun and the detestable symbol of the so-called system. The method Goebbels employed was wickedly cunning.

"He was held responsible for every injustice perpetrated at the Alexanderplatz; and unlike many other big bosses of the system, he reacted with the sensitiveness of a mimosa. This had only a stimulating effect on National Socialist propaganda that made him into a comical figure, without deigning to take him seriously as a political adversary. He was mainly depicted in cartoons, and usually in not particularly flattering situations, which apparently satisfied the natural taste of the Berliner, who will never tire of humor, wit, ridicule, and a sense of smiling superiority."

Goebbels was successful. Berlin laughed. Even Goebbels' enemies laughed, and the physiognomy of Dr. Weiss looked at the Berliners from a thousand cartoons, photographs, comic weeklies, from the pages of the *Angriff,* and from brochures. And Berlin's police vice president, straining to give the impression of a punctilious correctness, in his personal appearance as well as in his public service, was no mean subject for a cartoonist. He sported a little mustache *à la* Adolphe Menjou (a famous Hollywood actor of the time), and the visible part of his pocket handkerchief presented a geometrically perfect triangle. Weiss happened to have a big, very crooked nose and ears that stuck out. Goebbels' cartoonist Mjoelnir fitted him, gratis, with bowlegs and flat feet.

Mjoelnir's drawings of "Isidor" were not witty, but rough, provocative, and often barbaric. A particularly infamous cartoon showed how "Isidor" would love to spend Christmas. The decorations on the Christmas tree consisted of strung-up SA men, and "Isidor" himself held in each hand one of the SA men dangling from a noose. The text read: "Daughter of Zion rejoice." Another cartoon showed "Isidor," on his right the police manhandling SA men and dragging them to prison; on his left, SA columns bravely marching on. The text was "who sows the wind will harvest the storm." The third cartoon depicted Goebbels' most sinister forecast: "For him too, Ash Wednesday will come." From rooftops swastika flags play in the wind, and "Isidor" sits on the pavement leaning against a lamppost with a rope around his neck.[37]

Dr. Weiss took Goebbels to court several times and usually won his actions, but the gauleiter had the laughs on his side. Yet Goebbels was jubilant when the court in Munich (where the party publishers had published the book *Isidor*) acquitted him. The court substantiated the acquittal by saying it could not see an insult in calling a Jew a Jew, as little as in calling a Catholic a Catholic, or a Protestant a Protestant. And the triumphant Goebbels:

"If a certain group of citizens would suddenly get the idea of calling a certain Fridolin by the name of Max—would Fridolin ever get the idea of taking them to court? Why does Dr. Bernhard Weiss cite us before a judge only because we call him 'Isidor'? Does he perhaps find that this name does not fit him? Or does he find it fits him only too well? Only because 'Isidor' indicates a Jew. Well, is then a Jew something inferior?"[38]

Yet this was precisely the heart of the matter: The court drawing an analogy between Jew and Catholic or Protestant offered but a dry interpretation of pure law. But the question was not whether the Jew belonged to a religion but something very different, clearly formulated in the Introduction to the book *Isidor:* "Isidor" is not just an individual, not a person in the sense of the law, "Isidor" is a type, a face or, better still, a hideous face. . . . "Isidor" is the *ponim* [Yiddish expression for face. Translator's note] of the so-called democracy disfigured by cowardice and hypocrisy, the same democracy that in November 1918 conquered empty thrones, and wields over our heads today the rubber truncheon of the freest of all republics. . . . The literal translation of Isidor is . . . the Gift of the East. No name could more aptly characterize today's Germany.[39]

The case of "Isidor" was a classic example of the destruction of a man: "We just wouldn't stand for the enemy playing dead and simply trying to ignore us. So we dragged one from among their midst and set to work on him. A sample of the November Germany . . . and we exposed him to the public without charge, nicely tamed for the people to look at, and we did this with wit and gall, anger and malice, and a piercing laughter already sounding the day of doom. . . . This man couldn't stand a joke and that's why he lost. The laughs were on our side."[40]

The hate campaign against Dr. Weiss fell on fertile ground. It kept half Berlin laughing, and the target was a police official against whom the public ipso facto nurtured a prejudice. Even among the police force itself hatred against their superiors increased. When during a demonstration of the Red Front fighters on June 2, 1928, street fights ensued, necessitating police action, some police truncheons came down on the head and back of their own chief, "by mistake," as the official statement explained. Goebbels wrote an open letter in the next issue of the *Angriff,* addressed to Dr. Weiss, which ended with the following words ". . . faced with such an overwhelming force of Fate, the blind man regains his sight, the dumb sings a *Te Deum,* the friend of the Muse becomes a Homer and the theater doorman a dramatist."

The two enemies, Goebbels and Weiss, were locked in a fight to the end. Wherever the vice president of police saw a chance to get at Goebbels, he would exploit it to the full, and Goebbels would let him have it as good as he got, holding Weiss up to ridicule and branding him as the symbol of a doomed system. On January 25, 1932, Goebbels wrote in his dairy,

"When will the hour come when we enter police headquarters, knock at the Jew's door, and say, 'Herr Dr. Weiss, the time has come!'?"

Perhaps it was Dr. Weiss's luck that Franz von Papen, appointed Reich commissioner of Prussia on July 20, 1932, by Hindenburg, dismissed the Prussian government as well as the president and vice president of police. It surely saved him from being seized, six months later, by SA and SS men with the words, "Herr Dr. Weiss, the time has come!"

Mjoelnir's cartoon showing "Isidor" leaning against a lamppost with a rope around his neck was the first signpost showing the way to a hell called Auschwitz.

The Jews

Goebbels' relationship to the Jews passed through three phases. The first, starting with Goebbels' joining Hitler, reached its climax with the fight against the police vice president, Dr. Weiss, and the Jewish journalists in Berlin. The second phase, starting with Hitler's advent to power, included the purge of all Jewish persons and all Jewish influence from public life. It lasted until November 1938. The first significant measure of the second phase was the boycott of all Jewish enterprises, which Goebbels organized in April 1933. Its pretext was the economic boycott initiated by the West as an answer to Germany's anti-Semitic measures. And it was Goebbels again who organized the biggest pogrom in German history, in November 1938, the Crystal Night.

Yet, there are some contradictions in Goebbels' anti-Semitism. The facts are that he had to be prodded into action by other officials, even by Hitler personally, and seemed rather dilatory in carrying out purges in the cultural field. The third phase of Goebbels' anti-Semitism commenced with the war against Russia, when the destruction of the Jews became a top-secret government matter. Goebbels shrank back from the enormity of the plan, but called it a "hard necessity," and actively supported the planned genocide by his propaganda, using press, radio, and film to make the Jews the scapegoats for all the misery that had overtaken the world. He depicted the Jew as racially and morally subhuman, a monster, a poisonous bacillus that had to be destroyed. In its third phase Goebbels' anti-Semitism was not far behind that of the organizers of the actual destruction of the Jews. He played, one might say, the grim accompaniment to the wholesale murder of the Jews, hoping it would drown their death cries lest they reached some ears and weighed on some consciences. After all, those people were "only Jews."

But what makes Goebbels' anti-Semitism even more damnable is the fact that it did not come to him naturally. It did not stem from the so-called racial "instinct" the National Socialist "doctrine" liked to regard as the only valid assessment, unprepared, or unable, to see that this so-called instinct was nothing else than an acquired prejudice, nourished by a constantly replenished reservoir of hatred. Goebbels had read Heine, Börne, Rathenau, and Marx and not minded that they were Jews. In his younger days he had often studied the Bible and worshiped Jesus Christ without taking exception to the Jewish origin of the Holy Book. He studied at the University of Heidelberg with Gundolf and Waldberg, and admired both professors, though both were Jews. He loved a girl who had a Jewish mother, without finding that his Aryan instinct particularly inhibited his sexual passion. His own appearance, the weedy body and the clubfoot, was bound to be a warning to him not to assess the value of a human being by his physique.

Having been an ardent reader of the *Berliner Tageblatt* could hardly have furthered his anti-Semitic approach. Even the rejection of his applications for the position of news editor, or of a resident literary adviser at a theater, could hardly have appeared to him as the result of a Jewish conspiracy; nor the rejection of his novel, though he no doubt must have taken them as personal slights and humiliations.

Then Goebbels threw himself into politics and joined the party that had made anti-Semitism the cardinal point of its program. Yet the group to which he belonged in the Rhine and Ruhr districts rather tended to regard socialism as their most important issue. Deep down Goebbels hated the bourgeois more than the Jew. He regarded anti-Semitism as a sort of concession to the old nationalists in whose beards Wotan's ravens nested.

Anti-Semitism was a national heritage, the mere mention of which in a speech would assure the speaker a round of applause. But Goebbels' heart was not in it. He was much more attracted by the proletarian element in National Socialism, and the proletariat is essentially not anti-Semitic. During his activities as gauleiter in Elberfeld, Goebbels regarded the social revolution as the most important question. To him the bogey was the Jew as capitalist, but not as member of an "inferior race." This inner attitude broke down when Goebbels joined up with Hitler. In party circles in Munich the racial question was of supreme importance. Here the Jew was not looked upon as dangerous because he was a capitalist, but because he belonged to an inferior race, source of the Jewish blood that defiled this precious Aryan liquid when mixing with it. And that was not all: The Jewish racial soul, by introducing the spiritual poison, when added to the Jewish blood, completed the act of biological destruction. If the Jewish penetration of the Aryan world was not made an end to, then, so thought the National Socialist racial worshipers, the end of our Occidental culture would inevitably come. The National Socialist of the Munich brand regarded the Jewish blood as the new original sin of mankind. Goebbels was now bound to recognize that for the National Socialists anti-Semitism was not merely a slogan to be used in speeches in order to stimulate audiences, but a religion. Hitler believed in it and so did Rosenberg, both from innermost conviction. And the others believed in it because Hitler did. Since Goebbels, however, strove to become the master's favorite disciple, he, too, had to believe in anti-Semitism. It could have hardly been easy for him, as he was not dumb enough not to realize how many vulnerable points he himself possessed, and what an easy target he was for those preachers of the Nordic beauty idol. Perhaps that was the reason why, at first, he merely flirted with anti-Semitism. Only in Berlin did Goebbels become a fully fledged anti-Semite, and that for purely personal reasons. He felt that the Jewish press had looked through him. Their arrows stuck deeper in his flesh than those of other political adversaries. The Jews did not take long to recognize the spiritual treason he had committed. They found him superior to the National Socialist toughs, who with their strong bodies and their weak brains must have found Goebbels, that half portion of a man, a rather pitiful sight; yet the toughs followed his lead, recognizing his spiritual force, and impressed by the little cripple's courage.

Quite a different case, however, were the Jews, spiritually his equals; it was not so easy to pull the wool over their eyes. They knew he had violated his conscience only to satisfy his burning ambition. Anything to play a big part, even if it meant standing on the wrong stage and shouting louder than any other actor in order to draw attention to himself. Goebbels knew that his performance often had an involuntary comic effect, and how he resented it! Despite his own sense of humor and an inexhaustible well of ideas for holding up others to ridicule, he completely lacked any faculty for laughing at himself.

Immediately after the police ban of the party on May 5, 1927, Goebbels complained: "I learned then for the first time what it meant to be the chosen favorite of the Jewish press. Soon there was nothing they wouldn't accuse me of. . . . During my first working phase in Berlin I had to suffer greatly under the attacks of the press. At first I took everything far too seriously, and very often despaired of keeping my personal honor unsullied in the political fight. This changed radically as time went on. Whenever I knew of, or expected, some rabid personal attacks against me in the press, I simply didn't look at Jewish newspapers for weeks, in order to keep my faculty of deliberating calmly, and acting with cool determination. There are only two

possibilities of becoming famous in today's Germany. One has, if you
will forgive my saying so, either to crawl right up the Jew's—you know
what—or you must fight the Jew with all you've got to the bitter end.
The first is reserved for the careerist of the democratic civilization—
the literati and conviction acrobats. We National Socialists chose the
latter method . . . German intellectual circles often tend to over-
estimate the so-called farsightedness, cleverness, and intellectual
faculties of the Jews. The Jew has a clear judgment only as long as he
is in possession of every means of power. The moment a political
adversary faces him in a hard and pitiless manner . . . the Jew at
once loses his countenance and sober judgment. He suffers—and this
constitutes his main characteristic—under a deep feeling of inferiority.
We could call the Jew the personification of a suppressed inferiority
complex. We will, therefore, hurt him most by calling him just what
he is. Call him if you like, scoundrel, cad, liar, criminal, murderer,
and assassin—none of these words will touch him profoundly. But
look at him sternly and calmly for a while and say to him: 'You are a
Jew, aren't you?' and you will see, to your astonishment, how uncertain of himself he will become, how embarrassed and guilt-
stricken."[41]

It is significant how much of all this applied to Goebbels' own
person. He complained bitterly about attacks on his personal honor
perpetrated by the Jewish press, while he himself knew no bars when
besmirching any of his adversaries personally. He ascribed to the
Jews an inferiority complex while his own was as big as can be, try
as he did to overcompensate by a show of insolence and aggressiveness. Only when he became minister did he manage to overcome it
in some measure. Yet, whenever an enemy dared to point out his
physical deformation, he had some of his SA men beat up the culprit
mercilessly; when his own party colleagues did it, he went running to
Hitler crying for protection against such mean aggression. Only he
was permitted to depict his enemies, Jews or non-Jews, as physical
and moral cretins, and rub his hands when a section of the Berlin
public laughed about his malicious caricatures. Not that the Jews did
not try to hit back. But with all their malice, the attacks of the Jewish
press stayed within the limits of what was still humanly permissible.
A good example is Kurt Tucholsky, who published in the *Weltbühne*
[a leading left periodical—translator's note] one of his biting poems
which, no doubt, hit the target and enraged Goebbels:

> *Du bist mit irgendwat zu kurz jekommen,*
> *Nu rächste dir, nu leckste los.*
> *Dir hamm se woll zu früh aus Nest jenommen!*

Du bist keen Heros, det markierste bloss.
Du hast'n Buckel Mensch—du bist nicht richtig!
Du bist bloss laut—sonst biste Jahnich wichtig!
Keen Schütze—een Porzellanzerschmeisser,
Keen Führer biste—bloss 'n Reisser,
Joseph, du bist een grosser Mann!

(You've come into this world too short of something,
Now you cry vengeance and you kick with zest.
It seems they lifted you too early from your nest!
You are no hero, Joe—you must blow up your chest.
You've got a hump man—look you're not quite finished.
You're only loud—but otherwise diminished.
You're not a good shot—just a china smasher.
You are no Fuehrer—just a show-off flasher,
Joseph—no question you are great!)[42]

Goebbels gasped for air. He tried not to show it and wrote: "We've made it a principle to ignore rude personal attacks by the Jew press. We belong to those judicious people who cannot be insulted by Jews . . . and the scars we've acquired in our fight against Jews, are for us scars of honor."[43]

Scars of honor, all well and good, but Tucholsky's poem hit home like a blow from a sledgehammer. "They lie! They lie! With this battle cry we faced the Jewish dirt salvos. Here and there we picked out from this whole slanderous mass a few individual lies just to prove the baseness of those gutter journalists, and we concluded, 'Don't believe a word they say. They lie, because they have to.' "[44]

Journaille [a combination of the words journal and *canaille*. Translator's note] was the name Goebbels used for the Jewish press, though it would have fitted his own paper much better.

Whenever the *Angriff* wrote about Jews, it differed from Streicher's notorious sheet of hate *Der Stürmer* only by its superior German. The *Stürmer* had actually reached an all-time low of German journalism, and even succeeded in making many of the National Socialist leaders ashamed of it. But by sheer content the *Stürmer* had nothing on the *Angriff*.

"You cannot fight the Jew with positive weapons. He is something negative that has to be eradicated from German life or it will corrupt it for good. You cannot discuss with the Jew the Jewish question. After all, you will never be able to convince someone that you have the right, nay, the duty, to hang him."[45]

Even Streicher's conclusions were not worse. Goebbels, whom his own party colleagues had nicknamed *Schrumpfgermane* (Shrunk German), stated: "The Jew fills me with physical disgust."[46] There he sat once again in his glass house throwing stones.

And he went on: "Let the Jew cry 'terror!' We reply with the famous words of Mussolini: 'Terror? Never! It's social hygiene.' We get rid of these people the way a physician gets rid of bacteria."[47]

"Social hygiene," "get rid of bacteria"—the men who were shouting it did so at the top of their voices.

And, later, their soulless henchmen executed it punctiliously.

The System

Already under the Weimar Republic Goebbels succeeded in popularizing the word "system." National Socialist party propaganda called members of those system governments "fulfillment politicians," only because they had accepted the treaties of Versailles and Locarno, as well as the Dawes and Young plans. It would be idle to discuss today the wisdom of the Versailles Treaty or its positive or negative implications. The West, naturally enough, assessed the treaty more favorably than Germany or Austria, though there were also some important Western critics who considered it a grave political error. Certain German historians have lately pointed to some positive aspects of those treaties. Whatever the case may be, the treaties were unsatisfactory; yet cannot the same be said of the Congress of Vienna (1814–15) and Potsdam (1945)? It is notable that the most important treaties concluded during the past 150 years completely disregarded, if not actually betrayed, the basic tendencies of their times: the Vienna Congress—the principle of national states and political liberties; the Paris treaties after the First World War—the self-determination of the peoples and pan-European tendencies; and Yalta and Potsdam—every single one of these rights.

However, the Versailles Treaty permitted Germany to remain a united Reich. The worst was, therefore, not the loss of territory which, the German colonies excepted, amounted to 70,585 square kilometers or about 13 per cent of German territory, but the economic and moral impositions.

United States President Woodrow Wilson, who often lacked a sense of political reality, maintained that Germany's military hegemony was broken once and for all with the abdication of the House of Hohenzollern. It is hard to say if he might not have been proved right, had he only given the men who were willing to build a new republican Germany a fair chance, and the German people the proof that it was preferable to live in a democracy and in peace. But the Versailles Treaty did exactly the opposite. The German politicians who made peace had to tell their people that though they did not have to fight any longer, they would have to work even harder than before, and not to improve their own standard of living, not for themselves, but for their ex-enemies.

Times of crisis are always fertile ground for unrest. The old authorities have abdicated and the new ones are not yet firmly installed. Germany was no exception. Revolutions from the left alternated with those from the right, called putsch. But the word "revolution" seems an exaggeration for these actions, even for the Spartacist rising in Berlin and the establishment of commissar governments (*Räteregierungen*) in some towns. Neither the Spartacist leaders, Rosa Luxemburg and Karl Liebknecht, nor Kurt Eisner, who proclaimed in Munich the Commissar Republic, measured up to a Lenin or a Trotsky. But even more decisive was that neither the people nor the majority of the returned soldiers desired a Communist revolution. Nor did the German Social Democratic party, which had been deeply shocked by Bolshevik behavior in Russia.

In order to quell this unrest, the Social Democratic politicians, only to name those in power during this critical period—Friedrich Ebert, Philipp Scheidemann, and Gustav Noske—were obliged to call for help from officers and the Free Corps, originally formed for the defense of the eastern borders of the Reich, and the Baltic states. These Free Corps leaders, feeling they had been cheated of their reward, attempted several putsches, while the Army and its officers, instead of being the strong arm of the Republic, took the role of a referee, forming a state within a state. It was they who decided to what extent a left-wing revolution or a right-wing putsch should be allowed to succeed. And if neither had any success it was because the military opposed them. Only Hitler, once in power, succeeded in destroying the unique political position the Army had occupied in Germany up till then.

The officer corps, which had helped German governments in those first years after the war to stop revolutions and putsches, was neither prepared to share responsibility for the lost war nor accept the Versailles Treaty (or, as it was called, the Peace Diktat). When asked by their government whether a military resistance in the West would still be possible should they refuse to sign the peace treaty, they replied in the negative, even implying it would be irresponsible to refuse. But they were not willing to share with the political leaders the moral responsibility for signing the treaty. This attitude gave birth to the famous legend of the stab in the back (*Dolchstoss Legende*). The political leaders playing at revolution had stabbed the Army in the back. Germany had not lost the war at the front, but in the *Hinterland*. From then on the right-wing radicals branded all politicians who had signed the Treaty of Versailles, or those who had encouraged the signing, as traitors. Some of them—for instance, the Reichstag member, Matthias Erzberger, of the Catholic Center party—were murdered.

These unjustified accusations were the sources nourishing Adolf Hitler's faith in his calling to smite the traitors, avenge the German people, and clear the German name. The abrogation of the peace treaty of Versailles became from then on not only one of the main aims of German foreign policy (Germany had, in fact, a right to demand it in accordance with the statutes of the League of Nations, provided she used peaceful means) but also a pawn in the political game within Germany itself. The first act of the German tragedy had begun. Every German government striving to obtain reductions of the heavy demands of the peace treaty, especially in the economic field, was at once branded as pursuing the "policy of fulfillment," all the more as every concession had to be bought with a renewed affirmation of the treaty.

"Versailles," Goebbels hammered into his listeners and readers, "means enslavement of the German labor force for half a century, the cession of territory that was ours since eternity, subscribing to the lie that we have caused the war and have therefore to bear the whole burden, as well as the destruction of all German military power, leaving our whole future at the mercy of our enemies."[48]

And with true Goebbels cynicism he created the word *Schadre* (*schützt alle die Republik*), meaning "let us all protect the Republic." The word *Schadre,* with its pseudo-yiddish sound, meant to imply the connection between the fulfillment politicians and the Jews. The main target for Goebbels' propaganda was Gustav Stresemann, whose masterly tactics aimed at dismantling the Versailles Treaty step by step. Stresemann had formed his government in August 1923 when the inflation was at its worst. After being Reich Chancellor for a brief period, he became Minister of Foreign Affairs and held this post until his death on October 3, 1929. Six important achievements are connected with his name: the termination of passive resistance in the Ruhr; the Dawes Plan; the Locarno treaties; Germany's entry into the League of Nations; the Young Plan; and the initiation of a policy of understanding between France and Germany.

The Dawes Plan regularized German reparations payments after cessation of all German passive resistance against the occupational forces in the Ruhr. It was based on the report of a committee under the chairmanship of the American Charles Dawes. The report dealt thoroughly with the potential of the German economy and coined the notorious phrase: "The German people must be reduced to an utmost minimum of their needs." This sentence (it was actually not meant negatively), taken out of context, as well as Stresemann's words calling the Dawes Plan "the Bible of the economy," became the two main targets of National Socialist attacks against the Dawes Plan.

The plan provided for a yearly payment of 2.4 billion goldmarks, guaranteed by the mortgage on Germany's income from customs duties and consumer taxation, the sellout of the railways to private ownership, and some additional imposition on German industry.

The Dawes Plan was initialed on August 16, 1924, in London, and passed by the German Reichstag on August 29, 1924. Goebbels commented on it orally and in writing: "Dawes: It means we have to pay to the oppressor 2.5 billion [goldmarks] every year for nearly half a century, or daily 7 million. With this sum of money we could solve the whole housing problem. We have mortgaged our right to decide freely about our railways, the mint, and our economy. . . . No, ours is no longer a state, we have become a colony of slaves, an object for exploitation by the Stock Exchange financiers. . . ."[49]

At the end of September 1928, Goebbels arranged a Dawes week with the motto: "What does Dawes mean? Germany's poverty forever."

The mortgage on duties, consumer taxation, and railways guaranteed considerable credits that made it possible to revive the German economy. But the strain put upon Germany's economy proved too great after a time. After two years the army of unemployed had grown to two million. When in 1928 the nontransferable funds had dangerously accumulated, the Dawes Plan was substituted by the Young Plan. This plan, too, was based on a report of a committee of experts under the chairmanship of yet another American man of finance, Owen D. Young. The plan reduced the amount of yearly payments. They were fixed on a rising scale starting with the first half-year payment of 676.9 million reichsmarks, increasing until 1965 to 2.3527 billion, and from then on decreasing until 1988 to 897.8 million per year, when the total reparations debt would have been cleared.

A reparations bank was founded to arrange for Germany's necessary credits.

Many historians writing after 1945 present the Dawes and Young plans as special concessions the victorious powers offered to vanquished Germany. These plans certainly were an improvement on the limitless demands formulated by the Versailles Treaty. But the aspect

rather changes if we remind ourselves that at the time of the Young
Plan Germany had no less than three million unemployed, and yet
was expected to pay reparations over a period of another sixty years;
this meant that the three coming generations would have to carry
that burden. Under these circumstances the rise of the left and right
radical parties becomes perfectly understandable. The basic mistake of
the reparations payments was that they compelled Germany to live on
external loans. Catastrophe came with the great crash on Wall Street
on October 24, 1929, when the source of these loans suddenly dried
up. Germany's repayments dried up accordingly; banks went bankrupt, German production declined within two years by half, while the
number of unemployed rose spectacularly. It is easy to moralize as
some historians do who reproach the German people with having
simply given themselves over to Adolf Hitler. It is, on the contrary,
rather surprising that the NSDAP, even after having seized power,
failed to obtain an absolute majority. Economy stress in Germany had
grown so alarmingly, and the understanding the Western powers
showed was still lagging so far behind, that the outcry for the savior
in need, whether it came from the radical right or left, was bound to
drown out all other considerations.

Goebbels organized a petition for a referendum about the acceptance of the Young Plan, and let off political fireworks as rarely seen
before. His battle cry was: The acceptance of the Young Plan was
"the death penalty passed on the unborn." He was not able to prevent
the Reichstag from accepting the plan, but succeeded in alerting millions to the problem. Later, as Reich minister, Goebbels is reported
to have said he was actually not conversant with the contents of the
Young Plan, which was just as well, since it enabled him to organize
the campaign unfettered by details. Later he was joined in his struggle
by a most important ally whose expertise in economic matters could
hardly be doubted, Hjalmar Schacht. Schacht resigned his post as
president of the Reichsbank in 1930, in opposition to the Young
Plan.

The nonexpert Goebbels, ignorant of the details, as he said, reduced the Dawes and Young plans to a simple formula. The consequences of these two plans for the army of German unemployed,
as well as for the patriotic bourgeois, for the industrialists and the
shopkeepers who exhausted themselves in vainly running after
credits, Goebbels summed up as follows:

"The German people have been forced to tread between Versailles
. . . and London, the tragic path that led them from political slavery
into commercial serfdom. And when on October 29, 1924 [there was
acceptance of the Dawes Plan. Author's note] in the German Reichs-

tag . . . the last remnants of our sovereignty were mortgaged to the nameless powers of gold for the sake of a breathing spell, a pseudo-peace, a false success—a development was completed that converted a people of heroes into an army of helots, a nation of honor into a rootless community without substance, where profit, false glitter, poverty, and shame thrives. Versailles was a bleeding wound. The Dawes-Young Plan is a people with a wasting disease. Credits and loans are only shots of morphine."[50]

Pseudopeace and false success—these were Goebbels' main accusations against Stresemann's foreign policy. Under the same heading came also the Locarno treaties signed on December 1, 1925, by which Germany recognized the new borders in the North and West of the Reich, established by the Treaty of Versailles, as well as the demilitarization of the Rhineland. This move of Stresemann's was to a certain degree concordant with Adolf Hitler's concept: peace in the West in order to win greater freedom of action in the East. The guarantees of Germany's new borders contained in the Locarno treaties did not include her eastern borders. And yet Stresemann failed to get good marks from Goebbels; all Stresemann got was the reproach that the German Minister of Foreign Affairs was letting himself be used by the Western capitalists for a crusade against the Soviet Union. This absurd accusation was clearly contradicted by a treaty of friendship Stresemann concluded with the Soviet Union in 1926. Goebbels also objected to Germany's entry into the League of Nations, made possible by the Locarno treaties, as a capitalist conspiracy against the Soviet Union, although in fact it meant that Germany had taken her first step toward obtaining political equality. Stresemann was a man of slow advance, endeavoring to take the sting out of the Versailles Treaty by creating through a policy of rapprochement with France, a political climate that he hoped would finally result in a basic revision of the peace treaty. His efforts to find European solutions were publicly recognized by awarding him, and his French colleague Aristide Briand, the Nobel Prize for Peace in 1926. But how did Goebbels judge this man? For him Stresemann, the most successful Foreign Minister of the Weimar Republic, was the prototype of the German-educated philistine—"the bottled-beer doctor," "the democratic climber," "the risen syndicus," "the wild bourgeois," "the man with the proverbial elasticity," "a politicizing dilettante, propelled by a grotesque accident from chocolate merchandising into high diplomacy, who owing to the same accident became a pliable half-ignorant instrument of the world powers."[51]

Stresemann's portrait sketched by Goebbels testifies to Goebbels' acute observation and sharp characterization: "There he is for you to see in life size, a little fat, a little yellow, a little perspiring with this insufferable irritating smile on his lips. The small, sly eyes carefully protected by cushions of fat, a square, smooth forehead crowned by a gigantic bald pate, and there he stands in the midst of his dear Jews. . . ."[52]

But Stresemann was not the only one to be branded as typical of the system. He shared this doubtful privilege with many others, particularly members of the SPD (Social Democratic party—Sozialdemokratische Partei Deutschlands), whose initials Goebbels chose to reinterpret as "*Schamloseste Partei Deutschlands*" (Germany's most shameless party), granting them the rubber truncheon as their emblem. But also Hjalmar Schacht and Dr. Otto Meissner—both were later to hold leading positions in the Third Reich—Goebbels regarded them as typical of the "system."

But the true embodiments of the system were, for Goebbels, above all others, the Jews, together with the banks and the press they dominated. But also Walther Rathenau, whose writings Goebbels had once eagerly read, applauding the Treaty of Rapallo. This treaty Rathenau had concluded in 1923 with the Soviet Union, an action in complete accord with Goebbels' views on foreign policy at that time; Rathenau, too (he was assassinated on June 24, 1922, by right-wing extremists) was now included in the "system." The case of Rathenau clearly delineated Goebbels' inner transformation. He had worshiped Rathenau during his student days. Now he not only regarded him as belonging to the "system," but also extolled his murderers as heroes. In his book *Isidor,* however, Goebbels desisted from describing Walther Rathenau in his own words. He preferred to quote the obituary by Arnold Zweig, published in the *Weltbühne,* knowing full well how challenging Zweig's words were to the nationalistic reader and to a good many others:

"This Jew," wrote Arnold Zweig, "was very little of a Jew and had nothing of a genius. But he stood head and shoulders above everybody he encountered in the political sphere of today's, as well as yesterday's, Germany. He was too good, much too good for this nation. Poor Walther Rathenau! . . . There was nothing vulgar, native-rough any more about him. Nothing of the strong, laughing Eastern Jew. He walked around, his blood pregnant with his deeds. . . . And he was not the last Jew to face the rubble fearlessly. He had the courage of the Jew to die alone and ignore the bestial menace of the eternal Boche. But he did not die for this nation of newspaper readers, voting sheep, dealers, murderers, betrayers, lovers of operettas, and bureaucratic living corpses. . . ."[53]

Neither side, as can be seen, minced their words.

Goebbels becomes an I. d. I.

On October 29, 1927, Goebbels was thirty years old. To celebrate his birthday, his friends fetched him from his party office and presented him with a muzzle in the form of a "patented Isidor mask" with the inscription "perfectly constitutional." With this gag they gave him two precious gifts: a list of 2,500 new subscribers to the *Angriff,* and the torn-up IOU for the 2,000 marks he had signed personally when starting the paper—very likely the smallest sum of money any paper had ever been launched with.[54] Goebbels was now, at least temporarily, relieved of his worst material worries, and felt more than ever sure of the loyalty of his comrades-in-arms. For the Berlin party members he had become "our doctor," a unique honor; only Adolf Hitler had been invested with the royal title "Fuehrer," propagated by Goebbels.

Soon Goebbels extended his organization to the Mark Brandenburg, and surrounded the capital with a whole ring of National Socialist strong points. In addition to the *Angriff,* his supporters were supplied with various brochures, such as the *Nazi-sozi,* the *Damned Swastika-bearer,* and *The Little ABC of the National Socialists.* By the end of October the ban against his speaking in public was lifted, but Goebbels was required to obtain special police permission before every speech.

The party was officially admitted again on March 31, 1928, on account of the impending Reichstag elections due to take place two months later. It would have been difficult to maintain the ban much longer in any case for purely constitutional reasons. Goebbels threw himself into the election campaign body and soul. He organized one meeting after another, presenting himself as a candidate, while openly admitting he was doing it only for the purpose of using the Reichstag as a platform to carry on his fight against the system yet even more effectively. "We arrive as enemies, like wolves breaking into a flock of sheep," he wrote in the *Angriff* two weeks before the election.

The elections of May 20, 1928, brought the National Socialists in the whole of the Reich just over 800,000 votes—approximately 2.6 per cent of the electorate. Twelve Nazi members out of a total of 491 were elected to the Reichstag. In Berlin proper the NSDAP collected 39,052 votes, which represented only 1.5 per cent of the total; but one must remember that the party had been banned for almost a year, and that only six months before, Goebbels had taken over a totally ineffective party organization, which at the previous election had only obtained 137 votes. Taking this into account, it was obvious that Goebbels had made a great step forward. He had also, by being elected a member of the Reichstag, acquired immunity before the law, a precious advantage for someone who in the past had had to face one court action after another. In the second issue of the *Angriff* published after the elections, he declared: "I am an I. d. I.—*Inhaber der Immunitat* (possessor of immunity), possessor of free travel facilities; what do we care about the Reichstag? . . ."

"An I. d. I. is a man who is allowed to speak the truth occasionally —even in a democratic republic. An I. d. I. has free access to the Reichstag without being asked to pay entertainment tax. . . . With his free railway ticket the I. d. I. can travel for instance from Berlin to Essen, where he speaks to a thousand or more miners, praising the Republic for all its worth—most subtly, of course—returns again to Berlin without having paid a penny for his fare, where he receives as a token of the Republic's gratitude 750 marks monthly for faithful services rendered."

The free ticket and the 750 marks every month were most welcome to Goebbels—not less than the opportunity to speak his mind yet more freely, because an I. d. I. "differs from ordinary mortals in being permitted to think aloud. He is free to call a dung heap a dung heap, and need not talk around it by calling it 'state.' " And, indeed, Goebbels made no secret of what he thought of the state whose elected representative he now was.

On July 1, 1928, Goebbels appointed Reinhold Muchow chief of organization for the gau. Muchow, uncommonly gifted for the job, created the first comprehensive plan for such an organization. He kept close to the Communist model in subdividing the structure into cells, substreet cells, street cells, sections, and gau. The Berlin organization became the pattern for the whole Reich's organization of the NSDAP.

Goebbels also created strong points in Berlin that enabled him to rush SA men from all directions speedily to the points where street fights had started. The ordinary meeting places of the SA thus became the *Sturmlokale* (storm premises). They were a kind of home for the many unemployed who now were SA men. There they could enjoy a warm room, food and beer, and long chats with their comrades, exchanging tales of their street-fight heroics. These places were almost without exception public houses of a low type, usually shunned by the ordinary citizen. The landlord (in German, *Wirt*) was called "storm landlord" (*Sturmwirt*), and his wife, "little mother" (*Muttchen*). These strategic focal points came more and more into play as the tension rose between the Reds and the Brownshirts. Slowly but surely the system was crushed between the two radical movements of the left and the right.

Goebbels also infiltrated National Socialist cells into the factories under the name NSBO (Nationalsozialistische Betriebszellenorganization), "National Socialist Organization of Cells in Factories." From these grew later the DAF (*Deutsche Arbeitsfront*), "German Work Front." Its founder was Johannes Engel, who had, within a short period of time, succeeded in implanting Nazi cells in approximately seventy enterprises. The general attack, however, started only after the local Berlin elections of 1929, when the National Socialists had failed to get into the Red districts of Neuköln, Treptow, Köpenick, Lichtenberg, Weissensee, Pankow, and Wedding. From then on Goebbels concentrated on one main goal: to break into those Red districts at all costs, even if it entailed great risks. To the old marching order, "the conquest of the street," was now added a new one: "the conquest of the factories." This appeared at first completely impossible, as the left parties had at long last learned to take the boasting of "Big Mouth" Goebbels seriously.

In order to be independent of public hospitals, at least for lighter SA casualties (the Berlin hospitals were often staffed by a number of Jewish doctors), the gauleiter set up his own lazaret, which included huge-sized kitchens for fighting party activists. The lazaret was cared for by the German Women's Red Swastika-cross Order (Deutscher Frauenorden Rotes Hakenkreuz), which in turn served as a pattern for the party organization for women [Nazionalsozialistische Frauenschaft—"National Socialist Womanhood"].

Nowhere else in the Reich was the conquest of a city prepared with more intelligence and determination than in Berlin. Here Goebbels created the strategic center of the NSDAP for the whole Reich.

As a curtain raiser to the new election campaign, Goebbels invited Hitler to speak about German foreign policy at a closed meeting in the Saalbau-Friedrichshain on July 13. From then on it was full steam ahead. Goebbels wanted to prove that it was possible to work up within a year the minute Berlin NSDAP to a party of good medium size. As so often before, he stepped straight into the lion's den. He and 150 of his toughest SA men appeared on August 27 at a meeting of the Communist party and broke it up. This was too much for the Communists. When they were beaten up at National Socialist meetings they had at least the excuse that the advantage was on the other side. But now, when the Nazis had reversed the position and beaten them up at their own meeting, the Communists swore revenge. On August 29, the *Red Flag* published an appeal of historical significance. It presented the National Socialists with a blank check for all the brutalities they perpetrated later on at political encounters. It provided them with an alibi, at least in the eyes of the peaceful citizen. The Communist appeal, which ended with the words, "chase the fascists from the factories, beat them where you find them," was, after all, an indirect exhortation to murder. It was, in fact, the beginning of political gang warfare in Berlin.

On September 30, 1928, Goebbels dared to appear for the first time in the Berlin Sportpalast, which from that day on became the "historical" meeting place of the National Socialist movement. The most decisive speeches were held there. With an auditorium of over fifteen thousand capacity, it was Berlin's largest meeting hall. Even the two great left parties used it only on special occasions, for fear they might not be able to fill it. But Goebbels was not particularly worried. He knew that his party was still far from being a mass organization, but he also knew that his supporters were prepared to bring any sacrifice he asked of them. He set the meeting for September 30, which enabled him to make use of the roll call of the SA of Berlin-Brandenburg that had been arranged for the same day at Treptow, with the participation of visiting units from other gaus. They marched about four thousand strong across Lichterfelde-Ost, Steglitz, Friedenau, and Schöneberg to the Sportpalast. Altogether ten thousand people attended. Goebbels staged one of his provocative speeches, causing fights among the police, the SA, and the Communists, exactly as he had intended.[55]

Hitler's speech in the Sportpalast on November 16 was the climax of the year. It was the first time Hitler spoke in Berlin at an open meeting.[56] Goebbels had prepared everything meticulously. The Sportpalast was packed tight.

Hitler had chosen the theme "The fight that will one day break the chains" (*Vom Kampf der einst die Ketten bricht*), and in the end had the audience in a state of hysterical Heil ecstasy. Within six weeks Goebbels had fixed two mammoth meetings at the Sportpalast attended by twenty-five thousand people, or more than 60 per cent of all Berliners who had voted in May for the NSDAP. There was no other man but Goebbels in the whole of Germany who could offer his supporters such a splendid show.

The Fight Against the Young Plan

In 1929 Goebbels worked himself to a point of complete physical exhaustion. He would go on for sixteen, sometimes eighteen hours a day, constantly driving himself, constantly producing new ideas. In late spring, when the Young Plan became known, Goebbels hit his stride fully. In their fight against the plan, the NSDAP acquired an unexpected ally in Alfred Hugenberg, the leader of the German National People's party (Deutschnationale Volkspartei). Hugenberg had been managing director of Krupp from 1909 to 1919; a member of the Reichstag since 1919; proprietor of the biggest film company (UFA) in Germany; proprietor of a press agency; and proprietor of a publishing house that owned a number of newspapers all over Germany. Hugenberg wrote several thousand letters to various industrialists in and outside Germany, pointing out that the demands of the Young Plan could never be satisfied by the German economy and would ultimately lead to Germany's collapse. German economic circles were deeply impressed by Hugenberg's action. To popularize his fight against the Young Plan, Hugenberg joined Hitler, who demanded that Goebbels should be put in charge of all propaganda. This was accepted, and Goebbels had for the first time at his command sufficient money, as well as a propaganda network, including press agencies, newspapers, newsreels, and a chain of cinemas. He knew from the start that his action would not be crowned by success, since the majority of the parties were in favor of the Young Plan, while the Communist party remained neutral. Against this closed front, Hugenberg and the NSDAP combined could do little. But this did not bother Goebbels. What mattered was that he had been handed the means for attacking the system on a grand scale and had been helped by politicians and groups who in some way were part of it. It was an opportunity to use other people's money to strengthen the National Socialist position. Besides, Goebbels never minded a fight; fighting was his life elixir.

Goebbels spoke every evening, wrote a daily article, composed posters, invented slogans, gave guidance to other speakers, and was otherwise busy organizing the campaign—a prodigious task.

The referendum took place between October 16 and 29. In the whole Reich, 7.7 per cent of the electorate voted against the Young Plan; in Berlin however, 10.9 per cent, making all in all 5.8 million voters, perhaps not enough to prevent the plan from being accepted, but sufficient to give the NSDAP a powerful shot in the arm. On October 24, the Stock Exchange on Wall Street crashed and opened the eyes of economic experts to what the amateur Goebbels had predicted all along: The Young Plan was unworkable. The American financial catastrophe had put an end to the vicious circle of eternal loans and payments of interest.

Alongside his fight against the Young Plan, Goebbels conducted his campaign for the municipal elections to the Berlin Town Council, giving his special attention to some cases of corruption in the city's administration. Actions were brought against him for certain personal attacks, particularly against Dr. Weiss, as well as for other offenses, such as disturbance of the peace and insulting remarks against the person of the President. His immunity did not always work; the Reichstag acceded to the extradition demands of the courts. Goebbels, far from playing the part of the repentant sinner, appeared in court rather in the role of a high-handed accuser. He would shout at the public prosecutor, ridicule the charges brought against him, and transform the courtroom, packed with SA men, into a theater where the public seemed greatly amused by the successful performance of the accused.

The newspapers reported these court actions; Goebbels was pleased. He surprised the Berliners with a new, particularly crazy idea: He had a poster printed listing the sentences he had received, and underneath the words: "And you want to elect me!"—and the Berliners passing those posters by the thousands had to laugh at so much impudence. The little doctor had begun to impress them.

At the same time political gang-warfare between National Socialists and Communists continued unabated. On one occasion Goebbels himself had a narrow escape. On September 22, the Berlin SA undertook a propaganda march, parading before Goebbels on the Spreewaldplatz in front of the Goerlitzer Station. When Goebbels tried to overtake the SA group by driving through a side street, he was received by the Communists with a hail of stones; his chauffeur was hit on the head and injured. The accompanying SA men emptied their revolvers at their opponents, who withdrew. According to the SA men's own statement the shots were fired from alarm pistols. Police quickly arriving on the spot arrested Goebbels and the SA men, but released them again.[57]

On November 17, 1929, the municipal elections took place. Up until then the NSDAP had no representative. Now the party collected 132,697 votes, three times as many as at the last Reichstag elections in May 1928. It advanced from eighth to sixth place. The SPD counted 651,735, the KDP 555,277, the German National party (Hugenberg) 404,632, the German People's party (Stresemann's party—Stresemann had died in the first week of October) 154,250, and the State party 138,456 votes. The Catholic Zentrum, with only 81,404 votes, had fallen behind the NSDAP.

Goebbels could be well satisfied. In a mere three years, of which the NSDAP had been banned for nearly one whole year, he had raised the number of voters from 137 to 132,697. The party had now 13 representatives out of 225 in the city administration, and 40 district officials out of 480. Goebbels was one of the 13.

The first demand put forward by the NSDAP faction in the new Town Council was for a special Christmas aid to benefit the unemployed and people without means, small pensioners, and needy war-injured. The necessary means were to be obtained by imposing radical taxation on department stores, expensive restaurants, and luxury private houses. Goebbels' social radicalism, as we can see, had by no means weakened. He was still the terror of the bourgeois, still courting the votes of the poor. He himself would walk around shabbily dressed, parading a proletarian attitude and living modestly. But when work was done he would retire to his small, tastefully furnished two-room apartment in Steglitz. Here he could be quietly alone far from the vulgar crowd and would, if he did not fall into bed dead tired, read a good book.

The Making of a Hero

The year 1930 was decisive for Goebbels in more than one way. He had added to his post of gauleiter of Berlin that of chief of Reich propaganda (Reichspropagandaleiter),[58] with a seat in the party cabinet. Hitler considered propaganda to be of paramount importance and granted the new propaganda chief a privileged position.

Goebbels had not long to wait for a chance to prove what he could do in his new job. On January 14, Horst Wessel was shot dead. Goebbels at once saw that here was a martyr ready-made. It gave him an ideal opportunity to apply his propagandistic genius and score one of his most spectacular successes.

Horst Wessel, born 1907, son of a pastor and Freemason, left the parental home after his father's death, tired of its secure comforts. He became a "work student" (*Werkstudent*), one who preferred to frequent public houses rather than lecture halls. One evening when he was attending a meeting he heard Goebbels speak and was so fascinated that he joined the SA then and there. He soon commanded "Storm 5," which distinguished itself in battle by its particular aggressiveness against the Communists. Horst Wessel's insolent but charming ways had soon made him into a popular party speaker. This did not stop him from sitting around in low pubs and beer cellars. On the contrary, he sought and found in this environment a means of protest against the petrified bourgeois world.

At the end of 1929 he fell in love with Erna Jaenicke, described by several biographers as a prostitute. (At the trial at which she was a witness, it emerged that she had previously had an affair with Horst Wessel's murderer, Ali Höhler.)[59] She and Wessel lived together—another protest against the prudish ideas of a bourgeois society. His landlady was the widow Salm, whose husband had belonged to the Red Front fighters. It was she who allegedly divulged Horst Wessel's whereabouts to Höhler. Höhler went with a few of his men to the apartment, and when Wessel opened the door, fired a bullet into his mouth: "You know what for!" he called out to the collapsing victim (his motive was probably personal vengeance).[60] Wessel was rushed to the Hospital Friedrichshain. In every issue of the *Angriff*—it had appeared twice weekly since October 1, 1929—a bulletin of Wessel's condition was published. The gauleiter personally visited him in the hospital. At the end of a mass meeting called on February 7, 1930, the song written by Horst Wessel, and called after him, was heard for the first time, resounding from more than ten thousand throats. The "folksy," popular melody is said to have been "borrowed" from a book of Communist songs. On February 23, Wessel's condition worsened. Blood poisoning set in, causing his death.

Fearing clashes, the police banned the elaborate funeral arrangements planned by Goebbels. No more than ten cars were permitted to follow the hearse. Goebbels protested in the *Angriff*:

"Gentlemen, we are used to burying our dead with honor. Do not believe that by forbidding his friends to pay their last tribute to the murdered man, you can rob him of his honor. You even forbid us to bury Horst Wessel under the flag for which he died. Be it so. We have no intention to bury the flag with him in his grave. It shall unfurl above our heads when we march forward across other graves."

The funeral took place on March 1. The atmosphere was as tense as possible. The pavements of the streets through which the funeral cortege passed were lined with thousands of people, most of them wearing a black armband, giving the passing procession the Hitler salute. Approaching Nikolai Cemetery, the cortege was greeted from afar by the words the Communists had painted on the cemetery walls in huge letters: "A last 'Heil Hitler' to the pimp Wessel!" Just before the hearse passed through the gates, the Communists tried to overturn it and had to be prevented by the police. Inside the cemetery thousands had gathered. SA men and students formed an honor guard that reached from the gates to the freshly dug grave. While the coffin was being lowered into the earth, and the song of the *Guten Kameraden* was being sung, Communist groups started their own concert outside the cemetery walls, whistling and singing the "Internationale." They also bombarded the mourners, throwing sand and stones over the cemetery wall. But Goebbels, as always when it became really hot, kept cool and finished his burial speech: "A

Christ socialist! Who by his deeds calls out 'Come unto me and I will save you! . . ." At the end of his speech there was a moment's silence; then Goebbels called out, "Horst Wessel!"—and hundreds of voices answered, "Present!"[61]

The murderer Albrecht Höhler, called "Ali" by his friends, a carpenter by profession was, according to police records, a pimp. He was condemned to seven years in prison. Höhler was probably a member of the Communist party. The Nazi papers even published his membership number, not necessarily irrefutable proof—and as mentioned, the motive for the murder was very likely personal vengeance, political considerations taking second place.

But Horst Wessel himself was not a pimp. He was muddleheaded, contemptuous of society, a drunk, a womanizer, a fellow who liked a brawl; he might have let his mistress keep him from time to time, but he did not exploit her.

It was solely Goebbels' doing that Horst Wessel was converted into the greatest martyr of the National Socialist movement. It was a masterpiece of propaganda. Horst Wessel became a Siegfried-like figure—a young student who had relinquished the security of the parental home to give his all and everything to the people and fight against the injustices of society. Wessel became an "unknown SA man" who, following his "inner law," did his duty, rejecting the bourgeois world beckoning with its temptations. Wessel belonged to the nation's "new aristocracy," chosen to found the new, the Third Reich. He had been a courageous fighter, this *"Kamerad Horst"*!

"The mere sound of his name vibrates with something heroic, knightly, courageous. The name is brief and slim, grand and upright. A strange force lives in the name, incomparable youth. There is frankness in it and shining clarity without any frills. A young man shows the movement how you can die if necessary, even must die."[62]

During twelve long years the Horst Wessel *Lied* was sung in the Third Reich at every official occasion, along with the Deutschlandslied, as a second national anthem. During those twelve years every German knew the name of Horst Wessel. The Bülowplatz in Berlin was renamed "Horst Wesselplatz." The Karl Liebknecht House, headquarters of the KPD, would henceforth be called, after their own martyr, the Horst Wessel House. It became a kind of Horst Wessel museum. Squares and streets in many parts of Germany were named after Horst Wessel. No other fallen hero of the NSDAP could claim such honor. No one else's memory was held so sacred. And all this was Joseph Goebbels' doing.

Horst Wessel's glorification was Goebbels' last tribute to the dreams of his own youth. Wessel was far from being a hero, but he was essentially not an evil man. Having lost his inner equilibrium, he tried to drown his sorrows over his personal failure, his contempt for the world, and his hatred for society, in brawling, whoring, and drink. But Wessel had actually attained what the young Goebbels had longed for, fought for, and never achieved: an inner independence free of all outside ties. Wessel had descended into the lower reaches of human existence to live his life to the full; Goebbels had done the same, but with the intention of rising again and climbing as high as possible. Wessel was a libertine without any particular ambition. Goebbels was full of both. They both felt contempt for the world and society; that was why Wessel mixed with people whom society liked to call "the scum." Goebbels too mixed with the lower strata —at least with proletarians. But as soon as he had left them, he could hardly wait to wash his hands. Wessel might still have been saved by a friend, or the right woman, or a profound experience; Goebbels was already by then irretrievably lost. In Horst Wessel he erected a memorial to himself: a memorial for the lost Goebbels, the same man who had once intended to fight for his freedom and who now was in chains. Wessel had actually attained this personal freedom. He had not died for a cause. Only Goebbels knew how to make him into a martyr, a hero of the new Reich.

The Political Landslide

After his first propagandistic masterpiece, the Reich propaganda leader was all set to deliver his next: the electioneering fight for the Reichstag elections in September 1930. For the first time Goebbels was in sole charge of the campaign for the whole Reich territory. Goebbels' election fight is the first European example that measures up to American standards. It overshadowed everything done before in this field, either in Germany or in the rest of Europe. And Goebbels still lacked the two main instruments available to the great parties, namely radio and the daily press, with the exception of the *Völkische Beobachter*. The success was so overwhelming that when the election results became known, the whole party, including Hitler and Goebbels, was astounded, and their adversaries were dumfounded.

At the outset Goebbels said: "We will give those parliamentary boss-ridden parties an electoral fight as they have never seen before." In the meanwhile, difficulties mounted. Goebbels was cited in court on several occasions for the usual slanders, libels, and insults he showered on his adversaries in speeches and newspapers. But the authorities did not remain idle either, and made the election fight as difficult for him as possible. All legal means were used to stem the advance of National Socialism, particularly in Berlin. On June 11, 1930, the Prussian Ministry of the Interior banned the wearing of SA uniforms. But Goebbels' inventive mind found a suitable answer to every chicanery. Not only did he know how to circumvent all official bans, but he also succeeded in making the authorities look ridiculous. He knew his Berlin inside out, and knew that the masses would always sympathize with the victim, or even with those who appeared victimized by official action, hardly bothering to inquire who was in the right. Instead of the banned brown shirts, Goebbels' SA men wore white shirts. An SA man stopped by a policeman because he wore brown trousers took them off in public and proceeded in shirt and underpants for several hundred yards to the joy of the passersby and the helpless annoyance of the police. No one could say the little doctor was short of ideas, and the greater the pressure on him the more audacious and self-confident he would become.

Goebbels organized approximately six thousand mass meetings all over the Reich. He did not spare his speakers, particularly Hitler and himself, who never got a day's rest. He had trained a number of first-rate speakers who received precise instructions. He impressed upon them the necessity of using simple, clearly constructed sentences, accessible to all, irrespective of their level of education. This basic rule he borrowed from Hitler. But Goebbels was superior to Hitler in the art of simplifying, of making political aims concrete through slogans, and by using a black-and-white technique to delineate characters most effectively. He was also superior to Hitler in the art of clearing up vague notions so as to make them popular. Goebbels rented the biggest halls. He had tents erected and called mass meetings under the open sky, uncannily lit by thousands of torches carried by SA men. Goebbels catered to the ear, the eye, and the emotions. No other electioneering meetings were as impressive as those staged by Goebbels. He used any available space on walls, fences, or trees to stick his red posters with the swastika and a provocative text. The circulation of the few party papers, ordinarily around fifty thousand in all, was raised tenfold and passed to the party activists for distribution among the people, at the nominal price of one pfennig. Millions of election brochures were distributed freely in the streets and dropped into private letter boxes. Columns of cars with posters drove through the smallest villages, their loudspeakers blaring out NSDAP slogans. The fight against the Young Plan, so ably conducted by Goebbels, was now paying

off. The moneybags of the industrialists had been opened, and there
was no shortage of funds.

The strategy of the election campaign adopted by the new
Reichspropagandaleiter proved right. Everything seemed to fall into
place. The strategists of the other parties could not seriously com-
pete with him. They could not master that mixture of hatred and
love, of damnation and adoration, of servitude and freedom, of per-
dition and salvation. This was an art in which Goebbels was supreme.
The result was unbelievable. One of the smallest parties became the
second largest in the German Reichstag. The catastrophic economic
conditions; millions of unemployed; a situation of paralyzed foreign
policy; a lack of comprehension on the part of the victorious powers,
never short of beautiful phrases, but rather niggardly when it came
to meeting Germany halfway, or even granting a minor alleviation—
they would put forward their grand plans for general solutions, each
of them branding Germany as a vanquished nation forever: All
that, of course, was wind in Goebbels' propagandistic sails. But no
one knew better than Goebbels how to use this wind and sail vic-
toriously past the finishing line.

On September 14, 1930, Hitler and Goebbels sat together, exhausted and hoarse from too much speaking, tensely waiting for the
results to come in. The optimists predicted that 40 members would
be elected to the Reichstag. But even this estimate, mentioned
publicly by Goebbels once, was met with derision from the other
parties. At five o'clock in the morning Hitler and Goebbels, the party,
and, indeed, the whole world knew that the election had brought the
biggest political landslide in the history of the Reich. There still
might have been time to save democracy in Germany by strengthen-
ing the back of the democratic politicians, in granting them economic
and political successes, and by so doing take the wind out of the sails
of the two radical wings on the left and the right. But the world was
shocked, and that was all. Their statesmen wagged their wise heads,
sat back, and did nothing but wait.

The NSDAP had obtained almost 6.5 million votes, and entered
the Reichstag with 107 members. In Berlin the number of votes had
risen from 39,052 at the Reichstag elections of 1928 to 395,988.
They were now the third-strongest party in the capital, immediately
after the Communists and the Social Democrats. The KPD, with
739,235 votes, had for the first time become the strongest party in
Berlin, beating the Social Democrats by a mere 1,000 votes. The
election results showed a breakthrough of radicalism in Germany,
but not so much because the German people had become a radical-
thinking nation, but because they had fallen on bad times.

4. Hitler administering the oath of allegiance to members of the Nazi party. Left to right: Captain Goering, Dr. Frick, Hitler, Gregor Strasser, and Stoehr. In background is Dr. Goebbels. September 6, 1932.

5. Goebbels, minister for propaganda, speaking to a crowd at Neukölln, a suburb of Berlin, concerning a vote of confidence for Chancellor Hitler at the national referendum held August 19, 1934.

6. Goebbels introducing the new director of the German Broadcasting Service, Eugen Hadamowsky (at left in suit), to the staff of the company. July 20, 1933.

7. Goebbels during a visit in Rome, Italy. Shown here with members of an Italian fascist youth organization. June 13, 1933.

Lenin or Hitler? The choice was Hitler, thanks to Goebbels' masterly propaganda. Hitler, too, now threw his shadow over world events. Soon he would bestride the globe, and the world would tremble.

The Woman in His Life

One evening an elegant lady, attracted by the sound of lively military marches and the excited faces of thousands pushing their way to the booking office, also paid her entrance fee and found herself in the Sportpalast in the midst of ten thousand people frenetically cheering a little man who was just crossing the platform, past an honor guard of strong young men wearing brown shirts. In front of the stage was a forest of red flags displaying the swastika. The lean face of the man was set in a hard expression. The way he dressed and his behavior were proletarian, and yet he did not give the impression of being a genuine proletarian. The man began to speak; his quiet voice created a perfect silence in the hall. But then, suddenly, a torrent of words cascaded down on the enemies of the people, on the bosses, the November criminals; the eyes of the speaker sparkled, and his long, nervous hands menaced and drummed in accompaniment to the cacophony of irony and sarcasm, accusations and damnations. But then again the voice sounded warm, beautiful, and full, like an organ; he spoke of Adolf Hitler, the savior of the German people who would, as their Fuehrer, lead them out of their misery into the future Reich of German glory. The people jumped up, they shouted, they rejoiced, beyond themselves with ecstasy. The woman, who had at first felt out of place among those rough, fanatical people who smelled of sweat, sat there fascinated by what she had just heard, and even more by the man up there on the platform. According to certain reports[63] she joined the NSDAP local group of West Berlin on the following day. Her name was Magda Quandt, twenty-nine years old, divorced, and in a state in which her life appeared to her monotonous and senseless. She could not know that her fate had been decided on the previous evening, that she would, in fact, become the most interesting woman in the Third Reich, closely linked to Hitler's rise and fall, as no other woman was.

Maria Magdalena Behrend-Friedländer was born in Berlin on November 11, 1901. Her father, Oskar Ritschel, a well-to-do engineer, married her mother, Augusta Behrend, after Magda was born. Three years after Magda's birth the Ritschels divorced and her mother married shortly afterward a Jewish businessman, Friedländer. Thus Magda acquired a Jewish stepfather whom she dearly loved, and whose name she bore until she was ninteen. The six-year-old girl—the family lived at that time in Belgium—entered the convent school Sacré Coeur, run by Ursuline nuns in the Belgian town of Volvorde. Before the outbreak of the First World War the Friedländers returned to Germany, where Magda entered the *Gymnasium* and graduated in 1919. In the meanwhile her mother had again divorced, and Magda entered a most superior finishing school, Holzhausen in Goslar. On the train from Berlin to Goslar she made the acquaintance of the textile industrialist Günther Quandt, who fell in love with the pretty eighteen-year-old girl. He was thirty-eight, a widower with two sons, Helmut and Herbert. Quandt courted Magda, who was attracted by his wealth and the worldly manner of a mature man. She said "yes" to his marriage proposal, but at his insistence abandoned her Catholic faith. He also made her forsake the name of Friedländer and take that of her real father, Ritschel.

The wedding took place in January 1921 in Bad Godesberg. In November 1921 Magda gave birth to a son whom she called Harald. The marriage soon proved a failure and was only kept up as a façade. Magda's qualities as a society hostess, exploited by her industrialist husband, particularly during their journeys to North and South America, made it worth his while. But in 1929 the marriage was dissolved, when Quandt discovered Magda's liaison with a medical student. Quandt agreed to give his divorced wife 50,000 marks for the purchase and fitting out of an apartment, plus a monthly allowance of 4,000 marks for as long as she remained unmarried. Magda made her home in the West End of Berlin on Reichskanzlerplatz No. 2. There she rented an elegant seven-room apartment, which she furnished with great taste. Her love for the young student did not last very long; he soon began to bore her. Her life was without a care, but empty. She had been looking around for something worthwhile to do. Magda Quandt offered her co-operation to the head of the local group in West Berlin that was overjoyed to enlist such a superior lady, and asked her to lead the National Socialist Women's Group (Nazionalsozialistische Frauengruppe), hardly a fitting job for Frau Quandt, since the members of the local group, even in this fashionable district, mostly belonged to the lower classes. Among them were concierges, servants, small grocers' wives, etc. What on earth was Magda Quandt to do with her fine manners and her society connections with these good *Volksgenossinen?* Magda resigned her job and appeared at gau headquarters offering her unpaid services. The gau administration had been situated since May 1, 1930, in Berlin SW68, at 10 Hedemannstr. It was the fourth move of the party offices since Goebbels had taken over in Berlin. The spectacular growth of the party and its influence was reflected in the ever larger and ever more elegant premises it occupied.

Beautiful Magda's motive for appearing at gau headquarters to offer her services was not hard to guess. She wanted to be near the man who had excited her so deeply by his speech in the Sportpalast. First she was offered the post of secretary to his second-in-command. But later on, when Goebbels got to know her, he put her in charge of his private archives. In the course of this work she came across all sorts of articles that had appeared in Germany and abroad about Goebbels and the National Socialist movement. Both met daily and got to know each other more and more intimately. He, too, was fascinated by her, even if only because she came from a world and a class against which he may have always fought, but that held a certain magic for him. He advanced more cautiously than usual, and it took some time for the two to become lovers. In late summer 1930 they became engaged. What actually led to this engagement is told in a yet unpublished document that throws new light on the relationship between Magda Goebbels and Adolf Hitler.

Wagener's Notes About Magda Quandt

The Institute for Contemporary History in Munich has in its possession the handwritten notes[64] of Major General Dr. Otto Wagener, Ret., which he compiled from his diaries after 1945 and committed to the institute for safekeeping.

Wagener was head of the economic section of the party up to 1932; he resigned shortly before Hitler came to power. His notes are most interesting, particularly those passages that throw a new light on Hitler's personality and those of some of his close collaborators. The notes bear no date, but they deal with events that took place in the late autumn of 1930.

According to Wagener, Hitler met Magda Quandt for the first time at tea. Despite Goering's warning that Magda was "Goebbels' Pompadour," Hitler took an immediate liking to her. He was charmed by her elegant appearance, her vivacity, her winning smile. "There was no doubt," writes Wagener, "that a bond of deep friendship had begun to form between Hitler and Frau Quandt." Hitler was still suffering under the loss of his niece Geli Raubal, who had committed suicide. She had been very close to him.

Wagener's notes leave no doubt as to Hitler's vivid personal in-

terest in Magda, and he quotes Hitler himself as having confessed
how much Magda meant to him.

"I thought," Hitler told Wagener, "I was through with the world
and all human influence. And it may be that what touched me today,
and still keeps me spellbound, does not come from the earthbound
source of ordinary human emotions. There is something beyond and
greater that creates bonds between human beings and makes them
exert their influence on each other . . . there must be something not
of this world, but greater, that lives in us. Perhaps those are right who
call it the Divine.

"During my tender friendship with Geli I felt just that with her,
but never with any other woman. I have missed it ever since she
died. And I thought I had buried it with her in her coffin. Today,
much to my surprise, it overcame me again, and with great force.

"This woman could play a great part in my life, even without my
marrying her. In my work she could provide the opposing force to
my one-sided male instincts. . . . Pity she's not married."

This was the cue for the faithful Wagener.

As chance would have it, he happened to be driving Magda to
Braunschweig—a perfect opportunity for a serious talk. Wagener explained to Magda how important a role she could play in the life of
the "Fuehrer"—not as his wife, since he was not meant for that, but as
the feminine element, so to speak, that would establish the necessary
balance. But in order to play this part she would have to be married.
Preferably to Goebbels. Magda promised Wagener to think it over.
"I promise that you will be the first to know when I get engaged to
Goebbels. And then you will know that I made a still greater vow."

Two weeks later it was done. The engagement was celebrated
within a small circle of intimate friends. And Wagener "couldn't help
feeling that happiness had come to three people."

It emerges quite clearly from Wagener's notes that Goebbels' and
Magda Quandt's decision to get married was strongly influenced by
extraneous considerations. Magda had admired Hitler long before she
met him, perhaps less from having read his book than from listening
to her lover propounding in his speeches and in their talks his admiration for his "Fuehrer." She regarded Hitler as quite apart, and high
above any man she knew. And their first meeting had for her the
electrifying effect of an encounter with the hero already well known
to her from the imagery of her daydreams. And Hitler, sensing the attraction he exerted on this beautiful woman, was much too vain, and
also too sentimental, not to feel the extraordinary magic of the moment and enjoy it thoroughly.

Wagener's notes also help to explain Goebbels' later attitude toward his wife. Goebbels probably had no wish to marry; he rather wished to safeguard his independence. It was most likely Magda's account of her conversation with Wagener that made Goebbels change his mind. This, as he saw it, was the only way in which—without being made a cuckold—he could bind Hitler to him, and by means more powerful than personal merit or an oath of allegiance. Goebbels, an outsider who controlled no pressure group and had no friends within the party, entered the circle of Hitler's chosen few. And, notwithstanding an occasional deterioration in their relationship, he remained Hitler's most intimate collaborator to the bitter end. Even Speer who, bound to Hitler artistically by the Fuehrer's ambitious architectural plans, considered himself—if one is to believe his memoirs—Hitler's special favorite, could not claim to equal Goebbels as Hitler's confidant. This is not surprising if we remember that the artist in Hitler was after all the weaker part of his personality. In any event, what united Hitler with Goebbels was first Magda, Hitler's greatest consolation after the loss of Geli, and later the knowledge that they were both bound for life and death by the same pact with the devil.

Until the end Hitler felt responsible for Goebbels' marriage. He forbade them to divorce when their relationship had reached an all-time low, and succeeded in presenting the Goebbelses to the party and the people as the perfect German family. Later on, when Magda made some derogatory remarks about Hitler's female company, meaning Eva Braun, Hitler obviously took exception, and broke off with Magda, at least temporarily. Magda's jealousy of her idol Adolf Hitler was bound to lead to this deterioration of their relationship.

On September 19, 1931, the marriage between Goebbels and Magda was celebrated on the Quandt estate. Quandt's estate agent Granzow, an enthusiastic National Socialist, made all the arrangements for the festivities, which were preceded by a civil ceremony as well as a wedding ceremony in the Protestant church. The witnesses were Hitler and General Ritter von Epp.

Goebbels gave up his little bachelor apartment in Steglitz and moved into Magda's splendid apartment (the monthly rent was 450 marks). Magda lost her 4,000 marks' monthly allowance. Goebbels had earned as a member of the Reichstag and a gauleiter altogether 1,000 marks; Hitler apparently raised his income after the wedding to 2,000 marks. Goebbels also received royalties from his writings. By marrying they had no doubt worsened their financial position. This is another indication that love alone (which they could just as well have enjoyed without marrying) was not the decisive factor in their marrying.

Goebbels' and Magda's apartment on the Reichskanzlerplatz henceforth became Adolf Hitler's private headquarters in Berlin. Almost all important internal party conferences took place there. When Hitler was present, the Goebbels' apartment became the meeting place of party leaders. Frequent visitors were Goering; Himmler; Sepp Dietrich, the SA Fuehrer; Count Helldorf; and Hitler's adjutants. But Goebbels' apartment was also Hitler's Sans Souci. Here he would spend all his free evenings, recite his endless monologues—they would sometimes last for hours—or he would listen to records or to Ernst Hanfstaengl playing the piano. Hanfstaengl, called "Putzi" by his friends was, until he fled Germany, a member of Hitler's most intimate circle. Hitler also stayed with the Goebbelses in their rented weekend house in Caputh on Schwielow Lake. Magda was near him whenever possible—at least until he came to power.

The "Asphalt Democracy" Forced to Its Knees

After the elections of September 14, 1930, Goebbels brought off a coup culturally as decisive as the September elections had been politically. On December 5, 1930, Erich Maria Remarque's film *All Quiet on the Western Front* had a second showing in the Mozart cinema on the Nollendorfplatz. (The first performance, combined with a lecture, had been given before an invited audience.) The film had been shot in Hollywood after the German best seller of the same name, and promised to be as successful as the book had been. The novel was most realistic, showing the war through the eyes of a simple soldier at the front. It was written without false pathos, without any inkling of heroics, simply presenting the brutal soul-destroying existence, consisting of killing and surviving. "Ready to die" and "sacrifice oneself" were for Remarque empty slogans. A man's life was his most precious possession, and death was his greatest catastrophe. This made Goebbels' "heart of steel" glow red hot. Since he had not been in the war, he regarded it as a heroic experience. In "storms of steel" man must prove his mettle. Goebbels had blocks of tickets bought for the film performance, and distributed his SA men in the audience. He himself sat in the gallery, from where he could overlook the impending show he was going to direct.

And what a show it was! Within a few minutes the SA men threw their stink bombs and released white mice from briefcases. Many women jumped up, shrieking, and climbed up on their seats. Complete chaos ensued. The film show had to be interrupted.

"To the Nollendorfplatz! Down with the filthy film! For the fallen of the great war! Save their honor! Honor their memory!" Goebbels wrote in the *Angriff*. In the following five days SA men and party members marched to the Nollendorfplatz shouting "Down with the film!," "Hitler at the gates." The police were helpless; they succeeded in pushing the crowds back and clearing the square, only to see it soon invaded again from all directions. No one dared to enter the cinema. And after five days the film had to be taken off.

On December 11, 1930, the chief film censor banned the film for the whole of Germany, as being detrimental to German prestige and dignity.

Goebbels had won. All papers printed his name and discussed his action. The fact that most of the comments were negative left him completely indifferent. What was decisive was that the party had imposed its will on the system. Triumphantly Goebbels summed it up:[65]

"The film of shame has been banned. With that action the National Socialist movement has won its fight against the dirty machinations of the Jews all along the line. The occasion . . . was, it seemed, not very important. But it did raise a question of principle. Would the asphalt democracy [one of Goebbels' word creations. Author's note] be permitted to continue offering the German public unpunished such mockery of German honor and German tradition despite the growing national consciousness of the great masses? It was essentially a fight for a principle. We were the carriers of the ethical perception of the state and maneuvered the Prussian government into an increasingly untenable position. They had to use a grotesque display of power to protect a work of filth, more and more rejected in disgust by the public. In the end the means used no longer stood in any relation to the object they protected, and this was the undoing of the Prussian government's position. . . . It was a fight for power between the Marxist asphalt democracy and the consciously German ethical concept of the state. Let us put on record that for the first time the asphalt democracy has been forced to its knees."

The Stennes Putsch

In the years 1930–32 the NSDAP was in a state of fermentation. The dissatisfaction emanated mainly from the SA, who felt that their position in the party was not what it should have been. They particularly objected to Hitler's course of action, which aimed at coming to power by legal means; they saw in this a betrayal of the revolution. The SA leader corps had also most serious misgivings about the gauleiter's right to influence the appointment of high-up SA leaders.

The rebellion broke out in Berlin, and not without good reason.

Goebbels' radical fighting tactics, his policy of provocation, leading to
a succession of street fights and battles in meeting halls, had put the
main burden on the SA. They had incurred many casualties and demanded a greater participation in regard to policy. To make matters
worse, Hitler and Otto Strasser had quarreled when Strasser rejected
Hitler's tactics, which consisted of abandoning the fight against the
"capitalist" right parties in favor of intensifying the struggle against
the left. But Hitler needed money and could not afford to shock the
industrialists and the bankers. Otto Strasser had the benevolent support of the ex-Captain Walter Stennes, OSAF (Oberster SA Fuehrer)
East (supreme SA commander). Stennes had, at the time, disapproved of the co-operation between the NSDAP and Hagenberg in
their common fight against the Young Plan. Stennes had come into
the public eye when he attacked with his men the offices of the gau
headquarters in Berlin. The police had to be called in, much to the
delight of the party's political enemies.[66] Goebbels happened to be
absent from Berlin; at his request Hitler hurried to the capital to
pacify the rebels. But Stennes and his men remained discontented
with Hitler's course and the prepotent ways of the Munich party
bosses. To a certain degree, Goebbels understood how they felt. On
March 31, he invited several SA *Ober-* and *Standartenfuhrer* to his
apartment, and they all agreed that the liberation of Germany had to
come from Berlin, Prussia, and not from Munich, Bavaria. But
Stennes conspired with Otto Strasser in a plan to initiate an independent movement. When Goebbels left for Weimar to attend the
Fuehrer meeting on March 31, Stennes proceeded with his plan. He
occupied the Berlin *Gauleitung* and printed an appeal in the *Angriff*.
A delegation was sent from Berlin to Weimar in order to win over
Goebbels. But he remained faithful to Hitler. In party circles the
views persisted that Goebbels had sympathized with Stennes; but the
chief originators of this accusation were Goebbels' archenemies,
among them Rosenberg[67] and Hanke. Otto Strasser maintained that
in Weimar Goebbels was still undecided.[68]

It was not impossible that Goebbels' heart was with the Stennes
rebels, since he too rejected the *Reichsleitung* in Munich, and condemned their "bourgeois" course. Anything beyond that remains pure
speculation. From the day Goebbels had joined Hitler, he never
wavered in his loyalty. He sometimes tried, especially during the war,
to win Hitler over to an idea he considered to be right; but once Hitler
had said no, the matter was settled for Goebbels. The same applied to
the case of Stennes. Goebbels probably tried in Weimar to persuade
Hitler to adopt a political line that was more to the left, and make, at
the same time, some concessions to the SA. But as soon as the

Fuehrer had said no, Goebbels no longer insisted, and accepted the Fuehrer's decision.

Indeed, Hitler rewarded him for his loyalty. The *Völkische Beobachter* ceased publication of its Berlin edition, leaving the field to the *Angriff*, which became a daily paper on November 1, 1930. Furthermore, Hitler renewed the powers he had granted Goebbels in 1926:

". . . I empower you to carry out forthwith a new purge of the movement with all necessary determination. . . . You should act pitilessly and not deviate from your decision for any considerations whatever in regard to any consequences that may follow. . . ."[69]

Hitler released an appeal addressed to the SA clearing Goebbels of the accusation of having conspired with the rebels. "I need not defend your gauleiter, he stands so high above the rubble who work with such means, that to defend him would only mean insulting him. You should all follow your Fuehrer and gauleiter, Joseph Goebbels, with unconditional loyalty. Give him your full trust, just as he has all mine."[70]

The Fight Against Bruening

In March 1930 Dr. Heinrich Bruening of the Catholic Center (Zentrum) party had taken over from the last Social Democrat Reich Chancellor, Hermann Müller. Goebbels had counted Müller among the "system" politicians, and had depicted him colorfully in an underhanded and sarcastic article in the *Angriff:* "a little plump, self-satisfied, a double chin, even a third chin beginning to show, voice rusty but oiled with mucus—this is the man who today occupies Bismarck's chair."[71]

Bruening had been a captain in the war and had been decorated with the Iron Cross, making it rather difficult to call him a "November criminal." Modest, personally disinterested, and dutiful, he attacked a problem that seemed insoluble. He dissolved the Reichstag after he failed to have his budget passed. At the ensuing September elections the National Socialists had become the second-strongest party in the Reichstag. In refusing to pass the budget the Reichstag had only succeeded in letting the devil into the house.

Bruening was only able to govern by special decree. He had to rely on the tolerance of the Social Democrats, officially in opposition. In the meantime, the number of unemployed increased day by day. The government was actually in the minority. In January 1931 Bruening declared that the "radical verbiage" was responsible for the catastrophic worsening of the situation. After the September elections, a flight of capital took place, amounting to billions of marks, depriving Germany of the financial resources sorely needed for financing employment. This, Goebbels replied to the Reich Chancellor, was only a further proof of how totally dependent the German Republic had become on international financial trusts, which, by simply calling in short-term credits, could ruin it at any time.

In the following summer the Danat Bank and other financial enterprises collapsed as a direct consequence of the calling in of short-term French credits. This was the French revenge for the Austro-German customs union of March 1931. German Foreign Secretary Curtius and his Austrian colleague, Schober, were forced to annul the customs union in September after a "humiliating defeat" in Geneva. This annulment was in Goebbels' opinion "without equal even among the many defeats of German foreign policy since 1918."[72]

Bruening's home policy brought a lowering of wages, salaries, and unemployment benefits; at the same time taxation went up for everybody, sufficient reason for the Nazis and Communists to give Bruening the name "Hunger Chancellor." With the failure of the Austro-German customs union and the financial and economic pressure exerted by France, Germany's foreign policy had suffered a defeat that had its inner political repercussions, and a particularly adverse effect on nationalist circles.

On October 10, 1931, Hitler was received by Reich President Hindenburg for the first time. The meeting had been arranged by General Kurt von Schleicher, an officer with great political ambitions who, while personally remaining in the background, had all along influenced political events in the Reich to a considerable extent. He had been Bruening's strongest backer. (Schleicher owed his special position, which enabled him to influence Hindenburg, to his friendship with Hindenburg's son Oskar. Schleicher also played an important part in the build up of the so-called *Schwarze Reichswehr* (black armed forces) and in the making of a secret arrangement between Germany and the Soviet Union that provided for the training of German tank and air force officers in Russia, in exchange for German technicians and managers to help in the development of the Soviet armament industries.)

The day after Hitler's audience with Hindenburg on October 1, the "nationalist opposition" held a protest meeting against the Reich government and the Russian government in Bad Harzburg. Hugenberg's German National party, the "steel helmet" (*der Stahl-helm*), and the NSDAP founded on that occasion the so-called Harzburg

Front, which agreed to concert their actions on certain selected questions; in actual fact, Hitler never allowed anybody to tie him down in any way whatever. The Harzburg Front was only meant to serve him as a means for obtaining the necessary financial backing. Goebbels called the Harzburg Front a tactical move.[73]

Indeed, Hitler needed money at that moment more than anything else. One had better therefore tone down the socialist demands and modify the propaganda line, so as not to shock the financial providers too much. Goebbels, who now belonged to the inner circle, began from then on—and it could not have been easy for him—to play down the socialist note to a practically inaudible pianissimo. It was no longer the fight against communism and social democracy. And Goebbels only transferred his hatred more and more from the bourgeoisie to the Jews.

From Kaiserhof to the Reich Chancellery

After the Nazis had come to power Goebbels published his diaries covering the period from January 1, 1932, to May 1, 1933, in book form under the title *From Kaiserhof to the Reich Chancellery*. It became a best seller and a bone of contention among the party leaders. But also Goebbels' biographers, such as Heiber, criticize the book for serving only to glorify Hitler and Goebbels. They were right enough, but this was exactly what Goebbels had set out to do, and it proved most successful.

Goebbels' idea was to build an imperishable memorial for Hitler, and simultaneously an idol for his contemporaries: Hitler the greatest German statesman, who possessed courage, tenacity, and something that only history's great men had shown—the gift to divine the right action at the right moment. He could wait when others were in a hurry. He remained steadfast when all others began to waver, and would strike just when the enemy felt most secure. And as he had outwitted the parties of the Weimar Republic and broken all resistance, he would, thanks to his determination and cleverness, his wisdom and prophetic vision, also triumph in his foreign policy.

And Goebbels would not have been what he was had he not erected his own memorial next to Hitler's. A little less gigantic perhaps, but still large enough to tower over all the other party leaders. He actually mentioned only two of his party colleagues with any respect, Goering and Roehm, whose power he had to recognize, and with neither of whom he could afford to quarrel. . . . Himmler did not play a big part as yet, and no one, not even the prophetic Hitler, could foresee that Roehm would have to be destroyed one day.

What Goebbels intended to impress on the readers was, basically: There is Hitler for you, Hitler the unique, Germany's savior and Fuehrer; and at his side Goebbels, the only one who really understands the Fuehrer's innermost thoughts, the only one capable, thanks to his propagandistic genius, of transmitting them to the German people and the admiring world; also personally the nearest to Hitler, the only real confidant among the Fuehrer's so-called confidants. It was this last point the other party leaders disliked most. Rosenberg grimly noted down in his diary, Gauleiter Wilhelm Kube's summing-up of Goebbels' book: *"I* about myself."[74]

Moreover, Goebbels had succeeded in presenting himself to the whole German people as the man with the shortest direct line to Hitler. For the historian, the book is doubtless an important source of information covering the two decisive years immediately preceding Hitler's advent to power, and almost the only one that came from Hitler's inner circle.

Practically all authors who wrote about Hitler and the Third Reich used the book extensively; but not all succeeded in conveying what Goebbels actually meant to convey; some of them, rather the opposite.

Hindenburg or Hitler?

The year 1932 was memorable for two presidential elections, two Reichstag elections, and one for the Prussian State Diet (Landtag). During that year triumphs alternated with disappointments for the National Socialists. Behind the scenes Goering, Frick, and Roehm, acting as Hitler's negotiators, no doubt, played an important part, but Goebbels, who planned and organized the great electioneering battles, was—for all to see—the real hero of the year.

Ever since Goebbels had moved into the Fuehrer's shadow—from 1931 onward Hitler had stayed more and more frequently in Berlin, and usually at Goebbels' house—he had felt a growing paralysis stifling his own initiative. Before then he had been inferior to no one in Berlin and free to indulge unhindered in his propagandistic exhibitionism. But now he had to take Hitler into account, who above all wished to give the impression that he was fit to govern, particularly to the so-called high society. Goebbels confided his mood of frustration to his diary on January 1, 1932: "Tired of the prolonged quiet. A life without a wild pace sweeping you along does not appear to me worth living." He was getting stale, like a racehorse that had remained too long in the stables.

It suited Goebbels to be in opposition. He knew no other alternative than total power or absolute opposition. And he regarded with suspicion all movements that aimed at a compromise: "The chess game for power has begun . . . and the party will be played to the end—with tempo, astuteness, and a certain cunning. The main thing is to remain strong and not compromise."[75]

Goebbels knew the man who was ready to compromise, and knew that his policy was supported by a considerable number of party leaders. On January 6, Goebbels recorded a conversation with Hitler: "We discussed the internal position of the party. There is one man in the organization whom nobody really trusts. There is a danger that he will desert us at the decisive moment, inflicting on us possibly considerable, if not irreparable damage. This man knows no solidarity and is incapable of being anybody's friend. His name is Gregor Strasser!"

This touched on the question of what attitude the NSDAP was to adopt when Hindenburg's seven-year term of office came to an end in the spring of 1932. Bruening planned to secure an extension for the old field marshal without the constitutional referendum; for this he needed the votes of the NSDAP. Meetings among Hitler, Bruening, and Schleicher came to nothing. The leaders of the NSDAP were divided. Strasser was in favor of accepting Bruening's offer. Goebbels, Roehm, and Goering were against it. Hitler tried to strike a bargain directly with Hindenburg. He wrote the President a letter in which he offered his support for Hindenburg's re-election in exchange for Hindenburg's promise to drop Bruening's plan of prolonging the presidency by a simple vote in the Reichstag. Hindenburg refused.

Such an understanding would have compelled Goebbels to stop his propaganda completely. His joy at the failure of the negotiations showed in his diary note of February 14: "We must bring him [Bruening—author's note] down by every means at our disposal. He stands in the way of the German awakening. Only when he is gone will there be air to breathe."

The practical politician Bruening, who only needed a working majority in the Reichstag and some visible support from abroad to succeed, was a thorn in the flesh of the National Socialists, and particularly of Goebbels. The National Socialists feared that Bruening might succeed after all. In the meantime the problem of the presidential election became more and more pressing, but Hitler remained still undecided. Goebbels tried his best to get a decision out of him, but in vain. They drove together to Munich. The Brown House was in a fighting mood: "Only defeatists in the party are weakening—they refer themselves to Strasser. . . . I strongly advocate putting Hitler forward as a candidate." But Adolf Hitler avoided the issue, as always when asked to take an important decision. Yet to encourage his Reichspropagandaleiter he discussed with him his future ministry. "It is planned to introduce a new kind of ministry for the education of the people, which would combine film, radio, new educational institutions, art, culture, and propaganda—an immense project, the kind of which the world has never seen before. I have already started drawing up the basic plans for such a ministry. . . ." (January 19 and 22, 1932).

Hitler discussed problems that could only arise after he had taken over. But he was still undecided as to what to do with the actual problem before him. Even as late as February, he had still not made a decision. A discussion among him and his party leaders had failed to clear up the position. "Everything is in suspense," writes Goebbels; but for him there was only one solution: Hitler should put himself forward as a candidate for the presidency. "It is a risk, but one worth taking." (February 9, 1932).

On February 15, Hindenburg announced his candidacy. Hitler could no longer avoid the issue. He empowered Goebbels to announce his candidacy for the presidency on February 22, at the general meeting of party members in the Sportpalast. Goebbels, beating the big drum, announced: "I am not saying he is our candidate, because if he were that, it would mean that he was as good as elected."[76]

Hitler had two problems to face. One was that he was not a German national. This was not difficult to solve. There were already some National Socialist Ministers of the Interior in office, in the Länder, and they were only too eager to help. Hitler was simply appointed government councillor (*Regierungsrat*) of Braunschweig and sworn in as German official as well as citizen of the German Reich on February 25, at the Braunschweig legation in Berlin.

More thorny was the other problem. Hindenburg was a living memorial, a national legend. His glory went back to his great victories over the Russians at Tannenberg and the Masurian marshes in August and September 1914. Now Corporal Hitler was going to put himself up as a candidate against him! Hitler knew from the start that he had no real chance against Hindenburg. He presented himself only because Hindenburg was the candidate of all those factions Hitler fought as "system parties," comprising the Social Democrats, the trade unions, the Catholic and Liberal parties. Hitler refused to march together with the Social Democrats and "the party of the prelates."

Accordingly, Goebbels' propaganda refrained from attacking the candidate Hindenburg, but attacked the parties that championed him, particularly the Social Democrats. Speaking in the Reichstag on February 23, Goebbels coined the phrase of the candidate of "the party of the deserters," provoking the Social Democrats, whose storm of anger engulfed him with a spate of abuse and menace. The session was interrupted, and Goebbels was expelled. "A mad show," he noted, self-satisfied, in his diary. His insolence was so provocative that the *Augsburger Zeitung* of February 27 wrote: "Goebbels deserves a good caning."

Goebbels, too, knew quite well that there was no real chance of beating Hindenburg. His sole aim was to use the great election fight to stimulate the masses and further the progess of the NSDAP. Once again he adopted his old successful recipe of Lenin or Hitler, duly changed to Hindenburg or Hitler. In each case Hitler was the only alternative. The day would come when it would be adopted and Hitler emerge victorious.

With ample financial resources behind him, Goebbels organized an election campaign with a yet more lavish display than the one he had used in the Reichstag elections of 1930. The great orators, particularly Hitler, and Goebbels himself, as well as Gregor Strasser, who was then still in the game, were continuously on the move. Propaganda headquarters organized up to three thousand meetings a day. Millions of posters, handbills, brochures, and special editions of party newspapers flooded the country. But Goebbels also had something quite new to offer: a filmed ten-minute speech, which was projected in the evenings in the open air in big cities, as well as in cinemas (the cinema proprietors obviously preferred to avoid a quarrel with the SA). Fifty thousand small-size records of a Goebbels' speech were sent to the people who mattered.

Things were not made too easy for Goebbels. The opposing side had the radio at its disposal, perhaps the most powerful means of propaganda, of which it made full use. And there were other difficulties put in Goebbels' way. Newspapers, posters, and handbills were confiscated daily.

"Ban after ban. Thus they blunt the point of our attack. Our best posters and handbills are rendered useless. That is how the Reds hope to frustrate our victory."[77]

Goebbels' cardinal aim was to make Hitler the symbol of German unity. And nothing better for creating the Hitler myth than the two election campaigns for the Reich presidency: "Hitler, the Fuehrer . . . has made it his aim to unite the German people and weld them together for the greatest show of their power yet. . . . In his hard, arduous, and sacrificial ascent he led the ridiculed and laughed-at small sect to become the most imposing mass party in Europe.

> Hitler the Prophet!
> Hitler the Fighter!
> Hitler Reich President!

"Whoever stands up against the class war and fratricide, whoever seeks a way out of the bewildering jungle of our time, will give his vote to Adolf Hitler! He represents the newly awakened young German idealism. . . ."[78]

On March 9, Goebbels organized a mass meeting in the Berlin Lustgarten for the first time in the history of the NSDAP. Braving the piercing cold and the snow, 80,000 people attended. No other party had ever succeeded in attracting so many people in one place. Hitler spoke from the ramp in front of the palace, and the 80,000, their arms raised, swore to remain faithful to the aims of National Socialism.

The elections took place on March 13; 85.1 per cent voted:

Hindenburg	18,651,497	(49.6 per cent)
Hitler	11,339,446	(30.1 per cent)
Thälmann (KPD)	4,983,341	(13.2 per cent)
Düsterberg	2,547,729	(6.8 per cent)
(German National party)		

Goebbels noted in his diary: "We are beaten: our prospects are terrible." Hindenburg missed by only 100,000 votes getting an absolute majority. This necessitated a second poll. Hitler, who had never lost his countenance, wrote in a special edition of the *Völkische Beobachter* on the following day: "The first electoral battle is over. The second has started today. I will also lead this one personally."

The last sentence was aimed at Hindenburg who, apart from one dignified broadcast, had not taken part in person in the election campaign.

Goebbels threw himself into the second election campaign with even greater obstinacy: "There must not be any talk of coalition. One does not look for peace after a defeat, but for victory! If we were bourgeois we would capitulate. But the Fuehrer remains steadfast and firm."[79]

This attitude, disastrous as it proved during the war, was in this particular case psychologically right. True, Hitler would still not be able to beat Hindenburg, but by attracting Düsterberg's votes he would reach the biggest number of votes any single party had ever obtained in Germany before. It was an object lesson in Hitler's and

Goebbels' perfect co-ordination of propaganda. It was, incidentally, the first time in history that a candidate used an airplane, enabling him to speak in a number of places, situated far apart from one another, on the same day.

In the first campaign Goebbels had appealed to the electorate by depicting Hitler as a prophet and the unifier of all Germans; now he preferred to play on the voters' sentimental and emotional receptivity.

"Any kind of pose, any exhibition and 'attitude' is completely alien to his [Hitler's] nature. He appears as he is, natural, and without any kind of makeup. What has made him into the people's greatest orator of our time is his genius to be able to draw from the deepest well of human emotions and never say a word he does not believe himself."[80]

The results of the second election, on April 10, showed a slightly diminished participation, and gave the following results:

Hindenburg	19,359,983	(53 per cent)
Hitler	13,418,547	(36.8 per cent)
Thälmann	3,706,759	(10.2 per cent)

This second round was a personal success for Goebbels. In Berlin the Nazis beat the Communists for the first time; the Communists had been the strongest single party in the first poll. The results of the first poll were:

Hindenburg	1,307,661
Thälmann (KPD)	685,411
Hitler (NSDAP)	666,053

The second poll recorded:

Hindenburg	1,328,941
Hitler	863,621
Thälmann	573,099

The presidential election campaigns—exactly as Goebbels had predicted, and against the views of many party leaders, including Strasser—had very much furthered the progress of the NSDAP. The general situation remained rather unclear. Hitler still had a chance to form a coalition with the Bruening government and the Reichswehr. But this would have meant a further suppression of the revolutionary elements with the NSDAP. A partisan of this coalition was Gregor Strasser, no longer leader of the party's left wing. The revolutionary line was now represented by Goebbels and Ernst Roehm, chief of staff of the SA.

Revenge on Bruening

The Prussian police had allegedly confiscated papers and documents found at SA headquarters, from which emerged the fact that the SA had planned a *coup d'état* in case Hitler obtained a majority in the presidential elections. The logic of this allegation seems rather feeble, since it is hard to understand why a *coup d'état* should have been necessary after an electoral victory. Those who accept this as being true, as, for instance, Shirer[81], base their assumption on an entry in Goebbels' diary dated March 11:

"Discussed measures to be taken next day with SA and SS leaders. Great alarm. The word 'putsch' is making the round."

If the word 'putsch' was being used, it was rather in government and police circles, who felt strong enough after their election victory to carry out a *coup* against the NSDAP. General Groener, Minister of the Interior, induced, in fact, the somewhat reluctant Reich President to sign a decree dated March 13 to safeguard "the security of the state authority, banning the SA, SS, HJ, and the NSKK within the whole Reich territory."

Goebbels replied in his ingenious and ruthless manner. He called upon the people to gather at a mass meeting in the Sportpalast on April 15. On April 9 Bruening broadcast his last speech of the election campaign, from Koenigsberg. Goebbels had recorded his speech. On April 12, giant red posters announced that, as well as Goebbels, Reich Chancellor Bruening would speak at a National Socialist meeting in the Sportpalast on April 15. On the following day, a second poster appeared, printing a letter Goebbels had addressed to Bruening, in which Goebbels suggested that each of the two orators should have nine thousand entry tickets at his disposal. Goebbels assured Bruening of the perfect behavior of his followers. Each speaker would have an hour at his disposal, and the conclusion would be left to Bruening, a gesture by which Goebbels was eager to prove his good faith.

The second half of this poster contained Goebbels' comment: Bruening had not even bothered to answer this fair offer. May the Berliners judge for themselves how precarious the government must consider their own position to be, if their chief does not dare to take part in such a discussion. On April 14, pasted across these posters, appeared the announcement that the Herr Reich Chancellor would speak after all. Bruening, who had arrived in Berlin after his journey through Germany only on April 10, the day of the election, could not have received Goebbels' letter before the eleventh; the second poster accusing him of trying to avoid the discussion had appeared all over the town before Bruening even had time to answer. Goebbels had pulled a fast one on the Reich Chancellor.

On April 15, the police had to shut the doors of the Sportpalast, which was packed to overflowing. The SA who, after the ban, were forbidden to appear in their uniforms, wore top hats or paper hats. Goebbels arrived shortly after 8 P.M., with his escorts carrying several suitcases, which they placed on the platform next to the speaker's desk.

But where was Bruening?

Goebbels began:

"Herr Reich Chancellor Bruening has preferred to leave my generous offer unanswered. But never mind, I have brought him with me all the same."

Goebbels left a pause filled with suspense. The puzzled audience looked up at him.

"At the moment," he continued, "the Herr Reich Chancellor still inhabits these suitcases. I have carefully recorded his last speech. May I now have your attention, please: The Herr Reich Chancellor has the word."

Goebbels gave a sign and left the speaker's desk. And there came Bruening's voice. After a time the record was stopped and Goebbels, smiling, engulfed by tumultuous applause, returned to the speaker's desk. This procedure was repeated several times. And every time Goebbels nailed the Chancellor. He hacked into the defenseless Bruening like a vulture into a corpse. When he had finished with him, there was little left of Bruening; the raging crowd roared with laughter, shouting and giving Goebbels a standing ovation.

Goebbels proudly entered in his diary, on April 16: "The verbal duel with Bruening has stirred up the whole *journaille* (gutter press). Even the most evil-minded admit that the Reich Chancellor was soundly beaten. Now they rail at me like a bunch of fishwives, because somehow they know that the whole system has taken a beating. . . ."

On April 24—that is, eleven days after the ban of all National Socialist formations—the elections for the Prussian Diet took place. During the nine days preceding the elections, Goebbels spoke daily four times, exhausted as he still was from the presidential election campaign; he was actually ill and had himself carried to the meetings, showing a fanatical will power, matching only Hitler's.

During this election campaign Goebbels created the term "Prussian National Socialism." He never tired of presenting Berlin and Prussia as the main pillars of National Socialism, trying to push the South German element into the background, which was naturally dominant, as Hitler was Austrian, and Münich the birthplace of the movement.

Goebbels attributed the vagueness of National Socialism to its South German origins:

"National Socialism has a right to claim to be today's Prussianism. Wherever we are, anywhere in Germany, we National Socialists are the Prussians of today. The ideals for which we fight are born of the Prussian spirit, and the aims we try to realize are, in a rejuvenated form, those of Frederick Wilhelm I, of Frederick the Great, and of Bismarck."[82]

In fact, Goebbels succeeded in Prussianizing even Hitler to a certain degree, a condition entirely against Hitler's nature, the very opposite of Prussian. Nevertheless, Hitler too accepted—at least outwardly—Frederick the Great as the hero of National Socialism.

The Prussian Diet elections of April 24, 1932, brought the National Socialists another sensational success. Their representation rose from 9 seats (obtained in 1928) to 162, making them, with over 8 million votes, Prussia's strongest party. In Berlin they displaced the Communists from second place, and became with 765,909 votes the second party after the SPD, which had obtained 798,214 votes. Goebbels entered in his diary:

"Now something has to happen. We must get into power before long, or we shall keep on winning elections until we die of it."[83]

This worried not only Goebbels but others too. It was once again General Schleicher who made contact with the NSDAP, in particular with Hitler and Roehm. Schleicher's idea was to integrate the SA into the Reichswehr, so as to be in a better position to control it. Roehm agreed, hoping his SA would permeate the Army with the spirit of National Socialism. But Hitler strictly opposed such a move. For him, as for Goebbels, the SA was above all a political army.

Schleicher intended, furthermore, to include Hitler in the government, equally hoping to control him more easily. These were the true motivations that induced Schleicher to advocate lifting the SA ban. Goebbels entered in his diary on May 8, 1932:

"The Fuehrer had a decisive meeting with General Schleicher. A few gentlemen belonging to the intimate circle of the Reich President attended. All goes well. The Fuehrer was able to convince them. Bruening will fall in the near future. The Reich President no longer has confidence in him. The plan is to install a presidential cabinet. The Reichstag will be dissolved, all decrees rescinded; we will get a free hand for our propaganda and, trust us, we will surpass ourselves. If this plan succeeds, then our negotiators, headed by Chief of Staff Roehm, will have done a job they can be proud of."

On May 13, General Groener, who had proclaimed the SA ban, resigned. With him Bruening lost one of his strongest supporters. On May 12, Reich Chancellor Bruening had coined the famous phrase of being "100 meters short of the winning post." He had already obtained the promise from the victorious powers to abrogate completely German reparations and grant Germany the right of equal rearmament. This would have been a remarkable success for the Chancellor's foreign policy. As for his interior policy, he planned a large agrarian settlement program, for which the Government was to buy the large bankrupt East Prussian estates. This, more than anything else, cost Bruening whatever was left of Hindenburg's favor. The Reich President himself owned an estate there, a present from the East Prussian big landowners. Goebbels' propaganda wasted no time. His diary shows an entry on May 18:

"Bruening is under the sharpest attack by our press and propaganda. He must fall at whatever cost. The undercover action against him continues unabated. He is practically isolated. Wringing his hands in despair, he searches for collaborators. A kingdom for a minister. General Schleicher was offered the Reichswehr ministry and refused. Our intriguing little rodents are working hard to undermine Bruening's position."

At long last the goal was reached. Bruening resigned on May 30, 1932. The last democratic Reich Chancellor of the era between the two wars had abdicated. Bruening was doubtless a man of honest intentions, of limitless personal devotion, and of a certain political ability. He took over when Germany's foreign policy stood before half-closed doors, when Germany's interior politics had brought the country to the verge of economic disaster and civil war. With a man like Ebert as Reich President, and an SPD government in power with enough courage to be unpopular, Bruening might have succeeded in making those sorely needed last 100 meters to the finish line. But history would have it otherwise.

"Herr Dr. Weiss, the time has come!"

On the day of Bruening's fall, Hitler and Goering, who from then on emerged more and more into the foreground, were received by the Reich President. Hitler promised not to oppose the presidential cabinet installed by Hindenburg, but demanded in exchange the rescinding of the SA ban, and the dissolution of the Reichstag.

Perhaps the most fatal element in this development was the great attraction the National Socialist party exerted on the bourgeois masses. The National Socialists achieved this by keeping their program vague, their promises generous, by their appeal to patriotism, and their fight against communism, which had become the great bogey for all who still had any possessions to lose; the bourgeoisie were also impressed by the Nazi conquest of the streets, which up till then had been ruled by the Red battalions. They really thought Hitler could improve conditions.

On June 1, 1932, Hindenburg appointed, on the advice of General Schleicher, the fifty-five-year-old Franz von Papen as Reich Chancellor. Papen was a member of the Catholic Zentrum Party and of the conservative Herrenklub. [The Herrenklub was a highly exclusive, archconservative, mostly aristocratic club.] He was a Westphalian aristocrat who had come into money by marrying the daughter of an industrialist. The Zentrum Party expelled Papen after his obvious betrayal of Bruening, obliging the new Chancellor to form his Cabinet without the support of a party. It was called the "Cabinet of the barons," since a number of aristocrats held ministerial posts, the key figure being the Minister of Defense, General Schleicher.

On June 4, Papen dissolved the Reichstag and fixed new elections for July 31, thereby implementing the first promise he had given Hitler in exchange for his support of the Cabinet. Hans Bauer wrote on June 14, in the Social Democratic newspaper *Abend:*

> With bowlerhat merrily lifted
> On the occasion of the election fight
> The Cabinet of the Ruhr barons
> Needs you my
> Swastika proletarian!

Fulfilling the second promise he had given Hitler, Papen lifted on June 17 the decree of April 13. The SA, and all other formations of the Nazi party, were again made legal; the civil war between National Socialists and Communists began anew. Even during the SA ban, street battles had taken place between the two radical parties. One party had counted casualties by the hundreds and even some dead; losses on both sides were about equal.

But on June 22, hell broke loose. In Moabit, the Communists rehearsed an uprising in protest against the lifting of the SA ban. They systematically smashed street lamps, plunging the district into darkness, and erected barricades with cement blocks. To quell the revolt the police were obliged to use armored cars. On July 17, the confrontation between the KPD and the NSDAP reached a new high. In the working district of Altona Communists attacked marching SA columns. There were nineteen dead and nearly three hundred injured. Hardest hit this time was the SA. Now indignation rose from all sides. The democratic parties demanded that the government make an end to the terror. The KPD shouted their slogan: "Down with the fascist assassins of the workers!" And Goebbels in a speech threatened the government: "If you cannot establish order, then we will do it for you."

Goebbels nurtured a personal resentment: In his hometown, Rheydt, which he had visited during the election campaign, the workers had chased him out. On July 15, he wrote in his diary: "I have to leave my own hometown like a criminal pursued by curses, contempt and abuse, stoned and spat upon."

The events in Altona gave Papen a chance to use emergency paragraph 48 and depose the Prussian government. The reason given was that those events had proved that the Prussian government was no longer in control of the situation. Furthermore, proofs existed that the Prussian authorities had been co-operating with the Communists. In April the Reich government had used material about an alleged SA putsch to ban the National Socialist private army. Now they repeated the performance, using material that inferred that the Communists and the Prussian authorities had conspired to depose the Prussian government. But there was an essential difference between these two measures. The SA ban had been ordered to end a state bordering on civil war, and the rule of terror employed by a private army against specific sections of the population, while the second measure had served the Reich Chancellor to depose the legal Prussian government, which had been democratically elected. In fact, one could no longer speak of Germany as still being a democracy. With Bruening's fall the die had been cast in favor of a dictatorship. Papen's action presented Goebbels with a personal triumph: Together with the government, Dr. Bernhard Weiss had to relinquish his post.

Papen's energetic measures, very much after the heart of most NSDAP leaders, yet created among some of them a feeling of anxiety: "Many of us fear that the government does too much, leaving nothing for us to do," Goebbels remarked in his diary on July 22. He had then obviously not yet realized the inexhaustible possibilities of evildoing.

The NSDAP Becomes the Strongest Party

On July 31, a total of 13,745,000 people voted for the NSDAP, which thus became the strongest party in the Reich. In Berlin, too, the Nazis topped all other parties; their 137 votes of the year 1925 had grown into 756,745 in 1932! A stupendous result, even if their

230 Reichstag members were no more than a good third of the total
608. The Social Democrats with 133 (minus 10), and the Communists with 89 (plus 12), were the second- and third-strongest parties.
All parties representing the bourgeoisie showed losses, except the
Catholic Zentrum, which rose from 68 to 73. With the exception of
the Catholics, the greater part of the bourgeoisie voted for the
NSDAP.

Hitler immediately went to Berlin to negotiate with Papen and
Schleicher. Goebbels reported: "Hitler insists on securing the posts
of Reich Chancellor, Prussian Prime Minister, and the Prussian
Ministry of the Interior, Ministry of Agriculture, Air Ministry, Min-
istry of Justice, and a new ministry to be formed for the People's
Education and Propaganda (Volkserziehung und Propaganda).
Should the Reichstag refuse to pass the enabling act, granting the
Fuehrer full powers, it will be dissolved. Once we are in, we shall
never again let go—unless they carry us out feet first."[84]

But the NSDAP was not yet in power, and Goebbels was less
optimistic than Hitler: "It is just as well to view future developments
with skepticism," Goebbels said. And he watches with a certain degree of discomfort the development within the party: "The whole
party is already tuned to our being in power. The SA are leaving
their jobs so as to be ready. Political party officials are making preparations for the great moment. Should everything go all right, all will
be well. But if it does not, the deception will be terrible."

And, in fact, deception came. Although the SA was concentrated
around Berlin with "impressive precision and discipline," Schleicher
who, after all, had the Army, refused to be blackmailed. Hitler's
meeting with Papen and Schleicher took place on August 13, the day
before Goebbels had written in his diary:

"The Fuehrer . . . will have to make grave decisions. We need
special powers to be able to master the situation; if he is refused
these special powers he will have to decline, which will cause great
depression within the movement and among the voters. If he is prepared to face this situation he will give a proof of boundless courage.
And we have only this *one* iron in the fire."

The negotiations among Hitler, Papen, and Schleicher led to nothing: "They offered him the post of Vice Chancellor. This reveals
their intention to use him and the party only for their own ends.
What an impossible offer! If the Fuehrer accepts he is lost. It is out
of the question—he refused out of hand."[85]

On the afternoon of August 13, Hitler was received by the Reich
President, who only confirmed the offer Hitler had already heard
from Papen and Schleicher: Vice Chancellor in a presidential
government. "Painful, tormented waiting; in a short half hour he

[Hitler. Author's note] returned. Failure . . . everything refused . . . after two to three hours of complete consternation, we rally again. The Fuehrer never lost his calm. . . . Late in the evening he leaves Berlin for Obersalzberg. In the weeks to come he will need stronger nerves than ever before."

Hitler would not give up so easily. After all, the NSDAP was the strongest party, without which no coalition government could possibly be formed, unless it was prepared to include the Communists. A left coalition of SPD and KPD would not have commanded a majority in the Reichstag. On the other hand, a coalition of all other parties could not have formed a government against the united opposition of the NSDAP and the KPD.

It was not Hitler who was in a tight corner, but German democracy.

Hitler still remained the central figure of the inner political situation. Goebbels had complained in his note of August 12: "We have only this *one* iron in the fire." Many National Socialists thought differently. There was the other possibility of forming a coalition with the Catholic parties. But Goebbels was bitterly opposed to this. As early as August 2, he wrote: "Go together with the Zentrum?! . . . Unthinkable!" And on August 25, he, ex-member of the Catholic Unitas, recipient of a loan from the Albertus Magnus Society when a student, wrote:

"We have contacted the Zentrum, if only to exert some pressure on the other side. The question of a coalition with them does not seriously arise. A certain faction of the party is in favor of such a coalition. But the Fuehrer favors the old line. I fully agree with him . . . the mere idea of proffering one's hand to those political prelates, giving them a chance to come in again, makes you sick."

Basically, the reasonable NSDAP leaders—and there were quite a few—had more in common with the Zentrum than with the barons and the intriguing generals. The Zentrum, after all, was for social reform, for settling small holders on the bankrupt large estates; their program in foreign policy aimed at achieving equality of German rearmament, the quashing of all reparations, a peaceful revision of the Versailles Treaty; it flirted with corporative ideas, such as Othmar Spann had put forward, and Mussolini had actually realized in Italy, and which were even included in the encyclical *Quadragesimo Anno* of Pope Pius XI. The Zentrum advocated a strong governmental authority and was deeply anti-Communist. Even their views on the Jewish question were not too far removed from those of the National Socialists. The Zentrum did not oppose in principle a certain limitation of Jewish influence.

The main points of divergence between the Zentrum and National

Socialism (at that time not yet fully developed) were the racial
theory, which contained anti-Christian elements; the complete abolition of democracy, which presupposed the one-party system under
exclusion of all other parties; and the use of political terror. Yet the
racial theory, together with its most distinguished representative,
Rosenberg, was also rejected by a number of National Socialists.
Hitler was more concerned with power than with the so-called racial
soul. Many National Socialists considered the continued use of terror,
once in power, as senseless. The parties, with the exception of the
Communists, might at first be tolerated within limits, and slowly replaced by a corporative structure. A continuation of the trade unions
was, at least in the beginning of the movement, never questioned,
not even by Hitler. And, after all, Italy's concordat with the Church
had brought Mussolini certain advantages. Why should not a similar
course be possible in Germany?

The idea of a coalition with the Catholics was solely undermined
by Goebbels' excessive radicalization of political propaganda, and
the terror techniques of the SA. Nowhere else had Goebbels' negative influence on Hitler such disastrous consequences. Not that Hitler
would ever accept taking directives from anybody, but Goebbels once
again divining the innermost thoughts of his "Fuehrer," supported
them, whereby he only confirmed Hitler in his views and made him
less amenable to considering more reasonable alternatives.

Nevertheless, the contact with the Zentrum brought the NSDAP
two advantages. On August 26, Goebbels had entered in his diary:
"I could see in Berlin that General Schleicher already got wind of
our tentative contacts with the Zentrum." Goebbels visited Schleicher
the next day and had the impression that the general was worried at
the possibility of a coalition between the NSDAP and the Zentrum.

The second advantage was that on August 30, Goering was elected
president of the Reichstag with the votes of the National Socialist
members and those of the Zentrum. Thus the ex-fighter pilot, decorated with the highest order—Pour le Mérite—had obtained one of
the most influential posts in the Reich. From then on he became
Hitler's most important and, thanks to his energy and perseverance,
most successful negotiator.

The Fall of Papen

A meeting of the top NSDAP leaders took place on the same day.
Only Hitler, Goebbels, Goering, and Roehm were present. In this
most intimate circle the decision was taken to withdraw support from
the Papen government. Goebbels fired the first salvo against the

Reich Chancellor. Under the heading "Political Legacy Hunting," he
wrote on September 9, in the *Angriff*:

"The feudal gentlemen of the Herrenklub pretend that anything
that happens in Germany outside the Wilhelmstrasse [seat of the
Chancellery—translator's note] would be no concern of theirs. They
write in their gazettes that the Reichstag, and the possibility of a
majority coalition, has become completely irrelevant and uninteresting. This, they say, belongs to the thoroughly outdated institutions
of democracy, no modern-thinking man would even mention any
more. Important was that the country was governed, and that a "conservative state authority" guaranteed peace and order. . . .

"They do not say as yet 'by the grace of God,' but that is what
they mean. The people have no longer a say in it, and the gentlemen
have been called upon by kind Providence to govern Germany. . . .
What they really want is . . . a restitution of their political influence
they lost by their cowardice in November 1918, and which they now
try to regain by making use of the National Socialist force and energy.
They have learned nothing and forgotten everything. They have
since then done nothing for a renaissance of the nation, except to
make plans and projects, draw up lists of names for posts, giving
their tail coats a good brush so as to be ready when the call comes,
to appear before the public as perfect gentlemen in a new impeccable
rig. . . . They are naïve and stupid enough to want to divide the
people into two classes. The ones born to serve, meaning us and all
the ordinary people, and the others born to rule—chosen by wise
Providence to do so. . . .

"They have thought out for themselves a dumb-witted sly little
plan: The idea is to pursue a policy entirely in keeping with their
whole feudal-bourgeois arrogance, but cleverly disguised in form and
language, they borrow National Socialist slogans, with the hope of
deceiving the masses and luring them slowly away from the Hitler
movement. There is a good German word for it: Legacy hunting!
They sit down to the table that we have set, and attribute to us the
humble role of the pauper who has to be content with the crumbs
they kindly deign to drop. . . .

"The time has come to show them who we are. Up till now we
have shown them a leniency they hardly deserve. But this has now
come to an end. From now on it is an eye for an eye, and a tooth
for a tooth. You have the power; we want it. We throw you the
gauntlet. . . . You came to power by using the back stairs, appearing suddenly in the parlor. We have been too proud to do that. We
prefer, as we have always done, to use the main entrance, and if the
gates are shut the people will break them down for us."

Three days later, on September 12, Papen learned the hard way

what Goebbels really meant by his article: The Reichstag defeated
the Chancellor in a vote of confidence put by the Communist member, Ernst Torgler, which did not prevent the National Socialists
from voting with their archenemies. Before the session, Hitler had
briefed his faction in the palace of the Reichstag president.

New elections were fixed for November 6.

Goebbels was probably even more pleased about the fall of Papen
than Hitler was. Yet the party leaders agreed that the new election
might prove a most critical test:

"The election campaign costs money, and money is at the moment
difficult to find. Let us see how we can somehow get around this
financial calamity," Goebbels wrote in his diary on September 20.

In addition, the people were tired of voting—they had had enough.
Two presidential elections, several elections for the Landtag, and
now on top of it a second election for the Reichstag, which appeared
rather senseless since it was not likely to show any significant changes
and only lead to the same political merry-go-round. The position
of the National Socialists was most unfavorable. It was obvious that
they could not obtain an absolute majority. On the contrary, their
contingent of voters was exhausted. They could only lose. No other
political party—with the possible exception of the German National
party, which would not suffice to make up a parliamentary majority
—was prepared to form a coalition with the NSDAP. A coalition with
the Zentrum was out of the question. Hitler rejected, in principle,
the parliamentary system with its bargaining and concessions. Perhaps the "Fuehrer," unused and unprepared to be contradicted, was
afraid he might cut a poor figure in the Reichstag. He would hardly
find there a religiously attentive audience he could easily mesmerize,
but tough politicians instead, who knew all the tactical tricks, and
might with their poisonous interjections or sharply argumentative
speeches make him lose his countenance. Hitherto Hitler had only
known the monologue.

Goebbels could see the difficulties ahead even more clearly than
Hitler. But he had subscribed to the "radical phrase," and could not
simply change his course. Besides, he was gauleiter of Berlin, a city
predominantly Red, which could only be conquered by aggressive
methods and radicalism. At mass meetings he was in his element,
because he derived strength and comfort from the shouting crowd,
their indignation and their cheering. There he would feel his whole
power; there he felt supreme, superior to any other party leader.

The election campaign fatigued Goebbels more than any of the
others. It was just as perfectly organized as the foregoing elections,
but it lacked their panache and enthusiasm and, above all, the gen-

erous money gifts. All this contributed to Goebbels' irritability, expressed in his diary:

"An editor . . . has in his sensationalist newspaper attacked my
wife's honor in the most infamous manner. An SS man asked to see
him, and beat him up with a riding whip until he collapsed covered
in blood. Then the SS man left his visiting card on the table, and
walked out unhindered by any of the press reptiles present. It is
the only way to deal with those slandering bastards."[86]

The whip as a political argument has made its first successful appearance. Why argue, if the bludgeon can settle the matter?

Immediately before the elections, Goebbels appeared once again
as the bogey of the bourgeoisie. The workers of the Berlin Transport
Company went on strike for higher wages between November 2
and 8. The initiative came from the Communists, but the representatives of the NSBO (National sozialistische Betriebsorganization)
joined in, and the two together formed the strike committee. A
member of the committee was a certain Walter Ulbricht. It was a
wildcat strike, which the Social Democratic and Christian trade
unions disapproved of. Goebbels saw in it a means of approaching
the workers: "If we had not acted the way we did, we would no
longer have been a socialist workers' party. I released the slogan:
'There is no need to stab the worker in the back to be a good nationalist.' "[87]

The money sources for the election, meager enough as they were,
now dried up completely. Goebbels was happy to be able to find
10,000 marks two days before the elections, "which we threw into
propaganda Saturday afternoon. We have done what we could. Now
may Fate decide."

But Fate was less kind this time. At the election of November 6,
1932, the National Socialists lost approximately 2 million votes,
equivalent to 34 seats. Instead of 230, the National Socialists now
counted only 196 members in the Reichstag, but they still remained
the strongest party by far. The real victors of this election were the
Communists, who gained 11 of the 12 seats lost by the Social Democrats, whose number fell from 133 to 121, while the number of KPD
seats rose from 89 to 100. The losses of the NSDAP benefited mainly
the German National party, which had supported Papen. Their numbers rose from 37 to 52. The Zentrum party remained more or less
the same.

In Berlin, too, the Communists were the main beneficiaries of the
political dispute between the NSDAP and the Papen government.
They once again became the strongest party, displacing the NSDAP
from first place. The 830,837 KPD votes were the highest number any

party had ever obtained in Berlin in a democratically conducted free election. Compared with the last Reichstag election they had gained 108,854 votes, while the SPD, with 656,644, had lost 75,420 votes. The 720,613 votes (a loss of 36,132) the NSDAP obtained in Berlin were not sufficient to keep them in first place, but were slightly superior to the average number of votes the party obtained in the whole of the Reich.

The NSDAP had, admittedly, suffered considerable losses, but was not mortally wounded, as some historians would have it. They had lost the myth of invincibility, but at the same time had proved that they had behind them a solid and powerful mass of supporters. They had remained the greatest party and had only 26 seats less than the two left parties put together (at the previous election they had obtained more votes than both the left parties put together). The fact remained that without the NSDAP no parliamentary government could be formed, unless the democratic parties were prepared to include the Communists in any coalition. This was quite out of the question. The bourgeois parties would have never agreed to that; the German National party refused to consider a coalition even with the Social Democrats, let alone the Communists. In fact, without Hitler, one could only govern dictatorially.

Obviously, the attitudes of Hindenburg, Papen, and Schleicher were now of decisive importance. What were they to be, after all that had happened? Notwithstanding Goebbels' attack on Papen in the *Angriff,* Papen wrote Hitler a letter the day after the elections, on November 13, proposing a meeting "to talk over the whole position."

But Hitler, following exactly Goebbels' line, raised his demands in his answer. He was not prepared—he made that abundantly clear—to tolerate a Papen government. Schleicher once again took the initiative and advised Papen to resign, so as to give the Reich President a free hand for his negotiations with the parties. Papen resigned on November 17, and two days later Hindenburg received the leader of the strongest party, the NSDAP. The President offered Hitler an alternative: Reich Chancellor in a coalition of a parliamentary majority, or Vice Chancellor in a presidential Cabinet headed by Papen. But the only parliamentary majority available to Hitler presupposed a coalition with the Zentrum, the only party prepared to support Hitler as Chancellor providing he did not aim at setting up a dictatorship. The German National party, led by Hugenberg, refused to form a coalition with Hitler. Goebbels had done too much damage there.

On November 21, the Reich President received Hitler once more,

asking him to form a majority government. Gregor Strasser proposed
to renew negotiations with the German National party, but this time
Hitler "strictly refuses—maybe later on, but at the moment there can
be no question of it. Now only a personal solution imposes itself."[88]
Hitler wrote to Hindenburg that he was bound to decline the
President's offer as "impracticable," but would suggest "resolving the
crisis within three days if given a free hand."[89]

Hindenburg would not agree to giving him a "free hand," fearing
that a presidential Cabinet headed by Hitler would "of necessity
develop into a party dictatorship."[90] Hindenburg's refusal showed
that the senile old man still had moments of clearsightedness.

The Party Menaced by a Split

Now, so it seemed, Schleicher's opportunity had come. Hitler was
invited through an emissary to negotiate with the general. But
Hitler, regardless, went to Weimar on September 1, to a meeting of
the party leaders attended among others by Goering, Frick, Goebbels, and Strasser.

"Strasser advocates tolerating the Schleicher Cabinet. To support
his point of view he paints the party situation in the blackest colors.
He shows a pessimism we should hardly have expected of him. The
Fuehrer rejects sharply this negative attitude. He remains steadfast
to the last, and we support him wholeheartedly. . . ."[91]

In the meantime Schleicher had quite cleverly outwitted his own
protégé, Papen, and was actually appointed by Hindenburg
Chancellor of the presidential Cabinet on December 2. Goebbels
comments: "That is their last throw. If Schleicher falls, it will be our
turn. Goering returns to Berlin; he has got orders to negotiate the
details with Schleicher."[92]

The inner crisis of the NSDAP was about to come to a head. At
the Landtag elections in Thuringia the party lost around 30 per cent
of their votes. "This defeat comes at a bad moment. From now on
there must not be another election at which we lose one single vote,"
Goebbels noted on December 4.

Schleicher, who desperately searched for an ally, noticed the inner
crisis of the NSDAP, which was predominantly a crisis among the
leaders, and tried to use it for his own ends. He first offered Hitler
the post of Vice Chancellor in his Cabinet, and after Hitler had refused, contacted Strasser, offering him the same post. The plan was
transparent: Through Strasser's entry into the Cabinet, the NSDAP
would be split, thereby losing its dangerous momentum. The more

reasonable leaders among the National Socialists who, according to Strasser, veered more to the left, could be brought together with the Social Democratic and Christian trade unions, thus affording Schleicher more time to build a broader basis for his Cabinet, which rested solely on the authority of the Reich President and the support of the Reichswehr.

The idea in itself was not bad, but the partners would not play— neither the Socialist Democratic unions, which got the red light from their party, nor Gregor Strasser, who missed the chance of his life. On December 5, 1932, Goebbels wrote:

"By a sheer accident we got to know the real reason for Strasser's policy of sabotage. He had a meeting with General Schleicher Sunday evening, at which the general offered him the post of Vice Chancellor. Strasser, while refusing this offer, informed him of his decision to put up his own list in a future new election. This then is the worst treason against the Fuehrer and the party. It does not surprise me— I have never expected anything else."

On the same day, December 5, a meeting of party leaders took place in the Hotel Kaiserhof, with Hitler, Goering, Goebbels, Frick, and Strasser attending. Once again Strasser demanded a policy of tolerating the Schleicher government; he was supported by the chairman of the faction, Frick, but opposed by Goering and Goebbels, who were backed by Hitler, but who were prepared, however, to negotiate with Schleicher, providing the general agreed to the following: to proclaim an amnesty, approve the right of defense against aggression, reinstitute freedom of assembly, and postpone convening the Reichstag. As his negotiator, Hitler named Goering, and not Strasser.

That same day Hitler called the whole Reichstag faction together and, according to Goebbels' account, "castigates most sharply the growing tendency of seeking compromises: There could be no question of giving in. It is not a matter concerning only his own person but also the honor and prestige of the party. Whoever now commits treason only proves he has never understood the greatness of the movement."[93]

On December 7, Hitler and Strasser met for the last time. Hitler accused Strasser of disloyalty and worked himself up into a fit of rage. When he finally stopped to catch his breath, Strasser asked: "Herr Hitler, do you really mean what you say?" When Hitler affirmed, Strasser picked up his briefcase, drove to the Hotel Excelsior (his permanent quarters), and wrote Hitler a letter of resignation, putting at Hitler's disposal all party posts he had held. He then, thoroughly disgusted with everything, climbed into his car and drove

8. Goebbels attending a meeting of the leaders of the film industry. Left to right: the general manager of the UFA, Ludwig Klitzsch; unidentified; Prince Augustus of Prussia; Goebbels.

9. Wilhelm Furtwängler acknowledging applause of audience after concert of the Berlin Philharmonic. In front row left to right are: Goering, Hitler, and Goebbels. January 17, 1939.

10. Goebbels testifying at the Reichstag fire trial. 1933.

11. Goebbels and his wife arrive in Rome. June 1, 1933.

South. This, in any case, was Strasser's version. Goebbels' version added only:

"Midday the bomb explodes: Strasser has written a letter to the Fuehrer resigning his party posts. He furnishes worthless and irrelevant reasons: One should now lead the party toward the state; now the moment has come to make concessions; the movement is using itself up in frustrating opposition; he, Strasser, could no longer support this course and would have to decline all further responsibility. Of course, none of these reasons hold water. They only prove that Strasser's ambition to become minister is stronger than his loyalty to the Fuehrer and the party."[94]

Strasser was, as chief organizer of the party, second only to Hitler. Strasser should have used his position to build up his personal influence and controlling power. But all his attempts in this direction remained rather halfhearted. He had no control whatever over Goebbels, nor over the Reichsleiters, who were completely independent. And even most gauleiters did not accept much interference from him. Strasser had practically no influence on propaganda, which Hitler considered to be of paramount importance. Worst of all, he was in no position to get the SA—the real center of power within the party—on his side.

Strasser was looked upon as the leader of the party's left wing. But the left elements were rather represented by his brother Otto, whom Goebbels, acting on Hitler's orders, had expelled from the party in June 1930. After Otto Strasser's expulsion, the party's left wing was led by Goebbels. Gregor Strasser was, in fact, prepared to work together with practically anybody: with the German National party, the Zentrum, the trade unions, or the generals. He saw the party's empty coffers and knew of the heavy debts that had accumulated. In his view the movement had passed its peak, and this was the last moment to cease being an obviously unsuccessful opposition party and use the chance to turn the tide by joining the government. He even risked a break with Hitler, resigned all his posts, and left, instead of entering Schleicher's Cabinet and automatically taking with him a number of Reichstag members and party officials. Even if only a quarter of the NSDAP's members and officials had followed him, he would have succeeded in splitting the party.

Goebbels' diary bears out that Hitler and his entourage recognized the danger. But a politician who prefers in the hour of decision to retire and take his resentment into the woods, and let his anger erupt in solitude, instead of giving fight and using his chances, is obviously not made of the stuff political leaders are made of. He rather acts like a general who goes hunting when the battle is at its peak, leaving his

troops to fight on without command. They are bound to surrender
sooner or later. Strasser was, in fact, essentially loyal to Hitler. He
felt that Hitler had treated him unjustly by giving preference to
Goebbels, Goering, and Roehm; in short, he was jealous. He probably could not make himself assist in the destruction of the party to
whose growth he had contributed so much. All this points to his
personal integrity, but shows that he was not cut out to be the leader
of the party. This had already become apparent in 1926, when he
had clashed with Hitler for the first time in Bamberg; Goebbels had
noticed it then, and drawn his conclusions. He did not support Strasser, but neither did he engineer his fall, as some commentators say.
Strasser brought about his own fall. Strasser parted company with
Hitler because he disapproved of Hitler's course. Yet, when offered
a chance to act accordingly, he refused to bar Hitler's way. To his
friends he said: "From now on Germany is in the hands of a born
liar from Austria, a perverted ex-officer, and a clubfoot, and believe
me, the last is the worst of the lot. He is the devil incarnate."[95]

Despite his contempt for these three, Strasser once more offered
his services to Hitler in mid-January 1933, but in vain. Strasser remained in Germany after January 30 [the date of Hitler's takeover].
Strasser was "on Hitler's special orders never molested; on the
contrary, he was given a leading position in the Pharmaceutical
Association."[96] But later, following the so-called Roehm putsch,
Schleicher and Gregor Strasser were executed. It is uncertain if this
was Hitler's, Goering's, Himmler's, or Goebbels' revenge. In any
case, historically speaking, Strasser was a dead man long before he
actually died. His execution provided only a further illustration of
the barbaric system he himself had helped to establish. Gregor Strasser might have given German history a different turn. But the call of
Fate had fallen on deaf ears.

The Miracle of Lippe

The first task of the NSDAP leaders was to rebuild the shaken organization and prevent it from falling apart. Hitler himself took
Strasser's position as chief of organization, and made Dr. Ley his chief
of staff. The *Volksbildung* (people's education) was given to Goebbels. He wrote in his diary on December 16: "Traveling all over the
country, addressing party officials, exhorting them to keep steadfast." Hitler, Ley, and Goebbels were doing most of the work. The
greatest worry was the lack of money and the debts incurred during
their last election campaign, amounting to approximately 8 million

marks. The financial position in the gau Berlin was also bad: "We must reduce salaries or we will go bankrupt. All officials show an admirable spirit of sacrifice."[97]

When on November 23 his wife was taken ill suddenly and had to be transferred to a clinic, Goebbels lost some of his *sang-froid,* and the entry in his diary sounds depressed: "The year 1932 was one long succession of ill luck. We must break this evil spell. Outside in the streets the spirit of Christmas is at large. I am sitting alone at home brooding over so many things. The past was difficult, and the future looks dark and troubled; all prospects and hopes have vanished completely."

On the first day of Christmas Goebbels traveled to Berchtesgaden to see Hitler. Goebbels' wife was supposed to follow him on New Year's Eve. Instead, a telephone call came from the clinic that Magda was in critical condition. Goebbels took the train back to Berlin. On this journey, prolonged by snowstorms, Goebbels, according to Riess,[98] suddenly got the inspiration of how to save the party: One would have to throw in every ounce of one's strength and try to win the local elections for the Landtag in Lippe. Although Goebbels speaks about it in his diary—and, in fact, these elections were to play an important part—they were not the key to a successful solution of the party's problems. Someone else supplied this solution: Franz von Papen. He had not forgotten that Schleicher had eased him out of his post as Chancellor. Thus Papen arranged a meeting with Hitler, which took place in the house of the banker Kurt von Schroeder, in Cologne. There are two versions of what happened at that meeting—that of Papen, who claimed he had only tried to persuade Hitler to enter the government of Schleicher, and that of Schroeder, who says that Papen proposed to Hitler to form a new government in which both should share responsibility.[99]

In the light of what happened later on, Papen's version appears less credible. Yet even more decisive than the question of how Hitler and Papen would divide the cake between them was Schroeder's promise to find the necessary financing for Hitler, to enable him to pay the party debts and secure the considerable resources needed to finance the NSDAP organization and keep the SA going.

In the middle of the election fight in Lippe, Goebbels staged a grandiose funeral procession, one of many to follow. On January 1, a member of the Hitler Youth, Walter Wagnitz, had been killed by Communists. Goebbels gave him a truly royal funeral. The procession, consisting of tens of thousands of SA and SS men, Hitler Youth, and party officials, started moving from where the body had been lying in state. It proceeded for 2½ hours through the streets of Berlin toward the cemetery, past mourning crowds of hundreds of thousands thronging the pavement.

The procession was timed so as to arrive at the cemetery at dusk, where in the midst of a sea of tens of thousands of torches, Goebbels gave the farewell speech. After he had finished, the various party formations filed past the grave until far into the night. At the same time Goebbels held a protest meeting in the Berlin Lustgarten at eight in the evening, attended by 150,000 Berliners.

With this grand show Goebbels pursued—and rather successfully —three main aims. The National Socialist masses were once again united; Communist terror was demonstrated on this murder of a youth, which could hardly fail to frighten once more the good German bourgeois; and it also gave the German people an opportunity to see for themselves the masses the NSDAP could commandeer if need be, and how well the party knew how to honor their dead heroes.

But Goebbels offered the people yet another, even greater proof of the living force of National Socialism: the election campaign in Lippe.

Lippe, with its 170,000 inhabitants, was the smallest province in the Reich, hardly worth bothering about. And, in fact, all other parties treated the election campaign rather perfunctorily. Not so Goebbels. For him this was yet another opportunity to prove his propagandist genius once again. He knew that the party's waning prestige needed a victory at any price. For him Lippe was in no way insignificant. All the money he could scrape together—and there was not too much of it—he threw into the campaign. He established his headquarters in Detmold. His enemies mocked: "Goebbels goes into the villages because he has come a cropper in the big city." And, indeed, Goebbels went to the villages, and so did Hitler, and Goering, and all the other famous orators of the party. Instead of addressing mass meetings, as they had been used to doing before, they now spoke in local inns. Brochures, newspapers, and handbills were delivered to every farm. Swarms of trained party propagandists descended on every single household, spoke to the people, and described the wonderful times ahead once Hitler was in power. They promised the farmers that their troubles would be over then. They promised exactly the same to the small shopkeepers, artisans, and workers. Everybody's troubles would be over once Adolf Hitler had won. And the decision lay in their own hands, in the hands of the people of the smallest province in Germany. Theirs was the privilege to bring about the great change in the Reich's fortunes. The whole small province was covered with swastikas and by NSDAP posters. Every fence, every wall, every tree, every barn was adorned with Goebbels' slogans, crying out their messages in red letters. "Everything depends on the results of the elections in Lippe," he wrote in his diary on January 9, 1933. "If we manage to succeed there, the government will fall."

While Goebbels threw himself body and soul into the election campaign, his wife hovered between life and death. The doctors had given up hope. Only Hitler knew about it, but did not tell Goebbels, so as not to divert him from the campaign. Goebbels was only told about it when the danger had passed.[100]

The elections took place on January 15. The NSDAP got 38,000 votes, almost 40 per cent; compared with the Reichstag elections in November, they had gained no less than 20 per cent; all other parties, except the SPD, had incurred losses. By securing votes in numbers hardly more than a third of those who usually attended one of his mass meetings in Berlin, Goebbels had proved that National Socialism, far from declining, was growing faster than ever. He had confounded the glum forebodings of Strasser, of the gazettes, and of the "government clique." Hitler was back again, and stronger than ever.

The victory in Lippe was in itself not very important—the gain of a few thousand votes made no difference to the structure of Reich policy. Important was how Goebbels exploited this victory. His propagandistic maneuver belongs among the most brilliant ever carried out. The actual election results would have scarcely interested anybody in Germany, not even Lippe itself; and yet everybody in the Reich talked about the new great success of the National Socialists. The service Goebbels rendered Hitler with this victory can hardly be overrated. Goebbels baptized it the "miracle of Lippe," a phrase widely used, soon to become a kind of legend, which Goebbels took up again in the last year of the war to resuscitate the declining hopes of the National Socialist supporters, holding out to them the prospect of a similar miracle.

For Hitler the miracle of Lippe came just at the right moment. Papen, determined not to be beaten by Schleicher at the game of political intrigue, opened negotiations with Hitler in the house of the banker, Schroeder. Furthermore, Papen arranged another meeting, on January 22, in the house of his friend Joachim von Ribbentrop, among Hindenburg's son, Oskar; the President's state secretary, Dr. Meissner; and Hitler, Goering, and Frick.[101]

Hitler and Oskar Hindenburg conversed for one full hour strictly *tête-à-tête*. Hitler, no doubt, used on Oskar Hindenburg his personal magic, supported by certain promises and, as it proved, successfully.

Hindenburg's intimate entourage had been won over. All Hitler needed now was Bruening's "100 meters" to reach the winning post.

Schleicher was presented with the bill. Having spun his intrigues over the years, he now fell victim to an intrigue himself. By conspiring with Strasser, he had barred his way back to Hitler once and for all. He had ever since been continuously attacked by the NSDAP, particularly by Goebbels personally. Though calling himself a "socialist" general—he had, in fact, rescinded Papen's reduction of wages and unemployment benefits—Schleicher failed to win over the trade unions or the Social Democratic party. On the other hand, the industrialists and the big landowners opposed him on account of his socialist policy (in particular the big landowners, for reviving Bruening's plan to turn over 150,000 hectares belonging to the bankrupt large estates in East Prussia to 25,000 settlers).

Goebbels had in the meantime concentrated all NSDAP forces for a show of strength. The SA and the SS gathered on the Buelowplatz and paraded past the KPD headquarters in the Karl Liebknecht Hause. A counterdemonstration planned by the KPD was banned by Schleicher. Goebbels triumphed; the KPD was rendered powerless. The Communists had not really suffered a defeat, as they had been deprived of a chance to defend themselves, but Goebbels trumpeted his victory from the rooftops; and this time all good citizens believed him only too willingly. That same evening the "Fuehrer" dedicated a tombstone to Horst Wessel in Nikolai Cemetery, and an hour later sat in Von Ribbentrop's drawing room to remove the last obstacles on his way to becoming Chancellor of the Reich. On January 28, General Schleicher handed in his resignation. There followed twenty-four hours of a confused melee of intrigues between Papen and Schleicher—the one still trying to become Chancellor without Hitler, the other toying with the idea of a military dictatorship—but nothing came of it. The Weimar Republic had been ill fated from the beginning to its ignoble end. Finally, the barons and generals had lost the game by their own intrigues against one another. Their historical guilt lies in their having snatched the Chancellor's chair from under the democratic politicians and putting Hitler on it.

On January 30, Hindenburg appointed the Fuehrer of the NSDAP, Adolf Hitler, Chancellor of the Reich.

Hitler had arrived—he had made the last 100 meters to the finish line. For this he had to thank Goebbels and his ingenious propaganda trick of proclaiming the election results in Lippe a great victory, and thereby impressing the German people; Papen's ambitious nature and his desire to take revenge on Schleicher who, great as he may have been in the art of intrigue, was but a mediocre politician; Hitler had to thank the industrialists for it, who supported his party, and saved it by a hair from bankruptcy; and, last but not least, he had to thank the change of attitude toward him of Hindenburg's close entourage as well as the old President's senility. But the deeper causes lay in the decline of the democratic spirit—a majority of the German people gave their votes to the antidemocratic parties, the NSDAP and the KPD, because parliamentary democracy had failed to solve their problems. It also lay in the lack of comprehension of the victorious powers for the need to support the democratic governments in Germany; in the catastrophic economic position that had created over six million unemployed; in the general hopelessness and the desperate faith, so often appearing in the wake of such hopelessness, that a miracle would happen, a man would appear, a savior, who would solve with one stroke everything the others had only complicated and made practically insoluble. Messianic hopes have always appeared in history whenever evolutionary development broke down.

In the evening of January 30, 1933, the whole of Berlin seemed to be on the streets. Goebbels wrote:

"Then the torch procession started. Endless . . . endless . . . from seven in the evening until one o'clock at night they marched past the Reich Chancellery. . . . Indescribable joy everywhere. Only a few yards from the Reich Chancellery the Reich President is seen framed in the window, a magnificent figure of a hero, dignified, in an aura of legendary magic. . . . Hundreds of thousands march past the window in never-ending waves. . . . Long after midnight when the procession had come to an end, tens of thousands of people stand in front of the Reich Chancellery and sing the Horst Wessel song. I address the masses with a brief speech and finish with a Heil for Hindenburg and for the Fuehrer. In a crazy rapture of enthusiasm, the night of the great miracle comes to an end.

"Only now the square empties. We shut the windows and find ourselves with a great silence surrounding us. The Fuehrer puts his hands on my shoulders without saying a word."

A hundred thousand torches lit up Berlin. Twelve years later a hundred thousand bombs would light it up again. And Hitler will once again put his hands on Goebbels' shoulders, but this time not any longer to go forward together to accomplish great deeds, but to die together, accompanied by a chorus of curses from innumerable millions.

3

Propaganda
Devours Culture

The Hitler Ministry—Goebbels Becomes Minister

We mentioned Goebbels' entry in his diary of January 22, 1932, in which he spoke of a ministry that would surpass anything known before. Some skeptics may suggest that Goebbels had later inserted this note to enhance his own prestige.

But there is an authentic source that proves that Hitler had chosen Goebbels early to head a future Ministry of Propaganda. Dr. Wagener (his notes about Hitler's meeting with Magda Quandt were referred to earlier) also mentioned an art discussion that took place on one of the many evenings Hitler spent in the Goebbels apartment in Berlin before he became Reich Chancellor. Referring in this conversation to an exhibition that had recently opened in the Munich Glaspalast showing the works of the younger "Sezession" [a group of young artists in opposition to traditional art. Translator's note], Hitler called their paintings "rubbish, ill-designed rickety figures" and "spiritual excrements of diseased brains."

Having stated his views on modern art with "unfailing instinct," Hitler turned to his host: "Goebbels," he said, "start turning over in your mind what we should do to put an end to this calamity once you are appointed Minister of Propaganda. Granted that art, being the most profound expression of the soul of the people, has nothing to do with propaganda; but this soul, defiled by Jewish and secessionistic propaganda, is misled and driven off course. . . . To that extent it must be the task of propaganda to help the people to regain their freedom and their right to follow their healthy instincts."[1]

Goebbels knew he would be appointed minister in a Hitler government. Hitler considered the Ministry of Propaganda to be of utmost importance, and knew he could find no better man than the little doctor. There were several reasons for the fact that Goebbels was not made minister immediately when Hitler came to power. It had been agreed between Papen and Hitler that eight non-National Socialist ministers, headed by Papen as Vice Chancellor, should be appointed, as against three National Socialists: Hitler as Reich Chancellor, Frick as Minister of the Interior for the Reich, and Goering as Minister Without Portfolio. Goering became at the same time Minister of the Interior for Prussia, which gave him command of the Prussian police force.

Hitler's first aim was to delude Hindenburg, Papen, and Hugenberg as to his real intentions. This made it impossible for him to appoint Goebbels immediately; neither Hindenburg nor the other ministers would have accepted it, and it would have only revived their old suspicions. Besides, Goebbels had still another task for the party to fulfill: He had to organize the campaign for the Reichstag elections set for March 5, 1933. It was the last election in which the National Socialists still had to observe democratic rules, although the NSDAP had exclusive control of all official means of propaganda, including the radio. In true National Socialist style Goebbels denied other parties the use of radio (with the exception of their ally, the German National party, though even they were treated rather parsimoniously). This would not have mattered so much (only a relatively small proportion of the population possessed radios at that time) if the National Socialists had not taken some other measures against their political enemies that either impaired their electioneering or made it impossible. It soon showed how cunningly Hitler had acted when he demanded Goering's appointment as Prussian Minister of the Interior. Goering had become the most powerful figure next to Hitler. And Goering did not waste much time.

"Goering cleans up Prussia with heartwarming vigor. He has got it in him; he has iron nerves and the necessary staying power for a hard struggle ahead. . . . Goering cleans out the stables. . . . We have a new weapon against the press, and the bans are coming down with a vengeance. *Vorwärts* and *Acht-Uhr-Abend Blatt,* all those Jewish rags that have annoyed us so much and often had us worried, have vanished from the streets of Berlin. It calms and comforts one's soul."[2]

On February 24, the Berlin police carried out a razzia on Goering's orders in the Karl Liebknecht House, headquarters of the KPD; but the Communists had removed their most important material in time.

Goering's blow misfired badly. On February 27, the Reichstag fire broke out. It happened to be so perfectly timed for the National Socialists that many historians tend to regard them as the incendiaries. Who else but Goebbels could have conceived such an idea?

At the Nuremberg trial, Hans Gisevius[3] testified that the idea to put fire to the Reichstag had originated with Goebbels, who had actually discussed it with the SA leader, Ernst. Ernst had with ten of his most reliable men entered the Reichstag building from the palace of the Reich President. All the participants had been either wiped out later on during the Roehm putsch or had fallen on the eastern front.

This and similar statements are rather dubious. There was a general tendency during the Nuremberg trial to unload as much as possible on the dead Goebbels. It will probably never be proved who the actual incendiaries were. The version advanced by Fritz Tobias in *Der Spiegel,* submitting that the sole perpetrator of the crime was Marinus van der Lubbe, appears to me the most likely of all.[4] The thesis that it was Goebbels who initiated the Reichstag fire is contradicted by the fact that he never mentioned it anywhere, although it was later his boastful habit to lay claim even to certain acts he could hardly have carried out. Besides, it was not in Goebbels' nature to keep a secret for long.

Goebbels recounts how he sat together with Hitler in Goebbels' apartment when Hanfstengel telephoned, "The Reichstag is on fire!" Goebbels took this at first for a hoax and sought confirmation from other sources before telling Hitler about it. They both then hastened to the Reichstag, where Goering and Papen had also arrived.

"There can be no doubt that the Communists have a last try to create confusion through fire and terror, and use the general panic to usurp power. The decisive moment has come. Goering is going full steam ahead . . . he bans at once all Communist and Social Democratic newspapers. The Communist officials are arrested the same night."[5]

The next day the Cabinet published a decree that partly suspended seven articles of the Constitution. It limited personal freedom, freedom of speech, freedom of the press, right of assembly, and permitted official interference with the privacy of mail, postal, and telephonic communications. More serious cases of disturbance of the peace became punishable by death. Hindenburg put his signature to the first document that sanctified Hitler's reign of terror. On February 28, Goebbels recorded triumphantly: "One arrest after another, now we'll pull the Red pest out by their roots and destroy it once and for all."

The Reichstag fire gave the National Socialists a lucky break. It gave them a pretext for arresting the leaders of the Marxist parties, leaving their supporters orphaned, without guidance, and terrorized into a state of fear. Only Bruening appealed to Hindenburg to "protect the oppressed against the oppressors."[6] But the Reich President was already dozing away in the twilight of senility. The Father of the Fatherland had become politically blind and deaf.

The day preceding the election had been baptized by Goebbels, "The day of the awakening nation. . . . Everywhere on the mountaintops the fires of freedom have been lit. All Germany is one big flaming torch,"[7] Goebbels rejoiced.

Hitler delivered the final speech in Koenigsberg, and the German people gathered around their radios and listened to his sermon to the nation. In the end the *Niederländische Dankgebet* (the Netherlands prayer of thanks) came over the air, and during the last verse the bells of the Koenigsberg cathedral began to toll. The whole performance was a typical cocktail *à la* Joseph Goebbels, a wizardly mixture of politics and religion.

Considering the means at the disposal of the National Socialist propaganda machine, the election results looked rather poor. The NSDAP obtained 17,277,180 votes, or 44 per cent, but the absolute majority they had gone for eluded them. This obliged them to seek the support of the 3,136,760 votes (8 per cent) of the German National party. The Zentrum party had even been able to increase their votes, and obtained together with the Bavarian People's party (Bayerische Volkspartei) 5.5 million votes. Despite the terror exerted by the NSDAP, the Social Democrats had lost a mere 70,000 votes, obtaining 7,181,620, and even the Communists, who had been put under pressure by every possible means—most of their leaders had been arrested or had to flee the country—still obtained 4,848,058 votes. They had lost around 1,000,000 votes, but remained an important party. Practically the entire million the Communists had lost had gone over to the National Socialists.

The NSDAP and the DNVP had together 340 seats in the Reichstag, giving them the rather precarious majority of 18. Despite Goebbels' colossal propaganda display and Goering's terror, no less than 56 per cent of the German people had clearly cast their vote against a Hitler dictatorship, but, at the same time, the great majority had voted against a continuation of the Weimar type of parliamentary democracy. It had been rejected not only by the National Socialists and German Nationals, but also by the Communists.

Goebbels' victory celebration once again proved what a splendid theatrical producer he would have made. On March 21, the beginning of the National Era was solemnly inaugurated in the Garnisonskirche (Garnison church) at Potsdam. This was the great historical seat of Prussianism, the location of the tomb of Frederick the Great. Everybody of rank and renown from the times of the Empire, including the crown prince, was present. Hindenburg gave the new government his blessing. Even he seemed to be fascinated by Goebbels' stagecraft and touched by Hitler's praise extolling Fate, which in its wisdom had chosen the great field marshal to be the fatherly protector of the new rising of the people.

When Goebbels staged this Potsdam celebration he was already minister, and at thirty-five the youngest member of the Cabinet. His appointment came immediately after the elections, despite the objection of some ministers, particularly Hugenberg. But Hitler insisted on Goebbels' appointment, perhaps not so much because Hitler wanted to keep his promise but because he badly needed this new ministry. On March 23, the enabling act was passed in the Reichstag by 441 votes, with 84 Social Democrats dissenting. The Communist members had been prevented from taking part in this session. Most of them were imprisoned or had gone underground or into exile. Before the vote was taken, Hitler had promised not to touch such institutions as the Reichstag or the Reichsrat (Reich Council), nor to interfere with the rights of the Reich President; he had further promised to respect the existence of the *Länder* and the rights of the churches. He would make use of his special powers only when it was necessary for the reconstruction and benefit of the German people.

The events of the next few months proved Hitler a liar: The other parties as well as the trade unions were dissolved, the *Länder* fitted into the Reich structure, and the NSDAP closely associated with the state. The unions were substituted by the German Workers' Front (Deutsche Arbeitsfront—DAF), which occupied a position similar to the position of the unions in today's Communist countries. The DAF guaranteed "just" wages, not too onerous for the employers, yet sufficiently high to afford the employees a certain standard of living. Strikes were forbidden. The "Trustee of Labor" (*Treuhänder der Arbeit*) negotiated the contracts. The employee had, in effect, been put under tutelage.

The organization "Strength Through Joy" (Kraft durch Freude—KDF) took care of the cultural side and organized the leisure of the working population. For the first time in German history millions of workers and employees were systematically directed to visit theaters and attend concerts. And hundreds of thousands were given a chance to travel in great liners to all parts of the world. The great financial wizard Schacht put his notorious *Mefo-Wechsel* (money vouchers) into the people's pockets, which enabled them to buy a great variety of goods. The number of unemployed fell daily. Roads, factories, and apartment houses were built. The wheels were turning, the factories were working again.

Germany moved toward a dictatorship, but this was in keeping with the times. In Italy and Russia great dictatorships had been in existence for some time. Almost all countries east of the German border were governed by semidictatorships. In hardly any European country did the peaceful democratic and socially just conditions prevail that would guarantee the basic rights of peoples and minorities. It now remained to be seen whether a dictatorship would be installed in Germany that was at least tolerable. Indicative was the policy pursued in the cultural field.

In the religious sector, so it seemed at first, the government tried to keep the peace. Papen concluded a concordat with the Vatican that could have secured religious peace and might also have acted as a brake on the growing political demoralization if it had been adhered to correctly. But Hitler kept neither agreements nor promises.

Hitler had more difficulties with the Protestants, since the Catholic Hitler mistakenly thought he would be able to wield them into one unified organization similar to that of the Catholic Church. His efforts failed, and only earned the Protestants Hitler's undying contempt.

But at first Hitler was not particularly preoccupied with religious questions. He actually avoided a fight with the churches. He preferred to probe for weak points before launching an attack, and not risk an open trial of strength. He also hoped that a well planned anti-Christian education of the German youth would solve the problem automatically.

It seemed more rewarding to tackle first the cultural sector. Goebbels created a ministry according to his own ideas of culture—the Reich Ministry of Information and Propaganda (*Volksaufklärung und Propaganda*—incidentally, the only original creation of a National Socialist ministry)—and appointed as its chief the only intellectual among his close associates. This ministry—living up to its name—had the task of informing the people and propagating the intentions and actions of the government and the party to which, as in the Soviet Union, the state was subordinated. But above the party stood the Fuehrer whom Goebbels equated with Germany.

Under this ministry came all cultural branches: literature and journalism, music, theater, the fine arts, and films. But it was precisely in this sector that Goebbels failed. In fact he was bound to fail. He was National Socialist only in the power-political sense, but not in his *Weltanschauung*. He actually had no definite *Weltanschauung*—little socialism, a dash of heroism administered in different doses at various periods of his life. He did, however, possess a fanatical devotion to Germany and an almost mystical allegiance to Hitler. Otherwise Goebbels was a relativist, a man without any definite scale of values.

In the field of art and culture, Goebbels was at bottom a liberal, and this was why he failed. From the start he defended the thesis of a thousand flowers, all of which should be allowed to blossom forth. This was enough to mobilize the party against him, particularly Rosenberg, with his cultural following, as well as the many unimportant artists and officials dealing with art who had been loyal supporters of the movement and were now expecting to reap their harvest.

Rosenberg violently opposed the co-ordination of culture and propaganda: "I have never made a secret of my view that this solution was basically wrong, and doubly wrong to put this important instrument in Goebbels' hands."

For Rosenberg art was "a matter of conviction and not a subject for tactics or politics."[8] Yet this was exactly what Hitler wanted: a fusion of politics, propaganda, and art. He considered politics to be the greatest of all arts, and propaganda the most important arm of politics. And Goebbels was in full agreement with Hitler; only their views on art differed.

Goebbels' liberalism was alien to Hitler; the Fuehrer had formed certain opinions in his youth to which he adhered all his life. And whatever he learned later served only to confirm these preconceived notions. In all other fields, such as economy, military questions, transport, and technical questions, Hitler was open-minded, constantly trying to develop and eager to learn; but in his religious and artistic views he remained arrested in his development. We can, therefore, talk of a well-informed Hitler who would astonish technicians, military men, and economists by his general and detailed knowledge, fond of displaying his knowledge of the very latest developments, as well as of a narrow-minded Hitler, who constantly bored his listeners with the same old primitive clichés about religion, race, and art. In this field his education was practically finished when he left Vienna and moved to Munich.

Goebbels was often faced with this narrow-minded Hitler, no less dogmatic in his fanatical views on art than he was in his views on racial questions. Hitler would not only be content to deliver speeches at the Nuremberg party rally, laying down the law on culture, but he would also actually interfere with all cultural questions. It was forbidden to criticize his taste, and it usually was bad taste.

As for Goebbels, he was not particularly interested in art, with the exception of films. His taste had no definite direction, only it often differed from Hitler's. But as Goebbels could hardly afford to show a different taste from Hitler's, he forced himself to revise his own, and defend Hitler's so vociferously that it appeared to be his own. At the beginning of his ministerial activities, Goebbels—as can be seen in existing records—apparently made a big effort to induce as many famous artists as possible to stay and work in Germany. What really mattered to him was their fame and not what artistic line they represented. This, no doubt, was the right approach, but the party upset his plans. He might perhaps have weathered Rosenberg and his Cultural Fighting Association (Kampfbund), but he was obliged to capitulate before Hitler, who also condemned his policy.

In his speech in the Reich Cultural Chamber (Reichskulturkammer) in June 1934, Goebbels said:

"We National Socialists are far from being old-fashioned. On the contrary, we feel we are the standard-bearers of the most advanced modernism, not only politically and socially, but also spiritually and artistically. Because to be modern means to be close to the spirit of the age, or even in advance of it. In art, too, there is no other form of modernism than seeking in accordance with the political term of the common nationhood (*Volksgemeinschaft*) a stronger and more vital relationship to the people."[9]

This was a typical Goebbels formulation. He wanted to be regarded as modern, and he exhorted the artists to be audacious, while sticking at the same time to Hitler's view that art had to find a more "vital relationship to the people." His obvious attempt to please both sides simultaneously was doomed to failure, since it was bound to bring him up against the views of the highest court of appeal—Hitler himself. And Hitler was pitiless about what he and his art apostles called "depraved art," which included practically all modern art.

Against such an attitude Goebbels felt powerless, all the more as his own "liberalism" did not come from an inner conviction. He would have liked to keep all painters, sculptors, architects, and musicians in Germany, if only to give the impression abroad that the German dictator of art (which, in fact, he was not) was magnanimous and broad-minded. But art was certainly not worth getting into a fight with Hitler about, with precious little hope of winning anyway. Goebbels therefore chose the course of least resistance. Deep down he was not genuinely interested in art. Art was but another means of exerting power, of enhancing his own standing and Germany's prestige. But Hitler would have none of it. As soon as Goebbels had started building bridges that led to artistic tolerance, Hitler blew them up. All Goebbels could do was prevent the worst from happening. Had Rosenberg been Minister of Culture, the provincialism of the National Socialist cultural concept would have become infinitely more dominant. Goebbels at least succeeded in partly concealing it by propaganda. And yet Rosenberg's reproachful summing-up was not so wrong: "In all these years Goebbels has not said one single original, creative word."[10]

From Futurism to "Photorism"

Hitler had three hobbyhorses: architecture, painting, and music. Goebbels had hardly anything to do with architecture, which was entirely Hitler's prerogative. Hitler's architectural intimate was Albert Speer, who took the place of the dead Ludwig Troost, whom Hitler had looked up to like a devout pupil to his master. Hitler took personal responsibility for Berlin's new architectural plans designed to make it the "biggest and most beautiful" city in the world. He had put Speer in charge, which relieved Goebbels (though he was gauleiter of Berlin) of this worry at least.

Rather different was the position with regard to painting. Hitler directed Goebbels personally to take all necessary measures to put painting back on the map: "This is your greatest duty toward the movement, the German people, and the coming centuries."[11]

Goebbels' original taste can be traced in his novel *Michael*. Michael visits an exhibition in Munich and writes: "A star: Vincent van Gogh. In this environment he looks almost tame, and yet he is the most modern among the moderns. Modernism has obviously nothing to do with heroic gestures. That is only a false veneer. Modernism is a new world feeling. . . . Van Gogh combines all that is important: He is teacher, preacher, fanatic, prophet, mad. After all, we are all mad when we produce a creative idea. . . ."[12]

This concept was a clear challenge to Hitler's. Like every tyrant, Hitler disliked "mad people," particularly in art, since it was rather difficult to shut them up in asylums like other lunatics. Hitler favored concrete realism, not unlike the "socialist realism" upheld as the only valid artistic ideology in today's Soviet Union. The first important exhibition in 1937 in the House of German Art (Haus der Deutschen Kunst), called by real art experts "Palazzo Kitschi," was organized by Hitler's personal photographer, Heinrich Hoffmann. The Schwabingers [Schwabing is a district in Munich where many painters and artists live] said about him that he had changed futurism into "photorism."

From this exhibition all abstract and "mad" art was banned. It was a show of conformist pedestrian painters, which most likely revolted

Goebbels. He adored a few watercolors by Nolde, which Speer had given him for his apartment. But when Hitler, visiting Goebbels, saw them and expressed his dislike, Goebbels took them down immediately.[13] If only Hitler had been content with his gigantic architectural plans and not taken any interest in art, Goebbels might have loosened the reins and let many things pass. But this not being the case, immortal foreign painters like Picasso (whose early works even Rosenberg had praised), Chagall, Gauguin, Matisse, Braque, and even Van Gogh had to disappear, as well as German painters and designers of international repute, such as Klee, Liebermann, the Austrian Kokoschka (who lived in Germany), Corinth, Dix, Grosz, Pechstein, Kirchner, Kandinsky (a Russian who since 1922 had worked in the Bauhaus in Weimar), Nolde, and the great sculptor Barlach. They had to give way to painters like Wissel, Petersen, Stahl, Padua, Wilke, Buehler, Willrich, Hitz, Pitthan, and Hitler's favorite painter, Kriegel.

In the year 1937, Professor Adolf Ziegler, president of the Reich Chamber of Fine Arts, organized an exhibition of "depraved art" in the Galeriestrasse in Munich, showing paintings of officially banned painters to demonstrate the decadent products of the "system era" and the "destructive Jewish concept of art." In his opening speech Hitler said, "These prehistoric Stone Age culturists and art stammerers can, for all we care, return to their ancestral caves to produce there their primitive international doodlings."[14]

By that time Goebbels had already capitulated. The decisive influence came from officials responsible for art, such as Ziegler and Schulze-Naumburg, and the preachers of the National Socialist *Weltanschauung,* particularly Rosenberg. Also, the magazine *Die Kunst im Dritten Reich* (Art in the Third Reich), later called *Die Kunst im Deutschen Reich* (Art in the German Reich), which laid down the guiding line for art, was not edited in the Propaganda Ministry but by Rosenberg and his staff. Supreme, however, were Hitler's views.

In 1933 Goebbels had still permitted the painter Otto Andreas Schreiber, assisted by his friend, Hans Weidemann, an official in the Propaganda Ministry, to organize in a private gallery an exhibition called "Thirty German Artists," which included works by Barlach, Nolde, and Pechstein.[15]

The minister tolerated permanent exhibitions of modern art in Berlin. He even succeeded in persuading Reich Minister Rust to leave works by Edvard Munch, Lyonel Feininger, Emil Nolde, and Franz Marc in the modern part of the National Gallery in the Berlin Kronprinzen Palais. But after the Olympic Games in 1936, Goebbels gave up the struggle.

The Case Furtwängler

Music presented Goebbels with a similar problem. His musical taste was different from Hitler's. For Hitler nothing greater existed in music than Wagner. In all Goebbels' writing, Wagner's music, compared with that of other composers, is rarely mentioned. In the company of his mistress they would together play Brahms, Wolff, and Schubert. During one of his visits to Munich he listened to Schubert's *Winterreise* and wrote: "Viennese musician who speaks about death. This is doubly moving. They know how to make music in Munich. Munich is a German station on the way to Austria's love of music."[16]

When visiting Vienna in September 1932, he made a point of going to the opera. *"The Magic Flute*—never before have I heard Mozart played that way. The perfect style! This is making music as nobody else can."[17] For Goebbels, Mozart was "the greatest musical genius of Western civilization."

Goebbels was hoping to be able to show his tolerance and broadmindedness toward Germany's musical life, even more than toward the fine arts, where he felt less independent, faced with Hitler and the art officials. Goebbels actually succeeded in getting Richard Strauss, doubtless the most important opera composer of his time, appointed president of the Reich Chamber of Music, and conductor Wilhelm Furtwängler, one of the greatest interpreters of classical and romantic music, as vice president. Goebbels intended to interfere as little as possible with musical life, and gave his departmental chiefs, who knew his liberal attitude, a free hand. They would, he hoped, act accordingly. At the same time, he could always unload the responsibility on his departmental chiefs should there be any trouble with the party. At first Goebbels was on the fence. It was the State Opera, for which Goering was responsible, that started dismissing Jewish artists, including Otto Klemperer and Lotte Schöne; Arnold Schönberg and Franz Schrecker were expelled from the Prussian Academy, not by Goebbels but by Dr. Bernhard Rust, Reich Minister for Science and Education.

The dismissal of artists and scientists, particularly the continuous attacks and demonstrations by Rosenberg's Kampfbund against Jewish performers, insofar as they were still performing in public, had a bad effect. Goebbels preferred to bide his time, hoping things would calm down. His main preoccupation was to assure that internationally known Aryan artists, whose departure would have meant a loss of prestige, should remain in Germany. The two most important were

Richard Strauss and Furtwängler. Furtwängler's popularity, his personal integrity, and his international renown made him into a key figure.

On April 11, 1933, Furtwängler wrote in the *Vossische Zeitung* that he should like to take the liberty of drawing the minister's attention "to certain events that took place in the country's musical life which . . . were not necessarily bound up with the restitution of national dignity, which we all welcome so gratefully and joyfully. . . . Art and artists are there to unite and not to divide. I can recognize only one dividing line, the one between good and bad art.

"While a dividing line is being drawn nowadays between Jews and non-Jews . . . with inexorable severity, the other, so important, if not decisive dividing line, namely that between good and bad music . . . has been rather neglected.

"Our musical life of today . . . cannot afford any more experiments, we cannot treat music like other essential daily products such as potatoes and bread. If concerts have nothing to offer, the public simply stays away. It follows that the qualitative standard offered in music is not only an ideological question but rather a question of survival. It has to be stated clearly that men like Walter, Klemperer, Reinhardt, etc., should have a chance in the future to pursue their artistic activities in Germany. I appeal in that sense to you in the name of German art lest things happen that might prove to be irreparable."

Goebbels' answer appeared on the same day in the *Berliner Lokal Anzeiger*.

"In response to your letter I gratefully welcome the chance to clarify the attitude of the National German life forces to art in general, and music in particular. I was exceedingly pleased to see your assurance, given early in your letter in the name of German artists, that you gratefully and joyfully welcome the restitution of our national dignity.

"I have never assumed it could be otherwise; . . . it is your right to feel as an artist and to look upon matters from the living artistic point of view. But this does not necessarily presuppose your assuming an unpolitical attitude toward the general development that has taken place in Germany. Politics, too, is perhaps an art, if not the highest and most all embracing there is. Art and the artists are not only there to unite; their far more important task is to create a form, to expel the ill trends and make room for the healthy to develop. As a German politician I therefore cannot recognize the dividing line you hold to be the only one, namely that between good and bad art. Art must not only be good, it must also be conditioned by the exigencies of the people . . . no longer must there be art in the absolute sense, as hitherto known to the liberal democratic concept. . . . Any attempt to serve this art would ultimately lead only to a state where the people have no more an inner relationship to art, and the artist, living in the vacuum of the *l'art pour l'art* concept, would find himself isolated from the driving forces of his time. Certainly art must be good, but over and above it must be responsible, skilled, close to the people, and aggressive. I readily agree that we cannot afford any more experimenting.

"It might have been perhaps just as well to protest against artistic experiments at a time when German art was almost exclusively dominated by the obsession with experiments conducted by elements alien to the German people and the German race, who only succeed in dragging down and compromising the name of German art. . . . You will always be able to pursue your artistic activities in a future Germany. But to complain that men like Walter, Klemperer, Reinhardt, etc., had to cancel their performances, appears to me hardly opportune at this particular moment, still less, as truly German artists had been condemned to silence during these last fourteen years; the events of the last few weeks—incidentally not approved by us either —should, therefore be taken as a natural reaction. Be that as it may, I am of the opinion that every real artist should be given a chance to work here without . . . hindrance. . . ."

Goebbels' answer was devilishly clever. He picked out, and underlined, what Furtwängler only mentioned in passing—his joy at the restitution of national dignity—a phrase without which it would have been impossible to write this letter. He took up Furtwängler's warning "to stop experimenting," but again most adroitly perverted its original meaning. Furtwängler's phrase had of course not referred to creative experimenting, without which no art can ever evolve. By "experimenting" he had clearly referred to the ban of great non-Aryan interpreters, a measure bound to lead to a lowering of the general standard of public performances. But Goebbels deliberately talked about the creative experiment, since it gave him an opportunity to propagate the National Socialist thesis, whereby only art that was profoundly connected with the people was real art.

But Goebbels' assurance that every true artist should in the future be given a chance to work without hindrance was pure hypocrisy, since Jewish artists were forbidden by law to continue with their activities. It also showed how powerless Goebbels actually was. . . . In any case, this open controversy with Furtwängler was, as far as Goebbels was concerned, not so unwelcome. The continuous interference with cultural life by Rosenberg's Kampfbund and other similar National Socialist organizations worried him, if only on account of Hitler. The fact that such an important musician as Furt-

wängler had raised his voice in protest gave Goebbels an opportunity
to make public his point of view, which justified him in Hitler's eyes
and, while avoiding a break with Furtwängler, at the same time
struck a hard blow at those intriguing National Socialist art officials.
Goebbels' letter served the double purpose of veiling somehow Furtwängler's complaints and confirming before all party members his
own basic National Socialist attitude.

Goebbels continued his policy of preventing grave conflicts from
disturbing German musical life. But the national revolution and those
artists who profited by it, far from being content, demanded further
victims. One was Paul Hindemith.

Hindemith, too, who soon found himself the center of the storm
unleashed by Rosenberg and his group, remained for a long time
under Goebbels' protection. At a concert of the Berlin Philharmonic
Orchestra in October 1934, when Furtwängler performed a symphonic
adaptation of Hindemith's opera *Mathis der Maler* (Mathis the
Painter), he brought upon himself violent attacks from the former
Kampfbund, now rebaptized Nationalsozialistische-Kulturgemeinde
(National Socialist Cultural Association). They declared the com-
poser as "unacceptable from the standpoint of cultural policy."[18]
Furtwängler answered them in an article in the *Deutsche Allgemeine
Zeitung* of November 25, 1934, in which he passionately defended
the composer.

"Where would we be if political informers were given a free rein
in art? What is here at stake . . . is not only the particular case
Hindemith. We cannot afford—considering the terrible poverty of
genuinely productive musicians that exists in the whole world today—to do without a man of Hindemith's stature."

When the audience in the State Opera gave Furtwängler a demon-
strative ovation the same evening, the bubble burst. Goebbels, no
doubt, would have preferred to spare the government this embarrassing situation, and probably cursed Rosenberg and his Cultural Association. But after the incident in the opera, Hitler was bound to get to
know of it. The "Fuehrer" did not tolerate any demonstrations—
even by implication—against the party. Now Rosenberg's Kulturgemeinde could freely extend its witch-hunt by attacking Furtwängler,
which led to his resignation as vice president of the Reich Chamber
of Music, Prussian state councillor, and general musical director of
the State Opera (December 4). The shock of his resignation rever-
berated around the world, resulting in rather unfavorable reactions
to the German leaders.

Goebbels was probably afraid that Furtwängler might emigrate,
which would have resulted in a painful loss of prestige abroad and
upset people at home. Luckily for Goebbels, Furtwängler had an

enemy in Toscanini, who vehemently attacked the German conductor for exactly what, after all, he himself had attempted in Italy
at the beginning of the Fascist era, while he was trying to save in the
field of art whatever there was left to save. Toscanini's accusations
against his German colleague and rival created great resentment
against Furtwängler abroad. On February 28, 1935, Furtwängler and
Goebbels met for what was to be their last discussion. Goebbels
personally had the highest respect for Furtwängler. Wilfried von
Oven, Goebbels' personal adjunct during the last war years, quotes
the minister in his memoirs:

"An artist like Furtwängler has my greatest admiration. There is
for you a personality without a flaw. He was never a National Socialist,
nor did he ever make a secret of it; reason enough for the Jews and
the emigrees to regard him as one of them and as the center of a
so-called inner emigration within Germany. How high he stands above
all that rubble, Furtwängler—whose attitude toward us, incidentally,
did not change in any way—has clearly been shown by his behavior
during the bombing raids on Berlin. Not only did he refuse to run
away, as many so-called artists have done, but during these difficult
weeks and months, he gave his whole art to those who had suffered
under the bombardment in Berlin, the ordinary people as well as the
workers in the armament factories. The Fuehrer offered to build a
private bunker for him. He declined with thanks and asked that the
bunker offered to him should rather be built in one of the working
districts threatened by bombs."[19]

Furtwängler was a personality who stood in the center of public
attention, respected by friend and foe. He was one of the few who
tried to stem the tide without being able to assess correctly its overwhelming force. Once he had realized the extent of the peril he did
not try to save himself but stayed on, and not because he sought to
gain some advantage by doing so, but from a sense of duty. He felt
he was a German through and through. He knew that the barbarians
were in power; but he also knew that Bach and Beethoven, Wagner
and Brahms would outlive and survive the passing storm of the
barbarians.

The Case Knappertsbusch

Hans Knappertsbusch had been general musical director of the
Bavarian State Opera since October 1923. When the National
Socialists took over they appointed Oskar Walleck general adminis-
trator in order to curtail Knappertsbusch's sovereign position. The

conductor had earned the wrath of the Bavarian National Socialist bigwigs by his outspoken pronouncements, which had made the rounds in Munich. Knappertsbusch protested against Walleck's appointment and put before the responsible authorities the alternative: either himself or Walleck. The immediate official reaction was Knappertsbusch's suspension.

Unluckily for him, a letter containing serious accusations against him had arrived at the Propaganda Ministry on January 25, 1935. It had been sent by the attaché to the German embassy in The Hague, K. O. Faber, who at a party given by the German ambassador after a concert conducted by Knappertsbusch, reported the following conversation with the conductor:

"To my question how the atmosphere was at home, he said: 'In Bavaria we have the pure brand of National Bolshevism; the people like it, because they have got what they always wanted.' When I retorted it surely could be only a small, somewhat radical group in the party, known to the government and not really dangerous, Knappertsbusch replied: 'In the government sit men who indulge in their own fantasies without knowing what's really going on around them, because they're lied to on all sides.' When I said that I could not share this view, Knappertsbusch retorted with a question: 'Are you a Nazi?' When I replied in the affirmative, he inquired sarcastically whether I was 'a must-Nazi.' And on my astonished answer: 'What do you mean by "a must-Nazi"? I am Nazi by conviction. What makes you say that?' Knappertsbusch replied: 'Well, many officials *had* to become party members.'

"The mere tone of this conversation told me that Knappertsbusch was no friend of the new Germany, and has, no doubt, shown this even more clearly in his conversations with foreigners than when talking to me."[20]

Upon this letter the Bavarian cultural authorities pensioned Knappertsbusch off on March 1, 1936. As he was banned from giving public performances, his monthly pension of 600 marks created serious financial difficulties for him. Knappertsbusch wrote to Goebbels asking for an audience, but his letter was left unanswered. In the meantime invitations came from all over Europe inviting Knappertsbusch to give concerts, but he was refused permission to leave Germany. The change came about when Knappertsbusch wrote a letter on March 21, 1936, to the president of the Reich Theater Chamber, Dr. Rainer Schlösser. In this letter Knappertsbusch informed Schlösser that he had received two offers: one appointing him director of the Viennese Opera, the other permanent conductor in London. Through his retirement he had been put in a difficult financial position and was obliged to look for work. He would not like to leave Germany because "I will admit openly it is a horrible thought for me to leave my fatherland, which would put me, particularly in Vienna, just as happened to me in the beginning of my career in Munich—surely you must know that—entirely in the hands of Jewish scoundrels! No! I want to stay in Germany and continue to serve my fatherland to the best of my modest ability, but I must find work and earn money, and I must—and this is for me the most important of all things—regain the trust of my Fuehrer, which others have stolen from me."

This letter contributed without doubt to the conductor's rehabilitation. It is hardly a beautiful letter, but those who knew Knappertsbusch also knew his colorful way of expressing himself. He very likely did not give a damn for "the trust of my Fuehrer," but he had to try to get out of the fatal position into which some Bavarian party bigshots had put him.

Knappertsbusch was given permission for concert tours abroad: "We can't let Knappertsbusch starve," wrote Goebbels' state secretary, Funk, on March 11, 1936, in red ink on the file. He was even allowed to conduct at the Viennese State Opera, but when Director Kerber offered him Weingartner's place as first conductor with a yearly salary of 100,000 schillings, Hitler personally decreed on May 14, 1936, that Knappertsbusch should no longer be allowed to conduct in Vienna, since it was contrary to the interests of the Reich for German artists to perform in Austria. This brought forth a letter from the German ambassador in Vienna, Von Papen, addressed to Goebbels on May 29, 1936, in which he warned that Chancellor Schuschnigg might take offense.

On July 11, 1936, an agreement was signed between Hitler's Germany and Austria; and sixteen days later, on July 27, Goebbels informed Knappertsbusch personally that "there was no longer any objection to your accepting any engagement in Vienna or anywhere else."

Once again the political horizon darkened for Knappertsbusch when Viennese music critic Professor Dr. Max Graf published an article in *Die Bühne* (The Stage) entitled *Knappertsbuschiana,* in which he reported that the conductor had passed favorable remarks about non-Aryans, and had made fun of the *Deutsche Gruss*—Heil Hitler.

The head of the Organization of Germans Abroad in Vienna, who reported this to the Reich Chamber of Music, however, added in his letter: "The Jew Graf has written this article without consulting Knappertsbusch. Challenged by Knappertsbusch, Graf said, he 'would not permit anybody to interfere with what was common journalistic usage.' From this emerges clearly that this article is an intentionally malicious distortion, since Knappertsbusch had always been a severe critic of the Jewish mismanagement prevailing at the Viennese opera."

There can be no doubt that Knappertsbusch had actually made the remarks quoted by Graf. But if Knappertsbusch had admitted it, he would have been compelled to emigrate from Germany; he obviously wished to avoid this. He therefore initiated the *dementi* of Graf's quotation, and the Organization of Germans Abroad was only too happy to shift all the blame onto the Jews.

The Propaganda Minister, who'd had his fill of the case Furtwängler, also preferred to avoid further complications.

Knappertsbusch worked most of the time in Vienna, or went on concert tours abroad. He was rarely seen in Berlin, although, after Furtwängler, he was the most popular conductor of the Philharmonic concerts. In fact, his popularity was great enough to afford him a few other Knappertsbuschiana turns without falling into disgrace. To be in grace or not was not what really interested him. All he wanted was to conduct and be left in peace, and to be able to say a true word from time to time. And if the "Fuehrer" had not regarded frank pronouncements as *lèse-majesté,* Goebbels might have let them pass.

The Case Richard Strauss

In the beginning of the Third Reich it was vital for reasons of cultural prestige to retain Richard Strauss in Germany. His position as a composer placed him between two musical eras. Endowed with an incomparable talent for finding new creative ways for known musical forms, with a new approach to a highly musical concept, Richard Strauss had obtained world fame. He was the uncrowned king of music. It was somewhat disturbing for the National Socialist ideologists that the librettos of Strauss's operas had been written by the non-Aryan Hugo von Hofmannsthal. But the poet was dead, and his works were only rejected by a few overzealous art officials.

Strauss was already an old man and not particularly interested in politics. He loved Germany, liked to live in his fatherland, and did not feel like changing his domicile. Here at home, the greatest conductors vied with one another to be the first to perform his new works; they were proud to be counted among his friends, whether it was Clemens Krauss, Karl Boehm, Hans Knappertsbusch, Erich Kleiber or Karl Elmendorff. Since Richard Wagner there had not been another composer so deeply respected by every leading conductor. Goebbels, who saw him as the finest monument in his culture façade, did all he could for him. He offered Richard Strauss the presidency of the Reich Chamber of Music, which Strauss accepted all the more willingly, as he knew that Furtwängler would be at his side as vice president. Strauss probably thought things couldn't be so bad after all, if so many eminent non-Nazi musicians occupied important posts. The first measures taken against certain Jews were perhaps hard, but not yet cruel; many people possibly saw in those measures an excess of revolutionary zeal. Reason, so they thought, would win in the end.

Furthermore, the new minister had promised to invest important sums of money into the development of Germany's cultural life. It was almost considered chic among the high and mighty of the Third Reich to play the patron. It was precisely in this general mood that the composer made a speech when opening the Reich Chamber of Music that is held against him to this day. But all the speech proves is that Strauss was no more capable of provident political thinking than hundreds of world politicians active at the time. Strauss began his speech by saying that the creation of a Reich Chamber of Music had fulfilled the dream of musicians after the many years they had lost in wasting their strength, split up into many different associations (about 150), fighting one another. He was convinced that this creation of the Reich Chamber of Music was but the first step toward the aim to: "Unite the German people with their music, as it had been done once before—I am thinking of the sixteenth century—but very differently from the way it was done during the last decade." After the Nazi takeover "so much had been altered not only in the political but also in the cultural field," all of which seems to show that the new Germany "earnestly searches to find ways and means to give in particular our musical life a new stimulus."[21]

The speech probably pleased Goebbels as much as, not without reason, it displeased the emigrés. Strauss, no doubt, was hoping that magnanimity would be repaid in kind. And Goebbels was very likely prepared to be magnanimous, but difficulties inevitably arose, as always when an artist enjoying a privileged position in a dictatorial state tries to go "his own way," irrespective of the prestige of the authorities. Stefan Zweig had written the libretto to the Strauss Opera *Die Schweigsame Frau* (The Silent Woman). Hitler had promised to attend personally the first world performance, set for June 29, 1935, in Dresden. Goebbels had secured Hitler's attendance as a defense against Rosenberg and his clique, which had even tried to make rehearsals at the Dresden opera impossible.

Rosenberg had violently opposed the performance, stressing that Strauss, who "accepted an important position and the honors of the Third Reich, would have to abandon Zweig. . . . Either he sticks to his old friends or gives up his representative and culturally important posts in the Third Reich."[22]

Goebbels, with Hitler behind him, shrugged Rosenberg's protests off with a smile. But his smile soon disappeared when the Gestapo intercepted some correspondence[23] between Richard Strauss ˑand Stefan Zweig, which, in the eyes of the Gestapo and the National Socialist leaders, weighed heavily against the composer. Strauss wrote he was only "acting the president . . . to prevent worse from happening." But the letter also had a bad effect on the opponents of National Socialism, who had no time for Olympic irony and political vacillation. To make matters worse came Zweig's statement that he dedicated his royalties to Jewish charitable institutions.[24] Be that as it may, Goebbels was no longer able to back Strauss, and asked him to resign as president of the Reich Chamber of Music. Strauss complied on July 30, 1935, asking in a letter of the same date, addressed to Hitler, to be received "in order to vindicate myself personally." But Hitler did not even bother to answer.[25] Only Goebbels sent Strauss a personal letter of thanks, mainly to save face for both parties in the eyes of the public. The official reason given for Strauss's resignation was age and ill health.[26]

Goebbels actually saw to it that Strauss was left in peace, and this was all the over-seventy-year-old composer really wanted. The relationship between the authorities and Richard Strauss remained rather cool after the letter incident. The problem was only revived when on June 11, 1944, the composer reached his eightieth birthday. It was difficult for the Reich to ignore this event, all the more so because the Strauss conductors, Krauss and Boehm, as well as State operas in Berlin and Dresden, were making plans to celebrate the anniversary in great style. The Propaganda Ministry drew up a memo for Hitler:

"On the occasion of Richard Strauss's eightieth birthday on June 11, 1944, leading opera houses plan many performances, some of them entire Strauss weeks. Clemens Krauss originally intended to play all Strauss operas in Munich. This plan has been rendered impossible by the destruction of the opera house. Krauss therefore plans to stage several Strauss operas in the opera in Paris.

"Considering certain events in connection with Richard Strauss, the Reich Minister, Dr. Goebbels, considers such a plan to be undesirable, and proposes to limit presentations of Strauss's operas to two or three productions. Reich Minister Goebbels requests agreement to the proposed restrictive measure."

Despite this introductory note, the list of works attached included considerably more than two or three productions. From the Fuehrer Chancellery came the following reply:

"There is no objection to honoring the works of Strauss as listed, but not his person by giving any official reception. On this point a tight rein should be kept. For reasons of political considerations, however, the composer and his wife should attend these anniversary performances in a box, and permission should be given to the general administrators of the respective opera houses to invite him. Muethel [general administrator in Vienna], Elmendorff [general musical director in Dresden], Tietjen [Berlin State Opera], and Clemens Krauss should be permitted to invite Strauss to luncheon or dinner, which the more important departmental chiefs may attend, but not political personalities or representatives of cultural policy."[27]

The cases Strauss, Furtwängler, and Knappertsbusch show that Germany's musical life had greater artistic problems than is usually assumed. Admittedly, Goebbels tried to show some independence of party doctrine and a certain broadmindedness. But even in the musical field he failed to attain any measure of real freedom. He only succeeded in erecting a magnificent-looking façade. With the exception of a few famous Jewish conductors, practically all important composers and conductors stayed in Germany. The loss of Schoenberg, Schreker, Weill, and Krěnek found less resonance at home than abroad. With the exception of Kurt Weill (and mainly because of his collaboration with Bertolt Brecht), none of these modern composers had been really popular. The German opera houses in Berlin, Munich, Dresden, and Vienna were institutes of world renown; the Berlin and Vienna philharmonic orchestras were still the most sought-after abroad. Furtwängler, Knappertsbusch, Krauss, and later Karajan were conductors of world renown and made up for the loss of Walter, Klemperer, Busch, and Kleiber (after 1935).

Other modern composers such as Werner Egk, Rudolf Wagner-Regeny, Carl Orff, and Gottfried von Einem had come onto the scene. True, the great experiment was lacking; there was no exciting spiritual challenge. The people were driven into concerts by the organization "Strength Through Joy," and had for the first time an opportunity to listen to first-rate orchestras led by first-rate conductors playing Bach, Mozart, Beethoven, Brahms, Schubert, Bruckner, and Wagner. It was meant to acquaint them with racially pure music, and, indeed, never before had the works of the great masters been presented to the masses on such a scale. This development was helped by musical broadcasts. But most of the composers whose works were played were dead and buried long ago.

I Always Think of Thomas Mann

Goebbels had to admit his greatest, and perhaps most painful, defeat in the field of literature. To make it even worse, it was there that he felt at home and less afraid to meet with Hitler's disapproval; Hitler who, apart from technical books, read only Karl May. [Karl May was a very popular writer of adventure and Western stories, written for and read by adolescents. Translator's note]. But just in the field of literature (the National Socialists called it *Schrifttum*), Rosenberg's and his clique's protesting voices were loudest. Many poets and writers who Goebbels would have liked to retain in Germany, or induce to return, had gone abroad and refused to come back.

Yet it was Goebbels himself who committed the first and fatal error. On May 10, 1933, the "Burning of the Books" took place in several university towns, including Berlin; and Goebbels took part in it. His heart was probably not in it, and he actually arrived rather late for the ceremony, but he was not going to miss an occasion to prove he was a National Socialist revolutionary. But trying to be simultaneously a revolutionary and a liberal, he failed in both respects. Goebbels told the students: "The era of the overclever Jewish intellectualism has come to an end, and the breakthrough of the German revolution has opened the way for what is truly German. You are right in this hour of midnight to commit these products of the very negation of all spiritual meaning to the flames. It is a strong, great, and symbolic action designed to show the whole world: Here you see the entire spiritual structure of the November Republic crashing down in flames. . . ."[28]

Goebbels, who was almost obsessed with carrying out symbolic acts, was obviously not expecting the degree of horror with which this particular symbolic act was received by the whole world. Other dictatorial regimes such as the Soviet Union or Italy had taken similar measures, but much more discreetly, by simply letting undesirable books disappear from the library bookshelves.

Suppression of unwanted literature was nothing new, but the National Socialists had managed to find the clumsiest way of displaying their spiritual terror: The public burning of the books reminded the world of the darkest periods of the Middle Ages and the Inquisition.

They put the writers who had remained in Germany into a most unenviable position and barred the return of those who had gone abroad.[29]

Immediately after the Reichstag elections of March 1933, the German Academy of Writers, which had belonged to the Prussian Academy of Arts since 1926, underwent a thorough purge.

The following writers were expelled: Franz Werfel, Georg Kaiser, Bernhard Kellermann, Ludwig Fulda, Jakob Wassermann, Alfons Paquet, Bruno Frank, René Schickele, Fritz von Unruh, Rudolf Pannwitz, and Alfred Mombert. They were replaced by new members appointed by Reich Minister Bernhard Rust: Hans Carossa, Agnes Miegel, Wilhelm Schäffer, Emil Strauss, Erwin Guido Kolbenheyer, Hanns Friedrich Blunck, Boerries von Muenchhausen, Hans Grimm, Paul Ernst, Peter Doerfler, and the radically National Socialist writers Werner Beumelburg, Hanns Johst, and Will Vesper. Later on the members of the Academy voted in a few other members, including Enrica von Handel-Mazzetti and Johannes Schlaf, as well as Ernst Jünger, who declined the honor gratefully. And Ricarda Huch [a well-known German authoress. Translator's note] resigned her membership.

Goebbels had at that time actually nothing to do with the Writers Academy, which came directly under the authority of Reich Minister Rust; yet Goebbels took it upon himself to persuade Stefan George to become president of the Academy. But George had already left for Switzerland, where he died in Locarno on December 4, 1933. In his last work, *Das Neue Reich* (The New Reich), published in 1919, George had prophesied the coming of a young Fuehrer who would lead the people out of the "hated era of liberalism," but he did not see in Hitler the incarnation of his prophecy. The Austrian upstart hardly fitted into George's aristocratic spiritual concept. For him Hitler was not the Fuehrer with "the chaste, clear barbaric eye," but a mere barbarian. And the upheaval of the masses, which found an expression in the National Socialist manifestations, was bound to give George almost physical pain: "In my dreams I fled from the people . . . with a few of my brothers I flee from the noisy mob. . . ."

Goebbels' plan with George had come to nothing, but the poet's timely death was at least preferable to a categorical refusal, such as Goebbels had received from Thomas Mann. As late as 1934 Goebbels was still trying to persuade Mann to return to Germany. As early as December 5, 1925, Goebbels, after a visit to Lübeck, had written in his diary: "I can feel here the old Hansa spirit, and it makes me think continuously of the Buddenbrooks. I always think of Thomas

Mann." Goebbels greatly admired Thomas Mann, and Goebbels' disappointment must have been considerable when Mann refused to return and became a sworn enemy of the Third Reich.

All the same, to say that the whole élite of German writers had emigrated in 1933 would either be overestimating the emigrants or underestimating those who stayed on in Germany. Admittedly, the emigration of so many poets and writers meant a serious loss. Yet those who had stayed represented still an important creative potential: Gerhart Hauptman, Ernst Jünger, Gottfried Benn, Ernst Wiechert, Ricarda Huch, Hans Carossa, Agnes Miegel, Werner Bergengruen, Kasimir Edschmid, Hans Fallada, Ina Seidel, Wilhelm Schäfer, Reinhold Schneider, Erich Kästner (who could only write under a false name), and Rudolf G. Binding. The actual bloodletting was not the worst aspect. Worse was the poor quality of writers who now came to the fore. The spiritual terror caused the few good writers to retire into their ivory towers and only take up themes far removed from actual events. Their muted voices could no longer be heard in all the clamor drowning the Reich.

At first it was rather unclear who was really responsible for the banning or the admission of books and other literature. There were at first as many as twenty-one official agencies that arrogated for themselves the right to make the relevant decisions. This resulted in a flood of complaints from publishers and booksellers. With the foundation of the Reich Chamber of Literature and its correlated literary department in the Propaganda Ministry, Goebbels succeeded in achieving at least a certain degree of centralization. The chamber was an organization to which all authors, publishers, and booksellers had to belong. Whoever was expelled or whoever's membership had been refused could not publish, be published, or sell. There were always sufficient party writers or business competitors, particularly at the beginning, who made life rather difficult for authors and publishers by denouncing them politically. The chamber drew up lists of "harmful and undesirable literature," reserving their special attention for the so-called "asphalt literature." Under this category came practically all works of Jewish authors, as well as those of the German emigrés and foreign authors hostile to the Third Reich. Also banned was all Marxist and all pacifist literature. The chamber also decided, in concert with the relevant department of the Propaganda Ministry, which works should be banned under the term *Schmutz und Schund* (dirt and rubbish)—for being a corrupting influence on the younger generation. The number of banned authors varied, according to different sources, and was between 150 and 250; the number of banned titles was between 8,000 and 12,000.

With a membership of 35,000, the Chamber of Literature appeared to be a comprehensive organization comprising practically all writers. But there was also the Office for Cultivation of Literature (Schrifttumspflege), under the Fuehrer's special plenipotentiary, Alfred Rosenberg. Here too, an enormous apparatus was at work staffed by 1,400 chief and auxiliary readers whose task it was to analyze all works in regard to their ideological trustworthiness, their artistic quality, and their educational relevance. This office published a monthly called *Bücherkunde* (Book Information), which contained the most important evaluations. Rosenberg's office constituted a kind of competitive enterprise vying with the Reich Chamber of Literature and the Propaganda Ministry. It fought Goebbels' literal policy and tried to promote its privileged Nazi authors. In addition, there was the Party Examining Commission (Parteiamtliche Prüfungskommission—PPK), whose chief was Reichsleiter Philipp Bouhler.

Goebbels was less successful in the literary sector than in music, theater, and films, where, at least, he succeeded in hiding the actual inner emptiness behind a splendid façade. In the field of literature, even the façade showed too many cracks. Goebbels was able to save a writer from the fangs of the writing party wolves here and there, but he failed to secure any appreciable margin of creative liberty. All he did was to allow a few oases to survive in the spiritual desert.

Ruler of the Film Industry

Among all the artistic sections under his ministry, Goebbels felt closest to the Film Division. It was virtually an obsession with him. In each of his three private residences he had a cinema installed and viewed one or two films almost every night, including a considerable number of foreign films which, during the war, were obtained through neutral countries. His greatest enemies, headed by Rosenberg, were within his own party. But he had also to reckon with Hitler, who was a great film fan and very critical in the bargain. On March 28, 1933, a mere two weeks after his appointment as minister, Goebbels invited the heads of the film industry to the Hotel Kaiserhof for the purpose of outlining to them the future film policy of the Third Reich. He used all his charm and skill to calm the fears that had arisen within the film industry since the Nazis had come to power. The Nazi statistics claiming that 90 per cent of all German films were distributed by Jews, 86 per cent produced by Jewish producers, and 70 per cent written by Jewish screenwriters, were exaggerated. On the other hand, Jewish capital, Jewish authors and composers, as well as Jewish

12. Goebbels, his wife Helga, and daughter vacationing by the Baltic Sea at Heiligendamm. August 16, 1935.

13. Goebbels, his wife and children. November 1, 1937.

distributors, occupied a very strong position before 1933. Hitler's advent to power therefore resulted in a shock to the film industry that Goebbels had to neutralize. The minister underlined his determination not to interfere with artistic freedom but merely to help overcome the actual crisis. As "a passionate admirer of filmic art," he believed in the advent of a great new era for German films. And to prove his broadmindedness, Goebbels named his favorite films: the revolutionary Soviet film *Potemkin,* a bow to the intellectual left and to his own past; the American film *Anna Karenina* with Greta Garbo, giving America its due; to please the revolutionary elements in his own party, he added the Louis Trenker film, *The Rebel;* and pandering to the appreciation of the German myth, he finally included the film *The Nibelungen.* The last two were favorites of Hitler's; neither the Fuehrer nor his Minister of Propaganda seemed to mind that Fritz Lang, the director of *The Nibelungen,* was not a pure Aryan. Goebbels even tried to persuade Lang to stay on in Germany. Lang asked for time to think it over and left Germany quietly.[30]

But Goebbels' real favorite was probably *The Blue Angel,* with Emil Jannings and Marlene Dietrich. Goebbels was anxious that "la Dietrich," too, should return and work in Germany. But she preferred her director, Josef von Sternberg, and the United States.

On July 22, 1933, the Reich Film Chamber was founded, comprising ten divisions. All people working in the film industry—producers, directors, actors, architects, and technicians—had to be members. The Propaganda Ministry had a special department on "Film" that examined each film before it went into production.

The Film Law of February 16, 1934, installed a special bureau that decided whether a film violated religious, moral, artistic, or National Socialist concepts; it also categorized each film. This censorship had to consider image, dialogue, and music. Before a film was submitted to the bureau it had been read in the office of the special Reich film reader. The Reich film director general was responsible for the artistic and spiritual line of all productions. Simultaneously, the Film Credit Bank was founded, which advanced money for productions; the money was only awarded if the Reich film reader and the Reich film director general had recommended the film. This meant that every film was guided centrally from beginning to end, including scenario, cast, production, and distribution. In general the authorities acted generously and saved the producers and directors much trouble and detailed work.

At the beginning there were not many politically tendentious films, or the political tendency was so cleverly infiltrated that the public hardly became aware of it. An example is the Tobis film *Der*

Herrscher (The Ruler) after Gerhardt Hauptmann's *Vor Sonnenun-tergang* (Before Sunset) directed by Veit Harlan, with Emil Jannings in the lead. Jannings, Germany's most famous film actor (in 1927–28 he was the first to receive the highest American film award, the Oscar, for his part in *Way of All Flesh*), initiated also a film with a scenario close to the original text of Kleist's *Der Zerbrochene Krug* (The Broken Jug) with Jannings playing Judge Adam. *The Broken Jug,* although very successful, was soon taken out of circulation because Goebbels saw in the limping Judge Adam an allusion to his own de-formity. Albert Speer reports that Hitler found the film magnificent and gave orders that it be shown again in Berlin's biggest cinema.[31] Yet even judged from an international point of view, most of Jan-nings' films, such as *Robert Koch, Entlassung* (The Dismissal), *Der alte und der Junge König* (The Old and the Young King), and *Traumulus* were considered to be top productions. Jannings had in his contract the right to choose his subjects. Accordingly, his films were more or less free of political tendencies despite Goebbels' at-tempts to infiltrate National Socialistic ideas into the script. But when war broke out Goebbels exerted sufficient pressure on Jannings to play the title role in the anti-English *Ohm Krüger* (Uncle Krüger), knowing it would commit the actor irrevocably to the Nazi cause and at the same time compromise him abroad.

The Harlan film *Die Goldene Stadt* (The Golden City), after Billinger's play *Der Gigant* (The Giant), received in 1942 the Volpi Cup and the first prize of the German International Film Chamber. The German film industry declared certain films as "State politically and artistically valuable." Later on, top productions were awarded the title of "Film of the Nation" and presented with the German Film Ring. This distinction was only attributed to politically tendentious films that were technically excellent and cast with eminent actors. Examples are the film *Heimkehr* (The Homecoming), 1941, directed by Gustav Ucicky, with Paula Wessely and Attilla Hörbiger in the leading roles, and the film *Kolberg,* shot in 1944. This film was de-signed to exhort the German people to stand fast by showing them the successful resistance of the town of Kolberg against the French; it was directed by Veit Harlan, with Heinrich George, Kristina Söderbaum, Paul Wegener, and Horst Caspar in the cast.

There was also the National Film Prize. This, among others, was awarded to *Der Herrscher* as well as to two films directed by Leni Riefenstahl: a documentary of the party rally in Nuremberg called *Der Sieg des Glaubens* (Victory of Faith) and the film about the Olympic Games of 1936 called *Der Triumph des Willens* (Triumph of the Will). The Riefenstahl films are not only interesting as political documentaries of this period but also as records of the highest standard of camera technique achieved at the time.

Before the war the top films, even those containing a political bias, were of considerable artistic quality. The main responsibility for the later decline of standards and the crude politicization of German films must be put at Rosenberg's door. Rosenberg recounts[32] in December 1939 how, during a luncheon with Hitler, the "Fuehrer" had severely attacked the lack of political content in German films. There was hardly anything in any of them dealing with the National Socialist revolution and its problems, he complained.

Soon afterward a spate of tendentious and particularly anti-Semitic films such as *The Rothschilds, Der Ewige Jude* (The Eternal Jew), and the worst of all, the film *Jud Süss* (Jew Süss), descended on the German public. The producers were not ashamed to use, in crowd shots of the anti-Semitic *Jud Süss,* Jews taken from the ghetto. The Purim feast, which is the gayest of Jewish feasts, became in the film a feast of vengeance on the Gentiles, and the ritual slaughter of animals a scene of sadistic animal torture.

Films that dealt with National Socialist *Weltanschauung,* so much after the heart of Rosenberg and his staff, found only little interest with the public. The production of such films remained therefore small, and soon fizzled out. The most important of this kind were *S.A.-Mann Brand* with Otto Wernicke; *Hitler-Junge Quex* (Hitler Youth Quex), with Heinrich George; and the film about Horst Wessel, rebaptized by Goebbels *Hans Westmar.*

In 1937 all important film companies had been nationalized: Bavaria, Terra, Tobis, and the most important of all, UFA. After the occupation of Austria and Czechoslovakia the Reich also appropriated the companies Wien Film (Vienna Film) and Prague Film. Within the occupied territories the German film industry had reserved 80 per cent of the market for its own production. The remaining 20 per cent was divided between French and Italian films.

Goebbels remarked in his diary on May 19, 1942: "We must take a similar course in our film policy as pursued by the Americans on the North American and South American continents. We must become the dominant film power in Europe. Films produced by other states should only be allowed to have local and limited character. We must, therefore, prevent any rising national film industry other than German, from engaging actors, artists, or technicians that could be useful in Berlin, Vienna, or Munich."[33]

Goebbels was more interested and more successful in film and radio than in any other branch under his jurisdiction.

Admittedly, by centralizing the film industry he destroyed the

smaller film companies, which before 1933 had supplied the film
market with roughly 50 per cent of all films; but one must give him
credit for having tried his best to avoid politically tendentious films
—at least before Hitler (duly influenced by others) reproached him
for a lack of National Socialist *Weltanschauung* in German films.
Even in nationalistic films Goebbels gave preference to a patriotic
rather than a National Socialist line. Goebbels planned to write a book
about the artistic side of film production after the war. With his
usual modesty he predicted that his book would become a standard
work for films, as Lessing's *Hamburgische Dramaturgie* had been
for the theater.

"We Lived on an Island . . ."

Goebbels did not succeed in dominating the theater to the same degree as the film industry, where his absolute rule was never questioned. The two top theaters in the Reich capital, the Berlin State
Opera Unter den Linden, and the Staatliche Schauspielhaus on the
Gendarmenmarkt, came under Goering's patronage. The other cultural centers of the Reich, such as Munich and Dresden, as well as
Vienna, were to a great extent able to preserve their independence.

Yet, they, too, were under Goebbels' political control, and even
artists who enjoyed Goering's protection, or later on in Vienna,
Baldur von Schirach's, had to be very careful not to arouse the
Propaganda Minister's wrath. Like all other branches of art, the
theater had its own professional association, the Reich Theater
Chamber, founded in May 1933. And just as he had done before
when convoking leading film personalities, he now invited theater
directors and administrators to a meeting in the Hotel Kaiserhof to
give them a similar treatment:

"It is not my intention to put any artistic activity into a strait-
jacket. Nowhere has the law of personality a greater claim to the
right of self-expression than in art. All we demand is that the great
swing of the pendulum of our time should not stop at the doors of
the theaters. . . . We want to bring art to the people in order to
bring the people back to art."[34]

Goebbels pursued this aim by taking three steps. On October 15,
1933, he proclaimed for the first time "The Day of the Theater," on
which one whole hour was devoted in all German schools to discussion of theatrical problems. The second step was the so-called Reich
Theater Weeks, which took place each year in a different town. They
were meant to give a concentrated picture of the general theatrical

effort, so as to assess the development of the German theater. But the crowning idea of a theater closely allied to the people was the *Weihespiele,* open-air performances, called *Thingtheater,* which, as Goebbels imagined, would go into theatrical history as "National Socialism turned to stone." In 1935 already twenty-five "thing theaters" existed all over the Reich; the biggest, the Dietrich Eckart Stage, was founded in 1936 on occasion of the Olympic Games in Berlin. It was equipped with amplifiers and an auditorium that could seat twenty thousand people. It was opened with Eberhard Wolfgang Möller's *Frankenburger Würfelspiel.* Goebbels in 1934 had founded the Poets' Circle, which included forty authors charged with the special task of writing "thing plays." But the idea did not catch on. These plays (consisting mostly of speaking choruses and group movements) attracted an ideologically interested public at first, but in time people found them boring, and attendance dropped.

"Thing plays" aside, the theater continued working after its usual fashion. First-rate actors and producers gave first-rate theater performances, even though their ranks had been somewhat thinned by the absence of their Jewish colleagues—the most painful loss being the forced emigration of master producer Max Reinhardt, who had from Berlin creatively stimulated the whole European theater for over thirty years. And, what had sadly been lacking under the Weimar Republic, money, was now plentiful. By 1934 the number of theaters (248) had increased by 12, and the number of actors (a total of 25,663) had increased by 3,600. In 1936 the number of theaters rose to 299.[35]

Goebbels had not intended to offer theater with a *Weltanschauung.* This brought him once again into conflict with Rosenberg who, however, found little support from the great theater patrons. Neither Goering, Baldur von Schirach, nor Hitler himself cared very much for the *Weltanschauung* theater.

At the Reich meeting of the National Socialist Cultural Congregation (NS-Kulturgemeinde) in Düsseldorf[36] on June 7, 1935, Rosenberg launched a direct attack against Goebbels' cultural policy in general, and his theater policy in particular; but apart from a certain excitement it caused in the Propaganda Ministry, Rosenberg's speech made no real impact. Goering had appointed Gründgens as the head of the Staatliche Schauspielhaus and took him under his protective wing. In Jürgen Fehling, Gründgens had one of the greatest theatrical producers of his time. He had an ensemble of first-rate actors and actresses, including Käthe Gold, Hermine Körner, Elisabeth Flickenschild, Lola Müthel, Werner Krauss, Friedrich Kayssler, and Paul Hartmann, who helped Gründgens to make the Staatliche Schauspielhaus into Germany's foremost theater. Yet the "Goebbels theaters" did not lag far behind. At the helm of the Deutsche Theater (the former Reinhardt theater) stood the eminent Heinz Hilpert, who had in Paula Wessely, Käthe Dorsch, Edwald Balser, Attilla and Paul Hörbiger, as well as in Rudolf Forster, actors of an equally high standard. The constant competition between these two theaters only resulted in more and more outstanding productions.

A famous actress of that epoch later remarked: "We lived on an island and didn't know what was going on around us."[37] There was no contact or true exchange of ideas with the world outside Germany. Both film and theater lived in a world of illusion Goebbels had created. He did all he could for the actors. His efforts to improve their social position had Hitler's support who, outside his close circle of intimates, preferred the company of actors to any other. With Hitler's help Goebbels succeeded in creating for the theater and film actors a socially dominant position in the Third Reich. This had never happened before.

Most of the National Socialist leaders had a proletarian or *petit-bourgeois* background and found in actors their perfect courtiers. Actors did not care much about politics, were usually handsome, and were generally popular.

Goebbels founded the house of "Comradeship of German Artists" situated in Viktoriastrasse in Berlin. It was a modern club, complete with reception rooms, dance floors, a winter garden, a bar, and a tavern in the cellar. The head of the club was architect and Reich stage designer Benno von Arent, who was also president of the National Socialist Theater Artists. Goebbels was a frequent guest, Hitler an occasional visitor.[38]

The minister appointed himself as the ruler and protector of all theater artists. By the Reich theater law of May 15, 1934, the old professional law (*Gewerberecht*) was rescinded and substituted by the new art law (*Kunstrecht*), which placed all theaters under the artistic leadership of the Reich Propaganda Minister, leaving administration and direction in the hands of the theater proprietors. The law gave Goebbels the right to license new theaters or close down already existing theaters; to ban certain plays; and last but not least, the right to confirm the appointments of leading artistic personalities, such as general administrators, general music directors, and important theatrical producers. (An exception was Goering's Staatstheater and some other theaters that to some extent remained outside Goebbels' sphere of influence.)

The Propaganda Minister also founded in 1936 the Dr. Joseph Goebbels Foundation called *Künstlerdank* (A Thank You for the

Artist), which provided for old, retired actors. Goering, refusing to be left behind, founded a year later under his wife's tutelage, (she had been the actress Sonnemann) the Emmy Sonnemann Foundation.

Goebbels made the artists yet another, if somewhat dubious, gift: On November 25, 1936, he banned all art criticism, branding it as Jewish overalienation; it was replaced by "Art Commentary." He had, as a first step, abolished the so-called night criticism, arguing that a critic needed sufficient time to form a conscientious opinion. The idea of banning traditional criticism had not sprung from his own conviction. Rather, Goebbels was carrying out Hitler's wish, motivated by the fact that, as the Fuehrer explained, many men of genius had in the past been suppressed by critics, at least during their lifetimes.

It was frequently said that the artists themselves were but little pleased with the ban of the critics. The files of the Propaganda Ministry contain a letter Heinz Hilpert addressed to Goebbels on October 15, 1940, in which this eminent theatrical producer—he had never been a National Socialist—complained about an "Art Commentary" by Alexander Runge, who had called the play *The Café* produced in the Deutsche Theater a "coarse situation comedy."[39] Goebbels gave orders the next day to the head of the Theatrical Department in his ministry: "Herr Fritzsche is to reprimand Herr Runge. Would you inform Herr Hilpert that this is being done."[40]

From 1941 onward Goebbels had lists submitted to him every year with brief progress reports of conductors, theatrical producers, actors, directors, administrators, and singers. Seven such lists still exist,[41] and they must be unique. There can have been no other Minister of Culture in the world who followed with so much interest the development of artists.

Practically everything was decided in the Propaganda Ministry: tours abroad, salaries, appointment of general administrators. Quarrels and jealousies among the artists were also dealt with. When war broke out, Goebbels was even obliged to protect Berlin's nightlife because the Wehrmacht, the police, even some of his ministerial aides demanded severe measures against nude and seminude shows.[42]

The most delicate problems arose at the opera houses, where the handling of conductors, jealous of one another, was not always easy. When Karl Boehm wanted to leave Dresden to go to Vienna, Goebbels even had to bring Hitler in so that Karl Elmendorff was confirmed to fill the vacancy in Dresden, against the opposition of Mutschmann, gauleiter and Reich governor of Saxony. Elmendorff had been proposed by Boehm and Furtwängler, apparently to prevent Karajan's appointment. A memo from Goebbels to Hitler reads:

"Karajan's appointment could perhaps be premature, but Elmendorff fulfills all necessary conditions. . . ."[43] Hitler refused at first to appoint a new man in Dresden and commented, in view of Boehm's contract with Dresden, which actually ran until 1944: "In principle, contracts in the cultural field should be fulfilled."[44] A little surprising, coming from Hitler.

The "List of the Immortals"

When war broke out, Hitler personally tore up the draft papers of all artists whose names Goebbels had drawn up in a special list.[45] This meant they were exempt from military service. But in the autumn of 1944 Goebbels, newly appointed Reich Plenipotentiary for the Total War Effort (Reichsbevollmächtigter für den Totalen Kriegseinsatz), decreed that artists were no longer exempt. A new list was drawn up of artists drafted, but temporarily exempt from military service or work in the armament industries.[46] This "List B" was called "The List of Divine Talents." It contained a few hundred names drawn from every artistic branch, including writers. Theatrical and film artists whose names were on these lists were obliged to offer their services to the Propaganda Ministry without pay. Whoever refused was called up for work in armament factories.

There was, however, another list of artists "who represented eminent national capital." This "List A" was called "List of the Immortals"—those who continued to be exempt without any condition or obligation. The twenty-one people contained in "List A" reveal who constituted, in the eyes of the National Socialist cultural dictator, "eminent national capital." Among them were six writers: Hans Carossa, Gerhart Hauptmann, Erwin Guido Kolbenheyer, Agnes Miegel, Ina Seidel, and Hanns Johst. Missing were Ricarda Huch, Ernst Jünger, Werner Bergengruen, Ernst Wiechert; Gottfried Benn, also missing, had been expelled from the Reich Chamber of Writers in 1938. Nor can Heidegger be found on the list. It is significant that Hanns Johst had been preferred to the great poet Josef Weinheber.

Proof of Hitler's preference for the fine arts was the fact that no less than twelve of its representatives were put on "List A": Arno Breker, Georg Kolbe, Joseph Thorak, Fritz Klimsch, Hermann Gradl, Arthur Kampf, Willy Kriegel, Werner Peiner, Leonhard Gall, Hermann Giessler, Wilhelm Kreis, and Paul Schultze-Naumburg.

The three musicians on "List A" were Richard Strauss, Hans Pfitzner, and Wilhelm Furtwängler.

"List B" contained the writers Bruno Brehm, Hermann Burte, Hans Grimm, Max Halbe, Wilhelm Schäfer, Wilhelm von Scholz, Josef Weinheber, Heinrich Zillich, and some dedicated National Socialist writers. It also named seventy-three painters, thirty-four sculptors, fifty architects, and twenty-three industrial designers. Among the eighteen composers were Johann Nepomuk David, Werner Egk, Carl Orff, Josef Marx, and Theodor Berger.

Among the fifteen conductors mentioned in "List B" were: Karl Boehm, Karl Elmendorff, Eugen Jochum, Robert Heger, Oswald Kabasta, Herbert von Karajan, Hans Knappertsbusch, Clemens Krauss, Josef Keilberth, Hans Schmidt-Isserstedt, and Carl Schuricht. Among the seventeen pianists listed, the four best known were Walter Gieseking, Elly Ney, Wilhelm Kempff, and Friedrich Wührer. Among the nine violinists were Georg Kulenkampff, Wolfgang Schneiderhan, Max Strubb, and Gerhard Taschner. The four cello players chosen were Paul Grümmer, Ludwig Hoelscher, Hans Münch-Holland, and Adolf Steiner; also, the Schneiderhan, Stoss, and Strubb, quartets, as well as the organists Fritz Heilmann and Günther Ramin. Nine top orchestras were included in "List B." They were the Berlin and Vienna philharmonic orchestras, the Prussian State Orchestra, as well as the State Orchestra of Saxony, the Leipzig Gewandhaus Orchestra, the Bruckner Orchestra of Linz, and the Prague and Hamburg philharmonic orchestras.

"List B" also included 88 actors (from among 4,500), including Heinrich George, Ewald Balser, Friedrich Kayssler, Gustaf Gründgens, Raoul Aslan, Paul Hartmann, Werner Hinz, Eugen Klöpfer, Werner Krauss, Erich Ponto, Hermann and Hans Thimig, Gustav Waldau, Paul Wegener, Paula Wessely, Käthe Dorsch, Hermine Körner, Liselotte Schreiner, and Maria Eis.

The most famous singers on the list were Felicie Hüni-Mihacsek, Ann Konetzny, Adele Kern, Viorica Ursuleac, Maria Reining, Margarethe Klose, Erna Schlüter, Gerda Sommerschuh, Maria Müller, Martha Rohs, Erna Sack, Elisabeth Schwarzkopf, Irmgard Seefried, Gertrud Rünger, Elisabeth Höngen, and Alda Noni, as well as Hans Hotter, Paul Schöffler, Walter Ludwig, Max Lorenz, Hermann Nissen, Heinrich Schlusnus, Karl Schmitt-Walter, Marcel Wittrisch, Willy Domgraf Fassbaender, Josef Greindl, Hans Reinmar, and Ludwig Weber.

Film and radio proposed 700 names, of which 150 were accepted.

Those in radio on "List B" included conductors Hans Rosbaud and Fritz Zaun, and composers Nico Dostal, Werner Eisbrenner, Albert and Ernst Fischer, Franz Grothe, Peter Kreuder, Eduard

lcke, Theo Macketen, Alois Melichar, Norbert Schultze, and
ang Zeller.

October 10, 1944, all theater activities were stopped, and the
theaters were used for housing armament workers or storage.

radio and film were maintained as being useful to the war effort. Some theaters were taken over by the film industry and made
into studios.

An official file shows the following note, dated November 30,
1944: "Protected artists cannot be exempt from People's Militia
duties [The People's Militia (Volkssturm) consisted of civilians recruited for local military service. Translator's note]. In the Furtwängler case, the minister has decided that no one should be exempt
from People's Militia duty, not even he, although his name is on the
list of the Immortals."

If Hitler had to die, who would be left in Germany, anyway, worthy
of being considered as "eminent national capital"?

Information and Propaganda

After Hindenburg had appointed Goebbels as Reich Minister for Information and Propaganda (Volksaufklärung und Propaganda),
Goebbels made known his aims and objectives on March 15, 1933:
"The people must begin to think as one unit, react as such, and put
themselves at the disposal of the government wholeheartedly." The
following day Goebbels explained to the press what he meant by
active propaganda: "To belabor the people so long until they suc-
cumb to us." The layman may see in propaganda something "con-
temptible," but the true propagandist has to be an "artist" who
understands the "secret vibrations of the soul of the people."

On March 22, Goebbels moved into his ministry, the "Leopold
Palais," specially assigned to him. It was a baroque palace originally
built in 1737 and converted a hundred years later by Von
Schinkel, Prussia's greatest architect, for Prince Karl of Prussia, son
of Friedrich Wilhelm III. During the Weimar Republic it housed the
"press bureau of the Reich government" and belonged to the Ministry of Foreign Affairs. Goebbels left the large reception rooms untouched, but changed the rest of the interior, particularly his own
office, where he ordered the removal of the wooden paneling and the
heavy plush curtains: His ministry was to be light and modern.

The minister called upon a small number of experienced civil
servants, but the greater part of his staff came from the Reich Propaganda Office and the Berlin gau administration. The young minister

surrounded himself with equally young aides. They were full of enterprise and initiative, but had first to be introduced, by civil servants
of the Finance Ministry, to the basic functions of an administrative
apparatus. Goebbels started with a staff of 315, which increased in
the next four years to 1,000. Then work had grown accordingly and
they needed more space. The ministry finally occupied 22 houses that
they owned, and 23 that they rented. Between 1934 and 1941 the
ministry spent 14 million marks on building alone.[47]

The center of Goebbels' realm was his office, roughly three times
the normal size of an ordinary minister's office. He had obviously let
himself be inspired by Hitler's and Mussolini's offices. Here then sat
the little man behind an enormous desk, controlling his vast empire.
On a wall, in a place of honor, hung a portrait of Friedrich II, whom
Goebbels greatly admired. Also truly Prussian was the meticulous
order on his desk. Goebbels would make a note on his writing pad
of every task, to be crossed out only when it was done. He worked
with great concentration. His secretaries had to be changed constantly; none of them could stand the terrific pace of their chief for
long. Unlike Hitler, Goebbels adhered to a most sensible timetable.
He was regarded as a severe chief and knew how to keep his staff to
a strict discipline. On the other hand, he could be generous with
praise and was not resentful by nature.

The ministry was financed by the payments of radio licenses, which
rose from 29 million marks in the year 1934 to 97 million marks
in 1939. Expenditure of the ministry between 1933 and 1943
amounted to 881,541,376 marks. The income during the same period
was 1,308,233,707 marks, of which 1,283,700,000 marks came from
radio licenses alone. The Goebbels ministry was the only one with a
sound financial balance and in a position to put excess capital at
the disposal of the Ministry of Finance.[48] Some decrees and cir-
culars[49] throw light on the spirit prevailing in the ministry. "To pass
letters from one department to another is the typical method of
bureaucrats. I should like to draw your attention to the fact that such
a cumbersome method hardly befits a ministry that has only been
founded a few weeks ago. . . . Every member of the staff should
remind himself of the fact that we are in the middle of a revolution
and can safely leave it to future generations to bureaucracize this
revolution." (May 30, 1933).

"Since I cannot get through the flood of proposals, memoranda,
and exposés, try as I may, I should like to inform chiefs of departments that I cannot in the future accept any documents exceeding
five pages." (July 31, 1933).

"The minister requests that in letters going out from this ministry, words such as 'most obedient,' 'devotedly yours,' etc., should be omitted." (September 29, 1933).

". . . In the future I will not approve, not even in special cases, any expenditure exceeding sums laid down in the budget, or expenditure not originally provided for in the plan. I should like to emphasize that officials and employees shall be held personally responsible for such budgetary excesses." (December 17, 1937).

The ministry consisted of twelve departments. The five most important were: Propaganda, Radio, Press, Films, and Theater. Other departments were: Law, Administration, Budget, and Personnel, as well as the departments of Literature and Music, the Fine Arts, and Foreign Countries. In 1938 the Press Department was split into separate sections dealing with the German press and the foreign press. And in 1944 Goebbels combined the departments of Theater, Literature and Music, and the Fine Arts into the General Cultural Department. During the war new departments were added: the Occupied Eastern Territories, Technique, Armaments, and Building.

Seven departments corresponded to seven professional chambers: Press (Reichspresse), Literature (Reichsschrifttum), Theater (Reichstheater), Music (Reichsmusik), Radio (Reichsrundfunk), Film (Reichsfilmkammer), as well as the Chamber for the Fine Arts (Reichskammer für die Bildende Kunst). All these chambers were part of the Reich Cultural Chamber (Reichskulturkammer), with Goebbels as president. In accordance with the Fuehrer principle, this position gave Goebbels full powers, including legislation, administration, control, and jurisdiction.

The Propaganda Ministry opened propaganda offices in forty-one gaus, which by the law of September 9, 1937, became official state offices (Reich propaganda offices). As state and party were one, these offices were at the same time gau propaganda offices, and, as such, under the authority of the gauleiter in all questions concerning local affairs. By necessity, this led to continuous disagreements between government and party officials. There was nothing Hitler liked better. May his barons continue to fight among themselves for power, leaving him the final say in even the smallest detail.

In addition to a number of theaters in Berlin, the Propaganda Ministry had under its control the Deutsche Theater in Wiesbaden, the German Philharmonic Orchestra, the German College for Politics, the German Congress Hall, the Leipzig Fair Central Bureau, the Office of Tourism, the German Library in Leipzig, the Stock Exchange Association of German Booksellers, the Film Academy, the Economic German Propaganda Council, the Reich Co-operative for the Prevention of Damage, and the Archives of Photos and Records.

The Propaganda Division encompassed an immense variety of activities: mass meetings, exhibitions, conferences, fairs, Winterhilfe, folklore, racial policy, the Jewish question, medical care, economic and commercial publicity, advertising, direction of labor, large sports rallies, German sports abroad, official holidays, inaugurations, launching of ships, and state funerals; also operations aimed at helping "the will of the people" to manifest itself, such as in the boycott of Jewish shops.

The true center of command was the minister's office, consisting of the administrative director, the minister's personal aide, his press officer, and his personal secretary. It was the focal point connecting the different departments, including the liaison to other ministries. The Propaganda Ministry had three state secretaries: the minister's permanent representative, the Reich chief press officer, and the head of German tourism.

Goebbels' first state secretary was Walther Funk, lawyer and son of an architect. He had taken up journalism in 1912, joined the *Berliner Börsenzeitung* (Berlin Stock Exchange Gazette) in 1916, and was appointed editor-in-chief in 1922, remaining in this post until 1930. He joined the NSDAP in 1931 and was appointed economic plenipotentiary to the Fuehrer, chief administrative officer at the party office in Munich, chairman of the Commission for Economic Questions, and vice chairman of the Economic Council of the NSDAP. In 1932 he was elected NSDAP member of the Reichstag. Hitler valued him mostly for his ability to establish liaison between the party and industry.

After the takeover Hitler appointed Funk chief Reich officer of the press. Funk knew the Reich President personally (both were East Prussians), and reported to him daily—a perfect occasion to influence the old man in Hitler's favor. After the foundation of the Reich Propaganda Ministry, Funk became, at Hitler's express wish, Goebbels' state secretary to help Goebbels build up the ministry's administration and organization. Goebbels also made Funk his second in command and vice president of the Reich Cultural Chamber. There was perfect understanding between Funk and his minister. Owing to his past collaboration with Jews at the *Berliner Börsenzeitung,* Funk rather avoided clashing with high party officials. Funk knew many prominent people and had excellent connections with Berlin society. He was short, fat, and ugly, but convivial company, and he knew how to drink hard; in cultural matters he was rather open-minded. He admired his minister, particularly as a "propagandist of genius."[50] In February 1938 Funk took over the Reich Ministry of

Economics; Schacht had resigned in November 1937. At the Nuremberg trial Funk was sentenced to life.

Funk's successor as state secretary in the Propaganda Ministry was Karl Hanke. He came from Silesia and was the son of an engine driver. As a youth, when attending the *Gymnasium,* he had worked in his spare time as engineer in a locomotive workshop and later in a mill factory. Hanke obtained a teacher's diploma in engineering, taught for three years in Berlin, but lost his post because he belonged to the NSDAP, which he had joined in 1928. Goebbels took him on, employing him as local head official before making him his close collaborator, first adjutant, and later head of gau organization. Hanke belonged to the SS.

When Goebbels became minister, he appointed Hanke as his personal adviser, soon afterward as chief of the ministerial office, and, after Funk's departure, as state secretary. Hanke was the only collaborator whom Goebbels trusted blindly. But his trust was to be bitterly betrayed. During Goebbels' marital dispute, Hanke took Magda's part and tried everything to make the minister lose his position and his wife. But when Goebbels' marital difficulties had been cleared up, Hanke joined the Army and was appointed gauleiter of Silesia a year later. His name came up again at the defense of Breslau, where he showed a callous disregard for the survival of its inhabitants and the preservation of its monuments. He intended to defend Breslau to the last inhabitant and leave it in utter ruins to the advancing Russians. When Breslau's mayor, Dr. Spielhagen, warned against this madness, Hanke had him publicly shot in the marketplace in front of the monument of Frederick the Great. Hanke's motto was: "Who refuses to fight honorably must die shamefully."[51] Shortly before Breslau capitulated, Hanke disappeared. Rumor had it that he had tried to escape by helicopter and was killed by the enraged populace.

Hanke's successor was Leopold Gutterer. The minister appointed him state secretary mainly for his ability to organize mass meetings; his rather nondescript personality suited Goebbels at first. Hanke's "treason" had made him more distrustful than ever. But in time Gutterer became too boring for Goebbels, who transferred him to the office of the Association of Film Companies (Fachschaft der Filmgesellschaften—UFI).

It was now Dr. Werner Naumann's turn to become Goebbels' state secretary. He joined the ministry in 1941, and had been wounded at the Russian front, where he had fought as a volunteer with the SS division (SS Leibstandarte) "Adolf Hitler." He quickly rose from Goebbels' personal assistant to the position of chief of the ministerial office. Naumann was clever, energetic, determined, and most hard-working, but he was completely lacking in humor. Goebbels used not only Naumann's efficiency but also his good relationship to Himmler. Naumann occupied a similar position as Hanke before him, but without being made privy of the minister's private life.

Goebbels' secretary for tourism was Hermann Esser, one of Hitler's early fighting companions who, before the takeover, had even addressed Hitler with the intimate *Du*. Goebbels' relationship to him remained impersonal; he had never thought much of him. Esser's position was unimportant and rather a sinecure offered by Hitler to an old cofighter.

Propaganda, as Goebbels saw it, had the task of persuading the German to approve National Socialist actions and effectuate a congruence of views between the people and their leaders. His efforts were most successful.

During the war, at least until the first military setbacks, Hitler personally determined the topics of propaganda and, up to a point, the degree of emphasis he wished to be applied. It was Goebbels' task to execute the Fuehrer's plan. The minister also created slogans, determined tactics, and gave propaganda his own personal note. Funk declared at the Nuremberg trial, "Goebbels' position in the planning and execution of propaganda was so exclusive and total that no one else had a chance to make himself felt."[52]

Was Goebbels' propaganda, then, nothing but a huge factory of lies? Opinions vary. Some say Goebbels only manufactured small lies while the big ones at least were products of his conviction. But Hans Fritzsche, one of Goebbels' most important associates, stated before the Nuremberg tribunal: "According to what I know, it would be wrong to think that the Propaganda Ministry turned out thousands of small lies. Work done there was neat in every detail, disciplined and technically even perfect. Had we actually lied in a thousand little ways, it would have been far easier for the enemy to deal with us effectively."[53]

Fritzsche was right: Lying in detail was not exactly Goebbels' way. He would blow up small events, embellish crimes that had been perpetrated, and would make a point of never correcting any errors once they had occurred. He was, if anything, wary of small lies. He never used them to invent fictitious successes. If worse came to worst, he would use them as a means of defense. Yet, even then, he would avoid employing the propaganda apparatus and would use other channels to set them abroad.

Goebbels' realm was the big fundamental lie. He talked of the integrity of the government, knowing it was corrupt. He spoke of

victory when defeat had become inevitable. Goebbels' propaganda
had no ideological basis; therein lay its strength and its weakness.
One of Goebbels' aides, Moritz August von Schirrmeister, declared
in Nuremberg: "You should know that Goebbels had no time whatever for dogma and the party myth. They are not the kind of thing
you can catch the masses with. For him the party was the great gathering point, where the German people, converging from all directions, should come together. And he particularly mocked at the
Herrenvolk idea—perhaps as a result of his own physical deformation;
he flatly rejected it.

"Hate propaganda against other peoples was absolutely opposed
to Dr. Goebbels' propaganda line, as he was hoping—and he stuck
to this hope like to a fata morgana right to the end—that one day he
might effect an about-face from "against England" and "against
America" to "with England" and "with America"; and to do that you
could not employ hatred against any nation. Goebbels wanted to go
together with other nations, not against them. His propaganda attacked first and foremost systems, starting with plutocracy—it was he
who made this term into what it means today. Later he took on
Bolshevism; then individual people with governmental responsibilities. 'Gentlemen,' he once said, 'if I could replace you by ten Jews
they would get things done all right.'

"The minister had no use whatever for employing passions in his
propaganda . . . what he needed was a firm, consistent line. . . .
Perseverance in hard times. Trying to whip up hatred or arouse
murderous passions would hardly have found much response among
the German people; and it was not what Goebbels really desired."[54]

Schirrmeister no doubt dealt too kindly with his chief, but his
summing-up of Goebbels' propaganda maxims was fairly correct,
with one exception: his hate campaign against the Jews. Nor should
it be forgotten that when attacking systems, Goebbels also aimed at
their representatives, and when talking of the destruction of
Bolshevism, he most certainly included murder. He was not in the
least interested whether propaganda pursued good or evil. He himself
called his propaganda "influencing the masses," and carried it out
unscrupulously. He was not at all concerned with the quality of his
aims, but solely with their success. During the fighting era when
power was still in the hands of the enemy, his propaganda possessed
the fire of aggression; after the takeover, it lost its panache. When
war came, he regained it again, but then events proved in the end
stronger than any propaganda.

Goebbels' propaganda technique was supreme. No political
propagandist before him had been so fertile in inventing catch phrases

and slogans. No one understood as well as he the mood and temper of the people. Taking the Catholic Church as a model, he drew up a National Socialist calendar. The year started with January 30, "the day of the seizure of power." On February 21, the foundation of the party was celebrated with Sunday Reminiscere, the Day of Remembrance of Heroes. In March he initiated a hero cult. On April 20, all Germany feted the Fuehrer's birthday. May 1, once the Workers' Day, now became the Day of the People's Unity; it was one of the most important official state holidays in Goebbels' calendar. In June, Midsummer's Day was celebrated. But the climax of the National Socialist year was the Nuremberg Reich party rally, which took place in September. It lasted, like the most important Catholic feast, Easter, a full eight days. In the beginning of October was Harvest Thanksgiving Day, the farmers' equivalent of the Workers' Day of May 1. On the Bückeberg near Hameln over a million people would gather, just as in September in Nuremberg, or in Berlin on May 1.

November 9 was Remembrance Day of the march to the Feldherrnhalle in 1923. Goebbels made this ceremony into the most solemn and the most dedicated of all. It featured a Ceremony of Resurrection and "The Last Post," a cocktail of all good things such as mysticism, religious rites, solemn dedication, the hero cult, and the national faith in sacrifice and immortality. Only Christmas, which the clique around Rosenberg and Himmler's SS intended to transform into the Germanic Feast of Light, Goebbels would leave untouched, helping to preserve its pure Christian character.

By the national socialist year-cycle of feasts Goebbels sought to anchor the National Socialist regime more and more firmly in the people's consciousness and identify it more and more with the life of the nation. Each festivity had its own rites and sumptuous production. There was so much to be seen, both solemn and amusing, colorful and somber; there were rapture and devotion, feasts under the blazing sun (Hitler weather), and feasts at night when "domes of light" would create the mystical atmosphere of dedication.

Such festive occasions in which millions of people participated did not fail to have their effect. They were among Goebbels' most successful propagandistic weapons. He would transform everything, including funerals, into a festivity. They were interspersed (as in the Catholic liturgy) with days of contemplation and sacrifice. The Goebbels collections, particularly the one for winter aid, were days of introspection and manifestation of the unity of the people, when no one was forgotten, not even the poorest.

And just as the Church had, besides its fixed cycle of feast days special festivities from time to time, so would Goebbels take great state visits and special events like the Olympic Games and Hitler's victories as occasions of special celebration. One of the highpoints was the visit of Mussolini in September 1937. The organization of the festive arrangements around the Olympic Games in Berlin in 1936 earned the admiration of foreign visitors and Germans alike. Berlin theaters played the best plays with their best casts. The cinemas screened the best films. Social events and receptions were the order of the day. The foremost metropolis of the Reich seemed a city filled with happiness and a sparkling *joie de vivre*. No propaganda chief had ever before succeeded in mounting such a magnificent show of deception, or in building such perfect "Potemkin villages."

The war put an end to Goebbels' attempt to wield the Germans by means of propaganda into one united mass and leave them without any individuality of their own. Unity came at first through the unbelievable victories, and later through the equally inconceivable misery. It cannot be denied that Goebbels proved himself an even greater propagandist in times of need, though reality made his propaganda appear more and more unreal, until in the end it was revealed as nothing but a mirage. All that was left was a desert—a devastated land, devastated souls.

Broadcasting

Goebbels considered the radio to be the most important instrument of his ministry, and he was able to secure Hitler's full agreement in this area. This in turn helped Goebbels to repel attacks from outside, including Goering's. No less than fifty Hitler speeches were broadcast in the first year and obviously made a great impact. This gave Goebbels exclusive control of the whole radio network accorded him by the Fuehrer. Division 3 of the Ministry, which was the guiding agency for all questions concerning broadcasting, was the most important, and was under Goebbels' strictest supervision. He knew he had in broadcasting the most modern instrument of propaganda. It was a far more effective means than the press to make the German people think and aspire alike, which remained Goebbels' cardinal aim.

"Broadcasting is no longer the instrument of Cabinet ministers; it is a means for putting National Socialist aims before the people . . . broadcasting may be the most important means of influencing the masses. And if we succeed in imbuing it with a modern spirit, in giving it a modern tempo, a modern impulse, we will be able to apply ourselves to the many tasks waiting to be fulfilled in National Socialist Germany."[55]

Goebbels, paraphrasing Napoleon, who had called the press the seventh great power, named broadcasting the eighth. Broadcasting lent itself to a more unified and forceful direction than the press. Here he could use revolutionary propaganda methods combined with a simplicity and clarity of language which, in his view, were essential to get at the people.

Goebbels tried to lighten radio programs and avoid encumbering them with National Socialist ideology. Exceptions were Hitler's and his own speeches. Broadcasting, he declared, should serve "to lighten the daily round. . . . No one could go around continuously wearing his Sunday best. Broadcasting, product of its time, must go with the times, and has to be up-to-date and modern."[56]

He changed broadcasting policy fundamentally. Before the take-over, the programs had been structured according to an encyclopedic concept that offered a news service, a political commentary, and a cultural and philosophical view as varied and as comprehensive as possible, assuring every listener a free choice. From now on the programs dropped the individual and cosmopolitan approach and were exclusively orientated toward German unity and nationalism. By race every German belonged to this unified community, with its common history and fate. All great common festivities, important manifestations, and the feasts of the National Socialist year cycle were presented over the air.

At the same time, when drawing up the programs Goebbels took the taste of the public more and more into account every year. The first year was culturally orientated, producing broadcasts of whole cycles of serious music and poetry. In the years to follow it became increasingly relaxed. In 1936 the minister declared: "The program must be drawn up in a way to interest the most demanding listener as well as be accessible and pleasing to the least demanding. It should offer in a clever and psychologically astute mixture, education, stimulation, relaxation, and amusement. . . ." In the middle of the war, in 1941, Goebbels ordered "Action Jollity" and directed his collaborators to draw up a "program for a positive attitude to life."

From the outset Goebbels used broadcasting to conquer the German people. Accordingly, soon after he was appointed minister, he ordered, "in remembrance of the rising of the people on January 30, 1933," the manufacture of a type of radio that everybody could afford. Chief Engineer Otto Griesing designed the receiver Volksempfänger VE 301, costing, aerial included, 76 marks. The enterprise soon proved a spectacular success. A year after the takeover the number of listeners had risen by one million; with a monthly payment of 2 marks for the license, takings increased by 24 million marks. The number of listeners rose every year.

Goebbels had obviously changed his opinion about broadcasting since he had first started in politics. He had written in his diary on December 14, 1925: "Radio in the house! At his radio set the German forgets his work and his fatherland! Radio! The modern means of bourgeoisification of the nation!" But by the end of the twenties he became aware of the propagandistic potential of broadcasting. Already in the fighting era he founded the Radio Division of the Reich propaganda office. The Chief of the Berlin Radio Division was Eugen Hadamovsky. Goebbels appointed Hadamovsky director of the Deutschlandsender in March, and in July of the same year, chief of broadcasting and director of the Reich Radio Company.

Hadamovsky was not quite thirty when he took up his new post. After graduation Hadamovsky had studied at the Technical Academy and the Political Academy in Berlin for a few semesters. Unable to find work, he traveled, visiting Austria, Italy, North Africa, and Spain, earning his living as auto mechanic and locksmith. In 1928 Hadamovsky returned to Berlin, joined the NSDAP, and in 1931 was appointed by Goebbels chief of the Radio Division, Berlin, and the head of the Radio Division in the Reich propaganda headquarters.

Hadamovsky was equally proficient in theory and in practice. He furthered technical research and was actually able to announce on March 22, 1935, in a telegram to Hitler, the start of the world's first regular television service (Berlin Witzleben).

It was perhaps just as well that the development of television did not continue at the same pace, thus sparing the world having the television era be inaugurated by Hitler's personal appearance on the small screen.

Daily radio broadcasts to foreign countries increased from two hours in 1933 to fifty-eight hours in 1939. In 1943 the news service comprised broadcasts in fifty-three different languages.

During his twelve-year reign, Goebbels changed the chief of the Radio Division five times, the last being Hans Fritzsche. Appointed in November 1942, Fritzsche held this post right to the end. Goebbels had a great regard for Fritzsche, particularly for his technical acumen. Fritzsche, born in 1900, had studied philosophy and economy. In the mid-1920s he had worked as a journalist for the Hugenberg Press, and was appointed Chief of the "Wireless Service" by Papen in September 1932. His political commentaries were an instant success. After the takeover Goebbels left Fritzsche in his post despite the fact that Fritzsche had once published an article criticizing Hitler.

Goebbels even added to Fritzsche's responsibilities, placing under him several smaller news agencies. And after the fusion of the two most important German news agencies, the Wolff Telegraph Bureau (Wolffsche Telegrafenbüro—WTB) and the Hugenberg Telegraph Union (Hugenbergsche Telegrafen-Union—TU), into the German News Agency (Deutsches Nachrichtenbüro—DNB), this, too, was placed under Fritzsche's authority. In 1938 Fritzsche became chief of the Department "German Press," rising from ministerial councilor to ministerial chief and finally, in 1942, to ministerial director. In summer 1939 he founded a special division within his Department, "Rapid Service" (Schnelldienst), which saw to it that editors were supplied with press material with the least delay. When war started Fritzsche broadcast regularly the "Political Press and Radio Review," later renamed "Hans Fritzsche Speaking." Fritzsche, commonly known as "His Master's Voice," became, next to Goebbels, the most popular member of the Propaganda Ministry.

Fritzsche took exception to the methods of Dr. Dietrich, the Reich press chief, in embellishing press policy and volunteered, in spring 1942, for the Russian front; but Goebbels recalled him in the autumn of the same year, appointed him chief of the ministry's Radio Division, and made him responsible for the political line of the entire radio network.

At the Nuremberg trial several witnesses confirmed that Fritzsche had always pleaded for greater press freedom and had, in fact, protected the *Frankfurter Zeitung* for several years by preventing dubious issues from being sent to Hitler's headquarters. Fritzsche was acquitted at Nuremberg—somewhat surprisingly, considering that he had been responsible for the political line of all radio broadcasts since 1942. Broadcasting, which was entirely in the hands of Goebbels, had been more successful than the German press. Broadcasting kept close contact with the people and offered, at least in part, what Goebbels had vainly tried to achieve within the press: many different voices that gave a semblance of divergence while belonging to one and the same choir that sang the same tune.

The Press

From the outset Goebbels established his unquestioned control in the field of broadcasting. But he had to fight for twelve years to obtain complete control of the press, which he was only able to establish shortly before the collapse of the Third Reich. His competitors in this field were Reich press chief Dr. Otto Dietrich and Reichsleiter Max Amann.

The reason for all difficulties that bedeviled National Socialist press policy was Hitler's personal attitude. He diligently read a number of German newspapers, as well as German translations of the most important foreign news reports every day, but nothing could change his deep-down enmity to the press as such. His main argument was that many men of genius had been suppressed in their lifetimes by an adverse press. Nor could he easily forget that the press had attacked him—yet another man of genius—and his movement with particular severity and hatred during the fighting era. And yet these reasons hardly appear sufficient to explain Hitler's profound antagonism to the press. He saw in it essentially a product of liberalism and the individualist concept—sufficient reason to despise it from the bottom of his heart. A press without freedom of opinion was bound to be a caricature. But freedom of opinion was something Hitler feared and rejected.

It was not so much due to Hitler's favorite policy of *divide et impera* that he divided responsibility among three men instead of giving it to one, as to his inner attitude toward the press, with the result that none of the three dared to arouse Hitler's wrath by showing tolerance to the newspapers.

Goebbels, Dietrich, and Amann among them were responsible for all measures concerning the press. The result of their action was a veritable press cemetery. Goebbels wished to maintain a great number and variety of newspapers. He would have nothing to do with Amann's personal press racket; he was rather hoping that a great number of papers would give a great variety of orchestral color. Yet it was he who initiated the first measure that inevitably led to the disappearance of any such variety. In order to make the editor, called in the Third Reich *Redakteur,* independent of the publisher, and get him more closely under the control of the Propaganda Ministry, Goebbels instigated the "law governing editors" (*Schriftleitergesetz*) on October 4, 1933. This law removed the publisher's influence on the editorial line and gave the editor-in-chief the status of a public official. From now on the editor-in-chief was to fulfill an "official task controlled by the state" and pursue an "activity similar to that of a civil servant closely attached to the state." He was obliged to adhere to the Reich Association of the German Press (Reichsverband der deutschen Presse) and never publish anything contrary to the interest of the nation. The Department German Press (Abteilung deutsche Presse) of the Propaganda Ministry had the task of controlling the German press and laying down policy.

The immediate consequence of this new law was that the journalists preferred to adopt the formulation of the Propaganda Ministry rather than use their own brains and risk arousing Goebbels' or Dietrich's anger and possibly have their professional licenses withdrawn.

In July 1933 Goebbels instituted a daily secret staff conference attended by heads of the ministry's departments, liaison officers to the supreme Reich authorities, and occasionally by a special adviser. At these meetings Goebbels would lay down policy for the daily output of news and propaganda. If the minister was unable to attend he was replaced by the state secretary or by the head of the Press Department, whose functions, however, were limited to passing on the directives Goebbels had communicated by telephone. Goebbels released these daily editorial directives, which were transmitted to the newspaper editors via the regional Reich propaganda offices. These staff meetings were followed by the official press conference for the Berlin press and foreign correspondents. They were presided over by Reichsleiter Dr. Otto Dietrich. Dietrich had been Reich press chief of the NSDAP before the takeover, with his own staff led by Chief of Staff Sündermann. Dietrich dealt with every professional question concerning all editors of the party press. On January 15, 1938, Dietrich replaced Walter Funk as press chief of the Reich government. Dietrich was at the same time appointed state secretary in the Propaganda Ministry. Goebbels, though he tried to oppose this move, had to give in, since his position had been much weakened by his affair with Baarova.[57]

But in Max Amann, Goebbels had an even more dangerous rival than Dietrich. Amann had been Hitler's sergeant major in the First World War and had been commissioned in 1918. Hitler persuaded him to take over party administration. Later, Amann became director of the main publishing house of the NSDAP, Franz Eher Nachfolger GmbH Munich. They published the *Völkische Beobachter* and all other party material, including pamphlets and books. Their most important authors were Hitler and Goebbels. Later on Hitler let Amann administer also his personal fortune, consisting mainly of royalties from *Mein Kampf,* which after the takeover grew into millions.

After Hitler's victory, Amann was made general director. As Reichsleiter for the press of the NSDAP, he was head of one of Germany's biggest trusts. Amann, far from being spiritual, was a man of ruthless brutality. He knew better than anyone else how to get rich, but little about journalism and the press. To fill that gap he engaged Rolf Reinhart as chief of staff. Reinhart came from a Saxon rector's family. He had studied law in Munich and started his career as a young solicitor attached to the party publishers. He belonged to the Gregor Strasser wing. But Amann, who found Reinhart indispensable, stood surety for him. Reinhart wrote Amann's articles and speeches and conducted the most important negotiations. Reinhart was a fanatical worker and superb tactician, an astute negotiator and an outstanding organizer.

In 1932, there were 4,703 newspapers published in Germany. Of these, 120 belonged to the NSDAP. By 1938 the "Press Group" Amann-Reinhart—the word "trust" was looked down upon—had taken over 2,383 privately owned publications, more than half the total. War brought them further appropriations. While in 1940 the private press still possessed as much as 33 per cent of all press publications, their share had dwindled to 17.5 per cent by the end of 1944. At that time 625 private newspapers had a combined circulation of 4,391,000 copies. The NSDAP newspapers, although there were not more than 352 of them, had a circulation of 20,694,000 copies, or 82.5 per cent of the total.[58]

This process of quiet liquidation and Nazification of the private press had been facilitated by the law banning all parties except the NSDAP. The press of the SPD and of the KPD were prohibited, and all their properties and printing presses were confiscated. This enhanced and enriched the NSDAP press. Goebbels founded the Reich Press Chamber and appointed Amann as president. Goebbels promulgated his first ordinance on November 1, 1933; it gave Amann the right to expel private publishers for having failed to reach the "necessary standard of ability and trustworthiness." This was the beginning of the great wave of Aryanization that swept over the Jewish-owned newspapers. Both publisher and editor had to prove their Aryan descent going back as far as the year 1800. Everyone who had anything to do with production and duplication, with the spiritual and technical process, as well as with the distribution of newspapers was obliged to be a member of the Chamber.

On April 24, 1935, Amann, in his capacity as president of the Reich Press Chamber, ordered "the closing down of newspapers in order to avoid 'unhealthy competition.' " All newspapers were included that were joint stock companies, co-operative societies, or foundations. This measure aimed at eliminating anonymous capital and consequently the influence of industry, big landowners, and the churches. It also banned newspaper publishers whose publications represented professional, corporate, or religious interests. They were no longer permitted to publish a daily paper. Prohibited also was the founding of newspaper trusts. No publisher, without special permission, was allowed to have an interest in more than one newspaper.

Reinhart coined for Amann's new decree the slogan "Aryanization, decommercialization, desubsidizing, deconfessionalizing, and decentralizing."[59]

None of these regulations applied to the Central Publishing House of the NSDAP and its subsidiaries, particularly the Deutsche Verlag (German Publishing House), which undertook the Aryanization of Ullstein and Mosse, and published, among other newspapers, *Das Reich* and *Die Deutsche Allgemeine Zeitung*. These two publishing houses, the party publishers Zentral Verlag and the Deutsche Verlag combined, were the biggest publishing enterprise in Europe. Their yearly income was approximately 700 million marks. Amann thus became one of the most powerful men within the party organization. His position enabled him to put important party members under a personal obligation to him through channeling special funds into their pockets.[60]

The division of power among three men had the effect that the press practically was gagged three times over. But even if Goebbels had been solely in charge—though this might have avoided the kind of personal pillaging Amann and Reinhart indulged in—it still would never have resulted in a free, or even partly free press. No dictatorship can afford a free press. Lenin, too, had promised to reinstate freedom of the press as soon as possible, calling the suppression of press freedom a "temporary measure." Yet after fifty years of Bolshevism a free press in the Soviet Union is still to come.

The journalist Goebbels might have known better, but the minister Goebbels had no real contact with journalists, particularly with foreign correspondents. He ignored them at first, and when he later tried to curry favor with them and failed, he simply expelled those who were particularly irksome to him. The first victim was Dorothy Thompson, wife of Nobel Prize winner Sinclair Lewis. Her expulsion in 1933 made her world famous. Goebbels recorded his opinion about her in his diary on April 5, 1932: "Dorothy Thompson made a completely demented speech against Hitler. It is shameful and insufferable that such a silly woman with a brain of straw should have the right to raise her voice in public against a man of such historical greatness as the Fuehrer."

What had become of Goebbels? The one-time merciless critic of the Weimar Republic was now the idolizing worshiper of Hitler's power politics. He had voluntarily foregone his freedom, and therefore hated all who loved freedom and were prepared to defend it.

4

From Reich Minister
to Reich Chancellor

The Minister

There was a strange ambiguity about Propaganda Minister Goebbels. In every field he displayed a mixture of ostensible liberalism and ruthless exertion of power. This dualism introduced into Germany's political life a great measure of uncertainty. Nobody quite knew where he stood. Goebbels had become but a replica of his master, whose complex personality was subject to constant changes.

Goebbels actually needed enemies to thrive on. But as the Third Reich had suppressed its enemies by terror, all that was left for Goebbels to do was to "obliterate them." But his campaigns brought him little luck. His early fight against the Communists with but a few hundred men was impressive; but now he attacked those who were weaker or, like the Jews, completely defenseless. Goebbels had become the spiritual henchman of terror.

As early as March 24, 1933, he wrote in his diary: "The horror propaganda abroad is becoming a problem. The many Jews who emigrated from Germany whip up hatred against us. We are defenseless against these attacks." In Goebbels' view a show of strength was required. They should be taught a lesson. He proposed a boycott against Jewish enterprises throughout the Reich. Hitler readily agreed.

In his note dated March 29, Goebbels stated that the appeal to boycott Jewish enterprises was passed unanimously by the entire Reich government; this was denied by Schacht and Papen at the

Nuremberg trial. They even claimed that they raised important reservations—particularly on economic grounds. There were still over five million unemployed in Germany at that time. This is borne out by the fact that the boycott, originally planned to last several days, was limited to one single day, April 1. On this day the Jewish shops were closed. Each shop window was covered with anti-Semitic slogans and marked with the Star of David. Every shop was picketed by SA men. Goebbels could report that thanks to the boycott the foreign horror propaganda had "diminished perceptively."[1] This surely happened out of consideration for the Jewish victims mercilessly exposed to Nazi terror. But the mere fact of the boycott showed how far the German government—and it consisted mainly of non-National Socialist ministers—was prepared to go.

Even the limited success of this action convinced Goebbels and Hitler that shock tactics were the best methods to impose their will on other countries. As time went on Goebbels became a master of these shock tactics, and employed them more and more frequently.

After the boycott, Goebbels turned his attention to a completely different enterprise: May Day. May 1, 1933, was going to be made into a great festive occasion for the people. It was Goebbels' influence that induced the government to declare May 1 an official holiday.[2]

The festivities surpassed everything Goebbels had undertaken hitherto. Hundreds of thousands of children gathered in the Berlin Lustgarten and Unter den Linden to render homage to the Reich President and the Reich Chancellor. In the evening, according to plan, factory workers and members of the party formations arrived at the Tempelhoferfeld. The crowd, including a large number of bystanders, had grown to over a million. Goebbels had also arranged for workers' delegations to be flown in from all over the Reich.

Goebbels opened proceedings, and Hitler delivered the festive speech. May Day demonstrations took place simultaneously throughout the Reich. The proceedings in Berlin and Hitler's speech were broadcast by loudspeakers. Proudly Goebbels recorded in his diary:

"A wave of boundless enthusiasm has swept over the people. Devoutly and powerfully the sounds of the Horst Wessel song rise into the eternal evening sky. The ether carries the voices of 1½ million people who stand together here in Berlin on the Tempelhoferfeld across the whole of Germany, into towns and villages, and everywhere they fall in . . . the workers in the Ruhr, the sailors in the harbors of Hamburg, the lumberjacks in Upper Bavaria, and the lonely peasant up in the Masurian lakes. No one can remain outside; we

belong together all of us, and it is no longer an empty phrase to say
we have become a people of brothers!" (May 1, 1933).

After this hymn extolling a united people of brothers, Goebbels
wrote in his diary the same day: "We shall occupy tomorrow the
trade union headquarters. We expect no resistance. The fight continues."

Perhaps the most terrifying aspect of all this is that Goebbels himself apparently failed to realize the cynical contradiction implicit in
the two actions. He seemed to find it quite natural that on May 1,
Hitler extolled the workers as a pillar of the nation, only to give orders on May 2 to occupy their union headquarters and seize their
funds.

Yet Goebbels did not give up trying to win over the workers.
On Christmas Eve 1933 Goebbels had an enormous Christmas
tree put up in the Berlin workers' district of Wedding. Tables piled
high with presents were waiting for the guests, thousands of former
political adversaries belonging to the left. He also persuaded Hitler
to pardon a few hundred Communists, who were immediately released from prison. The surprise of their families was as great as
their joy. They felt that their gauleiter's heart was, after all, with the
workers.[3]

Not less contradictory was Goebbels' performance abroad. He
had been sent to Geneva as special German plenipotentiary in place
of the Foreign Secretary, Konstantin von Neurath, to take part in
the plenary session of the League of Nations on September 25, 1933.

It was Goebbels' first trip abroad apart from his visits to Austria
and the Sudetenland, and his first appearance at an international
gathering. "We must pull ourselves together," he told his entourage.
"Nothing would suit those gentlemen at our Foreign Office better
than if one of us made a gaffe. I expect iron discipline from my
collaborators. We are here as soldiers facing the enemy."[4]

His attitude was typical. The League of Nations, to which, after
all, Germany still belonged, was "the enemy." But before his Geneva
audience he played the gentleman. He wore a "Stresemann" hat
and gloves. He adopted the Geneva jargon and, despite the initial
hostility of two hundred foreign correspondents, obtained a personal
success at a press conference he gave on September 28 at the Hotel
Carlton. He began by complaining about the suspicion of the new
Germany prevailing abroad. He took the bull by the horns and referred to the Jewish question: "I will not pretend that certain excesses perpetrated by uncontrollable elements have not taken place
during the national revolution in Germany. But we fail to understand

why foreign countries will not accept the overflow of German-Jewish emigrants."[5]

He invited the journalists to visit the concentration camps in Germany in which "the most humane and most proper methods are used." Germany was prepared, he solemnly affirmed, to make peace in Europe secure. Most of the correspondents applauded warmly. Goebbels knew he had won the day, and, naturally, he was immensely pleased: "This is the greatest success of my life,"[6] he said to his aide.

At the beginning of his ministerial career, Goebbels set great store on his good name abroad. He considered himself to be a born diplomat. His success in Geneva only confirmed him in this assumption. Alas, his promises concerning peace were not followed up by deeds. Only sixteen days later, on October 14, 1933, Germany left the League of Nations. Goebbels organized Reichstag elections to take place on November 12, and took Germany's departure from the League of Nations as the central theme of his campaign. At the elections the National Socialists, the only party permitted to put up candidates, obtained almost 100 per cent, as is usual in elections in dictatorially governed states.

More astonishing, however, is to what extent this man could fascinate foreigners too. On June 12, 1934, he gave a lecture at the "Union of Intellectuals" in Warsaw. The theme he had chosen was "National Socialist Germany: A factor in European peace." Talking about the National Socialist state, Goebbels said: "Germany's modern structure is a kind of purified democracy in which, owing to the mandate, the people reign in an authoritarian way, thereby excluding any possibility of falsifying and frustrating the will of the people by the process of parliamentary procedure."[7]

He furthermore stated that class war had disappeared and that a "heroic attitude to life" has supplanted the former "tired lassitude." Addressing Polish intellectuals, Goebbels strained to show how deeply concerned modern Germany was with its own intellectuals. National Socialism demanded of her intellectual workers, no less than of the man in the street, to recognize "the eternal laws of national existence"; but he, Goebbels, had no intention whatever of putting intellectuals under a "party tutelage," since this would impose upon them "coercive laws bound to suffocate creative genius sooner or later."

On the one hand, Goebbels talks of "the eternal laws of national existence" to which the intellectual worker (Goebbels never used the word "intellectual" in a positive sense, but supplanted it by "intellectual worker"), has to submit, but declares at the same time that he will not impose upon them any "coercive laws." What then were the limits of "the eternal laws of national existence"? National Socialism had extended those laws over the whole life of the nation, imposing upon it innumerable coercive laws, leaving only the smallest margin for the freedom of creation.

Goebbels finished his lecture with words that must have sounded sweet to a Polish audience anxious about its borders with Germany. These words, no doubt, came from Goebbels' conviction and testify to his antiwar spirit:

"We young Germans are deeply convinced that there is no problem in Europe that need lead to war. We are not a generation of saber-rattling conquerors, and consider it criminal to believe that the damage the last war caused, which could not be made good by a peace effort now lasting fifteen years, could be repaired by a new war."

Of course, this was the time of the progressive Nazification of Germany, which was still militarily weak. What Hitler, therefore, needed was peace and a suitably peaceful foreign policy. The word "peace" occurred at that time in practically every Hitler speech, most emphatically in the "peace speech" he held on May 18, 1933, in the Reichstag, in which he took up and supported Roosevelt's proposal to abolish all aggressive arms. Goebbels brought to Poland only the confirmation of what Hitler had initiated by concluding a nonagression pact between Germany and Poland on January 26, 1934. It is doubtful whether Goebbels would have taken a different political line even if he had visited democratic foreign countries. (Poland and Italy were not democratically ruled, and Switzerland was the only democratic country he knew. He had to refuse an invitation to the Century of Progress Exposition in Chicago on Hitler's orders.)

Apart from his campaign against the Jews, Goebbels' fight was conducted on three fronts: against the intellectuals, the conservatives (despite the fact that their representatives were still in the Cabinet), and the Catholic Church. He called the fight "elucidation campaign against denigrators and destructive critics." He organized two thousand meetings during this campaign. When the conservative ministers in the Cabinet, particularly Papen, rightly felt that they were attacked by Goebbels' tirades of hate against the "exclusive gentlemen in their club armchairs," and tried to hit back in public, the Propaganda Minister simply banned the publication of their speeches, as, for instance, Papen's lecture given on June 17, 1934, at the University Association in Marburg-an-der-Lahn. Aiming at Goebbels personally, Papen said: "Only weak men will not tolerate criticism. . . . You cannot manufacture great men by means of propaganda. . . .

No organization, no propaganda, even the best, can command trust forever. . . . The time has come to make fanatics shut up."[8]

Papen complained to Hitler on June 20: "It is insufferable that the Vice Chancellor of your government is gagged." Hitler's answer was a lie pure and simple. "This was an unfortunate action of the Propaganda Minister, I will ask him to lift the ban."[9] Papen only realized that Hitler himself was the instigator of this ban when Hindenburg informed him that the Reich Chancellor had asked State Secretary Funk to inform the Reich President that Papen had openly come out against the policy of the Cabinet and against Hitler, and should therefore be dismissed.

The campaign against the "denigrators and destructive critics" did not originate with Goebbels. But as soon as he had orders from Hitler to act, Goebbels once again overexecuted the Fuehrer's orders. He worked himself up into a pretended indignation, as though all over Germany lemurs had suddenly appeared from nowhere to undermine Hitler's great work of reconstruction.

Another, more effective attempt to hit back at Goebbels was made by the president of the Reichsbank, Hjalmar Schacht, in his speech on August 18, 1934, in Königsberg, which was also forbidden to appear in the press. Schacht did not mince words: "Nobody in Germany is outlawed. According to Point 4 of the National Socialist program, the Jew can neither be a German citizen nor does he belong to the German people, yet Point 3 of the party program includes legislation for the Jews, which means that they should not be subject to arbitrary rule but to the law."[10]

This view, which Goebbels shared, at least at the time, hardly fitted into Hitler's concept. Goebbels had the speech broadcast by the Deutschlandsender for listeners abroad, but forbade the newspapers to print it or even quote from it. But Schacht knew how to help himself. He had 250,000 copies rolled off by the printing press of the Reichsbank, all of which were sold quickly.

The radical tenor of Goebbels' campaign was also meant to humor Roehm and the SA, who saw themselves cheated of their revolution. Roehm coined the phrase "the second revolution," and the word "revolution" was enough to set Goebbels alight with enthusiasm. On April 18, 1934, he jotted down: "Everywhere the people talk of a second revolution that is bound to come. This means that the first revolution is not finished yet. Soon we shall have to deal with the revolutionary forces. The revolution must not halt before anything or anybody."

Roehm and Hitler differed fundamentally on the future of the SA. Roehm wanted the SA to become a part of the Reichswehr, as

Schleicher before him, but not in order to see it absorbed, as
Schleicher was hoping it would be, but to create the nucleus of a
revolutionary people's army. Hitler was, in principle, opposed to this
plan, seeing the SA as but a political fighting force that had done its
job, and for which he no longer had any use. Its very existence—
there were over two million—constituted a danger to his policy. What
he needed now for his vast plans at home and abroad, was the un-
qualified support of the Reichswehr. A confrontation between Hitler
and Roehm had become inevitable.

Goebbels' attitude on Roehm is once again hard to ascertain.
Strasser's followers say that Goebbels met with Roehm at the Munich
tavern Bratwurstglöckl. Others say that Goebbels had raised an alarm
on June 29, 1934, and warned that an SA rebellion was imminent.
He had telephoned Goering and Himmler on June 30, and had given
them the signal to strike.

It seems rather unlikely that Goebbels took an active part in this
murderous conspiracy. Rosenberg's version seems to be closer to the
truth: that Goebbels was only informed of what was happening on
Friday, June 29, and was told to stay where he was; but he had
asked specially to be taken along.[11]

Accompanied by his SS guard, Hitler and his entourage went on
June 30 to Bad Wiessee, straight to the Hotel Hanselbauer, where
Roehm was staying. Roehm's assassination set off a whole succession
of murders. Hitler had on this day arrogated for himself the position of supreme judge, synonymous with supreme assassin.

Hindenburg backed his Chancellor in his role as murderer. And
the whole conservative right wing went along with the Reich President, including the generals (despite the fact that one of them, General Schleicher, had also been a victim of the night of slaughter).
They all thought that Roehm's death and the destruction of the SA
would be the end of the party's left wing, and of radical National
Socialism. They obviously did not realize that radicalism—when compared with organized terror, helped by a suitably vociferous propaganda—was the lesser of two evils.

On August 2, 1934, Hindenburg died. The "father façade figure,"
as he was later called, with little respect, was no more. Yet it would
be an error to saddle him with the guilt for Hitler's rise. When, a
year before his death, he had made Hitler Reich Chancellor, Hindenburg was eighty-six years old and, as many testified, not any longer
in full possession of his faculties. Bruening, the parties of the center,
and the Social Democrats, had persuaded him to stand once more as
a candidate for the Reich presidency, although they knew that his
faculties were greatly diminished. Nevertheless, even when a dying

14. Goebbels speaking to the Senate of Culture, officially established in ceremonies at the Philharmonic in Berlin. November 15, 1935.

15. A meeting held by Goebbels for the diplomatic officials in Berlin. Left to right: Monsignor Oresnigo, Goebbels, and William Dodd, the American ambassador. March 14, 1934.

16. Hitler, Goebbels, and Vice Chancellor Rudolf Hess acknowledging crowd in front of the Chancellery in Berlin, when it was announced that the government had ordered general military conscription. March 27, 1935.

17. Goebbels collecting funds on a Berlin street corner. December 18, 1935.

man, he was still the only one who would put a brake on Hitler's ambitions. With his death, all resistance to Hitler collapsed. A mere three hours after Hindenburg's death, Goebbels broadcast the new decree that merged the two offices of Reich President and Reich Chancellor into one. On the same day Hitler made all officers and others in the ranks take the oath of allegiance to his person. The generals gave no sign of resistance.

The death of Hindenburg contributed to laying the foundations of the Hitler era in Germany. What had been a myth hitherto, now became reality. From then on Goebbels was no longer quite as important to Hitler as he had been before.

The events of June 30 had also taught Goebbels that playing with revolutionary ideas was a most dangerous game ending with the loser's death. A wise man would stop playing before it was too late. Goebbels made his decision. Henceforth he would simply carry out his master orders, regardless of whether he was asked to play the sweet tunes of peace or blow the harsh trumpet calls of war.

Goebbels' Fight Against the Catholic Church

Goebbels' combative attitude toward the Catholic Church was perhaps not as clearly defined as that toward the Jews, but it reveals even more clearly his split state of mind. Although he had turned away from the Catholic faith when he was a student, he, like Hitler, never formally seceded from the Church. (He had to continue paying the Church tax, much to his chagrin, although he had been excommunicated after marrying a divorced woman.) Whether Goebbels' attitude was motivated by political or private considerations—he might have thought of his pious mother—remains unclear. Although both Hitler and Goebbels had a similar approach toward Christianity, Hitler would deride Christianity in his private conversations while remaining discreet in his public pronouncements; Goebbels, on the other hand, would extoll Christianity and the Catholic Church when talking to his intimates, but would attack the Catholic Church in public with almost hysterical ferocity, particularly between the years 1934 and 1937.

Yet in his first speech in the Reichstag, on March 23, 1933, the newly appointed Reich Chancellor Adolf Hitler—the fatal enabling act was passed at this session with the support of the Catholic Zentrum and the Bavarian People's party (Bayerische Volkspartei)—had stressed the importance of the two Christian denominations, which were "essential factors in the preservation of our nationhood."

On July 20, 1933, Vice Chancellor Papen and the Secretary of State of the Vatican, Eugenio Cardinal Pacelli (later Pope Pius XII), concluded the Reich Concordat. It could not have come at a better moment for Hitler. Germany was politically isolated, and cold-shouldered practically everywhere in the world. Yet only ten days later the Catholic Youth associations were dissolved. This was the beginning of a systematic exclusion of the Catholic Church from Germany's public life. As a first measure, the Catholic press was to be gagged and religious tuition taken out of the hands of the Church.

On April 24, 1935, the president of the Reich Press Chamber, Max Amann, subordinate to Goebbels as president of the Reich Cultural Chamber, published the new regulation whereby newspapers were forbidden to take a policy line that "by its denominational or professional content furthered the interest of any particular section of the population. Any transgression would result in "the expulsion of the newspaper publisher from the Reich Press Chamber."[12] The protest Cardinal Bertram lodged with Goebbels in the name of all German bishops was to no avail. From then on the Catholic Church could no longer publish a newspaper. Other Catholic publications were also subject to all kinds of chicanery. They were continuously cautioned and threatened with being closed down every time they defended the Catholic Church or the Catholic faith against attacks of the National Socialist press. Excelling in this aggression were the *N. S.-Monatshefte* (N.S. Monthly—publisher, Alfred Rosenberg), with a circulation of 60,000; *Der Schulungsbrief* (Educational Letter —publisher, Robert Ley), with a circulation of 3,500,000; and *Das Schwarze Korps* (The Black Corps—publisher, Reichleadership of the SS), with a circulation of 500,000 copies. These publications were printed by the party publishers, whose chief, Max Amann, was at the same time president of the Reich Press Chamber, which made him at once lawgiver and judge. Justice had become a farce.

As a further repressive measure, the Catholic press was compelled to restrict its advertising, which resulted in considerable financial losses.

Goebbels had neither the power to give orders to Rosenberg, Himmler, Ley, or Amann, nor any means of protecting the Church against their attacks. He was even obliged to defend them whenever the Catholic Church dared to counter National Socialist attacks, or contradict false statements about Christianity. Goebbels probably disliked his role. He was in many ways an admirer of the Catholic Church. He admired its hierarchy; the simplicity of its propaganda; and its liturgy, which used Latin all over the world, the same texts, the same breviary, and the same method of stereotypic repetition.

The rosary Goebbels called Rome's magnificent propagandistic instrument.[13] He had borrowed much from Catholic liturgy, adopting it as a model for his own productions of party festivities. All the more astonishing that Goebbels played an active role in the fight against the Church instead of leaving it to his party colleagues over whom, in any case, he had no power. In principle, Hitler and Goebbels rejected the political struggle with the churches; yet Goebbels would use his propaganda machine to attack the Catholic Church over and over again. He raved particularly against the so-called moral crimes allegedly committed in monasteries and convents. The aim of this campaign was obvious: Priests had to be banned from giving religious instruction, on the grounds of constituting a moral danger to their pupils. The monasteries, together with all their properties, could be confiscated for "being breeding grounds of immorality."

All cases of alleged immorality involving Catholic priests were distorted and magnified by official propaganda, while *démentis* or rectifications put out by the Church were duly suppressed. Catholic publications were threatened with foreclosure if they published a factual criticism of the official presentation of a case. But then again, when the state needed the Church, all attacks were suspended. During the referendum in the Saarland and in Austria; during the occupation of the Rhineland and the Sudetenland; and during the Olympic Games in 1936, when Goebbels saw fit to erect beautiful façades for the benefit of foreign visitors, the Church was left in peace. Moral crimes allegedly perpetrated by Catholic priests, or infringements of the exchange laws—yet another point of accusation often leveled against members of the Church—all of a sudden vanished from the Nazi press.

The climax of the hate campaign against the Catholic Church was Goebbels' speech of May 28, 1937, in the Berlin Deutschlandhalle, before an audience of 20,000. In this speech, which was also broadcast, Goebbels raged against a "general decline in morals" among the priests and members of Catholic orders. He spoke of "thousands and thousands of cases," and this was "only one facet of the actual moral decline. . . ."[14] (Two days later Goebbels' statements were indirectly corrected by Reich Church Minister Hanns Kerrl, who in a speech[15] gave the total figure of moral crimes: All in all, 45 priests had been condemned, 176 male and female members of various orders, and 21 Church officials.) This speech was meant to provide an answer to various pastoral letters, in particular to the encyclical *In Burning Sorrow,* which Pope Pius XI pronounced on Easter Sunday 1937, in which he condemned National Socialism. The Berlin bishop, Count Preysing, stated in his pastoral letter of November 30, 1937:

". . . One anti-Church measure follows another. A spirit inimical to Christianity dominates public life more and more. The distress of conscience grows."[16]

Preysing lodged a protest with Goebbels against the minister's generalizing insults against the Church. Preysing defended his priests and reminded the Propaganda Minister that only a very small number of legal actions against the Catholic Clergy were actually being heard while, at the same time, equally serious offenses perpetrated by Hitler Youth leaders were being suppressed. Goebbels did not answer the pastoral letter of the bishop of Berlin. He played deaf, as so often when faced with uncomfortable accusations.

Goebbels' speech in the Deutschlandhalle was, in fact, his last important outpour of hatred against the Catholic Church. He had gone too far. Just as he had stirred up foreign opposition by his radical anti-Semitic speeches, he now produced a similar reaction among German Catholics (almost 40 per cent of the population). But the entries in his wartime diary show how his revulsion against the Church grew steadily from year to year, making his heart beat faster when he thought of the reckoning to come one day. It was worth swallowing one's anger and storing up one's hatred:

"The Catholic Church continues with its incredibly mean attitude. Before me lie a number of pastoral letters that have so little to do with reality and are so inimical to the state that they need no further comment. Nevertheless, we prefer not to take action against them. Let the wicked clergy do their worst; we shall present them with the bill as soon as the war is over."[17]

But the longed-for day of vengeance never came. The Catholic Church survived National Socialism, as she had survived so many inimical doctrines before. Yet National Socialism breached certain dams in this field, as in many others, and the floods took with them much that had previously appeared to be firmly anchored.

The Bourgeois

Goebbels' hope of becoming the great cultural renovator of the Third Reich foundered on the principles of National Socialism and on some leading personalities, particularly on Hitler himself. There is a type of dictatorship that will at least pretend to tolerate a limited form of cultural liberalism. But Hitler would have none of it. Liberalism of any kind was outlawed, with the exception of theater and film, where a most moderate form of liberalism was admitted precariously. Everything else, including the press, literature, painting, and music were made to toe the official party line. Goebbels' early attempts to allow for a certain freedom of development in art failed. It was bound to fail, and not only because of the official lack of tolerance, but also because of Goebbels' own lack of principles. He would execute the Fuehrer's orders and help destroy any seed of spiritual freedom, with the result that Germany's whole cultural life capitulated in the end. The only exception was the Catholic Church and a few thousand vicars who managed to hold out in their religious strongholds. But even they were no longer able to give any new impulse to Germany's spiritual life.

Goebbels' cultural policy had become bankrupt, reluctant as he was to admit this to himself. He would extol the high standard of theater and film as indicative of the generally high cultural standard. But also his political views had run aground. The liquidation of the Roehm putsch ended once and for all every revolutionary and socialistic tendency within National Socialism. Radicalism, such as could still be found, veered toward the cultural field, much to Goebbels' dislike.

Hitler, too, had undergone a change after Hindenburg's death when he had vested himself with the two highest state offices. He no longer needed Goebbels as a cofighter in his struggle for power, but only as his mouthpiece. The power was now Hitler's. And Hitler enjoyed it, used it, and abused it at his pleasure. Goebbels' star had begun to dim, and the time had come to catch up with all he had missed in life. Goebbels started enjoying life to the full.

"Get rich" was the watchword, as in all reactionary revolutions. Many did it shamelessly and openly, like Goering and Amann. Goebbels preferred to do it more discreetly. He did not amass a personal fortune, but spent the taxpayers' money, even during the war, on his various residences. He had them enlarged and made more and more luxurious.

When he became minister he was still living in Magda's elegant apartment on the Reichskanzlerplatz. Here the Goebbelses would often welcome Hitler as their guest and receive visits of top party leaders who attended important conferences. Now Goebbels requested an official residence, and not only to enhance his status, but also to improve his financial position. His official residence, its installation, upkeep, and maintenance—in fact, everything—was paid for by the state. Adjoining his personal office was an apartment, consisting of a sitting room, bedroom, and bathroom, which served more as a meeting place for his rendezvous and intimate conversations during office hours, than as a habitation.

Luckily for Goebbels there was a time gap between Hugenberg's resignation as Reich Minister of Food and the appointment of his successor, Walter Darré. Goebbels used this hiatus to claim for himself the former Palace of the Marshals of the Prussian Court (Palais de Königlich-Preussischen Hofmarschälle), which had served since 1918 as the official residence of the Minister of Food. It stood in a neglected park in No. 20 Hermann-Göringstrasse (the former Ebertstrasse, called after Germany's first democratic Reich President, Ebert).

Speer himself undertook the inner decoration of the apartment and added a new large hall.[18] But Goebbels was apparently not entirely satisfied with the work of Hitler's favorite architect, since he obtained the Fuehrer's permission in 1938 to rebuild the palace. This entailed the purchase of the garden belonging to the Ministry of Food and the tattersall of the Palais Blücher, which belonged to the United States Embassy. Another story was added, but this time the construction was not carried out by Speer, but by the architects Paul Baumgarten and, later, H. G. Bartels. Speer's taste was obviously too Hitleresque for Goebbels, who preferred his private residence at least to be more to his own taste.

Even during the war in 1940, further architectural alterations were undertaken; another story was added containing apartments for the minister's closest collaborators, and servants' quarters, spoiling the building's original beauty.

The position of the palace was quite exceptional. The considerably enlarged gardens bordering on the park of the Reich Chancellery were, with their centuries-old trees, an island of peace in the midst of the hectic metropolis. The once-neglected lawn was now beautifully looked after by professional gardeners. There was a fountain, a glass house, a tea pavilion.[19]

The interior of the palace was furnished with great taste which, according to reports, surpassed by far that of the most showy luxury apartments of other party moguls. This might have also been due partly to Magda's influence. The indirect lighting, the soundless working of the doors, the muted ringing of the telephones, and the discreet manner of the servants combined in creating the necessary peace for the minister to pursue his thoughts and ideas undisturbed.

Most of the paintings and precious pieces of furniture had been transferred from museums or other state property. The music room, smoking room, workroom, and sitting room had wood paneling put in specially. The workroom was all in red—the leather armchairs, the curtains, the carpets. The approaches to the banquet hall, the entrance hall, and all bathrooms were of marble. There was also a private cinema and a bar.

The carpets, the gobelins, silver and cutlery for several hundred people, crystal, porcelain, glasses, and linen—everything was paid for by the state, making a total of 3.5 million marks.[20]

Goebbels did not live in quite such obvious luxury as Hitler or Goering, but sufficiently comfortably for the little doctor from Rheydt, who had been unemployed for a long time, and had later in Elberfeld lived in a shabby little room.

But an official residence was not enough. Goebbels wanted a private residence too. He found it in a villa built in the style of an English country house, situated in Schwanenwerder on a piece of land jutting out into the Havel River. The ground bordered on a wooded rise sloping gently down to the shore, and densely covered in reeds. The region was inhabited by people of a superior class, whose neighborhood was agreeably appreciated by the former revolutionary and rabid anticapitalist. He bought the property in 1934 quite cheaply for 350,000 marks; of this, 100,000 marks came out of his own pocket, made up mostly of the money his wife had received from her first husband. In addition, he took out a mortgage of 100,000 marks and received a further 80,000 marks from Amann as advance royalties on his book *Vom Kaiserhof zur Reichskanzlei,* as well as 70,000 marks that Hitler gave him as a gift of thanks for the hospitality he had enjoyed, and hoped to enjoy in the future.[21]

The property consisted of three buildings, the main house, the "cavalier's house" used for guests, and a third complex, consisting of stables and storerooms. Part of this was converted into a private cinema.

Two years later Goebbels bought the neighboring property and had alterations made to the house originally built in the Jugendstil. He called this house his "fort"; nobody, not even Magda, was allowed in without obtaining his permission beforehand. He used it for work and some of his gallant rendezvous. In the gardens roamed the children, ponies, and Alsatian dogs; moored to the jetty was the white motor yacht *Baldur.* Here, in Schwanenwerder, Goebbels installed his private paradise. He had failed in his political aim to do away with capitalism, but he was at least able to benefit from his failure and live in the style of a capitalist, which apparently rather suited him.

But a "palace" in town and a villa at the lake were obviously not enough. On the occasion of the tenth anniversary of his appointment as their gauleiter on October 21, 1936, the city of Berlin made him a present of a "modest blockhouse" on a quiet lake. It was, in fact, the Château Lanke on the Lake Bogen, a property of the old Prussian nobility that had been acquired by the coal industrialist Friedländer-Fuld, knighted by Wilhelm II. The city of Berlin had bought the property at an advantageous Aryanization price, and presented it to its gauleiter and honorary citizen for life. The country house, surrounded by beautiful woods thick with pine and beech trees, stood near the village of Lanke in the district of Barnim. The road passing the property led to the Schorfheide, where Goering had built his ostentatious Château Karinhall.

The small mansion was not big enough for Goebbels, and he had a one-story house built on the opposite side of the lake, despite the fact that the ground belonged to the nature reserve of the Lake Liegnitz. The competent authorities objected. But the Prussian minister-president, the magnanimous Hermann Goering, simply ignored their protest. He had his magnificent Karinhall, and let poor Goebbels have his modest Lanke. The Propaganda Minister declared the house his official summer residence, contributed 500,000 marks of his own, once again advanced by his publisher, Amann; but the final bill was 3 million marks, which the Minister of Finance, Count Schwerin von Krosigk, refused to pay. The bills mounted up, but there was no money to pay them. On August 3, 1940, the sales administration of the Berlin furniture enterprise addressed a letter to the architect, H. G. Bartels:

"Settlement of your order on behalf of Herr Reich Minister Dr. Goebbels, due in November of last year, is still outstanding. Payment has been postponed from day to day, from week to week, and from month to month, despite our frequent polite requests, which were left unanswered. If we had approached the Herr Reich Minister Dr. Goebbels directly, we would, no doubt, have received payment long ago."[22]

The Berlin furniture firm knew quite well why they had preferred not to approach Goebbels directly; he was as little able to produce the money as his architect. Now the film industry came to the rescue of its supreme chief, Joseph Goebbels. Max Winkler, owner and proprietor of the Cautio-Treuhand, produced the necessary 2.7 million marks.[23] The film industry also paid the yearly upkeep, amounting to 80,000 marks. The house became "German film property," but was put at Goebbels' disposal for life "in recognition of his services to the film industry."[24]

The building was air conditioned and equipped with a hot-air heating system. The enormous windows in the hall were electrically operated and could be lowered into the ground, making the room appear to be in the open. A third private cinema was added to the

other two Goebbels had installed in his town palace and in Schwanenwerder. A special cable with twenty lines leading from the building
to the post office at Wandlitz had been laid; from the post office four
more cables secured a direct connection with the central exchange
of the Propaganda Ministry in Berlin. To obtain electric power for
lighting, the Berlin transformer plant had to be enlarged, with special permission of the mayor of Berlin.[25]

In Lanke, too, Goebbels had his little retreat built, "quite a modest
little blockhouse," with five rooms and all conveniences.[26] There
Goebbels could retire, as in the "fort" in Schwanenwerder, to work
and occasionally enjoy extramarital pleasures. Indeed, Dr. Goebbels
had become a connoisseur of life, combining work and pleasure in a
style reminiscent of that of the ancient princes.

In May 1942 the town of Rheydt put the former residence of the
Counts von Rylandt-Rheydt, a beautiful renaissance château, at the
disposal of their honorary citizen. Goebbels, finding its upkeep too
expensive, refused it as a present, but deigned to consent to use it
from time to time as a residence after the war was over. (See Goebbels' diaries.)

During the first years as minister, Goebbels enjoyed life to the full.
When difficulties arose with his wife about Lida Baarova, Goebbels'
state secretary and closest collaborator, Karl Hanke, produced copies
of love letters and a list of Goebbels' mistresses, including the names
of thirty-six film and theater actresses. With a few secretaries thrown
into the bargain, one is not surprised to learn that the people gave
Goebbels the nickname *Bock von Babelsberg* (the ram of Babelsberg). [Babelsberg was Berlin's film city. Translator's note.]

Unquestionably, Goebbels had changed beyond recognition. The
rather poorly dressed gauleiter of the past had become but a vague
memory. He was now dressed by the best tailor, introduced to him
by his adjutant, Prince Christian von Schaumburg-Lippe. In the end
Goebbels possessed so many suits that, according to his press aide,
he could afford a change every day. When Lida Baarova once wanted
to buy him a tie, he suggested she might just as well buy fifty. Goebbels would change his shirt at least twice a day; and they were by no
means the simple shirts he used to wear when still a simple gauleiter, but rather silk shirts, usually cream-colored, his favorite color.
He had his orthopedic shoes made by the top shoemaker, who did
his best to hide his client's malformation. His hands were manicured
—an expression of vanity for which he had once attacked the poor
Vipoprä, Dr. Weiss, with utter venom. Goebbels had a daily artificial
sun-ray session.

Prince Schaumburg-Lippe described the gauleiter Goebbels of the early fighting era as follows: "The light, slightly faded macintosh suited him. It gave him a modest, agile, sportsmanlike appearance, it matched the temper of his life. He avoided wearing anything that looked like a uniform. His light green felt hat, with the narrow black band, was impeccably clean. The brim was turned up in front. . . . He seemed to move in jumps when in a hurry."[27]

Later, when minister, he still sported macintoshes, but they were no longer faded. He still used to wear a hat, but also gloves. He would never go out without hat and gloves, in summer or winter. He dressed preferably in white: a white suit, white cap, and white gloves at the wheel of his white motor yacht. Like some TB cases who would take refuge in a euphoric state, Goebbels abandoned himself to full living. Always restless, he hated to miss anything Fate could offer.

And, indeed, he could afford it. From 1941 onward Goebbels regularly wrote the weekly leader for *Das Reich,* for which he was paid 2,000 marks each time. A yearly selection of these articles was published in book form. He also drew sizable salaries as minister, Reichsleiter, and gauleiter, and received royalties from his books.

It is not a historian's task to judge Goebbels' gallant adventures; but it is psychologically interesting to analyze the motivations for his hectic quest for amorous conquests. With one exception, his liaisons were indeed no more than adventures. The women who had yielded to him, some married and some not, knew this, although the amount of time he would spend on them, the many signs of his personal attention he would lavish on them (he would, for instance, always send them their favorite flowers), pointed to something deeper than mere sexual desire. Little did they know that the flowers were ordered by Goebbels' adjutant, whose task was to find out and cater to the wishes and whims of his master's momentary favorite.

The whole governmental machinery was at Goebbels' disposal, as in times of the worst absolutism. Goebbels could choose freely from among the film and theater actresses.

And what about Magda? She produced a child almost every year, and as a consequence was out of the game for several months each year. Like so many ugly men, Goebbels was hypersensitive to female beauty. The many children Magda bore affected her figure. After the party rally of 1936, she fell from grace with Hitler because of some female gossip concerning Eva Braun. Hitler presented Eva only to a small circle of friends, so anxious was he to preserve the legend that the Fuehrer had sacrificed his right to marry for Germany and was leading a saintly life; yet he himself, a violent and merciless critic, was, as is often the case, most vulnerable to the slightest criticism. Hence the withdrawal of his favor from Magda, who grieved much more deeply than over any of her husband's infidelities. Magda's fall from favor was also a shock to Goebbels. He had lost, at least temporarily, his queen on the political chessboard. Magda bore Goebbels six children:

Helga	Sept. 1932
Hilde	Apr. 1934
Helmut	Oct. 1935
Holde	Feb. 1937
Hedda	May 1938
Heide	Oct. 1940

She also had two miscarriages. The Goebbels' children were described as very pretty and intelligent. Only Hilde, a premature baby, was rather delicate, and Helmut, the only boy, clumsy and a daydreamer. He was the only one among the Goebbels children who did not get along in school. That the names of all the children started with an "H" was Magda's personal whim. She had started this mannerism in her first marriage, calling her son Harald.

Apart from Hitler, eminent party leaders were rather rare guests in Goebbels' house. Not until after the catastrophe of Stalingrad did meetings take place regularly every Wednesday at Goebbels' residence, usually attended—to name the most prominent only—by Funk, Ley, and Speer. Among the party higher-ups, the only regular visitors were the chief of the Fuehrer's Chancellery, Reichsleiter Philipp Bouhler, and his wife. And the Goebbelses had only one real friend: Reich Church Minister Hanns Kerrl.

Most of the time Goebbels was surrounded by people belonging to the film and theater world. He liked to be the life of the party and shine with his brilliant *esprit* and sparkling irony. He was not adverse to causing confusion by giving play to his spitefulness, and would thoroughly enjoy the embarrassment he caused. This was a trait he and the Fuehrer had in common; and if the two together were in good form, the victim they picked had nothing to laugh about. Goebbels particularly liked to see handsome people humiliated, preferably men, but women too, unless he was flirting with them; he would put questions to them, knowing they had no answer, just to make them look ignorant. But then again he would enchant his guests by his overwhelming charm, and, knowing he was nicknamed the Mephistopheles of the Movement, he would give a sparkling display of amiability, unless the mood took him to play the bogey.

The cuisine at Goebbels' residence was not remarkable and there was no abundance of drink, but it was highly entertaining to be a guest of this perhaps most spiritual and charming of all the party bigwigs.

The Case Lida Baarova

After Goebbels had dedicated himself to the Fuehrer body and soul,
only once did it appear as if a woman had supplanted the master in
his disciple's heart. The lady in question was Lida Baarova, a petite,
graceful woman with dark hair, Slav cheekbones, and extremely
expressive eyes. The story grew into a scandal. As no reliable material about the case Baarova has come down to us—the press maintained absolute silence—biographers have rather to rely on statements made by the people who were intimately connected with the
affair. The chief witness is, of course, Lida Baarova herself. Obviously,
her point of view is subjective and quite different from that of Magda
Goebbels' sister-in-law Ello (divorced Quandt). Even today Baarova
still idolizes Goebbels, proof, if needed, that she really loved him.[28]
Naturally, anything she has to say in this matter is likely to be biased
in her lover's favor. Ello, on the other hand, sided with her sister-in-
law. Then there are some statements of actors who, with their usual
penchant for gossip, were apt to make up stories about the fallen
tyrant Goebbels, who had kept them in fear for so long. Finally,
Rosenberg's diary contains comments made by some party potentates,
such as Goering, Himmler, and Darré—hymns of hate against Goebbels; but Rosenberg, Goebbels' archenemy, was completely incapable
of judging him fairly. Speer, too, mentioned the Baarova affair in his
memoirs, but has hardly anything new to add. Comparing these different, often contradictory, statements, it seems almost impossible to
form a clear view of the case. It is material for a novelist—the story
of a woman in love coming to grief in a political witch's cauldron.

Lida Baarova's career was finished. Wherever she turned she was
met by hatred, hated by the Germans, as much as by her own compatriots; not less hated by National Socialists than by their enemies—
and only because she loved a man in whom most people saw the living incarnation of evil. The only political significance of the Baarova
affair lay in the fact that Hitler adamantly refused to let his Propaganda Minister down.

Like so much else in this case, precise dates are difficult to establish.
However, all are agreed that the two met during the summer of 1936,
during the Olympic Games. Baarova then lived with Gustav Fröhlich (a famous German film actor), who had been her partner in the
film Barcarole, which was made in 1934 and released in 1935. These
two had lived together since making the film and were planning to
get married. They had moved into a villa a few hundred yards from

Goebbels' property in Schwanenwerder, and the two parties soon got acquainted.

The next milestone in their relationship seems to have been the Nuremberg party rally in autumn 1936. Goebbels had invited Lida Baarova to the rally, as well as many other leading artists. Before he was to speak, Goebbels asked Baarova to see him and discuss with him her future plans. The conversation ended with Goebbels kissing her. Lida had to wipe lipstick off his lips, using his handkerchief. He told her to watch for the moment during his speech when he would remove his wristwatch; this would be a secret sign that he was thinking of her. He would also frequently take out his handkerchief and wipe his lips to signify his love. Goebbels punctiliously gave their agreed secret love-signs, looking at her every time—she was sitting right in front among other prominent personalities. From then on the two became inseparable. They met almost every day. Lida would walk up and down in front of Goebbels' ministry on the other side of the street, and the minister would be at the window to watch her. Goebbels visited his mistress at her little apartment near the Kurfürstendamm practically every evening. She later rented a villa in Grunewald. She and Fröhlich had separated but, according to her account, remained friends. The rumor that Fröhlich had slapped Goebbels' face was pure fiction, born of a wish dream of Goebbels' enemies.

The love between the two had soon become common knowledge, and the story had also found its way into the foreign press. Only Magda ignored it, obviously regarding it as one of her husband's extramarital adventures, which she had become used to. There are different versions as to why, in the summer of 1938, it finally came to a showdown between Goebbels and Magda. According to Magda's sister-in-law, Goebbels had proposed to his wife to continue their marriage à trois.[29] Lida would live as Magda's guest in Goebbels' tower. And, in fact, Baarova recounts that Magda had offered her the intimate Du, telling her she had no objection to this liaison as long as it did not destroy the family.

From then on the story becomes obscure. It took a dramatic turn through the interference of a man from whom Goebbels had least expected it: his closest collaborator, Karl Hanke. Only a few months earlier, Goebbels had appointed Hanke as his state secretary. Hanke possessed a key to the minister's mailbox, which gave him access to Goebbels' official and private letters. Also, outgoing letters, both official and private, passed through Hanke's hands. Hanke knew all about Goebbels' adventures and kept a list of them, apparently at a time when he was still loyal to his chief. But following SS methods—

and Hanke held a high rank in the SS—it was always useful to have
something solid in one's hands.

Hanke's defenders put forward the idea that the good SS man saw
in Goebbels' action a betrayal of the National Socialist family ideal.
They also say that the anti-Semite Hanke remembered how Goebbels
during the fighting era had declared that any German actress could
only make a career by sleeping with a Jewish producer; and they say
Hanke now saw his master acting out the part of the all-powerful
"film Jew."[30]

Magda's sister-in-law described Hanke as a romantic who lived
in the world of Theodor Fontane's novels and felt it was his duty to
offer Magda his knightly protection.[31]

The facts, however, seem less romantic or idealistic. Hanke, it
seems, desired Goebbels' wife and wanted to marry her. He was also
hoping to bring down his chief, who trusted him blindly, and become
his successor. But Hanke had miscalculated. Hitler would not dream
of replacing Goebbels, whom he needed and considered irreplaceable.
Hanke's self-deception also applied to Magda's feelings for him. According to her sister-in-law, Magda said about Hanke: "He was a
simple, brutally upright vassal, an intelligent, educated man, but his
education had gaps. In fact, it was full of them."[32]

This characterization could be applied to the whole National Socialist leader corps, starting with Hitler. The few exceptions were
specialists: Dr. Todt, Speer, and Goebbels.

Hanke handed Magda the list containing the names of the ladies
who had been involved with Goebbels, and maneuvered the same list
into the hands of Reichsfuehrer SS Himmler. Some of the ladies,
persuaded by Hanke or possibly by Himmler (whose mildest form of
persuasion was the use of menace), were prepared to be witnesses
in divorce proceedings; they would say that Goebbels had used black-
mail to press them into acceding to his sexual demands. Hanke also
made copies of the love letters Goebbels had written or received.
These were meant to provide further proof against the minister.
Hanke also organized a hostile demonstration at the opening of a
film with Baarova. Even during the screening, sarcastic exclama-
tions were heard from the audience. But when, at the end, Baarova
appeared to take her bow, she was greeted with boos and catcalls,
including, "Get out, minister whore!"

The whole matter was now submitted to the highest authority:
Hitler himself. There are two versions of how this came about.

One version (the source is once again Magda's sister-in-law)
claims that Hanke had arranged for Magda to be received by Hitler.
Hitler, put off by what he heard from Magda, called for his Propa-

ganda Minister, but he accepted Goebbels' word of honor that all this was only hysterical female gossip; upon which Hanke personally saw Hitler and told him the truth. Hitler was most indignant, particularly because Goebbels had falsely given him his word.[33]

The other version is that Goering, in whom Goebbels had confided, telephoned Hitler, at the time in Berchtesgaden, letting him in on the case; whereupon Hitler returned to Berlin immediately and had a talk with Goebbels lasting two hours. Goebbels for the first and only time opposed the Fuehrer, defended his love, and asked Hitler to agree to a divorce and to send him as ambassador to Tokyo.[34]

According to both versions Hitler forbade the divorce—at least for the time being—and demanded that Goebbels wait one year, during which time he would not be permitted to see his mistress. Lida Baarova lived for three months under what practically amounted to house arrest, always hoping to hear from her lover. But in vain. Once Baarova succeeded in driving her car up alongside his. They looked at each other for about a minute, but Goebbels' face remained impassive. The minister signaled to his chauffeur to drive on.

Baarova returned home to Czechoslovakia, where she was shunned by her own people. All films in which she had a part were out of circulation, all her contracts annulled. For the Germans she had simply ceased to exist. Goebbels did not lift a finger to help her. As far as he was concerned the case was closed. He had decided for "duty" against love, as so many of history's great men before him. That, at least, was what he told his associates.

Far more interesting than the love story were the direct consequences of the scandal. There was not one party leader who was not hoping to see Goebbels' fall. We find in Rosenberg's diary some relevant notes. Rosenberg told Himmler: "You know that I never held a brief for Dr. Goebbels, but I preferred not to express my opinion. But today he is the most hated man in Germany. . . ."[35]

In the middle of May 1939 Rosenberg wrote in his diary after a meeting of the gauleiters: "A heart-to-heart discussion and the demand for a clear lead in the party . . . and then: the deep sorrow at Dr. Goebbels having discredited the party."[36]

Goering said to Rosenberg on May 21, 1939: "Dr. Goebbels ruins our credit at home and Ribbentrop [does] abroad." On September 24, 1939—war had already started—Rosenberg remarked to Hess that it had been pleasantly noticed that the Propaganda Minister had, so far, not been seen or heard from; but he would sure enough reappear when the moment was propitious to take credit for everything that had been accomplished by others. The old party members had finished with him completely. "Many gauleiters told me that the moment the Fuehrer would withdraw his protection from Dr. Goebbels, one would just 'inhale' him so that no trace was left. . . ."[37]

But the Fuehrer refused to oblige, because he needed Goebbels. This showed clearly that only Hitler could protect Goebbels from the hatred of the other party members, be it Goering or Rosenberg, Himmler or Darré. Hitler simply could not dispense with Goebbels, because only he was able to produce that particular kind of propaganda Hitler needed for his plans. No one else knew as well as Goebbels how to drive the masses toward a certain goal. Not that Hitler was not annoyed; he actually banned Goebbels for a certain period from his luncheon and dinner sessions, reducing their contact to strictly official business. He furthermore rejected Goebbels' plan to write a book *Den Menschen Hitler* (Hitler, the Man), on the occasion of Hitler's fiftieth birthday. At the same time, Hitler increased Ribbentrop's powers in the field of propaganda abroad, and Reichsleiter Dietrich's in the press sector.

Goebbels realized that he would have to adjust his marital differences before he could revive his former relationship with Hitler. The only stumbling block was his own state secretary, Hanke, whom Hitler had not removed from his post—probably so as not to expose himself before his own party leaders, in whose eyes Hanke had acted rightly, and upheld the party's honor and integrity. They were hardly put off by Hanke's real motivations, for as long as he gave them a chance to shoot down the hated Goebbels.

But Hanke was so much in love with Magda that, in the end, he dug his own grave. Speer comments: "In the meantime the relationship between Hanke and Frau Goebbels had developed to a point when, much to the horror of all who knew what had been going on, they seriously contemplated marriage. . . . Hanke pressed Hitler to agree to a divorce, but Hitler refused. At the beginning of the Bayreuth Festival 1939, Hanke appeared one morning at my house in Berlin in a desperate state. The couple Goebbels had made it up between them and were reconciled. . . ."[38]

"Reconciled" was hardly the right word, but they were, in fact, to continue their life together. Now it was up to Goebbels to regain Hitler's favor. In the meantime, the Fuehrer had made world history. The year 1938, when Goebbels' marital crisis was at its height, had been the most eventful since the takeover. On January 15, Hitler dismissed his War Minister, General Field Marshal von Blomberg, under spectacular circumstances, and personally assumed command of the Army. He appointed General Wilhelm Keitel to be chief of the newly formed Oberkommando der Wehrmacht (Supreme Command of the

Armed Forces), directly subordinate to the Fuehrer. On February 4, Hitler dismissed his Minister of Foreign Affairs, Konstantin von Neurath, and appointed in his place Joachim von Ribbentrop. He furthermore retired a number of generals, among them the supreme commander of the Army, General-Oberst Freiherr von Fritsch. Schacht had already handed in his resignation as Minister of Economics in December 1937. All Cabinet ministers and high-ranking officers who had opposed Hitler's plans had been removed. In March followed Austria's *Anschluss;* in the autumn, the Sudetenland crisis and the Munich agreement.

Goebbels, eager to regain lost ground, looked around for some special tasks to prove his loyalty, diligence, and capacity. He did not dare start up a new campaign against the Catholic Church. Hitler needed peace inside Germany for his plans, in particular peace with the churches. Only in Austria, where the Church was not sufficiently conversant with National Socialist methods, did Hitler permit some anti-Church actions; the main victim was Archbishop Innitzer of Vienna. On the other hand, the archbishop had soiled his reputation with Catholic circles abroad by signing a letter with "Heil Hitler." And after his affair with Lida Baarova, Goebbels could hardly assume the role of a judge of the moral offenses allegedly perpetrated by priests and monks. He therefore returned to the attack against an enemy he could smite without running any risk: the Jews. They would be saddled with the guilt for everything that had happened. By accepting eagerly Hitler's order to prepare the "spontaneous actions" of the *Kristallnacht* (Crystal Night), Goebbels hoped to regain Hitler's trust and favor.

The Kristallnacht (Crystal Night)

Most historians attribute the initiative for the *Kristallnacht,* which took place on the night of November 9–10, to Goebbels. This was borne out by several witnesses at the Nuremberg trial. Even Speer records in his memoirs, written more than thirty years after that night of terror: "Later, Goebbels inferred in his intimate circle that he was the initiator of this sad and monstrous night, and I consider it quite possible that he put to a still hesitant Hitler a perfectly worked-out plan in order to obtain the green light from him."[39] This passage, incidentally, is typical of Speer's endeavors to whitewash Hitler in his memoirs.

Particularly damaging appears to be Himmler's note of November 10, 1938: "The order comes from the Reich Propaganda Ministry, and I suspect that Goebbels, with his lust for power, which I have noticed from some time now, and his stupidity, initiated this action just at a moment when we have run into difficulties with our foreign policy."[40]

At the Nuremberg trial, Reich Minister of Economy Funk put the guilt squarely on Goebbels' shoulders. On the witness stand he gave an account of a telephone conversation he had had with Goebbels on November 10, 1938, in which he told the Propaganda Minister "that this terror [the actions against the Jews during that night, their shops and synagogues] was a direct attack against me, inasmuch as valuable and irreplaceable economic assets were destroyed and our foreign relations, on which we were so dependent just then, had suffered considerably. Goebbels replied that I had only myself to blame if it had come to that. I should have excluded Jews from the economy long ago. The Fuehrer would give orders to the Reichsmarshal [Goering, who at that time was only general field marshal] to exclude the Jews totally from Germany's economic life."[41]

This last sentence contains the key to one of the best-kept secrets of the Third Reich: who was basically responsible for the *Kristallnacht*. The answer, to my mind, is Adolf Hitler. Goebbels took the guilt upon himself, to cover for Hitler. This is rather confirmed by Goering's attitude; as plenipotentiary of the four-year plan, he was just as horrified as Funk about the extent of devastation wrought during that night of terror. And yet Goering—apart from unsuccessfully complaining to Hitler—did not dare to undertake anything against Goebbels, despite the fact that Goebbels' position had been considerably weakened by the affair Baarova.

The Propaganda Minister—and there can be no doubt about this—gave orders in the evening of November 9 to organize and carry out during the night "spontaneous" actions against Jewish shops, habitations, and synagogues. This was found in the records of the party court compiled shortly after the events, and made available to the international court at the Nuremberg trial.

The organizer of the pogrom was Reinhard Heydrich, chief of the Gestapo and the SD (Sicherheitsdienst—Security Service), after Himmler the most important man in the SS. It was Heydrich who gave orders over the teleprinter to all party and SS leaders to go into action during the night. The pretext used was the assassination on November 7 of Ernst vom Rath, secretary to the German Embassy in Paris, by a Jewish refugee, Herschel Grynszpan. The motivation of this act remains obscure. Grynszpan told the French police during his interrogation that he had actually intended to kill the ambassador, Johannes von Welczeck, but shot Rath because it was he who happened to receive him. Grynszpan had done it as a protest against the treatment of Jews in Germany, remembering particularly the sufferings of his father who, not long before, had been taken off, together with many thousands of Jews, and put into boxcars to be transported to the Polish border, where the Poles refused to accept the human cargo.

On November 9, during the anniversary celebrations of the march to the Feldherrnhalle of 1923, Hitler and his entourage received the news that Vom Rath had died from his wounds. Hitler left immediately, while Goebbels held a provocative speech, informing the audience that "spontaneous actions" had already begun in several gaus. So far the report is clear. But what came after remains obscure. It is most doubtful that Goebbels would have dared to take it upon himself to order such a far-reaching action as followed during that night. He must have had orders from the Fuehrer. Reich Press Chief Dr. Dietrich, an inveterate enemy of Goebbels' who can hardly be suspected of wanting to whitewash the Propaganda Minister, referred in his notebook to the events of the *Kristallnacht:* "One has attributed this action to Goebbels. The truth is that Hitler, spontaneously reacting to Vom Rath's assassination, personally gave Goebbels orders to carry out this action. . . . Hitler gave Goebbels this sordid order, which also led to great misgivings within the party, in his private apartment on the eve of November 9. According to a reliable source, Hitler had a fit of rage when some people charged with the execution of this action raised certain objections. The German people refused, as so often, to believe that Hitler was responsible as, in effect, he was, being behind the scenes the sole instigator and prime mover of this destructive action, even if the guilt was shared by many others."[42]

During the night the mob destroyed thousands of shops and habitations, and attacked practically all synagogues, burning them down or demolishing them. Over twenty thousand Jews were arrested; thirty-six are known to have been killed. Even if Goebbels was not the original instigator of the *Kristallnacht,* he shares, with Hitler, Goering, and Heydrich, the guilt for the ultimate mass murder of the Jews. Earlier the point was made that Goebbels, in our view, was not an anti-Semite in accordance with the Nazi racial theory, and that privately he had scarcely any objection to Jews. At the beginning of 1934, one of Rosenberg's associates complained that among fifteen theaters in Berlin, only three were free of Jews.[43]

There are some indications that Goebbels personally might have let the Jews alone, if he had not been so eager to match Hitler's radicalism.[44]

Thus in 1941 Goebbels pressed for the dismissal of judges in Ber-

lin who were half Jewish or had Jewish family connections, even those
whose sons had fallen in the First World War. When, during the
Second World War, many Jews were brought to Berlin, where they
were less conspicuous, Goebbels got into a fit of rage and declared
that Berlin was not a "rubbish dump." In April 1941 he ordered that
all Jews not only had to wear the yellow star, but also had to affix the
same sign to the doors of their domiciles. He even intended to forbid Jews to receive newspapers or any other publications, but he ran
up against the objections of the Reich Post Ministry, which refused
to be burdened with the considerable administrative work this
measure would have entailed, and also was reluctant to lose the income connected with it. In December 1941 Goebbels also had to re-
nounce for economic reasons his large-scale plan for window dis-
plays of anti-Semitic material in 307 districts of his gau. Each window
display would have cost 400 marks.[45]

On the other hand, he declared at a conference of ministers—a further example of his duplicity—"that propaganda dealing with the
Jewish question would have to be handled tactfully and astutely."
He was afraid to see "a seventy-year-old Jewess being forced by a
sixteen-year-old Bund Deutscher Mädchen girl (New Youth Organization), to give up her seat for her," lest it might lead to the active
disapproval of other passengers.[46] But this did not prevent him
from plastering posters all over U-Bahn stations with the slogan: "Do
not forget, the Jews are our undoing."

Goebbels had certainly lost every scruple. As in all other questions, he closely followed in his Fuehrer's footsteps. Even before the
takeover, Goebbels had written an article in *Der Angriff* with the
heading, "The Jews are Guilty," and used it again later in his lead
editorial of November 16, 1941, in *Das Reich*. This, and another lead
editorial of the same brand, published in 1944 in *Das Reich,* descended to the worst journalistic level ever reached by this publication: ". . . all Jews, by the mere fact of their birth and race, belong
to an international conspiracy against National Socialist Germany.
They desire Germany's defeat and destruction. The fact that they find
little opening for their activities in the Reich itself is not by any
means the result of their loyalty but entirely due to the measures we
have taken.

"One of these measures was the introduction of the yellow Jewish
star. It is a most humanitarian measure of hygienic prophylactic defense, so to speak, meant to prevent the Jew from penetrating our
community in disguise, in order to sow disunity among us.

"The Jews are a race of parasites, who cling like a corrosive mold
to the cultures of sound but defenseless peoples. There is only one

remedy for this: Remove it, get rid of it. There is a difference between one human being and another, just as much as between one animal and another. We know good and evil human beings, just as we know good and evil animals. The fact that the Jew still lives among us is not a proof that he belongs to us; as little as the flea does not become a domestic animal because he lives in the house. . . ."

In his capacity as gauleiter of Berlin, Goebbels was particularly eager to purge his town completely of Jews. On March 2, 1943, he commented on this subject:

"We shall now remove the Jews from Berlin once and for all. Last Saturday we picked them up by a surprise action, and will ship them with the least delay to the East. Regrettably, it showed once again that the better circles, particularly the intellectuals, do not seem to understand our Jewish policy and have partly sided with the Jews. This led to a leakage, which made our impending action known beforehand, with the result that quite a number of Jews slipped through our net."

In his comments on March 15, 1943, Goebbels claims to be the main instigator for the clearing out of Jews from the whole Reich territory:

". . . I impress once again on the Fuehrer that I consider it necessary to rid the Reich territory of all Jews as quickly as possible. He approves and gives me the order to persevere with all available means until the entire Reich territory is free of Jews."

Goebbels does not hesitate to call the Jews "parasites, potato beetles, and bacilli." There certainly is not much left in the wartime Goebbels of the former sentimental, oversensitive young man. Suspicion and contempt of mankind have hardened his heart completely. We search his wartime diaries in vain for one truly humane word. Goebbels' and Hitler's views are identical. The same two words are their leitmotiv: "extermination" and "destruction."

On the Eve of War

Goebbels did not want war. Various statements of his associates are agreed on this point. Moritz von Schirrmeister, head of the press section from 1938–43, declared at the Nuremberg trial "that even Dr. Goebbels did not belong to the war conspiracy contained in the accusation, since he did not want war, but, on the contrary, saw his job rather in advancing the unbloody conquest of foreign territories. In the case of Poland, Dr. Goebbels reassured us frequently, and he really believed it, that it would not come to a war. He wrongly assessed the attitude of the Western powers, convinced they were only bluffing, and consequently assumed that Poland, without the military aid of the Western powers, would not dare to go to war."[47]

In the summer of 1939 Fritzsche handed the Propaganda Minister documents containing analyses of public opinion in Western countries. They were all agreed that England was determined to enter the war in case of an armed conflict between Germany and Poland. Goebbels appeared "very worried" about it, and decided to go to Hitler: "Believe me, we have not worked successfully for six years to risk everything now in a war."[48] His warning made no impression on Hitler, who had received information to the contrary from his Foreign Secretary, Ribbentrop.

It is not difficult to explain psychologically why Goebbels did not want war: His experience during the First World War, when he volunteered for the Army and was rejected on account of his clubfoot, was still rankling. He had ever since nurtured a hatred against militarism, but he knew how to hide it—indispensable in a militant movement like the NSDAP—behind his attacks on the reactionary spirit among high-ranking officers. Goebbels knew only too well that in a war civilians had to take second place, not a prospect that appealed to him.

Indeed, there were several reasons why Goebbels should not want war, yet they were all on a personal and not on a humanitarian level. He also felt—and his intuition was usually right—that apart from a minority of young fanatics, war would be unpopular with the German people. During the six years of government, Hitler had achieved more than even the most fanatical National Socialists could have expected when they came to power. And all that without resorting to war. There were no longer any unemployed. Industrial production in practically every field had multiplied. Over the whole Reich, roads were being built, canals, factories, houses, and cultural institutes. Thanks to Hitler's foreign policy, Germany had won the Saarland, Austria, the Sudeten- and Memel-land, and thus had incorporated into the Reich over 10 million people and almost 100,000 square kilometers of territory. In the spring of 1939 Bohemia and Moravia had been occupied. Slovakia had become a German protectorate, and on May 22, 1939, the "Steel Pact" had been concluded in Berlin between Germany and Italy, binding both to come to each other's help in case of an armed conflict.

Up to the occupation of Bohemia and Moravia, Hitler had proceeded in accordance with a solid program that featured the unification of all Germans in one Reich. Hitler advanced step by step, acting with great astuteness. He would never tackle more than one problem at a time. He would give it time to mature and use every opportunity to reiterate his love for peace. Then, at a given moment, he would strike swiftly, letting Goebbels precede his action with such a deafening propaganda barrage that the whole world gave a sigh of relief when at last it was over.

Until March 1939 Hitler's actions appeared justified and did not entail any blatant acts of injustice against other nations. The occupation of the Rhineland was a breach of the Locarno Treaty, but it was in accordance with the idea of sovereignty of a people who not so unnaturally were loath to see a part of their own country unprotected. The *Anschluss* of the Sudetenland could be perfectly defended by invoking the internationally recognized right of self-determination of ethnic groups. Had not the three million Sudeten Germans, as far back as 1918, declared themselves a part of Austria and been forcibly integrated into the new Czechoslovakian Republic? More controversial was the integration of Austria into the Reich. Before 1933 the greater part of the Austrian people had favored the *Anschluss*. But after 1933 the majority no longer wished the *Anschluss* with National Socialist Germany. Yet, even in the case of Austria, Hitler could point to the almost 100 per cent confirmation of the *Anschluss* he had obtained by the Austrian referendum of April 1938. That this had been obtained by applying terrorist methods was another matter.

But there was no international law to fall back on to justify the occupation of Bohemia and Moravia. It was an act of naked force, and probably Hitler's greatest political error. He had broken his word for the whole world to see, and had lost all credibility. "We don't even want any Czechs," was still reverberating in every ear, for Hitler had said it in the Berlin Sportpalast as recently as December 26, 1938. Nor had the world forgotten the promise he had given the British Prime Minister Chamberlain, that once the Sudeten question had been solved to his, Hitler's, satisfaction, he had no further territorial demands in Europe.

Hitler's occupation of Moravia and Bohemia compelled the British government to revise its peace policy. It can hardly be doubted that without the rape of Czechoslovakia, or what was left of it after the Sudeten *Anschluss,* the Western powers would have supported Hitler's moderate, or limited, demands to Poland—that is, an integration of Danzig into the Reich, and an extraterritorial railway line and motorway through the Polish Corridor. But the question was no longer Danzig; it was the fact that Hitler openly used terror to achieve his political aims. Once more Goebbels' propaganda succeeded in convincing the German people that Poland alone was the guilty party. Even on the last day before war broke out, the Germans heard over the radio that Hitler had made a generous offer to the Polish government: "In reply to their offer to come to an understanding the German government received, instead of a statement announcing the arrival of an authorized Polish emissary, news of the Polish mobilization. . . ."[49]

The German people were bound to find the Polish attitude challenging to the point of megalomania. Little did they know that Hitler had already ordered the attack on Poland for August 26. He postponed it when Mussolini and the Swedish amateur diplomatist Birger Dahlerus, a friend of Goering's, made last-minute efforts to save the peace. But while still negotiating with them, Hitler had already decided on September 1 as the last and definite date for the invasion of Poland.

The German people as a whole wanted war as little as any other people. Only Hitler's enemies within Germany, as well as most German refugees abroad, wanted the war, knowing it was the only way to bring the National Socialist regime down. But above all—and this was decisive—Hitler wanted war. It is hard to say whether he wanted a limited war only. His Minister of Foreign Affairs had assured him that the Western powers would not come to the aid of Poland. Whatever the case, Stalin and Hitler had done good business together. According to the secret clause of the German-Soviet nonaggression pact of August 23, 1939, Poland was divided—for the fourth time in history —between them.

The Wartime Civilian

When war broke out Goebbels had to retire into the background. At first Hitler had no time for him because he wanted to be the "first soldier" of his people, as he had proclaimed in his speech in the Reichstag on September 1. Nothing stood in the way any longer of his career from corporal to the greatest warlord of all time. On the first day of the war Goebbels gave orders to all newspaper editors "to avoid" the term "war" in any reports. The term to be used was "the Polish attacks were repulsed."[50] Hitler and the German government were still hoping that the Western powers would stay out of the conflict.

But just as everybody had expected (except the wishful-thinking fantasists in the German Reich government), Britain and France declared war on Germany on September 3. They may have disliked declaring war—and there was, in fact, some hesitation—but Hitler gave them no chance for a second Munich.

War created a new situation for the German people, and they

needed some time to get on their feet. Also, Goebbels' propaganda machine had to adapt itself to the new situation. At first Goebbels showed some restraint (in which Rosenberg, who followed developments with great apprehension, saw the one ray of light in the darkness). The people were only interested in the Wehrmacht communiqués, and Goebbels had nothing to do with their formulation. It was their very sobriety that made the strongest impression at home and abroad. German arms rushed from one victory to another at a breathtaking speed, which made it rather easy for the Wehrmacht command to publish sober and truthful war communiqués.

The enemy, on the other hand, was in a more delicate position. They had to find attenuating formulations for their defeats. And since the German communiqués gave the true position, the news agencies of neutral countries aligned their reports with those of the Germans.

The Polish campaign was officially over after eighteen days. Fighting continued for some days against some remaining pockets of Polish troops. Warsaw held out until September 26. But in actuality, effective Polish resistance had been overcome by September 18. Now the secret clauses of the Soviet-German treaty, signed in Moscow on August 23, 1939, giving the Russians a free hand in the eastern parts of Poland, became effective. This treaty had been presented to the world as a nonaggression pact, but it was, in fact, a pact of common aggression, instrumental in making Hitler's war possible. On September 17, the Red Army marched into a crushed Poland, under the pretense of giving protection to the Ukrainian and White Russian minorities. The cynicism of the Soviet dictator obviously did not lag far behind that of his National Socialist peer.

Immediately after the fall of Warsaw, Hitler directed Goebbels to open the great peace offensive. Once again Goering called on the services of his Swedish friend Dahlerus. On October 6, Hitler gave in the Reichstag a peace speech, as he called it. He had his spoils and was not prepared to let them go, even less so since he was obliged to share with the Soviet Union. The Western powers simply ignored Hitler's offer.

From then on Goebbels directed his propaganda against the main enemy, which now was Britain. The first highlight of this propagandist campaign against Britain was Goebbels' broadcast against Churchill on October 22, 1939. It still dealt with the case of the British passenger boat *Athenia,* which had been sunk on September 3, not far from the Hebrides. Based on the information furnished by the German naval High Command, assuring the Propaganda Ministry that no German U-boat had been in the vicinity at the time of the incident, Goebbels put out a *démenti* of the British communiqué that said the

Athenia had been sunk by a German U-boat. All German U-boats had strict orders to conform to The Hague Convention, which forbade sinking a passenger boat without prior warning.

The German government only learned what had actually happened when the German U-boat *U-30* returned to base on September 27. It had mistaken the *Athenia* for a disguised raider and had sunk it.

But Goebbels, not prepared to admit his error, turned the tables, and accused the First Lord of the Admiralty, Winston Churchill, of having given orders to sink the *Athenia* so as to bring America into the war, since there had been a large number of Americans among the passengers. Goebbels accused the enemy of infamous murder of its own people, as well as of citizens of a friendly nation.

At the same time, Goebbels carried out a war of nerves against the bored French soldiers shut up in the fortifications of the Maginot Line. He brought into operation a secret broadcasting station called "Humanité," employing, among others, former Communist Reichstag member Ernst Torgler. The pact with the Soviet Union obviously proved a paying proposition in more than one way. Apart from furnishing the Germans with raw materials and wheat, the Soviets also put at their disposal some of their harbors, which enabled Hitler to circumvent the British blockade. Soviet policy also influenced Communist parties outside Russia and turned them against the war, as, for instance, the French Communists, who adopted a subversively defeatist attitude.

The radio station "Humanité" fed the French troops with false information. Goebbels fabricated *The Diary of an English Prisoner of War,* which described the joyous experiences of an Englishman in Paris. The aim was to put the French soldiers up against their ally: While they had to sit in their Maginot fortresses through boring days and nights, English soldiers slept with their wives. Goebbels considered pornography an excellent means of propaganda, and supplied the French soldiers in every possible way with that kind of material, hoping to create sexual tension among the idle poilus, who by then had had their fill of this quasi-behind-the-front existence.

Goebbels drummed in the message that the British would fight to the last Frenchman. There was no real reason for a war between the Germans and the French, since the Germans did not want anything from the French. It was the British politicians who wanted the French to die for Danzig. Goebbels was in his element. To unnerve and demoralize enemy soldiers was right up his alley. No doubt he waged a most effective battle before the shooting started in earnest.

Goebbels' tactics toward Britain were entirely different. Once again he spared the people and blamed the system and the "plutocracy," which became the dominant term in his fight against the Western powers. The most familiar figure of his broadcasts beamed to Britain became the Irishman William Joyce, whom the British had soon nicknamed Lord Haw-Haw on account of his Oxonian accent and his aristocratic intonation. Like so many Irish, he loathed Britain; he went to Germany, was naturalized there, and became an enthusiastic supporter of Adolf Hitler. He broadcast his "Talks," in which he tried to convince his listeners that Hitler's war was not directed against the British people but against the British warmongers. According to his colleagues, Joyce was an idealist. After the war Joyce was arrested and, unlike the great poet, Ezra Pound, who was shut up in a mental hospital, Joyce was condemned to death for high treason and executed.

Goebbels also created the so-called Propagandakompanien (Propaganda Companies—PK). They consisted of soldier-propagandists, who supplied photographic material and reports based on their war experiences. These photographs and reports could never be realistic enough for Goebbels. His aim was to give the public the impression that they had taken part in the fighting. The Propaganda Companies included 150 writers. The war experience was to be used as material for creative writing.

Hitler Gets Stuck with His Victories

After the invasion of Denmark and Norway, Hitler started his attack against France on May 10, 1940. This operation included the neutral countries Holland, Belgium, and Luxemburg. Germany won a blitzkrieg as surprising to the German High Command as to the Allies; Germany won because of an audacious strategic plan and a concentration of armor without precedent. Also, the mass employment of parachutists and troops sent in by air was being used for the first time. To complete the inferno came the howling Stukas, with their demoralizing effect on the enemy. This audacious plan originated with General Manstein and provided for a main attack through the Ardennes with a great concentration of armor, which would then cross the river Maas, roll on to the northern plains, and reach the Channel at Abbeville. The point of the plan was to launch the attack at the most difficult, and therefore least probable, sector in order to achieve a "sickle cut," separating the forces of the enemy. Hitler spoke about Manstein's plan as though it were his own. His sole merit was to have pushed it through against the initial resistance of the High Command. But then the audacious advance of the Panzers tried

Hitler's nerves. When the artillery had almost reached Dunkirk, he gave orders to halt the advance, against the protest of General Brauchitsch, commander-in-chief of the Army, and Halder, chief of the Army General Staff. Hitler acted on General Rundstedt's advice; Rundstedt did not want the artillery to advance any farther before stronger reinforcements of infantry had been brought in. Besides, Goering wished to claim part of the glory for the Luftwaffe, which would destroy the British at Dunkirk. This error of the German war strategy created the miracle of Dunkirk. Under the code name Operation Dynamo, the British succeeded, with the help of the Royal Air Force, in evacuating the greatest part of the British Expeditionary Force, together with several French units, although they had to leave their heavy equipment and artillery behind. At the meetings of the British Cabinet on May 27 and 28, Neville Chamberlain, then lord president of the Council, and Foreign Secretary Lord Halifax proposed to lay down arms, since Britain was likely to get better terms before the final collapse of France. They proposed asking Mussolini to act as mediator for the price of Malta and Gibraltar. The Prime Minister, Winston Churchill, and the two leaders of the Labor party, Clement Attlee (lord privy seal) and Arthur Greenwood, rejected this proposal.[51]

On June 10, when France was practically beaten, Mussolini hastened to declare war on France, hoping to get a share of the spoils in the southern parts of France and Tunisia. On June 21, a mere six weeks after the attack on France had commenced, an armistice was declared.

During these military victories, Goebbels had to remain once again in the background. He only introduced a ceremonial type of announcement, to be used on Hitler's orders, exclusively on the occasion of important victories. During the French campaign this could be heard almost every three hours, which did not fail to have the desired effect on the much-tried nerves of Hitler's opponents at home and abroad. The announcement was introduced with the words: "Attention! Attention! Here is a special announcement!" and followed by fanfares. Then came the announcement and more fanfares. It ended with a chorus, singing either the *Niederländische Dankgebet* (Netherlands Thanksgiving Hymn) or the *Choral von Leuthen* (Choral Song of Leuthen). After three minutes of complete silence Hitler's favorite, the *Badenweiler March,* was heard, which was only played on official occasions in Hitler's presence.

Goebbels, and indeed the whole German people, hoped that after the magnificent victory in the West, peace would come. After the French capitulation, the Propaganda Minister told his guests the same evening that peace was imminent and that Hitler's magnanimity would astonish the whole world.[52] And, in fact, Hitler proposed making peace with Britain for the mere return of the former German colonies, and even this demand was not a condition *sine qua non.*

In his speech in the Reichstag on July 19, 1940, Hitler practically implored Britain to make peace, prophesying, if they refused, the disintegration of their Empire, "which I never intended to destroy or even impair in any way." The King of Sweden offered the British government to mediate between Britain and Germany. Also, the ambassador of the United States, Joseph Kennedy, counseled peace negotiations between London and Berlin.[53] But Churchill refused to hold any peace talks.

Britain completely ignored the German offer. Hitler was at a loss to know what to do next. Once again Goebbels stepped in. He would mount a propaganda campaign as part of a strategic plan, starting with terror attacks from the air against Great Britain, in order to soften her up for peace negotiations. Simultaneously, a plan for an invasion of Britain from the sea was elaborated—the code name was *Seelöwe* (Sea Lion)—but its execution was never seriously considered. Hitler and his generals preferred to wait for the outcome of the air battle.

This combination of propaganda and terror that had proved most effective within Germany, as well as in other continental countries, brought no return whatever when applied to Britain. Goering failed to establish German air superiority over Britain, which was the aim of his operation *Adler Angriff* (Eagle Attack), just as he had failed earlier to destroy the British Expeditionary Force at Dunkirk or prevent their embarkation. This meant that Goebbels' propaganda campaign had no chance of succeeding either. It could have worked only if Goering's terror raids had broken the fighting spirit of the British—a hopeless task. Goebbels' propaganda produced such terms as "rubbing out" and "Coventryizing." Both terms were attributed to Goebbels, but it was Hitler who used the word "rubbing out" for the first time in his speech on September 4, 1940, when he opened the winter-aid campaign. The term "Coventryizing," which referred to the English town of Coventry, which had been particularly hard hit by a German air attack, was probably Goebbels' literary property. At least it has the sound of one of Goebbels' word creations.

The main target of Goebbels' propaganda between August 1940 and June 1941 was Churchill, who had succeeded Chamberlain as Prime Minister, and whom Goebbels accused of being responsible for the continuation of the war. These vitriolic attacks full of hate and brutality had no effect, not even in Germany, let alone in England. On the contrary, they only helped to popularize Churchill, and Goebbels was, therefore, almost relieved when the outbreak of the war with Russia gave him a pretext for discontinuing his attacks against the British Prime Minister.

Goebbels called Churchill a "double-or-nothing politician of the first order," or the "gravedigger of the British Empire."[54] He also quoted Hitler, who had told him "that all Englishmen he had received before the war thought that Churchill was a fool. Even Chamberlain had said so."[55]

Since, however, this "political archcriminal," Churchill, was Germany's worst enemy, he could, so argued Goebbels, be only a friend of the Jews; were "not the English all together," with "their lying, their pious hypocrisy, and their pietistical claim to resemble God, so to speak, the Jews among the Aryans?" The "Hebrew Kraal" in London had always puzzled Europeans.[56]

The best negative characterization of Churchill appeared in Goebbels' article in *Das Reich* on February 21, 1941, when the attacks against the British Prime Minister reached their peak. By then it had become clear that Goering had lost the Battle of Britain. The article opened with several Churchill quotations dug up from newspaper archives. It quoted the young Churchill who, as war correspondent during the Boer War, had written in the *Morning Post* that there was only one way to break the resistance of the Boers, namely by applying the most severe measures. One would have to kill the parents to make the children respect the British.

Goebbels went on quoting Churchill's description of the punitive expedition carried out in the Marmund Valley, when the British proceeded systematically from village to village destroying houses, stopping up the wells, overturning the water towers, cutting down the big shady trees, burning the harvests, and destroying the water reservoirs, converting the valley into a desert to revenge their honor.

After these quotations Goebbels gave a characterization of the British Prime Minister: "It is not easy to draw the character of a man who has none. He belongs to the species of political chameleon capable of changing its color a thousand times if need be, and who, indeed, makes full use of this ability. He not only tells lies from necessity but also from sheer lust, from the enjoyment he finds in lying which, so to speak, is his life element. . . . His face is devoid of one single kindly feature. It is entirely drawn by cynicism. These ice-cold eyes have never known what it is to be moved. This man walks over dead bodies to satisfy his blind and presumptuous personal ambition. The end of a cigar stuck between his lips is the last vestige of a voluptuous life coming to a close. . . . England will pay dearly for this man . . . as long as he remains in public life he will be the leader of that plutocratic cast that wanted the war to destroy Germany. . . . He wants war for war's sake. War is for him an end in itself. . . ."

Despite his hymns of hatred, Goebbels could not help admiring Churchill in some way. This can be traced in Goebbels' wartime diary. Churchill's ability to enjoy life fully while remaining hard and pitiless whenever Britain's interests were threatened, remained for Goebbels a riddle. Goebbels saw the ascetic life his "Fuehrer" led, and he, too, led a most abstinent life, at least where eating and drinking were concerned.

What Goebbels most admired in Churchill was his courage. Churchill's famous words that he had nothing to offer his people but "blood, sweat, and tears," Goebbels adopted for his own propaganda after the catastrophe of Stalingrad. When Churchill openly admitted in a speech in the House of Commons in January 1942 that the British offensive had foundered on Rommel's supreme strategy, Goebbels wrote not without some respect: "He [Churchill] compares England's position with that of a drowning man who just about manages to keep his head above water. He admits heavy losses in North Africa, and most astutely assumes all responsibility for the disaster, which relieves him of having to dismiss somebody or other. It makes a good impression that he covers up for the people who work for him. I will, therefore, when releasing his speech to the German public, omit this passage."[57]

But any admiration Goebbels may have felt he hastened to drown in hatred. He wrote on February 18, 1943: "Reuters reports that Churchill is ill and is running a temperature. I suppose this whiskey drunk has enough alcoholic power of resistance to be up again in a few days. Pity. His disappearance could be of great advantage to us." And on February 22, 1943: "It is reported that Churchill has a slight attack of pneumonia. It would be too much to hope that he'll kick the bucket. Such a tough beast usually has a long life."

Goebbels pursued Churchill with a far more ardent hatred than he ever displayed for Stalin or Roosevelt. Goebbels was rather impressed with Stalin's brutality, which showed a certain affinity with Hitler's. Roosevelt's personality was too far removed for Goebbels. The whole American world was a closed book to him. Besides, he regarded Roosevelt as a tool in the hands of the Jews.

Until March 1941 time passed almost peacefully. The war continued, but the German people hardly felt it, apart from some restrictions and sporadic air attacks on certain towns, by which Britain tried to prove that, notwithstanding Goebbels' boastful propaganda describing the German air victories, Britain was not likely to be "rubbed out" or "Coventryized." In the meantime, certain events took place that did not directly touch the German people and were discreetly passed over in Goebbels' propaganda, yet were decisive for the future German defeat. Hitler had conquered a great part of Europe, but did not rightly know what to do with it. His policy of pacification, as he liked to call it, carried out by his SS police contingents, far from pacifying the subjected peoples, only stoked up a growing hatred, and not against Hitler alone, but against all Germans.

Hitler had no real strategic concept. He was only preoccupied with the solving of immediate problems without thinking farther ahead. And as soon as he had occupied practically everything there was in Europe, he seemed stuck, without knowing what to do next. He didn't seriously believe in an invasion of Britain, nor did he accept Great Admiral Raeder's advice to hit Britain at its most vulnerable point, namely in the Mediterranean. Hitler's attempts to find allies for an all-out war in the Mediterranean remained unsuccessful. The French and the Spanish heads of government, Marshal Pétain and Generalissimo Franco, declined. And Mussolini, irritated by Hitler's arrogance and his own military failures, gave his troops in Albania orders to march into Greece on October 28, 1940. This fateful act, together with Hitler's strategic error at Dunkirk and the failure of the Battle of Britain, was responsible for the future disaster. It delayed Hitler's most important military enterprise, his war against the Soviet Union.

Operation Barbarossa

Long before the event, Hitler spoke in *Mein Kampf* of his intention to wage war on the Soviet Union. This was, on the one hand, motivated by his romantic concept of a Germanic invasion of the East and, on the other hand, by his wish to secure sources of raw materials that would assure Germany's economy the much-desired autarchy. Soviet moves against the Baltic states, Finland, and Romania confirmed Hitler's decision to go ahead with his Russian venture. The military setbacks of the Russians in their war against Finland during the winter of 1939–40 led Hitler to underestimate the strength of the Soviets. The deciding factor was Stalin's demands, which Molotov presented during his visit to Berlin (November 12 and 13, 1940). They included a military base for Russian terrestrial and naval forces on the Bosporus, and recognition of Soviet interests in the Persian

18. Hitler visiting Goebbels and his wife and three children, Helga, Hilda, and Helmut. December 29, 1938.

19. The cabinet meeting at which it was decided that Germany would return to military conscription. From left to right: Dr. Frank, Dr. Goebbels, Dr. Frick, Herr Popitz, Herr Rust, General Goering, Herr Kerrl, Baron von Neurath, Hitler, Dr. Lammers, General von Blomberg, Dr. Schacht, Dr. Gurtner, Herr von Schwerin-Krosigk, Herr Darre, Herr von Eltz Rubenach, and Herr Selote. March 27, 1936.

20. The Goebbels family at the circus in Berlin. November 2, 1937.

Gulf, in Romania, Bulgaria, and Yugoslavia.[58] On December 18, 1940, Hitler gave instruction No. 21 for Operation Barbarossa.

The date originally set for the German attack against Russia, May 15, 1941, had to be postponed because of the defeat of Mussolini's armies in Africa (Ethiopia and Libya) and Greece.

To make matters worse, a military putsch in Yugoslavia had succeeded in deposing the pro-German government. On April 6, 1941, German troops entered Yugoslavia, and a few days later, Greece. Yugoslavia capitulated on April 14, and Greece on April 23, after resisting the Italian onslaught for six months and inflicting some shameful defeats on the Italian Army.

General Erwin Rommel proved how important the African theater of war might have become when he reconquered Cyrenaica (it had been taken from the Italians by the English) in a mere twelve days with only one light Panzer division and limited support of the Luftwaffe.

After the occupation of Yugoslavia, Greece, and Crete, with Rommel's troops at the gates of Egypt, Hitler, using the Italian air and sea bases, could have created for the British a most dangerous situation in the Mediterranean. He had always dreamed of a "world empire," but he had no global concept, either politically or militarily. His campaigns were rather reminiscent of those of Genghis Khan's raiding hordes.

The Balkan campaign compelled Hitler to postpone the German suprise attack on the Soviet Union by precisely five weeks; he later failed to achieve the first objectives of his campaign. He had miscalculated in every way: the time needed, the enemy's strength, the hardships of the climate. He set out—as once upon a time the Crusaders had—into the immeasurable unknown.

It is difficult to assess exactly when Hitler informed Goebbels of his Russian war plans. Goebbels' press attaché, Semmler, wrote in his diary on April 28, 1941, that Goebbels had told him after dining with Hitler about the Fuehrer's preoccupation with such terrifying plans that even Hitler's closest collaborators trembled at the thought. Hitler, said Goebbels, had neither eyes nor ears for anything else and was working on these plans until two or three o'clock in the morning; but he was obviously thriving on it. He had never seen the Fuehrer more alert and in better humor. Goebbels added that the execution of those plans would bring Hitler his greatest triumph to date and secure for him the rank of the greatest European in history.[59]

This was probably the first time that Hitler had talked to his Propaganda Minister about his Russian venture. Yet it was only two

weeks since Semmler had recorded Goebbels' reaction when learning that Stalin had heartily embraced the German deputy military
attaché in Moscow, Colonel Krebs, with the words: "If we stand together like brothers nothing can ever happen to us. Do everything to
see that we remain good friends." Goebbels appeared "most excited" and commented approvingly: "Stalin's words open up completely new vistas. They could give Germany's policy a totally new
direction, and are likely to determine the shape of Europe for the
next thirty years. We shall see what the Fuehrer thinks about it."[60]

Although Goebbels, too, lacked a global political concept—one of
the reasons why his propaganda had no success abroad—he nevertheless had a greater understanding of world politics than Hitler, whose
thoughts would always turn in circles. And Goebbels must have
trembled when he heard for the first time of the Fuehrer's Russian
plans. But no one dared doubt Hitler's ideas then, let alone criticize
them. The Fuehrer had, after all, in a short year and a half defeated
Poland, Norway, Holland, Belgium, France, Yugoslavia, and Greece,
and had, in effect, become the greatest German conqueror of all time.
A civilian like Goebbels, who could not even correctly stand at attention, had better keep his mouth shut about such grave military
matters.

In this period of victories that outshone by far any diplomatic
failures, an event took place that any sane observer would have ob-
served as the writing on the wall. On May 10, the Fuehrer's deputy,
Rudolf Hess, flew to Scotland to contact the Duke of Hamilton, whom
he had met at the Olympic Games in Berlin. His intention was, as
Hess said in a letter he left for Hitler, to try to bring about an end of
the war by negotiation. Whether the British Secret Service had anything to do with it, or whether Hitler knew of this beforehand, still
remains obscure.[61]

In any case, the event made a devastating impression on the Germans, and Hitler ordered an official announcement that said that Hess
had suffered under "the delusion" of being able to bring about "an
understanding between Germany and England" by his personal initiative.

Semmler reports[62] that the formulation of this announcement
annoyed Goebbels, as it was bound to worry the people who would
ask themselves how Hess could have remained the Fuehrer's deputy
if Hess was suffering from delusions. But Hitler had specially underlined Hess's abnormal state, fearing Hess would tell England about
his Russian plans.

At the beginning of May Goebbels told a secret conference, attended by ten top members of his ministry: "Gentlemen, I know that

some of you believe that a military campaign is being prepared against Russia. It is my duty to inform you that it is not Russia we are going to attack, but England. The invasion is imminent. Take this line. You, Dr. Glasmeier [chief of broadcasts], prepare new victory fanfares for England."[63]

On June 13, 1941, the Berlin edition of the *Völkische Beobachter* published Goebbels' headline "Crete as an Example." It contained allusions to a military enterprise, and was designed to make the reader believe that an invasion of England was imminent. The edition was seized, but not before copies had been mailed to subscribers and foreign correspondents. On the following day rumors were rife in Berlin that Goebbels, owing to his careless indiscretion, had fallen into disgrace with Hitler, who even refused to see him. The fact was that they conferred together daily.

Goebbels failed to deceive the British government. He was possibly more successful in deceiving the Soviets. Stalin, who in May 1941 had assumed the position of chairman of the Supreme Council of the People's Commissars as well as that of Premier, did everything in his power to ward off any eventual aggressive plans of Hitler's. Stalin took special measures, such as shutting down all Russian embassies and legations in all countries occupied by Germany, in order to emphasize his loyal intention of keeping strictly to his agreement with Hitler.

In the meantime, the world press was talking about German troop concentrations on the Soviet borders, and Stalin had actually been warned by the American and British governments to that effect.

On June 14, one day after Goebbels' suppressed lead editorial in the *Völkische Beobachter,* the Soviet radio broadcast a Tass announcement holding Sir Stafford Cripps, British ambassador to the Soviet Union, responsible for spreading the rumor that war between Germany and the USSR was imminent.[64] It remains a mystery how the Soviets could have failed to notice the concentration of German troops on a front of 2,400 kilometers.

On June 22, 1941, at 3:30 A.M., German troops crossed the Soviet borders. Two and a half hours later, Goebbels gave the news over the radio. Reich Press Chief Dietrich, who—incredible as it seems—claimed he had had no knowledge of Hitler's plans beforehand and had himself been a victim of Goebbels' propaganda—recounts how Hitler, as someone had told Dietrich, remarked to the few people present, at three o'clock in the morning, only half an hour before the war started: "I feel as though I'm about to force open a door into an unknown, dark room—without knowing what I'll find behind the door."[65] Waiting behind the door was the greatest catastrophe into which any statesman had ever criminally dragged his people.

German troops penetrated deep into the Soviet Union. Only three months later, on October 3, 1941, Hitler announced in a speech that the enemy had been utterly defeated and would never rise again. This was one week after Kiev had fallen and 665,000 Soviet soldiers, caught in a cauldron, had capitulated. The morning after the town of Orel had been taken (October 8), Hitler, intoxicated with his victory, sent a message from headquarters to Press Chief Dietrich in Berlin ordering him to tell the press that the Soviet campaign had been practically decided.

This announcement compromised Dietrich and later served Goebbels to expose his rival's ineptitude.

Hitler had disastrously overrated his victories. To make matters worse, Corporal Hitler, wanting to be wiser than his generals, rejected their strategic plan, which proposed throwing the armies in the central sector against Moscow, which was not only the capital, but also the most important industrial concentration and traffic junction of the Soviet Union. Hitler wanted to conquer first the Donez Basin and the Crimea in order to insure the economic requirements the war imposed.

When Hitler finally, albeit too late, ordered the attack against Moscow on October 20, 1941, German troops were only 60 kilometers from the Russian capital. But now the rains came, and with them the notorious mud. The German attack got stuck in it. An early winter followed, revealing yet another unbelievable mistake of the German war leaders.

According to Goebbels' personal aide,[66] the Propaganda Minister approached General Jodl, Chief of Staff, asking if he should organize a collection of winter clothing and furs. Jodl firmly advised against it with the argument that such a collection might come as a shock to the soldiers and the people, as no one believed that the war would last into the winter: "When winter comes we'll be sitting in the warm quarters of Leningrad and Moscow," Jodl assured Goebbels.

General Wagner, general quartermaster of the Army, organized in the autumn of 1941 an exhibition at Smolensk that displayed, among other items, the winter equipment of German soldiers, wearing furs and fur boots. It also showed blockhouses with cozy interiors. To Goebbels' question, "But have you sufficient supplies of those items?", the general answered: "More than sufficient. Our stores are bulging with them. Heaps of them are already rolling toward the front." Thereupon Goebbels had a film documentary made of this exhibition, which was shown in all cinemas at home.

Winter came and the German soldiers did not sit in warm quarters in Leningrad or Moscow, but had to retreat in haste, if not in panic. Tens of thousands of soldiers froze to death. The temperature was −40°C, and they had no winter equipment. Some of the wounded froze to the wooden boards of the boxcars evacuating them, and had to be hacked free with pickaxes. Their frozen guns refused to function, and supplies of material, food, and fuel—in particular, gasoline—no longer reached their destination. The Panzers were stuck, and guns of all sizes had to be abandoned.

Against all this, the Soviets brought up well-rested troops from Siberia, fully equipped for winter warfare, and started their counteroffensive on December 6, 1941. The German armies, it appeared, had been singled out for the grim fate that had once overtaken Napoleon's Grande Armée.

The great moment had come for Hitler. He accepted the resignation of the chief of the army, General Field Marshal von Brauchitsch, dismissed a number of Army commanders (among them the two top Panzer commanders, General Guderian and General Hoepner), and forbade any further retreat at whatever cost. His view—that it was preferable to stand their ground under all circumstances, even if they were overrun at certain points, rather than to risk, by a retreat through ice and snow, a disintegration of the army—proved essentially right, but could not prevent a catastrophe.

Between June 22, 1941, and February 28, 1942, the German Army lost over 200,000 dead (of which more than half had frozen to death), over 700,000 wounded, and more than 40,000 missing.[67]

Despite his defeat in the East, Hitler had the audacity to declare war on the United States on December 11. The United States had been at war with Japan since Japan's attack on Pearl Harbor on December 7. Except at sea, there was no immediate danger of a clash between the United States and Germany. But once again Hitler overestimated his own strength and underestimated the economic war potential of his new adversary. He believed Japan would prevent the United States from taking part in the European war and would cause a reduction of American supplies of arms and goods to Britain.

The experience of the Russian winter campaign was a turning point for Goebbels. He had, up till then, remained in the shadow of the military; the civilian Goebbels now regained his self-confidence. His collection of winter clothes for soldiers at the front had been a great success. Goebbels lost his diffident attitude toward the military. He now felt not only their equal but even their superior. The last phase in Goebbels' life—one might call it his Frederican Period—had begun.

Vain Effort

Goebbels now reconsidered the whole situation. It was probably then
that the idea occurred to him for the first time that the war could be
lost. This effected a deep transformation in him. He became a militarist. Henceforth he would be the most passionate fighter and fanatic
advocate of total war. In any case he was the first among the NS
leaders who realized that the last chance had come and that only the
concentrated total force of the nation might still prevent a debacle.

Hitherto Goebbels had only been Hitler's mouthpiece and had refrained from forming his own ideas about the military and political
direction of the war. He now became a merciless critic of both.
And there was yet another significant change in Goebbels' attitude.
He had, up till then, always anxiously courted Hitler's favor; he had
feared Goering, Himmler, and Bormann; he had felt threatened
should Hitler ever withdraw his personal protection from him. This
feeling of insecurity had weakened him; he had been a tool in Hitler's
hands. Now his fear seemed to have vanished as with a single stroke.
He no longer feared Goering or Himmler, and even his fear of Bormann was not so much personal as factual. He feared, and not without reason, that Bormann would impede Hitler from making the
necessary changes in the badly disorganized political leadership.
Goebbels was conscious of his growing courage, and wrote in his
diary on January 21, 1942:

"I no longer consider it to be my main task to keep order in my
own ministry, but rather to fight the defeatism of Berlin's governmental circles, whatever the consequences. I fear nothing and nobody,
save the possibility of Germany's defeat. To fear any man is the most
dangerous thing in times of crisis: and as Nietzsche said, there is only
one sin: cowardice. . . ."

Goebbels recognized the need for creating not only the appropriate
military, but also the appropriate political conditions for winning the
war. He believed in Hitler's military leadership—a forgivable error
for a civilian who could only rely on what he actually saw, and was
in no position to discover for some time the inner crisis of the military
direction, which was a direct consequence of Hitler's amateurish orders and his dangerous disdain of professional advice. Goebbels
shared Hitler's opinion about the German generals, whose views were
completely devoid of any revolutionary impetus and who were mere
technicians without much military genius or ability to improvise.

And in Goebbels' view, Hitler possessed precisely these two rather decisive qualities, borne out by Hitler's actions during the winter months. When the generals had lost their nerve, Hitler stood his ground unshakably and proved his superiority to the military experts. Goebbels, too, showed a gift for improvisation when calling on the people to donate winter clothes for the soldiers at the front. He did not wait for Hitler's approval, nor did he consider the objections of the generals. He was the first German politician to draw the people's attention to the gravity of the position, and put an end to the people's illusions, created by the military and political leaders.

At the outbreak of the war against Poland, Hitler, in his speech in the Reichstag on September 1, 1939, proclaimed Hermann Goering as his successor. A "Council of Ministers for the Defense of the Reich" was created, with Goering presiding. This Council of Ministers was to be a Supreme Command at home in the event that Hitler's activities as Supreme Commander of the Armed Forces prevented him from devoting himself to his duties as Reich Chancellor. The rapid successes of the various campaigns until the summer of 1941 made it unnecessary for the Council of Ministers to go into action. At first Hitler's attack on the Soviet Union looked like a blitzkrieg, but then came the catastrophe of the winter of 1941–42, which should have been the moment for Goering to wield the Council of Ministers into a responsible instrument for conducting policy at home. Goering missed this chance.

With the loss of the Battle of Britain, Goering's decline set in. It seemed that the "Iron Hermann" was a man of iron only for as long as he faced those who were weaker. He did not dare to touch those who were strong, men like Himmler or Bormann, or even men of lesser strength, such as Goebbels. Yet, for him too, Hitler was a god. In the presence of the Fuehrer he was a yes-man like all the others. With the declining prestige of the Luftwaffe, Goering's prestige with the people, the party, and Hitler declined accordingly. The general disillusion with him was complete when allied air attacks on German towns began, and when Goering's promise to supply the Sixth Army in Stalingrad from the air remained unfulfilled, demonstrating only too clearly that the Supreme Commander of the Luftwaffe (after Prince Eugen, the second Reich marshal in German history) had no accurate idea of the actual strength of his Air Force. He had been mistaken at Dunkirk, again at the Battle of Britain, and at Stalingrad; and he had failed to protect Germany from enemy air attacks. It did not take long for the people to call him Herr Meier; had he not said his name would be Meier should an English plane ever succeed in bombing a German town?

The military direction of the war against the Soviet Union left

Hitler without enough time to conduct the political affairs of the
Reich. The disorganization which, owing to Hitler's undisciplined
working methods, had already started before the war, only grew from
day to day. The fact that the administrative apparatus of the Reich
continued turning over was only due to the seasoned bureaucracy,
which became more and more powerful, supplanting political leadership by organized disorganization. Government was, practically speaking, in the hands of three men: Hans Heinrich Lammers, chief of
the Reich Chancellery; Field Marshal William Keitel, chief of the
OKW (High Command of the Armed Forces); and Martin Bormann, chief of the Party Bureau. Bormann, personal secretary to
the Fuehrer, was the *de facto* chief of the party. Lammers and Keitel,
with but little character of their own, were only too eager to carry
out Hitler's orders. The dangerous man was Bormann, because of
his close position to the Fuehrer. Everything passed through Bormann's hands. Bormann had known how to make himself indispensable, even at the time when Hess was still the Fuehrer's deputy.
Bormann would carefully make notes of everything, which enabled
him to furnish any information the Fuehrer required. He was the
strongest influence on Hitler and, as all agree, an evil influence.
Bormann bore the main guilt for the general radicalization that took
place. Any pronouncement of Hitler's that might bring Bormann any
personal advantage, Bormann released as a decree. He was generally
feared.

"The three kings,"[68] as Goering used to call Lammers, Keitel,
and Bormann, were in charge of all business that belonged to the
Reich President, the Reich Chancellor, the Minister of Defense, and
the leader of the party. Being the only party in existence, it was at
least as powerful as, if not more powerful than, the Reich administration. A political leadership and a co-ordination between the Reich
ministers and the Reich administrative bodies were practically non-
existent. Goebbels took up the fight against this paralysis of the
Reich's political leadership. It took him three years to win this fight;
and when he had won it, it was too late.

Goebbels combined the fight for a functional political leadership
with his fight for a total war effort, which he started immediately
after the first military setbacks in the winter of 1941–42. Excluded
from the military conduct of the war up till then—his task was to report the military victories in special announcements—Goebbels was
aware of the fact that he would play the least significant role within
the party leadership after the war was over, since he had not been
able to influence the military course of the war. He actually toyed
with the idea of retiring after the war and writing books about

Christ, about German history from 1900 to the present day, and about films.

The winter campaign of 1941–42 woke him up. It only confirmed his poor opinion of generals, and, like Hitler and all the other dilettantes, he thought that a fanatical will to persevere at whatever cost was worth more than the factual and tactical considerations of military experts.

Hitler, who during his victories had rather neglected the civilian Goebbels, preferring the company of his generals, now turned to Goebbels once again, to confide his bitter disappointments with those same generals. Hitler's complaints acted like a balm for Goebbels' injured civilian soul. For the first time since the Baarova affair the old intimacy between Goebbels and the Fuehrer was re-established. The concord of their souls grew stronger from day to day, until, in the last year, it had become indispensable to them, a deep emotional need for both. They gave each other strength and consolation. Their relationship could only be destroyed by death, and even then they chose to act together.

In the winter of 1941, when the Russian front was beginning to crumble and the German people, used to victories and emotionally unprepared, were at a loss to understand what was happening in the East, Goebbels set to work to disabuse them of their illusion that victory was imminent. At the same time he tried to console them. This contradictory double massage applied to the soul of the German people—on the one hand Churchillian lamentations of sweat, blood, and tears, and on the other hand, the consoling assurance that history had always given victory to those who could heroically withstand the worst onslaught of Fate—was perhaps Goebbels' propagandistic masterpiece. His essay "When and How," published on November 9, 1941, in *Das Reich,* and especially his broadcast of December 21, 1941, imploring donations of winter clothing for the soldiers at the front, were the cries of Cassandra. They contradicted Hitler's prediction, as well as that of the Reich Press Chief who, on the Fuehrer's orders, had announced the impending defeat of the Red Army only one month earlier. Goebbels was too clever to build his propaganda on a lie that sooner or later was bound to be found out.

In his article Goebbels argued that Poland's rejection of Germany's modest demands for Danzig and a way through the Polish Corridor had led to war, which had opened up "all the old European problems which had never been solved, or solved only very unsatisfactorily." The "dying plutocracies" held "Germany, with its growing birthrate, pressed into a too-narrow living space, at her throat with a suffocating grip," excluding her "from the world's riches and raw materials," and thereby condemning her "to a long drawn-out agony and ultimate end of her people." As for the Soviet Union: She had condemned 170 million to a miserable existence in order to build up Bolshevik armed forces that would fall upon the ailing continent, overtaken by a crisis. Goebbels drew his conclusions:

"More important than the question as to when this war will end, is the question how it will end. If we win, everything will be won: free access to raw materials and food, *Lebensraum,* a basis for the social transformation of our state and a chance for the Axis powers to fulfil their national destiny; if we lose, all that will be lost, and more: our very existence as a nation. . . . Today's opportunity will never come again. The chance our nation has today is the best it ever had, but also the last."

Having told the people they should not expect a quick end to the war, since Fate never gave anything for nothing, Goebbels administered a sedative after the shock. In an article of December 7, 1941, headed "A Necessary Rectification," Goebbels pointed to the attitude of the Prussian people during the Seven Year War (1756–63), when Frederick II withstood a European coalition and was rewarded for his heroism by history, which accorded him victory. Goebbels also mentioned the conquest of Berlin by National Socialism, which he had begun with only a few hundred determined party comrades. If, then, the Prussian people could withstand an enemy forty times as strong, and the Berlin NSDAP could conquer with their puny forces the "reddest of all cities" in the world after Moscow, with how much more right might the German people be certain of final victory now, providing they would rise to a similar heroic spirit, backed by the world's strongest armed forces. A whole continent with its inexhaustible resources was manufacturing arms for Hitler's army: "Yes, we believe in our victory, it will be ours for sure. On this I'll bet my life."

Goebbels was usually more careful than Goering to take such personal risks, but he could safely do it this time. Years before the war, Goebbels had declared he would never survive a German defeat.[69]

In the spring of 1942, when the Russian offensive had come to a halt, the shock had been successfully absorbed. Both sides, thoroughly exhausted, needed a break. In March 1942 Goebbels had a long talk with Hitler who, still angry with the generals, received sympathetically Goebbels' proposals for a totalization of the war effort.

"In the mood he was in, my proposals to radicalize the conduct of the war have a most positive effect on the Fuehrer. I only need to touch on a problem and I have gained my point. Every detail I submit to him, the Fuehrer accepts without questioning."

At the end of their talk Goebbels is overjoyed, as always after having been in Hitler's company. "It is wonderful for me to be able to talk to the Fuehrer at length, also about my personal problems. Once again he has the effect of a power source recharging me with energy. After you spend an afternoon with him you feel like a recharged battery."[70]

The civilian Goebbels needed this emotional recharge even more than the militarist Hitler. As a civilian, Goebbels knew how susceptible the people were to peace rumors, which had originated abroad and infiltrated into the Reich. Goebbels wrote in his diary on March 6, 1942: "There is a lot of talk in the neutral countries of a separate peace between Germany and the Soviet Union. London has become rather apprehensive about it. They need not fear. The Soviet Union will and must be smashed, however long it takes us. . . ."

Hitler had told him when they met on March 20 of his plan to start a great offensive against the Soviet Union in the spring. Although "it was not his intention to prolong the war indefinitely, his aim is to occupy the Caucasus, Leningrad, and Moscow. As soon as this is done, he intends under all circumstances to halt the campaign at the beginning of October, and occupy winter quarters in good time. His idea is to build up a gigantic line of defense and keep the war in the East static. Another winter like the last will not happen again. The war in the East may, if need be, become a hundred years' war without being any longer a worry to us. We shall then occupy a similar position toward the remainder of Russia as the English occupy in India."

These words alone show why Hitler was bound to lose the war. His medieval idea of a hundred years' war in a world of modern techniques demonstrates his primitive way of reasoning. But quite apart from his false assessment of reality, Hitler's policy would have been fatal even if it had been possible to freeze the war in the East. In that event he would have needed the support of the peoples of the eastern territories in order to exploit their hostility to the Bolshevist regime; but his racial prejudices and his policy of terror against them had transformed potential friends into sworn enemies. And this was not the only reason. Hitler's inability to assess the situation in global terms was the deeper cause of why the campaign he had begun so promisingly in the spring and summer of 1942 was bound to end disastrously. In the meantime, the question of the inner German organization was pushed into the background once more.

All eyes were anxiously on what was happening at the Russian and North African fronts.

Rommel started his attack in North Africa on May 27. On June 21, Tobruk was taken, and on June 23, German troops crossed the Egyptian border. At the end of June they had reached El Alamein, 100 kilometers from Alexandria. Once again England was hit in a most vulnerable spot. With an additional number of Panzers and troops, and the necessary support of the Luftwaffe, Rommel should have found it not too difficult to cross Egypt and reach the oil fields in the near East. This would have put Britain—which, as it was, had great difficulty containing the Japanese in the Indian Ocean—in a catastrophic position. But Hitler was incapable of seeing this important tactical advantage.

He refused to send more Panzers or men; he did not even order the Luftwaffe and the necessary naval forces into action to neutralize Malta, which Britain used as a vital base for operations by air and sea against the German and Italian supply lines. Hitler's omissions soon proved disastrous. On October 23, Montgomery started his counteroffensive, and owing to the crushing superiority in men and matériel of the British forces, destroyed the greater part of Rommel's army and chased the rest back into Libya. Hitler's only answer was to order Rommel not to retreat any farther. But when Anglo-American troops, under Eisenhower's supreme command, landed in Morocco on November 9, 1942, Hitler shipped 250,000 German and Italian soldiers to Tunisia who, for the lack of supplies and insufficient air support, were in a hopeless strategic position from the start. If four months earlier Hitler had sent Rommel only a part of this army, the position would have been exactly the reverse.

But in June, when Hitler should have grasped the great strategic opportunity Rommel's advance to El Alamein had presented, his mind was not on Africa. It was, indeed, a unique chance, to use Goebbels' words, one that would never come again. But Hitler was entirely steeped in his Russian campaign, where at the time everything seemed to go wonderfully well.

On August 8, German troops reached the oil fields of Maikop, and on August 23, the German Sixth Army under General Paulus reached the Volga, north of Stalingrad, which gave them control of Russian oil transports going up the Volga from the Caspian Sea into central Russia. Instead of following the advice of his General Staff and ordering the Fourth Panzer Army to advance on Stalingrad and take it, Hitler withdrew his Panzers and ordered them to advance on the Caucasian oil fields. This was a grave error, but not less grave than turning a deaf ear on Rommel's demands for further troops and matériel. These errors were the result of Hitler's inability to conceive strategy in global terms and his failure to assess correctly his resources. He underestimated the vastness of the Russian territory and failed to see that he had not enough troops, Panzers, artillery, and planes to meet the need for reinforcements with the means of transport at his disposal.

On September 23, 1942, Goebbels wrote in his diary that Stalingrad would prove to be the decisive battle of the war. On September 27, he had second thoughts about the official optimistic views, expecting an early fall of Stalingrad:

"My impression is that we have fostered too many illusions in regard to our military operations at Stalingrad. Especially the Reich Press Chief has pursued a policy that is simply irresponsible. Before one could even speak of Stalingrad having fallen, he had already special editions printed announcing our victory. Naturally, this became generally known, raising hopes that could not be fulfilled. And, as they failed to materialize, a mood of general disappointment set in. . . . Special editions should wait until we have actually taken Stalingrad."

The civilian Goebbels, with his premonition of catastrophe, saw the military situation more clearly than the "greatest warlord of all time," but also more clearly than even the military expert, General Paulus, who informed Hitler on October 25 that he estimated the fall of Stalingrad by November 10 at the latest.[71]

At the end of October a secret SD (Sicherheitsdienst—Security Service) report confirmed Goebbels' fear that his own anxiety was shared by the people. "The battle for Stalingrad," the report stated, "is often compared with the fighting around Verdun in the First World War, particularly with the heavy losses suffered then." Should it come to a "war of position, and to a battle of material annihilation," the report continues, Germany will once again be beaten in an armament race as she was beaten before in the First World War. Goebbels must have been particularly impressed with the closing paragraph of the report, which said: "Rumors about an armistice with the Soviet Union are spreading to all parts of the Reich, including the most remote and smallest villages. The impact of these rumors on certain sections of the population, particularly on women, is considerable. It was, for instance, reported from Freital, near Dresden, that on October 23, 1942, when the rumor of an impending peace with the Soviet Union had reached the population, a wave of enthusiasm swept the town. Scenes of joyful fraternization took place in the street, sweeping all restraint overboard. . . ."[72]

On November 8, Hitler announced at a memorial meeting on the anniversary of the march to the Feldherrnhalle that Stalingrad had fallen. He had based his announcement on a report he had received from General Paulus. But since the Fuehrer never lied, the Sixth Army was forbidden to retreat to the West when the Soviets opened their offensive on November 19. Hitler chose to ignore completely the advice of his Chief of Staff, General Kurt Zeitzler, who had succeeded General Halder, whom the Fuehrer had dismissed.[73]

In the meantime the German people and their Propaganda Minister got the jitters. They did not yet know the full extent of the tragedy being played out at Stalingrad. But they knew that Rommel's army had been defeated in North Africa and that the Western Allies had landed in Morocco and Algeria. The moment had come for Goebbels to propose to Hitler the necessary reforms for totalizing the war effort. The salient points were extension of working hours, mobilization of women's labor, and the closing down of all luxury shops and establishments. Hitler was hesitating, but as a sign of his appreciation, he sent Goebbels a Christmas gift consisting of ten pounds of coffee, five pounds of butter, and a magnificent ham. He also sent his Propaganda Minister an armored Mercedes, ordering him to use no other car. Goebbels had recently escaped an attempt on his life: Dr. Kumerow, the departmental chief of a radio factory, had made plans to assassinate Goebbels on September 19, 1942. The plan was to blow up the bridge leading to Schwanenwerder the moment the Propaganda Minister's car was crossing it. Kumerow was caught in the act of affixing an explosive charge under the bridge. He was put before a people's court a few days later, condemned to death, and executed.[74]

Goebbels' proposals for totalizing the war effort were put before a committee consisting of Lammers, Keitel, and Bormann. Goebbels attended in an advisory capacity. No action was taken. But then, on February 21, 1943, the news of the capitulation of the Sixth Army in Stalingrad struck the German people like a bolt from the blue. Of the 285,000 men, only 49,000 had been evacuated by air; 91,000 were taken prisoner, of which only 6,000 were to see their homeland ever again. Over 140,000 men had fallen, the most terrifying price ever paid for the obstinacy and vainglorious pride of a man prepared to sacrifice thousands of lives as long as he was not proved a liar. Hitler and his military and political advisers were at a loss to know how to impart to the people the news of this catastrophic defeat. Only Goebbels had no difficulty in plucking up enough courage to tell the people the bitter truth. For him, the news, grim as it was, was yet another challenge to his propagandist skill, in some way not less exciting than the announcement of a great victory. Had he not in the past successfully used funerals for great propagandist occasions? No fanfares this time, but muted drumbeats preceding the special announcement: "The battle for Stalingrad has come to an end. Faithful to their oath of allegiance, to their flag, fighting to their last breath, the Sixth Army, under the exemplary command of General Field Marshal von Paulus, has succumbed to superior enemy forces and adverse conditions."

The announcement was followed once again by muted drumbeats and, instead of the *Niederländische Dankgebet, Ich hatt ein Kameraden* was played. Then silence and, after the silence as consolation for the wounded hearts, came the tender A-major theme of the *Andante con moto* of Beethoven's Fifth Symphony, played by a violoncello. Newspapers appeared with a black border, and all theaters and places of entertainment were closed for three days. A people mourned their dead.

"Now, People, Rise, and Storm, Break Loose"

According to the Wehrmacht communiqué, Stalingrad was supposed to be a modern repetition of the battle at Thermopylae. It had no resemblance whatever to that famous battle of antiquity. If it had, the commander of the army, General von Paulus (promoted by Hitler at the last moment, on January 30, to general field marshal), would, as Hitler hoped, perish together with his army. Instead Paulus capitulated and was made prisoner, together with twenty-four other German generals. Paulus was hardly like Leonidas, who led the 300 Spartans defending the pass at Thermopylae against the Persians and died at their side. The sacrifice of the defenders of Thermopylae, fighting to the last man, gave the Athenian general Themistokles enough time to make preparations for the naval battle at Salamis, where he defeated the Persian fleet.[75]

The battle of Stalingrad, however, was totally senseless. It improved in no way the position of the German armies. The German soldiers at Stalingrad did not give their lives because the law demanded it of them, but because of one man's vainglory.

The catastrophe of Stalingrad was entirely unsuited to form the basis of a Thermopylae myth, however much Hitler wished it would. He rather resented that Paulus had not chosen death. It did not take long for Goebbels to size up the situation. He was determined to use Stalingrad as a torch to kindle the people's enthusiasm for a last supreme effort. Even the form he chose to present the grave news was designed to move the people and at once create a mood of heroism. Then his speech—and Goebbels was determined to surpass himself on this occasion—would do the rest and put them well on the road to total war.

Goebbels took more care in preparing this speech than ever before. He spent days dictating it, altering it, and, when he had finished it in the early morning of the appointed day, February 18, he rehearsed it in front of a mirror.

As early as February 15, after he had drafted the general outline of his speech, he recorded in his diary: "My speech in the Sportpalast. I think it's very good. It could be the *chef d'oeuvre* of my career as orator." At the same time he was not in a particularly happy mood. On the same day he admits to himself: "I sometimes feel an almost paralyzing anxiety if I think of our military position at the front." And: "My work presses like a nightmare upon my body, soul, and spirit. Late at night, dead tired as I am, I can't fall asleep."

On February 18, at 8 P.M., the Sportpalast was packed to capacity. Goebbels, greeted by a storm of "Heils!," stepped onto the rostrum. The entire radio network was geared to transmit his speech. The suspense was almost intolerable. One can still feel it, even today, when listening to the record of the speech.[76] Goebbels started quietly. His words penetrated the enormous hall clearly.

"The German people with their discipline can bear the truth." But soon came the first clarion call; his voice became steely:

"Stalingrad is the voice of Fate sounding the alarm. Time presses, there is none left for talk, we must act. . . . A savage, determined will lives in us to ward off the danger. A heart of steel equal to all assaults from within and from without . . ."

After that the speaker again became calm and his voice matter-of-fact: "We have underrated the war potential of the Soviet Union. It has only now revealed itself in its full magnitude. . . . If we were to fail in this struggle . . . history would lose all sense. . . ."

Goebbels elaborated three theses:

1. Should the Wehrmacht fail to crush the danger threatening from the East, it would mean that the Reich, and soon the whole of Europe, would be extradited to Bolshevism.

2. Only the Wehrmacht and the German people, helped by their allies, have the strength to save Europe from this mortal peril.

3. This peril is upon us. We must act quickly and thoroughly lest it be too late.

Bolshevism, Goebbels continued, "if it ever were victorious, would not halt at Germany's frontiers"; it was out to conquer all countries:

"We know that there, in the East, we have to deal with an infernal, politically diabolical adversary. . . . Bolshevism is not only a terrorist doctrine but also a terrorist practice. It pursues its aims . . . without any regard for the happiness, the well-being, and the peace of the subjugated peoples."

But because in the East "a whole people are forced into combat," and "men, women, well-nigh children, are not only used in the armament factories, but also driven into the fighting, total war"—and now Goebbels' voice rose in a powerful crescendo—"has become our urgent duty." The question was not whether the methods applied by necessity were "good" or "bad," but solely whether they were effective.

And Goebbels enumerated some impending measures—every single one being greeted with applause: closing down bars and night-spots, luxury restaurants, luxury shops, fashion houses, and hair-dressing salons. Reduction of bureaucratic procedure—offices will dispatch a greater number of their staff to the front.

Goebbels also demanded a complete cessation of private journeys and sojourns in spas, because "the Fuehrer had—since war started, and even long before that—not taken off one single day."

Theaters, cinemas, and concert halls should remain open, as they served the people by fortifying their "fighting and working morale." . . . "The people," Goebbels exclaimed, "demand a Spartan standard of living for everybody, high and low, rich and poor."

At the end of his speech, Goebbels put forth the famous ten questions:

"1. The English say the German people have lost their faith in victory. I ask you: Have you faith, with our Fuehrer and us, in the final total victory of the German people?

"I ask you: Are you prepared to follow the Fuehrer in his struggle for victory, however thorny the path may be, and however great your personal sacrifices?

"2. The English say the German people are war-weary.

"I ask you: Are you prepared to form, with the Fuehrer at the head, the phalanx at home, behind our embattled soldiers, ready to continue the struggle with savage determination, impervious to what-ever Fate may bring, until victory shall be ours?

"3. The English say the German people are no longer willing to continue the ever-growing war effort the government demands.

"I ask you: Are you, are the German people prepared to work ten, twelve, if need be, fourteen and sixteen hours a day, if the Fuehrer orders them to do so, and give all they possess for victory?

"4. The English say the German people reject the governmental measures for total war. They do not want total war but capitulation. [Shouts of 'Never! Never! Never!']

"I ask you: Do you want total war? Do you want war, if need be, even more total and more radical than any we can imagine today?

"5. The English say the German people have lost their faith in the Fuehrer.

"I ask you: Is your faith in the Fuehrer today greater, deeper, and even more unshakable than ever before? Are you absolutely and unconditionally prepared to follow him on his way and to do everything that is necessary to bring this war to a victorious end?"

The crowd jumped up, erupting with boundless enthusiasm. Many thousands roared as with one voice: *Führer befiehl, wir folgen!* (Fuehrer order us and we shall follow!)

A never-ending storm of "Heils!" for Hitler erupted.

"My sixth question: Are you prepared from now on to give every ounce of your strength to supply the Eastern front with all men and arms they need to strike Bolshevism the mortal blow?

"My seventh question: Do you give your solemn oath to the soldiers at the front, that those at home will stand firmly behind them with an unshakable spirit and give them what they need to win victory?

"My eighth question: Do you want, particularly you, women, that the government makes arrangements enabling the German woman too, to put her whole strength behind the war effort? To fill the gap wherever possible, free men for the front, and thus help our soldiers at the front?

"My ninth question is: Do you approve that the most radical measures be taken, if need be, against the small number of war shirkers and black marketeers, who, in the midst of war, play at peace, trying to exploit the people's needs for their personal advantage? Do you agree that whoever sins against the war should be put to death?

"My tenth and last question is: Do you want that in accordance with the National Socialist party program, all citizens should share rights and duties equally—particularly in war-time—and that all people at home should carry the war burden together, and that this burden should be distributed equally among the high and low, the rich and the poor?"

Each question was answered by a thundering chorus from twenty thousand throats, shouting "Yes!" The Sportpalast was like a witch's cauldron. The people, almost beyond themselves, roared their enthusiasm, practically drowning Goebbels' last words. His voice now sounded hoarse, but his words were filled with savage passion:

". . . We, the leaders of the party, the state, and the Wehrmacht, swear to you, swear to the front, and swear to the Fuehrer that we shall weld the people at home into one. Never again shall we fall into our old vice of indulging in too much objectivity, which has damaged us so much in the past.

"The nation is prepared for everything—the Fuehrer has given his orders and we shall obey. If ever in the past we believed in victory loyally and firmly, we now believe in it more than ever. . . . Just as proud as we are of the Fuehrer, he shall be proud of us. In times of crisis the truly strong show their mettle. . . . Victory is within our reach—we need only grasp it. We must only marshal the necessary will power to subordinate everything else to it. This is what the hour demands. Let, therefore, our motto be: 'Now, people, rise, and storm, break loose.' "

Goebbels' speech about total war was, in fact, an attack against "the three kings," and particularly against Bormann.

The Struggle for Internal Leadership

The Propaganda Minister wanted to mobilize the people against the delaying tactics of the three chiefs of the Reich Chancellery. Casting his eyes around for suitable allies, he found them in Dr. Robert Ley, chief of the party organization; in his former state secretary, Dr. Walther Funk, now Minister of Economy; and in Albert Speer. These three, joined later on by some other important party personalities, met, from the beginning of 1943, practically every Wednesday evening in Goebbels' apartment.

Speer had succeeded Dr. Todt in February 1944 as Reich Minister for Armaments and Munitions. The young gifted architect and technician who, before his appointment as minister, had constructed some buildings for the Fuehrer and designed plans for Hitler's even more ambitious architectural projects—Speer had, in fact, become Hitler's favorite architect—now took upon himself a task that, no doubt, appeared difficult but all the more tempting. Speer was a technocrat, in some ways a forerunner of Robert McNamara. He, too, preferred to work with statistics and calculations, and was far more interested in production figures than in political considerations. Speer's figures and statistics mesmerized and, to a certain degree, misled the nontechnicians Hitler and Goebbels.

According to a secret SD report,[77] many Germans already had by then some doubts about the accuracy of Speer's figure magic; lacking information about the respective enemy figures, they were unable to make any comparisons. Goebbels deplored Dr. Todt's death. He had considered him, next to himself, the only efficient minister in the Cabinet. Nevertheless, he admired Speer too, whose unconventional methods of running his ministry he vividly welcomed, at least at the beginning. Speer, Ley, Funk, and Goebbels agreed that it was high time to clear this jungle of administrative incompetence. In his memoirs Speer lays claim to having been the originator of the plan to totalize the war effort. But there can hardly be any doubt that Goebbels, well before Speer had become minister, was the first to understand that ultimate victory was not only a military but also a political affair.

But after the catastrophe at Stalingrad Goebbels realized the war could also be lost, unless one succeeded in mobilizing all available forces. From this moment on, the absence of leadership in the political conduct of the war becomes an almost traumatic obsession with Goebbels. With his speech at the Sportpalast he hoped to bring about the necessary change. After the speech, Goebbels' Wednesday meetings were attended not only by Speer, Funk, and Ley, but also by Goering's right-hand man, Field Marshal Erhard Milch; Otto Thierac, Minister of Justice; Wilhelm Stuckardt, state secretary at the Ministry of the Interior; and Paul Koerner, state secretary at the Air Ministry. They were still under the spell of Goebbels' speech and ready to support his plans. Allegedly Milch and Speer proposed to make use of Goering's special powers as chairman of the Council of Ministers for the Defense of the Reich to further Goebbels' plans.[78]

Speer took it upon himself to reconcile Goering and Goebbels. The Propaganda Minister had shut down all luxury restaurants in Berlin. When Goering demanded that an exception be made in the case of his favorite restaurant, called the Horcher, Goebbels gave secret orders to a few suitably outraged citizens to break the restaurant's windows. Speer, in fact, succeeded in arranging a meeting between the two in Goering's summer residence on the Obersalzberg, on March 1, 1943. Goebbels' diaries contain an account of their conversation:

". . . We didn't even touch upon the minor misunderstandings that in the course of time had bedeviled our co-operation. Compared with the historical problem before us they appear puny, and he made no attempt to refer to them in any way. He knows full well that everything is at stake, and that it is essential for us to take a long view and come to an arrangement.

"The question is whether we shall be successful in filling the gap created by a lack of leadership in our policy at home and abroad. One cannot burden the Fuehrer with everything. He must be free to devote himself entirely to the military conduct of the war.

"Goering sees quite clearly what our fate in this war would be if we became weak. He has no illusions whatever. We are, particularly in the Jewish question, so deeply committed that there is no escape for any of us. [This proves that Goering knew what was being done to the Jews. At the Nuremberg trial he tried to put all the blame on Goebbels, Himmler, Bormann, Hitler, and Streicher.] Just as well. A movement and a people who have burned all bridges behind them are known to fight far better than those who know the way of retreat is still open. . . ."

Goebbels asked Goering to do everything to transfer the political leadership of the Reich from the trio of Lammers, Keitel, and Bormann to the Council of Ministers for the Defense of the Reich. Goering agreed. He, Goebbels, "would himself win over Himmler. Funk and Ley are already on our side. Speer is 100 per cent with me," he added.[79]

But the conspiracy did not come off. Goering's prestige with Hitler had declined too much. Goering's failure to supply the German forces at Stalingrad from the air and his incapacity to effectively prevent Allied air raids had lowered his standing with Hitler so much that Goebbels could not pluck up enough courage to submit to the Fuehrer the proposed transfer of the political leadership, when they met on March 8.

There was nothing else to be done but to write off Goering. Later Goebbels even asked Hitler to depose Goering as supreme commander of the Luftwaffe. Hitler declined, possibly for sentimental reasons or fear that such a move might have an adverse effect on public opinion, despite the fact that Goering's stock did not stand particularly high with the public. Or did Hitler simply prefer to have the weak, drug addict Goering at the head of the Luftwaffe rather than some general of the Luftwaffe who, knowing his responsibilities, might have told his Fuehrer that the war in the air was finally and irrevocably lost?

Goebbels' plan to organize total war and reform the political leadership had gone awry. It was bound to fail, since Bormann and Lammers, and above all Hitler, opposed it; they were perhaps not so much against totalizing the war effort as against political reforms that were bound to upset the existing balance of power. Goebbels was, in fact, the only party leader with enough power and energy to effectuate such reforms. But Hitler's entourage at Fuehrer headquarters knew that Goebbels would never be content with titles and honors and would not hesitate to make full use of his power. It was therefore preferable to let matters drift rather than allow Goebbels to become too powerful.

Goebbels soon had assessed the situation, but far from accepting defeat, he continued his efforts in two directions: He would strengthen his ties with Hitler until he had become indispensable, and he would do his utmost to curry favor with the people. His weekly lead editorials in *Das Reich* became more and more popular, and he was admired for his courage in making an appearance at the most critical moments.

Before Stalingrad, Hitler and Goering were the two most popular men in the Third Reich, leaving all others far behind. This was due to the fact that Goebbels' complete control of the propaganda apparatus enabled him to determine the level of popularity of any leading personality. He alone had the power to elevate or—what was much more often the case—prevent someone from getting to the top.

Anybody Goebbels had chosen to popularize soon became a star. He would, as a rule, choose artists. Politicians were the exception. The only ones who would receive star treatment were those whose political support Goebbels needed for his own plans. Or Goebbels might crank up a war hero if Goebbels thought this would strengthen the morale of the German people. A typical example of a politician chosen by Goebbels for his political influence was Albert Speer. As Minister of Armaments and architect of the Fuehrer's future projects, Speer was constantly in Hitler's company and could, so reckoned Goebbels, be used as a counterbalance to the influence of the trio of Lammers, Keitel, and Bormann. In advancing Speer, Goebbels would advance his own interests. Speer commented on this: "I had requested him [Goebbels] in the summer of 1942 to use his propaganda apparatus on my behalf; newsreels, illustrated weeklies, and newspapers were told to go into action; my reputation rose. The Propaganda Minister had only to push the right button and I had, in no time, become one of the best-known personalities in the Reich. My increased standing helped at the same time my associates to cope with their daily difficulties with state and party officials."[80]

Speer's description sums up the position accurately. Goebbels had no effective control over administrative bodies, the police, or the military machine, but he had the power to make people famous or to kill them by silence.

A good example of a war hero made popular by Goebbels was General Field Marshal Erwin Rommel. Goebbels' idea was to create the image of the National Socialist type of general. Rommel had never been one of those "monocle-using aristocratic generals," but a professed National Socialist when still a young officer. Rommel's art of improvising, and the audacity he had shown during the African campaign, made him, in Goebbels' eyes, the perfect opposite to the older generals who Goebbels reproached for their lack of determination and original ideas. Goebbels seemed to forget that the generals commanding in European war theaters were for purely professional considerations and their sense of responsibility, obliged to put a brake on Hitler's irresponsibly audacious adventures, while Rommel was free to execute his grand military maneuvering in the enormous spaces of the North African desert without having to carry out Hitler's orders. Whatever the reason, Goebbels made Field Marshal Rommel into a greater star than any other Army commander.

Before Stalingrad, only Hermann Goering was in no need of Goebbels' propagandistic help. The Reich marshal was the most popular figure after Hitler, at least before Goering's decline. Goering's immensely powerful position warranted his popularity almost automatically. As head of the Four-year Plan, he held a commanding post in the Reich's economy. He was the highest-ranking officer of the Wehrmacht and chief of the Luftwaffe, which was at the beginning the most famous branch of the Armed Forces. As Prussian prime minister he had also a most important political function. He was president of the German Reichstag, and last but not least, he was Hitler's successor designate. Goering's colorful personality enhanced his popularity. His penchants for luxurious living and ornate uniforms were willingly forgiven because he made no secret of them. His weaknesses made him appear to the majority of the people only more human, more accessible; he had a sense of humor and even seemed to enjoy the contemporary jokes that made fun of him. Goering was just the opposite of Hitler, whom the people, for all their enthusiasm and devotion, could only regard with a certain awe. Goebbels was in that sense never as popular as Goering. Goebbels employed his propaganda apparatus on his own behalf, and became, together with Hitler and Goering, the best-known personality in the Third Reich, without however becoming really popular. From 1935 on, when Goebbels began to indulge in a truly bourgeois way of life, he even became most unpopular, if not hated, and not only by the party, but also by the people, who disliked the utter discrepancy between his radical pronouncements against the Jews, the Church, and the intellectuals, and his own private life.

During the war Goebbels had retired into the background, to re-emerge now, in time of need—and precisely when the two most popular men, Hitler and Goering, conscious of their failures, rather preferred not to show themselves in public. Hitler appointed Goebbels plenipotentiary for the bomb-damaged areas in the Reich, a job nobody was particularly anxious to tackle. Once again, Goebbels showed his propagandistic genius in using this obviously ungrateful task as a means of building up his popularity.

When, in the summer of 1943, the Anglo-American air raids were at their height, Goebbels would visit the worst-hit areas in the West, in particular Cologne, Dortmund, and Essen. He would speak at meetings and impress the people by his frank admission of the difficulties and errors that had been made. But he never failed to end his speech on a note of hope, depicting the impending retribution, final victory, and the paradise sure to come once the war was over. Yet he not only spoke at public meetings, but would also mix with the bombed-out people and duly pocketed some bitter remarks. He would talk to them, encourage, console, and manage to convince a good many how much their worries were his own, and how fanatically determined he was to meet their essential needs. He organized the so-called Aid for Victims of Air Warfare. These were motorized units, each consisting of three mobile kitchens. Carrying the names of Hermann Goering and Dr. Goebbels, they supplied the bombed-out population with food, coffee, wine, mineral water, hot drinks, cigarettes, and tobacco, as well as with blankets and first-aid kits. Goebbels found the necessary quarters to house them and mobilized an army of official helpers and volunteers.

He was genuinely affected by the fate of Berlin. He loved the place, and as gauleiter felt responsible for its welfare. He was, incidentally, the only member of the government to combine his ministerial post with that of gauleiter. In addition, Hitler made him, on April 1, 1944, president of the city of Berlin (Stadtpresident), which had no practical significance, as Goebbels had already exerted full control, politically, administratively, and culturally. Berlin, trusting Goering's boasts about the invincibility of the Luftwaffe, possessed hardly any air-raid shelters. Goebbels immediately took action.

He circularized all inhabitants, requesting them to leave Berlin if they had no professional obligations requiring their presence. The circular contained a vivid description of the frightful consequences of a heavy air raid; and, indeed, the intended shock had the desired effect. Over a million Berliners, particularly women, children, and old people, left immediately. He also dealt with the dire need for air-raid shelters. Disregarding the warnings of military and administrative authorities, Goebbels gave orders to make the *U-Bahn* stations (for Berlin's city trains) available for use as air-raid shelters. Again he was proved right. No catastrophic mishaps ever occurred, and, no doubt, the *U-Bahn* shelters saved the lives of tens of thousands of Berliners. Goebbels also included Berlin in the general aid scheme he had organized for the whole Reich territory. He would appear in districts that were particularly hard-hit, and had no difficulty in establishing an immediate contact with the inhabitants. He would always find the right word; he would console, encourage, or produce the appropriate brand of grim humor. His relationship with the Berliners became almost mystical. "I sometimes get the impression that the moral attitude of the Berlin population is almost religious. Women approach me, bless me, and pray God to preserve me."[81]

At long last Goebbels had managed to become the most popular party leader after Hitler. The people felt that he was the only one who was personally moved by their trials and tribulations, and that he did his best to alleviate their suffering. As Hitler's and Goering's stars dimmed more and more, Goebbels' star shone more and more brightly. In times of struggle and distress, Goebbels was at his best. He seemed to draw superhuman strength from adversity.

But Goebbels knew that popularity alone was not enough. He would have to obtain the necessary power if he wanted to reach his goal. Neither Goering, Speer, Ley, or Funk were in a position to induce Hitler to approve the necessary inner political reforms. Goebbels therefore sought a rapprochement with Himmler. Their go-between was Goebbels' state secretary and ministerial director, Dr. Naumann. Naumann—a member of the SS—had set his mind on bringing about a coalition between Goebbels and Himmler that should be strong enough to displace the trio committee (Lammers, Keitel, and Bormann).

Himmler was fully informed through his SS offices about everything that happened in the Reich. He knew all about Goebbels' growing influence on Hitler, and Goebbels' rising popularity with the people. He knew about Goebbels' Wednesday evening sessions, and also realized that Goebbels' energy was incomparably greater than that of any other party leader. Himmler had so far been one of the Propaganda Minister's enemies; but he was now prepared to become his ally.

The first problem was the SD secret reports, usually sent to all ministers and Reichsleiters. Goebbels was never shown up to advantage in these reports. Either the authors took into consideration their chief's dislike of Goebbels, or they were not yet aware of the fact that the Propaganda Minister was the coming man. These indirect attacks were bound to hamper Goebbels' efforts to bring about such inner political reforms as he deemed necessary. The first condition

for any alliance with Himmler was obviously Himmler's promise to
discontinue the SD secret reports in their present form. On May 12,
1943, Goebbels could already count one success:

". . . Himmler is prepared to suppress henceforth the SD reports,
which in the long run have a defeatist effect, at least their haphazard
distribution to Cabinet ministers. Himmler will from now on prepare
a special SD report for me personally which, up till now, had been
distributed to a larger circle. Himmler paid on this occasion warm
tribute to the work of the Propaganda Ministry and me personally.
He told Naumann that he considered me to be at the moment one of
the few strong men who, without making any concessions, fights
for our main war aims. I had already displayed the same tendency in
1932 with considerable success, and he could only hope that my plans
would succeed this time too. . . ."

Yet once again certain differences must have arisen between Goebbels and Himmler, the nature of which still remains obscure, for
Goebbels wrote four months later in his diary:

"Naumann had a long talk with Himmler. The differences between
me and Himmler were cleared up. Himmler is very anxious to work
in harmony with me, which is also my wish. Anyway, he will in the
future think twice before sending me such an insolent telegram as his
last." (September 11, 1943)

Goebbels and Himmler met two months later on November 8,
1943, to talk things over. The results of this meeting were slight. The
Reichsfuehrer SS, who in the meantime had risen to the post of Minister of the Interior, passed disparaging remarks about Ribbentrop,
which was enough to win Goebbels over. Himmler also referred to
a "circle of state enemies to whom Halder and possibly Popitz belonged.[82] This circle would like to contact the English in bypassing
the Fuehrer. They had already contacted the former Reich Chancellor Dr. Wirth[83] in Switzerland."

Goebbels, though considering this to be a "dilettantish attempt"
and, therefore, not really dangerous, nevertheless thought that these
people should be closely watched.

It is not impossible that Himmler wanted to probe the reaction
of the Propaganda Minister since he, himself, was hoping to come
to an arrangement with the West so as to be able to continue the fight
against the Soviet Union. Himmler's racial views about the Slavs,
and the ruthless actions of his SS police force (SS Ordnungstruppen)
in the East excluded any arrangement with Stalin. On the other hand,
Goebbels thought that Stalin's Realpolitik offered the sole possibility
of preventing defeat. Although Goebbels failed to reach his aim in
1943 and during the first month of 1944, he managed to strengthen

his position considerably. Even abroad one talked about him, which he noted with great satisfaction. On March 11, 1943, he wrote in his diary:

"The English papers make no bones about admitting that the German propaganda constituted a truly inspired force liable to cause great confusion in England and the USA."

The recognition Goebbels received at home and abroad could not deceive anybody that no progress whatever had been made in reforming German inner policy or German policy in the occupied territories.

German Foreign Policy a Failure

Hitler's foreign policy was a complete failure right from the beginning of the war. For every military victory he had scored, he had to chalk up a political defeat. He had failed to make peace with Britain or to draw Franco's Spain into the war. His Italian ally proved to be a liability rather than an asset. And with his third partner, Japan, it never came to any concerted military action. When Japan's Minister of Foreign Affairs, Matsuoka, visited Berlin in April 1941, Hitler did not reveal to him his intention to attack the Soviet Union. Worse still, when Matsuoka told him that on his way back he would stop off in Moscow and try to arrive at a nonaggression pact with Stalin, Hitler, obviously distrusting his ally, did not oppose this plan. Japan's underlying idea was to free her hands for her impending American war venture by concluding a nonaggression pact with the Soviet Union. Thus these two great military powers—Germany and Japan —operated isolated from one another, and were, in fact, separately defeated, one by one. A concerted attack of Germany and Japan against the Soviet Union would probably have changed the position completely. But each was only after his own particular prey.

In effect, the three axis powers never managed to concert their military actions, for Italy, too, resented Hitler's habit of putting before his Italian ally a *fait accompli,* without even bothering to inform her of his plans beforehand, let alone seeking her advice; Italy chose to attack Greece on her own initiative—a move that later proved very costly. All three powers mistrusted one another, with disastrous consequences for every one of them. Yet Goebbels at no time held the real culprit, Hitler, responsible for the complete failure of German foreign policy, but rather he blamed the Minister of Foreign Affairs, Joachim von Ribbentrop.

"Whenever Ribbentrop was mentioned," Goebbels' press chief, Semmler reports, "Goebbels would speak about Churchill in terms of great admiration . . . and deeply deplored that Hitler had chosen such a dilettante to be his adviser on foreign policy. Ribbentrop had bought the aristocratic 'von.' He had acquired his money by marriage and his position by intrigue. . . . Ribbentrop belongs to the category of yes-man at any price, who will always swim with the tide."[84]

Goering and Rosenberg shared Goebbels' opinion of Ribbentrop. And, indeed, the German Foreign Minister surpassed all his predecessors in vanity and weakness of character. Not once did Ribbentrop pluck up enough courage to oppose the "Fuehrer." Ribbentrop liked to boast that he had broken treaties. He was Hitler's ideal man—a big zero. In fact it was Hitler himself who conducted foreign policy, although he had never set foot in any foreign country apart from a brief state visit to Italy. His concepts were quite primitive: The democracies were decadent, the USA a conglomeration of different races, all Slavs racially inferior and only suited to be Germany's serfs. Only the British Empire got good marks for demonstrating the superiority of the white race over colored peoples.

Not surprisingly, Hitler's actual foreign policy was conducted on the low standard of his basic concepts, which involved either menacing people and making war on them or signing treaties and breaking them afterward. These two cards were all he needed to play his game. Nor did he need any advice. All he could use was an obsequious assistant, and Ribbentrop was an ideal cast for the part.

As long as Hitler's armies were overrunning Europe, the lack of a well-planned foreign policy was not apparent. The aim was to conquer countries, and to do this there was no need for a good Foreign Secretary; all one needed were victorious armies.

But already during the Polish campaign the absence of any foreign political concept made itself felt. Hitler, determined to impose his own will under all circumstances, ordered Ribbentrop to conclude a nonaggression pact with the Soviet Union. This was done in such haste that several questions had been left in suspense, the settlement of which could no longer be expected from a Hitler overrunning France in a triumphant blitzkrieg.

Ideologically speaking—if one may ascribe any ideology whatever to National Socialism—Hitler, when concluding a pact with Moscow, had carried out a *salto mortale*. During two decades he had played the role of defender of the West against Russia, and now his policy liberated the Soviets from their political quarantine, to which they had been confined since 1917, giving them a chance to break out and send their armies into Poland, Romania, the Baltic states, and Finland.

Today's Soviet historians endeavor to present Stalin's policy during that period as a defense measure, calculated to prevent a situation arising when Russia would have to meet a German attack alone, while the Western powers stood by and had time to husband their forces. But there exists convincing evidence that Stalin took the German-Soviet pact quite seriously. From the ideological point of view it could matter little to him who his ally was, for as long as it helped him to pursue Soviet interests. Stalin was prepared to strike a bargain, but Hitler was not even capable of that. In August 1939 Hitler pursued a policy which, in essence, was the same Goebbels had passionately advocated in 1926, and which then had led to a conflict between Hitler and the Strasser group. But Hitler never considered the pact with the Soviets as a long-term policy; he rather acted like one gangster combining with another against society, with the idea of killing off his partner as soon as they had succeeded together in carrying out their coup.

Goebbels, on the other hand, had fully accepted the Fuehrer's anti-Bolshevik course after he had joined up with Hitler. But Goebbels welcomed the German-Soviet pact because it removed the danger of a war on two fronts. The Moscow pact was indispensable for launching the Polish and French campaigns. Goebbels saw in this German-Soviet understanding a virtual guarantee that Germany could no longer lose the war. Small wonder that he could feel his knees shaking, to use his own description, when, later, Hitler told him of his intention to invade the Soviet Union. At first, though, the defeat of France, and the fact that Britain was not in a position to conduct a war against Germany on the Continent unaided, apparently excluded the danger of a two-front war, even if Germany attacked the Soviet Union. The situation became critical only when Japan had started its own war with the United States, and Hitler, renouncing his policy of restraint, declared war on the United States. The terrible specter of a war on two fronts suddenly reappeared, even if it did not materialize at once—the United States had its hands full with Japan; but it was only a question of time before the immense economic potential of the United States would come into play in the European war theater. The technicians of Hitler's entourage, particularly Reich Minister Dr. Todt, saw this at once. Todt perished in an air accident in February 1942, when returning to Berlin from the Fuehrer's headquarters in Rastenburg, East Prussia. Todt had had a long discussion with Hitler the previous night from which he had emerged "strained and tired."[85]

Goebbels knew that German foreign policy had generally failed, particularly in Europe and the occupied territories. He tried to in-

duce Hitler in various memoranda and discussions to take the necessary initiative to remedy the situation. But by then Hitler was
already the burned-out shell of a man. He would hide away in his
headquarters like a wounded beast waiting for the end. From there
he conducted a war of his own imagination—a war Germany could
no longer win, except in Hitler's fantasy. This split in Hitler's mind,
creating a dangerous gap between reality and fantasy, rendered him
less and less capable of facing facts and searching for political solutions or, at least, accepting advice.

Hitler only yearned for further military victories, but after the defeat at Stalingrad there was no chance whatever of that coming to
pass. The fact that Hitler had always succeeded in imposing his will
on his entourage now nourished his delusion that he would also succeed in imposing his will on the enemy. Right up to his last day, he
was still waiting for the miracle his will power would work in the end.
He who had often made fun of the miracles described in the Bible
now clung to his faith that Providence would work a miracle and
bring him victory against all logic and political reality, thanks to his
personal will power and genius. To be able to conserve his faith in a
miracle, he isolated himself from the world outside, lest the mere
sight of bombed-out ruins and innumerable dead destroy his faith in
this miracle.

Goebbels endeavored to convince Hitler in a personal discussion
that Germany had never yet won a war on two fronts and that Hitler
should, therefore, decide with which of the two enemy camps he
should try to conclude a separate peace. Notwithstanding the Anglo-
American decision to demand Germany's unconditional surrender,
taken at Casablanca on January 24, 1943, Goebbels still believed, in
September 1943, in the possibility of coming to an understanding with
the Western powers. He falsely assumed that the Western powers preferred National Socialism to Bolshevism. He might have known that
National Socialist policy in the occupied territories, particularly in
Eastern Europe, exceeding in brutality anything the Bolsheviks had
ever done, excluded them in the eyes of the West from being considered as partners in any separate peace negotiations. It took Goebbels some time to realize this bitter fact.

At the time he saw his main task in stoking up distrust among the
Allies and creating a fear psychosis of Bolshevism, especially in the
neutral countries. One particular event seemed to bear out fully Goebbels' propaganda. The Germans discovered, in the spring of 1943,
near the Polish town of Katyn—it had been occupied by the Soviets
during the Polish campaign in 1939—the buried corpses of several
thousand Polish officers who had been executed by a shot in the

back of the neck. The world was horrified and, at first, took it for a piece of typical Goebbels horror propaganda. Seeing, however, that the Germans made all efforts to invite scientific observers to come from neutral countries (it was not easy to persuade them to come, since nobody wanted to burn his fingers on this politically highly explosive matter), the neutral and Western world finally became convinced that the German statements were true and that the Soviets had actually committed this brutal crime.

German propaganda exploited the Katyn story to the full, much to the annoyance of the Americans and the British, who were, after all, conducting this war against Germany for "humanitarian reasons." Goebbels could record his deep satisfaction in his diary on April 29, 1943:

"The conflict with the Poles has taken first place. Since the beginning of the war no other event has stirred up public opinion quite so much. The Americans and the English have treated the Poles as though they belonged to the enemy camp. It is admitted that we actually succeeded in producing a deep rift between the Allies, and created a far bigger crisis than the one between Darlan and De Gaulle."

The next day Goebbels wrote: "Our propaganda is under suspicion from all sides of trying to inflate the case Katyn, in order to make a separate peace with either the English or the Soviets. This, of course is not the purpose, although such a prospect would, in fact, be quite welcome. . . ."

Goebbels' personal opinion was that it should be easier to come to an understanding with Stalin. Stalin was free of Christian or humanitarian "prejudices." He had always shown himself to be a realist who, among the possibilities open to him, would always choose the one that would bring him the greater advantage. It is not certain if Goebbels knew that in the beginning of 1943 Stalin had actually made tentative contacts in order to explore the possibility of a separate peace with Germany.

In the last two war years Goebbels seemed to return to the ideals of his youth. His initially vain attempts to organize total war were designed to bring about a complete social leveling of all Germans by an equal distribution of burdens and sacrifices. He finished the entry in his diary dated September 10, 1943: ". . . National Socialism needs a renewal. We must get even closer to the people in a socialist sense. The people must know that we are managing their interests in a just and generous manner. No ties must exist between the National Socialist leadership and the aristocracy, or the so-called society."

Goebbels' press assistant, Semmler,[86] reported that, in April 1944, Goebbels sent Hitler a forty-page memorandum in which he stated that a military victory had become impossible in the present situation. The war on two fronts drew so heavily on German strength that one could foresee the moment when the German people reached a state of complete exhaustion. This made it imperative to bring the war to an end at one of the two fronts as quickly as possible.

For the sake of saving Western civilization, it might have been worth a try to come to an arrangement with the Western powers. But by then, however, nothing was likely to move Churchill and Roosevelt to change their course.

But the fact that the existence of the Reich and eighty million Germans was at stake obliged the German leadership to overcome all scruples and prejudices and try to come to an understanding with the Soviet Union. Stalin's attitude was essentially anti-British, and in view of the position in the Far East, also anti-American. It should, therefore, be possible to make common cause with Stalin against the Western powers. And if one succeeded, with the help of the Japanese, in arranging discussions with the Russians, Germany should be prepared to make Stalin a concrete offer along the following lines:

Germany would recognize Finland and the northern parts of Norway as a Russian sphere of influence. Germany would also agree to an annexation of the Baltic states by the Soviet government. The general government in Poland should be ceded to the Soviet Union up to the Warta. Germany should also recognize Romania, Bulgaria, and Greece as spheres of Soviet influence. Only the future of Czechoslovakia should be left open.

Goebbels ended his memorandum by saying that Ribbentrop was incapable of carrying out this plan. Goebbels was therefore putting himself forward as Minister of Foreign Affairs to try to bring about an understanding with the Soviets. A whole year had elapsed since Goebbels had, for the first time, offered himself to the "Fuehrer" as Foreign Secretary. To Goebbels' criticism of Ribbentrop, Hitler had once replied: "Your assessment of Ribbentrop is wholly wrong. He is one of the greatest men we have, and history will put him above Bismarck."[87]

According to Semmler, Bormann suppressed Goebbels' memorandum, seeing in it "a betrayal of our allies, Finland, Romania, and Bulgaria." Hitler, when learning later of Bormann's action, took no exception to it. Perhaps he saw more clearly than Goebbels that Germany had missed the chance of negotiating with Russia. He himself had lost it when he arrogantly rejected Stalin's offer.

In any case, spring 1944 was too late to make such an approach with any real hope of success. In the meantime the Soviet Union had joined the Western powers in the declaration of Casablanca (October

1943). It demanded Germany's "unconditional surrender." It is, furthermore, an established fact that Goebbels was the only party leader who sincerely wished to come to an understanding with the Soviets. All the others still harbored illusions with regard to the West, while Hitler was hoping for a conflict between East and West before Germany's total collapse that, at the last moment, would stave off *finis Germaniae*. Only Goebbels realized that National Socialism and Bolshevism, though each using a basically different approach, arrived at the same result: the end of all personal freedom and all democratic rights. Collectivism had ultimately imposed itself on National Socialism too, even if disguised as a national community.

Goebbels knew that the only remaining hope was to come to an understanding with Stalin. Yet, paying tribute to his sentimental ties with the West—had he not always played the guardian of Western culture?—he called it a "perversion of history" that "two peoples of such a racially and culturally high standard" as the Germans and the English should kill each other to assure the victory of the two "barbaric upstart nations." He was at a complete loss to understand why the Western Allies should, apparently without the slightest objection, grant the USSR everything they denied Germany.[88] He failed to realize that ever since 1939 the key figure to all "perversions of history" was none other than Hitler himself.

The Debacle of Germany's European Policy

On March 16, 1943, the German embassy in Helsinki sent a telegram to the Ministry of Foreign Affairs in Berlin, asking if the guidelines Goebbels had given to foreign correspondents in his speech of March 13 should also be adopted by the German embassy in Finland. On March 20, Ribbentrop wired his answer, marked "strictly secret for the ambassador personally": "I beg you to avoid the topic of the new Europe in your discussions as much as possible. If someone refers to the pronouncements of Reich Minister Goebbels, I beg you to make it clear, in an appropriate manner of course, that these are not official views. . . ." Signed, Ribbentrop.[89]

In his speech to the foreign correspondents Goebbels had given the following four guidelines:

"1. The harsh measures taken in occupied territories due to special circumstances prevailing in war, are only valid for the duration of the war. The cohesion of the new Europe should not be obtained by compulsion, but by the voluntary adherence of member countries. There is no intention of using dictatorial methods in any European country whatever.

2. There is no intention of suppressing individual national entities.

3. All European countries should combine under the strong protection of big powers against all interference from outside.

4. No country in Europe will be compelled to adopt any particular form of government. Any country wishing to maintain its traditional democracy will be free to do so."[90]

Already at the beginning of the war against the Soviet Union, Goebbels had pondered a constructive plan to supplant the Bolshevik system. He did not know that on July 16, 1941, after the first spectacular successes of the German armies on the Russian front, Hitler had called Goering, Keitel, Rosenberg, Bormann, and Lammers to the Fuehrer headquarters for a secret conference and given them an outline of his policy toward the peoples of the Soviet Union: "The essential problem is to slice the cake handily, so as to be able first to control it, second to administer it, and third to exploit it."[91]

Briefly, Hitler's policy was to extend German rule to the Urals. The German people, as the *Herrenvolk*, were to be exclusively entitled to bear arms. The Baltic states, the Crimea, and the Kola Peninsula should be integrated into the Reich. None of the five sages Hitler had convened to this conference had raised any moral objections to the Fuehrer's concept. None of them, Rosenberg excepted, had any concept of their own, anyway.

And Rosenberg's concept was totally different from Hitler's. He envisaged autonomy for the Eastern peoples, as well as land reform and important concessions in religious and educational matters. Even Goebbels, who considered Rosenberg unfit to be chief of the ministry for the Occupied Eastern Territories, admitted that Rosenberg's ministry had actually worked out agrarian reforms for the occupied territories designed to bring about "a gradual abolition of the Kolchose system and a return to private landownership. I expect quite a lot from this reform once it has been put over to the peasantry as a whole; once we are really in a position to distribute the land among the peasants, they will scarcely look forward to seeing the Bolshevik back again."[92]

But Rosenberg's ideas, in particular their elaboration by his staff, did not get any farther than the paper they were written on. The reality looked quite different. In only a few months the Germans had managed to lose all sympathy shown to them at the beginning. Goebbels' disappointment clearly emerges from his diary note of April 25, 1942:

"In the Ukraine the people were at first more than eager to regard the Fuehrer as Europe's savior, and welcome the German Wehrmacht wholeheartedly. In a few months their attitude was completely transformed. Our harsh policy shocked the Russians, particularly the Ukrainians. The bludgeon coming down on their heads is obviously not a convincing argument, neither with the Ukrainians nor with the Russians."

On the suggestion of Goering (who as head of the economic Four-year Plan was also responsible for the exploitation of foreign peoples), Hitler appointed the gauleiter of East Prussia, Erich Koch, as Reich commissioner of the Ukraine. Koch, supported by Goering and Hitler, proceeded to build up his position independently of the Ministry for the Occupied Eastern Territories. He rejected the idea of a Ukrainian administrative and cultural autonomy and squeezed the last drop from the land and its people. Rosenberg called him "utterly ruthless," a *petit bourgeois* run berserk."[93]

Koch's attitude emerges unmistakably from the rules he laid down for the Ukrainian Working Organization: "Laziness is a crime. This must be drummed into their heads. The Ukrainian must be taught what it means to really work hard. . . . Nothing is impossible for Germans; therefore, nothing should be impossible for the Ukrainian Working Organization under German leadership. . . ."[94]

Whatever the case, Germany could never regain the sympathy of the Ukrainian people. An SD report of October 14, 1943, headed "The End of the Ukrainian Dream," makes it clear that the Ukrainians had realized that in Hitler they had been backing the wrong horse:

"All Ukrainian emigrées, including those of the left, swung over to Hitler's policy when he came to power. Likewise the Ukrainian inhabitants of Polish Galicia who already, under Austrian rule, had developed strong nationalist tendencies. They expected to pay a high price for their liberation and the independence the Germans promised them. But they were hoping that the price would be assessed in economic terms, and that Germany would, at least, grant them the kind of autonomy she had granted Slovakia. Today, after two years of German administration, and particularly after the countless 'systematic evacuations,' the Ukrainian nationalists have lost all illusions. . . ."[95]

Despite Rosenberg's protest, the police in the Eastern territories enjoyed complete independence which, notwithstanding the disorganization of the administrative apparatus, safeguarded a smoothly working system of exploitation and forced deportations. At the Nuremberg trial several documents of Rosenberg's Ministry for Eastern Affairs came to light. They provide shocking proof that

against the better judgment of a majority of German civil servants at
the Ministry for Eastern Affairs, and other German administrative
agencies, a small clique of people, aided by their henchmen, managed
to make the German people, who at first had been welcomed as
harbingers of freedom, into the feared messengers of terror. And
once again the main culprit was Adolf Hitler, who regarded the
Eastern peoples as inferior, born to be slaves and mere objects to
be exploited.

Goebbels' proposals for a European and Eastern policy compare
favorably with the official policy, which was actually carried out. Yet
one is entitled to have some doubts as to Goebbels' sincerity. He was
far more interested in the superficial impressions his proposals for
pacification were likely to make than in their implementation. Goebbels' entry in his diary of February 15, 1942, is revealing: In complete
contradiction to his ideas on what German Eastern policy ought to
be, he praises Heydrich's actions in the protectorates of Bohemia
and Moravia. Reinhard Heydrich—SS Obergruppenfuehrer and Chief
of the General Office of Reich Security (Reichssicherheitshauptamt),
doubtless one of the most sinister figures of the Third Reich—was
appointed acting Reich protector, because the Fuehrer considered
the policy of the nominal Reich protector, Konstantin von Neurath,
to be far too lenient. One should have expected Goebbels to condemn
this move. But this is what he wrote:

". . . Heydrich is a success. He plays cat and mouse with the
Czechs and makes them swallow anything he puts before them. The
Slavs, he says, cannot be treated like the German people; one must
break them or slowly bend them to one's own will. He has apparently
chosen the second method, which he applies most successfully.

"It is quite clear what our task must be in the protectorate.
Neurath completely failed to realize it, which led to the crisis in
Prague."

Heydrich continued playing cat and mouse so long with the
Czechs that two of them tossed a bomb into his open Mercedes on
May 29, 1942. The car blew up and the tyrant was fatally injured;
he died four days later. In retribution the whole population of the
village of Lidice was wiped out. This, then, was the result of Heydrich's policy in the protectorate, the policy that Goebbels had
praised so warmly.

Once again we can observe the duality in Goebbels' mind. He
could foresee the consequences of German policy in the East and
tried to change it by memoranda, proclamations, and even by certain
actions. Yet when it appeared that German victory was not imperiled
—as, for instance, in the protectorate—he condemned Neurath for his

21. Prince Paul of Yugoslavia visits Goebbels in Potsdam. Above, the Prince talking to Mrs. Goebbels; Goebbels with back to photographer.

22. Goebbels giving Christmas presents to the children of German workers, who were his guests at a Christmas party in Berlin. 1938.

23. Goebbels and his wife at a Berlin press ball in 1939, his first public appearance following his illness. At the left is Secretary of State Hanke, and next to him is Wilhelm Weiss, leader of the German Press Association.

24. Hitler, Goering, and Goebbels in Berlin. August 13, 1943.

policy of compromise and praised Heydrich for playing "cat and mouse" with the Czechs—or, in any case, before the mouse swallowed the cat.

The Wartime Diary

Goebbels' wartime diary of the years 1942–43, like that which he kept in 1925–26, contains observations primarily on contemporary events and personalities; however, the strong personal accent of his earlier diary is absent. In 1942 Goebbels was a mature man. He was no longer beset by griefs of young love, and in any case, times were far too serious for sentimental problems. He was fully preoccupied with the political or military position; everything personal had to take second place.

Historically this diary is interesting, insofar as it differs from that of 1925–26, in that it was written with an eye to posterity. Goebbels might have planned to use it as material for some books he expected to write one day; but as he became increasingly aware of the fact that the war might be lost, the diary more and more assumed the character of a political testament. Perhaps the most striking feature of this wartime diary is the author's complete amoralism. This amoralism had its predecessors in Nietzsche, Machiavelli, and, above all, in Hitler. It appears that Goebbels threw his own moral concepts overboard and adopted Hitler's. Examples are his praise of Heydrich's policy in the protectorate and his open admission that he was more concerned with an ostensible than a real pacification of the subjugated peoples. He did not hesitate to make promises for the future to certain countries, knowing full well they would never be kept. Goebbels' brutal policy of destruction of the Jews, as recorded in his wartime diary, is also new. All this painfully demonstrates his assimilation of Hitler's ideas. In the twenty years that elapsed between the two diaries, Goebbels' thoughts had cleared up considerably, but they had also become far more primitive and brutal. All humanitarian considerations had disappeared.

The wartime diary is also interesting as a critical analysis of that particular period. It covers two years, from January 1942 to December 1943. In these two years the tide turned against Germany. In December 1942 the tragedy of Stalingrad threw its chilling shadow over Germany's fate. In summer 1943 Italy joined the enemy camp. The Anglo-American air forces established their unchallenged superiority and dominated the airspace over the German homeland. One town after another fell in ruins; this, in fact, failed to destroy the morale of the population or diminish production appreciably, but it revealed Germany's impotence. The "Baedeker raids" that obliterated Germany's most beautiful towns and monuments were militarily useless and obviously barbaric, but destroyed much that the Germans were proud of. [The term "Baedeker raids" was used for the first time in connection with Germany's air attacks on English towns of no military importance. They preceded those mentioned here. Translator's note.] On the Eastern front the Soviet advance continued, and Germany's strong ally in the Far East, Japan, had begun its "planned retreat."

Interesting, also, in the diary are Goebbels' judgments of his contemporaries. His views on Churchill and Roosevelt have been mentioned, but they were not the only foreign politicians to get bad marks. Generalissimo Franco is called a "bigoted churchgoer," "an inflated peacock" who permits "Spain to be practically ruled by his wife and his father-confessor."[96] About Quisling, Goebbels says, "I have the impression that Quisling is just Quisling. I cannot feel much sympathy for him."[97]

For Stalin, however, in his diary Goebbels has only admiration. There is a marked divergence between his private entries in his diary and his official pronouncements. He was most impressed with Stalin's brutality. "He got rid of all opposition within the Army and thereby cut out any defeatist tendencies. The introduction of political commissars had a most salutary effect on the fighting capacity of the Red Army."[98]

Goebbels saw other advantages in Bolshevism, such as "the liquidation of all opposition in Russian society." Goebbels also welcomed Stalin's brutal methods used against all opposition within the Church, "which remains a real headache for us."

Goebbels' views on how to deal with France were profoundly deceitful. He had adopted Hitler's line. Reading Goebbels' notes, one never has the feeling that he was seriously concerned with the question of how to build a new Europe, since he proposed to exclude all peoples, including such a highly cultivated nation as the French, from playing any important role. He drew on Hitler for his moral excuses.

"Whoever possesses Europe will soon lead the world. In this context we cannot even begin to discuss the question of right or wrong. A lost war will put the German people in the wrong; victory will assure us every right. Altogether, only the victor will be in a position to put over to the world the moral justification of this war."

Goebbels accused the Ministry of Foreign Affairs of lacking initiative in its European policy; he published his own statements, promising all European peoples freedom and prosperity after a German victory. At the same time he confided to his diary his views on France, which prove that his promises were brazen lies.

"It would be a mistake to hope for too much from France. The French people are to my mind ill and worm-eaten. They are no longer able to make any significant contribution toward the construction of a new Europe. . . .

"The Fuehrer's policy toward France has proved correct in every way. One must put the French on ice. As soon as one flatters them it goes to their heads. The longer one leaves them hanging in the air the readier they will be to submit."[99]

While the Ministry of Foreign Affairs is inclined to support the French demand for a preliminary peace, all the more so since the French government declared its readiness "to actively take part in the war," Goebbels sided with Hitler who, reluctant to play his aces too soon, thought he could do without French armed assistance. He intended to obtain "truly historical results from the war against France."[100]

What are these "historical results"? "Whatever the war may bring, he [Hitler] says France will have to pay dearly; after all, she has caused this war and initiated it. . . . [This statement completely contradicts Goebbels' propaganda line up until the French campaign in May 1940.] France will be reduced to its frontiers of the year 1500 . . . which means that Burgundy will be integrated into the Reich. We will win a territory superior in beauty and riches to almost any other German province."[101]

But woe to any other nation that pursued a similarly egotistical and ruthless policy. This is exemplified by Goebbels' reference to Mussolini's fall. In May 1943 Tunisia had been lost, and on July 10, Anglo-American forces landed in Sicily. This appeared to be the moment for Italy to seek a divorce *à l'Italienne* from her Axis partners. Italy's inner political situation made this relatively easy: The Italians still had a ruling King, not to mention the Pope, in their midst. Mussolini was completely spent after twenty-one years of government. There was precious little left of his animal-of-prey nature, of being "the big wild cat," as Ezra Pound had described him once. Driven by sheer greed, Mussolini had entered the war too hastily. The ignominious defeats the Italian armies sustained in Greece and North Africa only revealed to the world Italy's military and economic weakness. This, in its turn, reduced Mussolini from his position as Hitler's partner to that of Hitler's factotum—if that. And when on July 25, 1943, Mussolini was deposed by the Great Fascist Council and arrested by the King, no one in Italy raised a finger to help Mussolini. Over twenty years of fascism seemed to have been blotted out overnight.

Goebbels had never set great store by Italy or fascism: "The Italians are not only incapable of any valid military effort, but they have also failed to produce anything important in art. One can almost say that fascism had a sterilizing effect on the Italian people. . . ."[102]

But when Goebbels was told of Mussolini's fall, he stared at his press officer "with a mixture of unbelief and horror." Goebbels sat down, incapable of uttering a word, for a quarter hour: "An expression of complete despair appeared on his face, slowly changing into grim bitterness. The first words he then uttered were 'What a shit of a man.' Then he added: 'Fascist Italy was never anything but a blown-up rubber lion. . . . And a clever ventriloquist made him roar, so that some people believed the lion had real teeth and claws. But one little pinprick and—puff—the whole monster collapses.' "[103]

Goebbels immediately left for the Fuehrer's headquarters in Rastenburg. Hitler, too, had been taken by surprise, since the German Diplomatic Service, as well as the Secret Service, had obviously been caught by surprise. As soon as Hitler heard that Marshal Pietro Badoglio had taken over the government, he knew the revolt was directed against Germany. Badoglio's declaration that he would continue the war on the side of the Axis powers could not deceive Hitler.

For once, Hitler managed to keep his composure better than Goebbels who, in his consternation, hardly knew how to break the terrible news to the German people. At first he broadcast that Mussolini had retired "for health reasons." Goebbels refused for three weeks to write an editorial in *Das Reich,* which gave rise to all kinds of rumors.

Events in Italy developed slowly but according to plan. On September 8, an armistice was proclaimed between Italy and the Western powers. Badoglio had already signed the agreement on September 3, when Anglo-American forces landed in southern Italy. Yet on September 8, the Italian marshal told the councilor of the German legation, Rahn, that he had not the slightest intention of quitting the fighting Axis powers. The Germans would see "how an Italian general kept his word."

Goebbels, who before had never missed a chance to employ aristocrats in his entourage, became after the events in Italy a real hater of the aristocracy: "The conspiracy that was built up against us in Rome consisted of the monarchy, aristocracy, society, high-ranking officers, Freemasons, Jews, industrialists, and clerics. The Duce fell victim to this conspiracy.

"The Fuehrer is taking all measures to exclude, once and for all, the possibility of anything of this kind happening over here. All German princes are expelled from the German Wehrmacht. I suggested to the Fuehrer that we confiscate without any further delay the great estates belonging to the former ruling families."[104]

Eighteen years earlier, Goebbels and the Strasser group had supported the proposal of the German left parties to dispossess the princes without compensation. At that time Hitler had opposed the Goebbels-Strasser group. Once again, Hitler recoiled from taking this drastic step, while Goebbels more and more reverted to the National Bolshevist ideas of his political beginnings. Goebbels openly leaned toward Stalinist policy, trying to prepare the German people for co-operation with Stalin.

Had Goebbels learned his lesson from the events in Italy? His diary reveals his determination to apply still harsher methods in order to prevent anything similar from happening in Germany. "I will from now on beat up anybody who says anything against the war or against the Fuehrer. Or I will put him before a court, or shut him up in a concentration camp."[105]

The Twentieth of July

An SD secret report of August 2, 1943, contained a remark that must have startled Goebbels. In the West of the Reich, the report said, many people talked about a future occupation by American troops, and apparently thought, " 'it might not be so bad to be under American occupation, perhaps even better than it is now'. The lack of faith in our victory is gaining ground daily."[106]

Ever since the military debacle of Stalingrad, Goebbels was tormented by fear that the war might be lost. This fear became worse after Mussolini's fall, although the hesitant military tactics of the Allies had made it possible to bring their advance to a halt. On the other hand, the position on the Eastern front looked bleaker than ever. The last great German offensive around Kursk, carried out with half a million troops and seventy Panzer divisions equipped with "Tiger" tanks, had collapsed. The Soviets had begun to strike back and had reached, by the end of the year, the Romanian and Polish borders. The Anglo-American naval forces, equipped with radar, had compelled the German Admiralty to halt U-boat warfare which, in 1942, had still been able to inflict grievous losses on Allied shipping. Now U-boat losses had become too heavy to continue. The Allied air raids by day and night on the German homeland increased spectacularly.

Whatever peace of mind Goebbels might still have possessed had now gone. His remarks to his staff became more and more pessimistic. According to Goebbels' assistant, Oven, the minister mentioned for the first time, on August 27, 1943, the possibility of Germany's defeat. And in September, when discussing the general situation with his intimates, Goebbels would often employ the words "if I were the Fuehrer."[107]

What then would Goebbels do if he were "the Fuehrer"? He would under all circumstances try to make peace with Stalin. His diary mentions, in September 1943, two discussions he had with Hitler when he, Goebbels, proposed to make peace with one of the two enemy camps. But each time the Fuehrer's reaction had been negative. During their second discussion, which took place during a dinner *tête-à-tête,* Hitler expressed his willingness to negotiate with Stalin, "but he does not believe," Goebbels writes, "it would yield any results because Stalin could never accept Hitler's Eastern demands."[108]

Yet Goebbels refused to let go, as though he knew that the last possibility of an understanding even with Stalin would soon be gone. Deep down Goebbels no doubt considered that Hitler's conduct of the war had failed, and Goebbels would not have hesitated to give the Soviets all territories up to the Warta and the borders of Czechoslovakia, if only to get out of the war in the East.

What else would Goebbels do if he were the Fuehrer? He would totalize the war effort and squeeze the last reserves from the German people. Yet Goebbels was just as unlucky with his total-war proposals as with his plans for a separate peace. Hitler had simply become blind to reality, and the more cruel reality became, the more he retired into his own dream world.

The general rejection of Goebbels' plans, starting with Hitler and ending with the least important gauleiter, made it difficult for Goebbels to pursue a credible and effective line of propaganda. All he had left to base his propaganda on was hope and hopelessness: hope of revenge, and the hopelessness of concluding an honorable peace with the enemy.

At a confidential meeting of all gauleiters on February 23, 1944, Goebbels said in his speech: "Retribution is at hand. It will take a form hitherto unknown in warfare, a form the enemy, we hope, will find impossible to bear. The creation of a new weapon naturally presents many problems, but they have been practically overcome, and the effort continues successfully.

"This retribution will come when the enemy no longer expects it and strike him on a scale he will hardly be able to survive."[109]

This allusion to a secret weapon, scarcely ever mentioned in official propaganda, and filtered through various channels to the German people, fortified their will to resist. Goebbels was chiefly thinking of the rockets, but also toyed with the idea of atomic weapons. On March 21, 1942, Goebbels called for a report concerning research into atomic fission. "It is so far advanced that it might still be possible to make use of it in this war. Its most sparing employment results in such immense devastation that one can only feel horror-struck when contemplating the technical development of this war if it goes on much longer—let alone the prospect of future wars. Modern technique puts means of destruction into men's hands that defy imagination. German science in this field is supreme, and, indeed, so it must remain. Whoever will be able to introduce any revolutionary innovations in this war will have the greater chance of winning."

It was Europe's lucky chance that none of the prominent National Socialist leaders, with the exception of Goebbels, was in the least interested in atomic physics. Those who would have been important, particularly the Reich Minister for Science and Education, chose to ignore nuclear research. Even Speer, who in June 1942 attended Heisenberg's lecture on nuclear fission and, at least partly, realized the significance of these new scientific discoveries, left it at that as soon as he heard Heisenberg's and Hahn's estimate that two years were needed to produce an atomic bomb.[110]

American scientists, in fact, needed approximately two years to build the first atomic bomb. The man who in Goebbels' view was mainly responsible for the official neglect of basic nuclear research was Dr. Rust, Reich Minister for Science and Education. But the real culprit was Hitler. Nuclear physics were rather suspect. He saw in Einstein the founder of modern physics and rejected him and his Theory of Relativity on racial grounds. Incidentally, Stalin, too, rejected the famous physicist and his Theory of Relativity.

Goebbels' double-pronged tactics of totalizing the war effort at home, while striving to conclude a separate peace with the Soviet Union, would, he hoped, prevent a German defeat and preserve National Socialism. Goebbels dreaded two events more than any other: first, a successful attempt on Hitler's life, fearing that with the Fuehrer's death National Socialism would disintegrate unless he, Goebbels, could take over quickly enough the whole governmental apparatus at home and abroad; second, a successful military putsch—and there were constantly signs that some were developing. In his conversation with Hitler on September 23, 1943, Goebbels said:

"Treasonable acts such as the Italian generals committed against Mussolini can be absolutely excluded considering the mentality of the German, particularly of the Prussian generals. Quite rightly, the Fuehrer asked me what I thought he would do if faced with such treason. I believe he would not hesitate for a moment to take such terrible punitive action that anyone who might have even faintly contemplated committing treason would soon be deterred from pursuing his plans once and for all."

Goebbels was particularly outraged by the anti-Nazi propaganda of certain German generals of the Sixth Army who had been made prisoners by the Soviets: "It is very sad that a number of German generals, particularly those of aristocratic descent, have joined the Free German Committee in Moscow, which entirely serves Stalin's aims. . . . To name the worst, a certain Count Einsiedel, who belongs to one of the oldest German officer families."

But the main target of Goebbels' hatred was General von Seidlitz: "I'm reading the last speech General von Seidlitz has broadcast from Moscow. This illustrious aristocrat is simply the worst swine of the German officer corps. It makes you want to spit between his eyes to show your contempt."[111] Goebbels' hatred of the generals was closely bound up with his fear that they could wake up one day and depose Hitler. Goebbels' fear grew with every defeat. He also worried that civilian circles could, in conjunction with the military, come to an arrangement with the Western powers that would spell the end of National Socialism. Goebbels' fanatic call for totalizing the war sprang not only from his desire for victory, but also from the fear that resistance groups might form within the Reich and successfully combine with the generals at the front in a common cause. Goebbels did not know that the German field marshals and generals commanding the armies at the front had been approached on several occasions and had rejected taking part in a putsch. Goebbels had been only too right when he said that treason was alien to the mentality of the German, particularly the Prussian generals. A determining factor of their attitude was the defensive war in the East. No general was prepared to be saddled one day with the odious responsibility for Germany's defeat caused by his "treasonable" action. The demand of the Western powers for Germany's unconditional surrender destroyed whatever will to resist Hitler they may have had. But then on June 6, 1944, the Allied forces landed on the beaches of Normandy.

Only then were some officers at last prepared to get rid of Hitler and put an end to National Socialism. This enterprise, even if it had succeeded, came at least a year too late. In fact, the main actors of the conspiracy, Colonel Stauffenberg, General Beck (retired), and

Dr. Goerdeler, asked themselves if it was still worth going ahead with the putsch. Their only reward would be to have acted as liquidators of the German defeat. Their decision to act after all was prompted by their desire to prove to the world, at the last moment, that there had been an active resistance movement in Germany.

If the action of July 20 is judged morally, German history will give it a good mark. But its organization was deplorable. The mere fact that the civilian Goebbels sufficed to stop the putsch proves the ineptitude of the military organizers.

Every military putsch planned during the war made the same fundamental error: Hitler was to be assassinated. Only Rommel, who joined the resistance group as late as January 1944, realized that it was essential to arrest Hitler and put him on trial. Hitler's assassination would have had several disadvantages:

1. It would have made Hitler into a martyr who, backed by Goebbels' Hitler myth, would have survived National Socialism after the war. It might have left behind a latent tendency among the German population to sympathize with the Fuehrer.

2. It might have created a new version of the old legend of the "stab in the back." The new secret weapon which, as Goebbels told the German people, would bring about a complete turn in Germany's fortunes might, in the event of Hitler's assassination, have convinced many Germans that the war would not have been lost if Hitler had remained alive. Or that Hitler would at least have secured better terms for a defeated Germany.

3. There was also the danger that Hitler's assassination would be followed by a German reign of terror. History shows that assassinations were almost regularly followed by such reigns of terror. This happened after the French revolution, after the Bolshevik revolution, and was hardly less likely to happen after a National Socialist revolution.

4. Hitler's assassination would have also inferred that the resistance regarded the person of the "Fuehrer" of such vital importance that his actual death was a *sine qua non* for bringing about a change. It shows that even German resistance, such as it was, had fallen victim to Goebbels' Hitler myth: "Hitler is Germany and Germany is Hitler."

The failure of the attempt on Hitler's life and the putsch of July 20, 1944, were almost a historical necessity. Its success would not have changed the Allied policy toward Germany that had been firmly established at Casablanca and Moscow. It ended Europe's spiritual supremacy. The prime movers were the two "non-European" major powers. The only military personality of importance and name who might have effectively pitted his weight against Hitler was General Field Marshal Erwin Rommel; the armies he commanded in France were an important asset. As it happened, on July 17 the car in which he was traveling was attacked by low-flying Allied planes, and Rommel was grievously wounded. The full significance of his elimination from active resistance—a heavy blow to the resistance group—can only be seen today. All other military, with the exception of Stauffenberg, lacked Rommel's courage and talent for improvisation, indispensable for a successful outcome of the putsch. It was perhaps historical justice that the enterprise was denied success, since it had come far too late.

The action of July 20, with its miscarried attempt on Hitler's life, its defective organization, and its ultimate collapse, was a mixture of bad luck, errors, omissions, short circuits, and moments of weakness. Quite a few of the main actors showed courage, but only two showed both courage and determination: Count Klaus Schenk von Stauffenberg and Joseph Goebbels.

Hitler, impressed with Stauffenberg's self-confidence, was said to have once remarked: "At last, a staff officer with imagination." Guderian had planned to propose that Stauffenberg—"his best horse" —be appointed chief of staff. The count had lost his right eye, his right hand, and two fingers of his left hand in North Africa. His position as chief of staff to General Fromm, supreme commander of the reserve armies, gave Stauffenberg an opportunity to take part in Hitler's military conferences at the Fuehrer's headquarters. This enabled Stauffenberg on July 20 to plant a bomb in the conference room at the Fuehrer's headquarters in Rastenburg, East Prussia, which exploded at exactly 12:42 P.M. The explosion killed one officer and injured several others. But Hitler survived. This presented Goebbels with a new propaganda weapon: The Lord's protective hand had saved the Fuehrer. Providence had spared him to accomplish his great mission. Why else should it have saved him? And, in fact, a number of incredible accidents had combined to save Hitler's life. Goebbels can hardly be blamed for seeing in it a miracle, an act of Providence.

"For a moment I felt as if the ground was shifting under my feet. Apocalyptic images rose before my mind's eye that would follow a successful outcome of this cowardly and infamous attempt, historically disastrous for our people, well-nigh for the whole of Europe. . . . Then my heart filled with almost religious and solemn gratitude. Often before had I realized, but never before so clearly and unmistakably, that the Fuehrer's mission was protected by Providence. No amount of baseness and infamy was able to impede or stop him: And Divine Fate, high above all work of men, had given us a sign that his mission, may it encounter ever so many difficulties, must be fulfilled, can and will be fulfilled."[112]

Stauffenberg flew from Rastenburg to Berlin, where the conspirators were waiting for his return. Three precious hours had been lost. The conspirators reckoned with Hitler's death. Surely they must have known that the failure of Stauffenberg's attempt on Hitler's life would endanger their own. Yet even three hours later they hesitated to throw themselves wholeheartedly into action, which might have given them at least some chance of success. Tragic as the individual fate of the conspirators was, the putsch of July 20 was, historically speaking, a tragicomedy. It was the caricature of a putsch.

The action *Walküre* had been planned in every detail, but nothing happened. No order for action was given, nor—and this proved their worst mistake—had they occupied the radio station, the central telephone exchange, or the telegraph center. The heads of the conspiracy, General Field Marshal von Witzleben and General Beck, arrived in the Bendlerstrasse, the conspiracy's headquarters, hours after they must have known that the bomb had exploded at the Fuehrer's headquarters. They seemed to have all the time in the world, as though they were going to attend a tea party.

Only when Stauffenberg, the only one who had the mettle of a conspirator, had arrived, did things begin to move. At last the action *Walküre* was started—but too late. In these three lost hours the news that Hitler had survived had time to reach Berlin. On the same morning, at eleven o'clock, Reich Minister Speer had given a lecture in the great reception hall of the Propaganda Ministry, before an audience of two hundred, including Goebbels and some other ministers, as well as Goebbels' state secretaries and several high civil servants. A company of twenty soldiers dispatched by the conspirators could have arrested all the leading official personalities in Berlin.[113]

At 4 P.M. one of the conspirators, General von Hase, commandant of Berlin, ordered the Grossdeutschland Battalion stationed in Döberitz to prepare for action. The commandant of the battalion was Major Otto Remer. The Orders were to surround the district where most government buildings and the SS Reich security head office were situated. The reason given was that Hitler had been assassinated and that the SS was planning a putsch.

Attached to the battalion was a National Socialist party officer, a member of the Propaganda Ministry, Lieutenant Dr. Hans Hagen. When Remer transmitted to him the orders he had received, Hagen rushed off to see Goebbels and tell him what had happened.

After Speer's lecture Goebbels was in his office with Speer and Minister of Economy Funk; a telephone call came through from the Fuehrer's headquarters informing Goebbels that an attempt had been made on Hitler's life, but that the Fuehrer had survived.

Goebbels could see from his window a company commanded by Major Remer surrounding his Ministry. He at once ordered Hagen to ask the major to come to see him.

Before receiving Remer, Goebbels, according to Speer,[114] put a poison vial into his pocket. But according to some members of his staff, Goebbels took a revolver from his desk and put it in his pocket.[115] Whether it was a revolver or poison, it shows that Goebbels realized the gravity of his position.

When Major Remer arrived, Goebbels reminded him of his oath of allegiance to the Fuehrer. Remer replied that the Fuehrer was dead, which obliged him to carry out the orders he had received from his superior. These were to arrest the Minister of Propaganda. Goebbels replied that Hitler was alive. A small ambitious clique of generals was planning a military putsch. He, Remer, Goebbels continued, was bearing a heavy responsibility at this historical moment. Already half swayed by Goebbels' words, Remer became a fanatic loyalist when Goebbels connected him by telephone with Hitler, who promoted Remer to the rank of colonel then and there, ordered him to quell the rising in Berlin, and obey Goebbels' further orders.[116] Remer at once put himself and his battalion under Goebbels' direct command. The civilian Goebbels, once rejected for military service because of his physical deficiency, now became a military commander. He addressed the soldiers massed in the garden with a fiery speech and gave Remer orders to proceed to the Bendlerstrasse and arrest the conspirators.

At 6:30 P.M. Goebbels broadcast a special announcement about the abortive attempt on Hitler's life; the putsch, which from the start had been miserably enacted, collapsed.

Those officers who had still hesitated to join the conspirators now returned to the fold. At 8:30 P.M. Keitel addressed all commanders over the teleprinter in the name of the "Fuehrer," informing them that Himmler had been appointed supreme commander of the reserve armies. All orders given by Fromm, Witzleben, and Hoepner were declared null and void.

The "Fuehrer's" new orders had their immediate effect. Field Marshal Kluge, supreme commander of the German troops in France, who had been prepared to join the conspirators, changed his mind at once.

At the Bendlerstrasse, General Fromm, supreme commander of the reserve armies, had in the meantime appointed himself supreme judge, and established an improvised military tribunal. His second-in-command, General Friedrich Olbricht; Colonel Stauffenberg; Colonel of the General Staff Merz von Quirnheim; and Stauffenberg's adjutant, First Lieutenant Werner Haeften, were tried in haste, condemned to death, and executed. Fromm hoped by this action to cover up every clue that might lead to himself and the discovery that he had been privy to the plot. This ignoble attempt to save his own skin was to no avail. General Fromm, too, was tried and condemned to death, regretted by neither side; both regarded him as a traitor. General Beck, designated to become head of state after the putsch, twice attempted to shoot himself. A sergeant had to give him the *coup de grâce* and put him out of his misery. Beck was one of the most cultivated but—and this was perhaps his undoing—one of the most undecided of all German generals.

That evening Goebbels' residence became the headquarters of all forces that combined to suppress the putsch—an *ad hoc* tribunal. A commission presided over by Goebbels and later joined by Himmler was quickly formed. They interrogated Fromm, General von Hase, and the police president of Berlin, Count Helldorf.

Shortly before 1 A.M. Hitler addressed the nation over radio. They should "hear his voice and learn that he was unscathed and well." They were also to hear some details of "a crime unique in German history." Since Hitler regarded himself as the greatest German who had ever lived, the attempt on his life must have necessarily appeared to him the greatest crime ever committed. . . . He saw in his escape "the divine affirmation of the task for which he had been chosen by Providence." He called the conspirators "a small clique of ambitious, irresponsible, and at the same time criminal and stupid officers." They were but an insignificant "coterie of criminals who would be mercilessly exterminated. . . . And this time we'll settle accounts in the truly National Socialist fashion."

Goebbels told his staff that night: "It was a revolution by telephone, which we finished off with a few rifle shots. If they had been only a little more clever, the rifle shots would have been in vain."[117]

Goebbels had nothing but contempt for the conspirators, with one exception: "This Stauffenberg, now, he was a real fellow! It's almost a pity he had to go. What *sang-froid,* what intelligence, what iron will power! Inconceivable that he surrounded himself with that guard of idiots. If the plot had succeeded only Stauffenberg might have been a real danger for us. . . ."

Hitler kept his word. The conspirators were mercilessly exterminated. Every one of them, whether officer or civilian, had to face

the People's Court. The first show trial of eight accused, headed by
General Field Marshal Erwin von Witzleben and Major General Erich
Hoepner, began on August 7. All prominent personalities of state
and party hierarchy were present. The long procession of cars arriving at the courthouse was worthy of a grand opera gala. All accused
were condemned to death and executed at the Prison Plötzensee. On
Goebbels' orders the trial and the executions were filmed.

They are among the most sinister chapters of the Third Reich.
They prove that Hitler acted against his enemies, even if they were
Germans descended from the oldest and most venerated families,
with the same cruelty and mercilessness he used against the Jews.
Both Hitler and Goebbels had a deep contempt for mankind and did
not bother even to hide it. But astonishingly enough, Goebbels succeeded until the very end in upholding the Hitler image: a true German, a good man who sacrificed himself for his people. And most
Germans believed Goebbels. Despite thousands of executions, battles
of retreat in which the lives of hundreds and thousands of German
soldiers were sacrificed senselessly, despite defeats in the East and in
the West hastening the day of collapse, in the midst of burning cities,
Goebbels had the audacity to publish on December 31, 1944, in *Das
Reich,* an article about the Fuehrer of unsurpassed Byzantinism:

"If mankind only knew how much he has to tell them and give
them, and how deep his love is and not only for his own people but for
all mankind, they would even at this late hour forsake their false gods
and pay tribute to him. He is the greatest of all personalities who
shape today's history. His gift of foreseeing what the future will bring,
places him high above all other world leaders. He towers above them,
not only by his genius and political instinct, but also by his knowledge, character, and will power. This man, who set himself the task
of redeeming his people and giving a whole continent a new face, does
not care for every-day pleasures and comforts; they simply do not
exist for him. He spends his days, and most of his sleepless nights,
surrounded by his closest associates. Yet even in their midst he is
alone in the chilly solitude of the genius who, as always, triumphantly
rises high above everyone and everything. Never will a base word
or a falsehood pass his lips. He is truth personified.

"He has a genius for simplification, that admirable gift to see things
as they really are before they fall into the hands of the specialists.
. . . In 1939, when the nations lined up to make war, he alone of all
national leaders pleaded for peace with fanatic determination, with an
almost self-immolating altruism—but they wouldn't listen to him. It is
almost naïve to ask: 'Does the Fuehrer know?' He knows, all right,
he knows the smallest detail; he is the first to know, and the less he

talks about it, the more it preoccupies him. . . . He is the classic example of a war leader. His universal knowledge and ability in all fields that appertain to leading the state and the people enable him to make the most mature assessments of all war problems, which he analyzes with penetrating logic and burning passion, to resolve them with his precise all-encompassing power of reasoning. When he talks about them all ambiguities seem to vanish. . . . While the world has changed profoundly under the impact of his will power, he himself remained unchanged.

"It is precisely this ability of remaining unchanged, refusing to fit in with the convictions and the faith of others, but change the others' convictions and faith to fit his own, that makes him the greatest man alive. . . .

"The pains of our tormented times are the birth pangs of a new era. It will come to us one day like a gift of grace won by our own efforts and granted to us by Fate. Only then will mankind realize fully what significance the Fuehrer had for our century, which will bear his name and his stamp. He is transforming mankind. He has given the world a new content and way of thinking. He stands head and shoulders above all living statesmen—which even our enemies have tacitly admitted by banding together against us despite their profound basic differences, because they know that that is their only chance to overwhelm him. They are hoping in vain. This man is far too great for them. . . .

"He is a superhuman example for us. To trust him means securing victory of our good cause. It cannot and will not founder because he leads us. May Providence combine to grant his life and his strength divine protection."

Here is the madness of a man glorified and magnified out of all proportion by the madness of a propagandist. We are listening to a satanic prayer that has no equal. The Son of Darkness is elevated to the Son of Light. The barbaric sacrifice of millions is made to sound a great hallelujah for the new god.

Das Reich *or the Consolation*

The weekly paper *Das Reich* appeared for the first time during the French campaign on May 26, 1940.

The idea for this paper, which soon became by far the most highly esteemed periodical in the Third Reich, originated with Carl Anders, assessor, who had the English weekly, *The Observer,* in mind. Anders was the personal assistant of Rolf Rienhardt, chief of staff to Max

Amann. In his confidential information sheet, however, Goebbels said: "The publication of this paper is due to the initiative of the Reich Minister for People's Information and Propaganda, Dr. Goebbels, and the Reichsleiter for the press of the NSDAP, Max Amann."[118]

The name itself, *Das Reich,* was meant to imply its purpose, which was to be the representative voice, the spiritual mirror of the rapidly expanding *Imperium Adolphi Maximi.* Propaganda was to be subtly used and always beautifully wrapped up. The paper's aim was to show National Socialism not as it actually was, but in the rosy light in which its most benevolent adherents saw it. Many traditional symbols re-appeared. The term "Reich" alone evoked romantic and sentimental associations. The old idea of the Reich was married to a concept of a new order; Germany the new power of order in Europe, no longer Christian but Germano-heroic. Consequently the war was a task set by Providence, and the soldier its executor.

Goebbels' first and foremost aim was to produce a good paper. Good style counted just as much as having the right convictions. Someone who only had the latter was not accepted if his writing was bad. On the other hand, a good writer was welcome even if he was not a convinced Nazi, as long as he was not opposed to Nazism. The idea was to produce a paper that would be a neat visiting card de-livered abroad and a true consolation for the intellectuals at home. The cultural page occasionally even took a slight liberal line, such as the favorable mention of writers and artists who had retired into ivory towers. A modern but dignified layout, a careful selection of photos, and high linguistic standards were the visible trappings of the new publication. A number of well-known personalities, who had little to do with the party, contributed. This was meant to demon-strate the paper's broadmindedness. The first editor-in-chief was Dr. Eugen Mündler, who had been the last editor-in-chief of the *Berliner Tageblatt*. He was replaced as editor-in-chief by Rudolf Sparing in February 1943. Sparing was more critical than Mündler of his con-tributors but no less loyal to his staff. He never overacted the role of National Socialist, he never wore the party badge. Only when the Soviets arrived did he put it in his buttonhole, was deported, and died in a Russian camp. He took his heroic attitude seriously, which rather testifies to his strong character.

The paper had its correspondents in almost all big European cities; in Helsinki and Stockholm, in Rome and Lisbon, in Ankara and Moscow, in Paris and Bucharest, in Madrid and The Hague. Among the correspondents were Louis Barcata, Martin Bethke, Rudolf Fischer, Fritz von Globig, and Alfred Rapp. From Thailand, Peking, and Shanghai, Herbert Tichy reported. From Tokyo Wilhelm Schulze, and from New York Paul Scheffer.

The deputy editor-in-chief was Dr. Werner Wirths. The resident editors were: Otto Philipp Höfner (foreign policy), Curt Strohmeyer (interior), Dr. Karl Korn (features), as well as the critics Will Grohmann, Fritz Nemitz, and W. E. Süsskind. The paper called upon a large number of contributors: Margret Bover, Hans Georg Brenner, Helmut von Cube, Schwarz van Berk, Christoph Freiherr von Imhoff, Werner Höfer, Ilse Urban, the later Bundespresident Theodor Heuss, Friedrich Luft, Erik Graf Wickenburg, Wolfgang Koeppen, Herbert Schöffler, Clemens Graf Podewils, Joachim Fernau, Bruno Brehm, Otto Gmelin, E. H. Busse, and Manfred Hausmann, as well as the scientists Max Bense, Eduard Spranger, Herbert Fritsche, Heinrich von Srbik, Willy Andreas, and military experts Rear Admiral Lützow (retired), General of the Artillery von Metzsch, and Wilhelm Ritter von Schramm.

The success of the paper was extraordinary. All educated people, or at least those who liked to be regarded as such, read *Das Reich*. The paper had a larger foreign distribution than any other German newspaper. It was on sale in all European capitals, with the exception of enemy countries. Widely read by officers and the more educated soldiers, it penetrated as far as the Russian steppes, the African desert, and the frozen North—in short, everywhere that German soldiers were fighting to realize the idea of the Third Reich.

In his confidential information sheet, Goebbels wrote: "With a circulation of 1½ million every week *Das Reich* is, together with the *Völkische Beobachter,* the most widely distributed German newspaper. We could easily double or treble circulation if we had enough newsprint. Long lines forming every weekend before newspaper stands to buy the new number of *Das Reich* demonstrate the population's high standard of morale, very different from what happened during the First World War, when the people preferred to buy *Die Zukunft* [The Future], edited by the Jew Maximilian Harden. A considerable number of copies, approximately 250,000, are sent abroad, mainly to European countries. In Lisbon the English carrier plane sometimes postpones its departure if the arrival of *Das Reich* has been delayed. . . ."[119]

But the real success of the paper was not its intellectual note and its unusual political reticence, but precisely the feature which, different from everything else, almost seemed an alien body: Goebbels' editorial. Originally, no contribution from the Propaganda Minister was envisaged; it was even considered undesirable. But since his approval was needed, as for every other publication, Rienhardt submitted the idea of such a weekly to the minister. Goebbels was enchanted and told Rienhardt that he himself would write the editorial. Stabsleiter Amann had no choice but to agree.

If one reads these articles today, particularly those that exhort the German people to remain steadfast, it is not easy to see why they had such a great influence at the time. They were eagerly read by friend and foe alike and were the only German articles Churchill took into consideration. They were written in a simple style, here and there interspersed with brilliant slogans.

They derived their great effect not from their style; many other articles in *Das Reich* were linguistically more accomplished. The secret of their success lay in their content. They began to make a real impact with the first German setbacks at the front, and their success grew steadily with every new German defeat. Goebbels succeeded in conveying to his readers that he was privy to the vital causes and motivations determining the conduct of the war, and that he, knowing so much more than the average reader, was clearly in a position to comment on events from a superior point of view. Giving himself the air of an incorruptible critic, he would analyze the precarious position to arrive at the rather illogical but consoling conclusion that German victory was assured. He depicted the first defeats as transient attacks of weakness every army was prone to, after so many victories.

But as soon as the setbacks had become a regular feature, Goebbels discovered the military advantage that lay in shortening one's lines of supply, a real boon to Germany's conduct of the war, apt to grow into a deadly danger for the enemy.

When the Anglo-American air forces bombed city after city into ruins, Goebbels explained the favorable effect these attacks had on the people. These attacks not only stoked up hatred against the enemy, but also relieved the German people of any moral scruples they may have felt once the new German miracle weapons had started raining death and destruction on their ruthless adversary. When enemy troops reached Germany's borders, or even later when they had deeply penetrated into German territory, Goebbels still spoke of one last effort needed to turn the tide. After all, the enemy, too, had used his last reserves and was bound to give in once he realized Germany would never capitulate. And when the crushing material superiority of Germany's enemies had become obvious to everybody, including the most devout National Socialists, Goebbels seemed most concerned with human material. The decisive factor, he explained, was man, not material. If it were otherwise, history would have lost its sense. Therefore Germany could not possibly lose the war, possessing in the Fuehrer the man of the century, vastly superior to any politician and military leader the enemy could call upon.

When, at the end, neither the new military weapons nor the Fuehrer's military genius, neither the supreme courage of the German soldier nor the unlimited bravery and sacrifices of the German people could stem the catastrophic tide, Goebbels intonated his plaintive chant about the horrors committed by the Bolsheviks. The neutral countries and the enemy powers in the West would soon realize what barbaric tornado threatened to devastate Europe. The clash between East and West was inevitable; the Americans and the British were about to understand that they needed the German armies to shield Europe.

Goebbels' ideological argument, submitting that Germany simply could not lose the war, had a far stronger effect than his reasoned conclusions (after all, they became less and less credible and less and less convincing daily). Goebbels would call on historical justice, which had always granted victory to the best and most courageous people, and as there were no better or more courageous people than the Germans, victory would be theirs in the end. Goebbels constantly found new variations of the same theme, which was that nothing could happen that had no right to happen. He fed this illusion to the German people and perhaps to himself, a consolation that the heart "made of steel" would not suffer in vain and not be forgotten by the goddess of justice. Not unlike the last philosopher of antiquity, Boethius, writing his *De Consolatione Philosophiae* in prison to comfort himself and the Roman people groaning under the yoke of the Goths, so offered Goebbels the suffering and despairing German nation the comforting hope that at the end of the rocky road of suffering stood triumph and victory as a reward for their steadfastness.

No doubt these mental hat tricks could hardly have been successful if the German people had not still believed in a miracle that would turn the tide. A nation that for years had rushed from one victory to another and had overcome the armies of the strongest powers was simply unable to absorb the image of a complete military collapse, followed by a disintegration of the Reich. Was it possible that all their sacrifices, all their suffering, all courage and heroism should have been in vain?

It was as though a magic circle had been drawn around a troubled people beset from all sides, with magician Hitler in the center, trying to work the miracle that would bring salvation at the last moment. And Goebbels was beseeching the people to defend this magic circle in order to give the magician time to work his miracle.

Apart from his vituperations against Churchill and against the Jews, which hardly harmonized with the general content of *Das Reich,* Goebbels' articles present a curiosity in newspaper history. No other journalist ever succeeded in pulling off such a lying deception or showed the stamina needed to keep it up for three long years. Goebbels' articles (which were also broadcast Saturday evening and Sunday morning) had become for many Germans like a drug. And Goebbels himself appears to have been addicted to his own drug. He seemed intoxicated with his own arguments. He worked on the weekly lead editorial almost every day for several hours, using minutely prepared documentation, careful never to make the smallest factual mistake.

Taken all together, Goebbels' articles falsified the truth. They not only depicted the world strictly from Hitler's and Goebbels' points of view, but they painted it upside down. It cannot be denied that Goebbels' propaganda chemistry, which succeeded in transforming any catastrophe into a stroke of luck, was nothing short of masterly. He poured contempt on reality and perverted the scale of values: He would present evil dressed in garments of virtue. But even more remarkable was the fact that his articles succeeded in bringing comfort even to some right-thinking people who rejected National Socialism but were not strong enough to face the idea of Germany's defeat.

Reaching the Goal at Last

After the putsch of July 20, 1944, Goebbels was at long last given the powers for which he had been striving so long. On July 25, 1944, the Fuehrer appointed him plenipotentiary by special decree, with full powers to organize the total war effort. For the short time still left, Goebbels became the most powerful figure, after Hitler, in the Reich. Goebbels had reached the pinnacle of his career and, like so many in this position, he overestimated his own capabilities and underestimated reality. He was virtually intoxicated with optimism and actually believed he could still turn back the wheel of fortune. He tried to transfer this optimism to his vast audience in a speech broadcast on July 26:

"The war is about to change in a manner that will make our enemies choke on their own shouts of triumph. They thought that the events of July 20 would finish us off; instead they only roused us! They will have to bear the consequences and not we." And to give his words more credence he once more referred to the new weapons being prepared: "Only the other day I was shown new German weapons the sight of which took my breath away. I don't say this to boast or to bluff."

With these miracle weapons and the miracle Providence had worked on behalf of Hitler, Goebbels was hoping to convince the people that the tide had turned and all would end well: "Let us surpass one another in our love and loyalty to him [Hitler]; to him and to our faith in his historical mission. We are actually in a position to turn the fortunes of war in our favor in the immediate future. All that's needed to bring this about is there for the taking. Let's take it! Never again will the Almighty reveal to us his presence as clearly as when He worked a miracle on behalf of the Fuehrer, saving his life."[120]

Goebbels now held full powers over all Reich and party authorities. He was responsible only to the Fuehrer. All complaints about Goebbels were forbidden, even if they were addressed directly to Hitler. As a first measure, Goebbels combed through all administrative bodies. And to set a good example, he started with his own ministry, demanding a 30 per cent reduction of staff, the extra bodies to be made available for the Wehrmacht or the armament industry.

He introduced the sixty-hour week for everybody, including workers, employees, and officials. The age limit for women liable to be called up for work, set at forty-five until then, was raised to fifty.

Goebbels shut down all theaters, music halls, schools for acting, and conservatories. All leaves were canceled, all traffic and transport reduced. All official forms and questionnaires were simplified. He cut down film production and broadcasting, the only two artistic institutions he had maintained as helpful to the war effort.

To organize the total war effort, Goebbels formed three committees, employing fifty people in all. They were unpaid, honorary appointments.

1. The Planning Committee was charged to deal with all plans for totalizing the war effort. The chairman was State Secretary Naumann.
2. The Executive Committee drafted the necessary decrees and regulations to put these plans into effect. As chairman, Goebbels appointed Paul Wegener, gauleiter of Oldenburg.
3. The General Secretariat assured the co-ordination of the two committees and the liaison with Goebbels. Its chief was Regierungspresident Dr. Faust of the Ministry of the Interior.[121]

Goebbels charged the party with the execution and control of his measures. Each gau had his part to play. The responsibility rested with the gauleiter. Goebbels instituted a special radio network, the Gauleiter Rundfunk, which enabled him to keep close contact with forty-three gauleiters, a number of Reichsleiters, and some other prominent party members, to whom he transmitted top-secret information concerning the military and political situations, and the necessary directives.

This sudden increase of the labor force put the armament industry into a difficult position. Unable to absorb so many additional hands at once—most of them unskilled and in need of specialized training—it lost at the same time great numbers of workers who were called up for the Wehrmacht. This created bottlenecks in production. The factory inspectors kept on sending urgent calls for help to Minister Speer.[122]

An additional Fuehrer decree of September 10 gave Goebbels additional powers, enabling him to comb through various administrative bodies attached to the Wehrmacht and pull out as many men as possible for service at the front.

Goebbels had reached the highest position for a civilian in a military setup. He likewise wielded dictatorial powers over the Wehrmacht apparatus at home. One of his confidential communications to his gauleiters shows how rigorously, even brutally, he fulfilled his task. This communication deals with the recruitment of men taken from the ranks of the military administration at home. Goebbels proposes to form front battalions consisting of men suffering from ailments of the stomach, ears, rheumatism, and gall- and kidney stones. He informs them that "under his new powers" he succeeded "in recruiting for the front in the Wehrkreis VIII alone 79,874 from a total of 336,766 men suffering from such ailments.

"The physician in charge of this Wehrkreis reckons that one could recruit in the whole Reich enough men suffering from these ailments to form one hundred such special battalions, all in all around two million men fit to be dispatched to the front. We are taking the point of view that, for instance, a chronic stomach ailment cannot be regarded as a life insurance and that it could hardly be the aim of this war to send the fit to die while the ailing are preserved."[123]

Goebbels' measures were obviously insufficiently reasoned and rather too hasty; but there was precious little time for making plans or experimenting. Hitler had charged him to produce an army at all cost. By mid-August Soviet troops had reached the borders of East Prussia. At the end of August Romania had to capitulate; Bulgaria and Finland had pulled out of the war. News from the West was no better. On August 25, the Allies took Paris, and on September 3, Brussels. A day later they occupied Antwerp, which Eisenhower used as the chief harbor to land supplies for the Allied armies. Goebbels' efforts were a race against time. He was determined to win the race and make the impossible possible. In this respect he was a worthy disciple of his master, who would inflict the most inhuman treatment on the people and demand of them superhuman efforts at the same time.

After the failure of Hitler's offensive in the Ardennes in January 1945, Goebbels realized that Germany's defeat was inevitable. "We are finished, bled white, it's the end. Nothing can help us now,"[124] Goebbels said to his intimates early in February 1945. And yet, at least outwardly, he stuck to his assumption that Germany could still win the war. His entire effort continued to be directed toward the coming victory. He seemed to go through the day like a blind man, with his eyes shut to reality.

As late as February 1945 Goebbels met with Himmler to discuss the forming of a new government, with Goebbels as Reich Chancellor and Minister of Foreign Affairs, Himmler as Minister of War and supreme commander of the Wehrmacht. Hitler was to be reduced to the position of Reich President.[125]

But all these combinations had no reality in fact, and Goebbels knew in his heart only too well that there was no real chance of any change whatsoever. He knew that with Hitler's fall the Third Reich, the party, and the party leaders would also fall.

The Iron Curtain

In the last week of January, Hitler moved to Berlin. In the meantime his former headquarters had fallen into the hands of the enemy. This meant the end of Goebbels' task as plenipotentiary for the total-war effort. Armament production had sunk to 30 per cent. The loss of the Ruhr and Silesia had robbed Germany of her most important industrial centers and most of her coal mines. The natural sources of crude oil had been lost with the fall of Romania and Hungary. Anglo-American bombers had destroyed the industrial plants producing synthetic gasoline. Brand-new German jet-fighter planes had come off the line and stood idle for lack of fuel. The new electrically driven U-boats, designed to revolutionize U-boat warfare, were no longer able to leave port. The ramps for the "V" bombs had been overrun by the enemy. Everything that might have favorably influenced the course of events came much too late. Goebbels' warnings had been in vain.

And as to his personal position, there were only two paths open to him: either make an end then and there, or fight on at Hitler's side to the bitter end. Goebbels chose the latter; perhaps less from heroism than from stubbornness. If Hitler and Goebbels had to leave this

world, they would do so with a cosmic bang! The foreign conqueror
was to find a Germany in ruins. Germany, Hitler's and Goebbels'
Valhalla, would go up in flames first. No "cowardly capitulation" for
them, but a fanatical fight for the last square foot of German soil, so
that history after hundreds of years should still tell the heroic legend
of the two greatest National Socialists, just as it recounts the last
mortal struggle of the East Goths and their King Teja, or the fall of
the Nibelungen.

It is difficult to say if Goebbels supported wholeheartedly, as Bormann and Ley did, the order Hitler gave on March 19, 1945, for the
destruction of all German military and industrial installations, as well
as of the whole network serving transport and communications.
Speer's deposition at the Nuremberg trial points to the fact that Goebbels supported this order. Other witnesses leveled the same accusation at Goebbels. Yet none of Goebbels' intimate collaborators confirmed this.

On the other hand, Goebbels' hatred of the British, who sent their
bombers to destroy German cities, had grown out of all proportion.
On May 29, 1944, Goebbels wrote an article in the *Völkische
Beobachter* that at the Nuremberg trial was judged to constitute an
open appeal to the German population to kill British pilots who had
been shot down.

"We have to use the help of our armed forces to protect the lives
of enemy pilots shot down during such air attacks; otherwise the
much-tried people would kill them. Who is in the right? The murderers who after their cowardly deeds expect to be treated in a human
fashion by their victims, or the victims who try to defend themselves obeying the old law, an eye for an eye and a tooth for a tooth?
It should not be too difficult to answer that question. It appears to us
to be no longer possible or tolerable to use German police and German
soldiers against the German people, when they are about to treat
murderers of children the way they deserve."

After two successive air attacks on Dresden—by the Royal Air
Force during the night of February 13–14 and by the U. S. Air Force
on the fourteenth, in daylight, Goebbels lost his control completely.
Dresden harbored no important military installations and had been
spared up until then.

The town was overflowing with hundreds of thousands of refugees
from Germany's eastern provinces. Dresden's world-famous monuments, such as the Residenz, the Zwinger, the Hofkirche, the National Theatre, and the Brühlsche Terrace, were completely destroyed. Approximately 60 per cent of all houses were leveled. The
many refugees among the victims make it almost impossible to estab-

lish the exact number of dead; an approximate estimate gave a figure of well over thirty thousand. To crown the horror, the first wave of attacking aircraft dropped incendiary bombs, which started fires, with the result that the heat drove the people out of their shelters into the streets, where they became defenseless targets for the second wave of bombers dropping explosives. Squares and streets in the center of the town, as well as in the suburbs, were covered with corpses. The daylight attack on the following day mainly bombed the suburbs, to which the bombed-out had fled. These Anglo-American air raids were an example of pure terror tactics—the destruction of a town and its civilian population of no particular strategic value. This was an action worthy of Hitler's obsessive extermination tactics.

Goebbels' press officer, Semmler, described Goebbels' deep shock; Goebbels wept with rage for twenty minutes; he looked like a broken man. Then his anger erupted and he cried: "If I had the power I would drag this cowardly good-for-nothing, this Reich marshal [Goering], before a court. . . . How much guilt does this parasite not bear for all this, which we owe to his indolence and love of his own comforts. . . ."[126]

Outraged by the bombing of Dresden, Goebbels is said to have advocated the immediate denunciation of the Geneva Convention and tried to persuade Hitler to act accordingly. The idea behind it was to put all captured Allied pilots immediately before a court, accuse them of murder, and have them condemned to death. Semmler added in his report that he informed a Swedish journalist of Goebbels' intention, and the journalist transmitted it immediately to Stockholm. From there it reached the British government; which immediately addressed a sharp warning to Berlin. Goebbels called a press conference at which he denied this rumor and declared it was not Germany's intention to denounce the Geneva Convention.[127]

Goebbels continued to console and encourage the people, although he himself had actually given up all hope. On February 25, 1945, he wrote an article in *Das Reich* entitled "The Year 2000," which was pregnant with predictions for the future: "In the year 2000 Europe will be one united continent. People will be able to fly from Berlin to Paris for breakfast—in a mere fifteen minutes. Our most modern weapons will have become completely obsolete, as well as so many other things. But according to the Yalta Conference Germany will still be under military occupation and her people trained by English and Americans to become good democrats. How empty must be the brains of these three charlatans, at least of two of them. . . .

"Because the third, Stalin, pursues his own aims, which are far more ambitious than those of his two companions. He is, of course, most careful not to show his hand, but makes his two hundred million slaves work and fight for it all the more. He sees before him a future in which the whole globe is subordinated to the dictatorship of the Moscow Internationale, that is, to the Kremlin. . . .

"These are his plans: As soon as the German people have laid down arms, the Soviets would occupy the whole of Eastern and Southern Europe and the greater part of the Reich. This enormous territory, including the Soviet Union, would be sealed off by an Iron Curtain [the term Iron Curtain was therefore not invented by Churchill], behind which the mass slaughter of certain peoples would take place, possibly applauded by the London and New York Jewish press. All that remained would be a certain raw material called man, a dull fermenting mass of millions of proletarized beasts of burden, who would not be allowed to know more about the other part of the globe than the Kremlin considered fit to serve its own ends. . . ."

Goebbels also predicted a process of diminution of Great Britain, which by then would no longer be able to pursue a European, let alone a world policy. The United States, Goebbels foretold, would return to isolationism, "accompanied by a withdrawal of American troops from the boiling witch's cauldron of Europe. . . . He [the President] would be applauded for this action by the entire American nation. . . ." This would leave the Western Hemisphere in mortal danger. The time would come when the United States would curse the day when a then long-forgotten American President had published a communiqué of the legendary conference at Yalta, which led to this disastrous development.

And Goebbels exhorted the German people to go on fighting to prevent these terrible prospects from materializing. On the other hand, a wonderful future was in store for the German people if they only remained steadfast. "In the year 2000 Germany, far from being occupied by her enemies, would be the spiritual leader of cultured humanity. We have earned in this war the moral right to be that."

Germany's moral right was, in fact, just as feeble as Germany's defense, which was collapsing on every front. A last attempt was made by the creation of the Volksturm. This Home Guard included all males from sixteen to sixty, who were put through a crash course in the use of arms. These men were not soldiers but poor souls who were thrown into the dying furnace of war by Hitler's madness. Joseph Goebbels duly joined in. He must have acted against his better judgment, knowing he could only delay the end at the price of still more terrible destruction. But perhaps he needed to dramatize his own end.

Hitler and Goebbels still remembered the activities of the partisans in the Soviet Union and Yugoslavia and tried to create something similar within the shrunken territory of the Reich—German partisans called Werwolf (werewolves). Goebbels launched a new slogan: "Every German a sniper." But Werwolf remained primarily a product of the imagination. Only a small number of young men volunteered. The great majority had only one wish—to finish the war as soon as possible. They had had their fill, and even the worst kind of peace appeared as a godsend from heaven, compared with the kind of war they had to endure.

Hitler and Goebbels knew only too well that the end had come. Yet they prolonged the war, clinging to their hope for a miracle. And one day it seemed as if it would really come to pass.

The Miracle Does Not Happen

Goebbels, a passionate reader of the letters of Frederick II and Thomas Carlyle's biography of the Prussian King, now made use of it to strengthen his "Fuehrer's" position. Had not, during the Seven Years' War, Frederick the Great been saved by the bell in an ostensibly hopeless situation by the sudden death of Czarina Elisabeth, which led to the breakup of the coalition of Prussia's powerful enemies, Austria, Russia, and France? Elisabeth's successor, Peter III, a great admirer of Frederick II, had become his ally, enabling the Prussian King to finish the war and keep Silesia, which he had occupied.

On April 12, 1945, Goebbels visited the Ninth Army at the Oder front and stayed at the headquarters of General Busse near Küstrin. Goebbels addressed the officers and reminded them of the miracle that had saved Frederick II. On his return his press officer told him that Roosevelt had died: "He grew pale, then he exclaimed, 'This is the turning point!' And rather used to bitter disappointments, he asked incredulously: 'Is it really true?' " The press officer confirmed it, upon which Goebbels immediately telephoned Hitler, talking to him feverishly: " 'I congratulate you, my Fuehrer, Providence has smitten our most powerful enemy. The Lord has not forsaken us. He saved you twice from the hands of savage assassins, now he smote your most dangerous enemy. A miracle has happened. . . . This is like the death of Czarina Elisabeth.' "

Goebbels put down the telephone and offered champagne to his associates. They drank to the great miracle Providence had worked on behalf of her favorite, Adolf Hitler.[128]

But Roosevelt's death changed nothing. The expected miracle did not materialize.

On April 17 or 18, Goebbels, aided by his personal assistant, burned all important papers to prevent them from falling into the hands of the enemy.[129]

The last week preceding his move into the Fuehrer's bunker Goebbels spent working on a speech and an article. He wrote the editorial for *Das Reich,* entitled "Resistance at All Cost." It was to be Goebbels' last article and appeared in the last issue of *Das Reich* on April 22, 1945; it was never to reach its readers. The article is psychologically interesting. Written by a man who had already known for some time that his life was finished, his arguments seen in the light of what actually happened—the Allied armies from the East and the West were now so close that they could join hands—appear to be those of a madman. Yet Goebbels was by no means mad. But he was caught in his own propaganda net and desired to go down in history as an undefeated heroic statesman:

"The war has entered a phase in which nothing can save us short of an all-out effort of the entire nation, of every single citizen. The defense of the nation's freedom is no longer exclusively the duty of our soldiers at the front, but also of the civilian population. Men and women, boys and girls must rally to do their share as they have never done before, with fanatical devotion. The enemy calculates that once his Panzers have broken through he will find no more resistance in the hinterland. . . . It's up to us to prove them wrong. There must be no village, no town that will ever submit to the enemy's might . . . as long as we remain determined to resist, whatever the cost, the insolent invaders of our land . . . we cannot be beaten, and not being beaten means being victorious.

"What the soldiers can no longer accomplish, boys and girls should accomplish for them." "There is method in the madness," one might say with Shakespeare. The German people were called upon to destroy their own country, the enemy was to find nothing but ruins. When the German people had descended to the lowest spiritual and material level, then at least the memory of the Third Reich, together with the glorious victories of the early war years, should remain alive —a glorious past to remember. Hitler and Goebbels would then be heroic figures, examples to emulate.

The climax of this hero cult was Goebbels' speech, broadcast on April 19, 1945, the eve of Hitler's fifty-sixth birthday. It is perhaps Goebbels' most impassionate speech.[130] Not only his language and delivery but also the inner excitement of the orator was irresistible. A man was speaking who knew that within three days he would move to the Fuehrer's bunker, there to die; who knew that the war was lost and that Hitler had failed everywhere; who knew from his own bitter experience that Hitler's failure was very much due to his obstinacy and lack of comprehension; who also knew that Hitler was a wreck in body and soul, deserted by his good fortune. Once again Goebbels tried to conjure up the Hitler myth he had himself created, make it reappear from the glorious past as though he could still compel Fate to turn back and transform the wreck Hitler into a Titan. For the last time Goebbels intonated the hymn of Hitler the Great, the Unique, the Savior.

Having told his audience that "all the dark powers of hatred and destruction were assaulting us" and that now "the somber question of our people's future is upon us," Goebbels speaks of "the last act of a powerful drama." He refers to Jacob Burckhardt's statement that "The fate of entire nations and states as well as the direction a whole civilization may take, can depend on the ability of one extraordinary human being to stand up to certain great pressures upon his soul and extreme efforts in times of stress." In Goebbels' eyes Hitler is such an extraordinary human being:

"If it is manly and German for the Fuehrer of a great and courageous people . . . trusting in his own strength and self-assurance as well as in God's help to brave the menacing storm of the enemy, instead of capitulating before it, then it is also manly and German for a people to follow this Fuehrer faithfully, without reservation, without excuse or limitation, to shake off any access of weakness or doubt, to trust in the lucky star that looks down on him and all of us now as before, and particularly when dark clouds have temporarily darkened the sky, calling upon us not to become cowards in misfortune but brave men, and on no account to give a gleefully watching world the satisfaction of seeing the spectacle of belly-crawling submission, and in the eyes of the enemy proudly unfurl the Swastika instead of the white flag of surrender he is expecting to see, renew the oath we have taken so often in happier and safer times of peace, to thank our God again and again that He has given us in this terrible but great time a true Fuehrer, to open our hearts to his worries and the trials he endures day and night, and show our enemies that they may well wound us but not kill us, smite us until our blood flows but never conquer us, torture us but not humiliate us.

"The war moves toward its end. The madness that the enemy powers have let loose on mankind has already passed its peak. All it leaves is but a feeling of shame and disgust felt in the whole world. The perverted coalition between plutocracy and Bolshevism is about to break up. The head of the enemy conspiracy has been crushed by Fate [Roosevelt's death. Author's note]—the same Fate that saved the Fuehrer on July 20, in the midst of the dead, the gravely injured, in the midst of shambles, leaving him unscathed so that he should be able to finish his task as Providence had ordained, though under trials and tribulations. Once more the armies of the enemy powers storm our defenses; in their wake, foaming at the mouth, international Jewry, which does not want peace because their diabolic aim is to see the world destroyed. But in vain, God will throw back Lucifer, as he has done before when the dark angel stood before the gates of power, back into the abyss from whence he came. A man of true secular greatness, of incomparable courage, of a steadfastness that elates and moves all hearts will be His instrument. . . .

"Germany will only need a few years after the war to blossom forth again as she has never done before. Her ruined lands and provinces will be resurrected with new, even more beautiful towns and villages, in which happy people shall dwell. The whole of Europe will take part in this task. We shall again be friends with all people of goodwill. Together we shall heal the deep wounds that now disfigure the noble face of our continent. . . .

"May the world now insult and abuse Hitler, pursue him with its base hatred. It will one day revise its judgment and regret it bitterly. He is the heart of resistance against the decline of the world. He is Germany's brave heart and our people's most glowing will. . . .

"We are at his side as he is at ours in truly Germanic loyalty, as we have sworn to be and as we shall be. There is no need for us to tell him because he knows it, as know it he must.

"Misfortune has matured us but not broken us. Germany is still the land of loyalty; she will in the hour of danger celebrate her greatest triumph. Never shall history say that the people have abandoned their Fuehrer, or the Fuehrer has abandoned his people. And this means victory. What we so often in past times of happiness [the eve of Hitler's birthday. Translator's note] on this evening begged of the Fuehrer has become today in the hour of grief and danger for us all an even deeper and more heartfelt wish: that he remains for us what he is and always was: our Hitler."

The End

On the afternoon of April 22, during the review of the general position in the Fuehrer's bunker, Hitler, as so often in these last months, completely lost his composure when told that the Soviet Panzer spearheads had reached Berlin. This was the end, he cried, everywhere nothing but treason, lies, corruption, and cowardice. Hitler probably decided then to make his last stand in Berlin.[131]

He obviously gave in to Goebbels, whose view it was that if the Fuehrer had to die, it should be in the capital. Goebbels had, in fact, the day before already recorded his farewell speech. His personal assistant Oven reports how the minister delivered his speech, calmly reading the text, apparently unruffled by the sound of the heavy Russian guns. One of the shells even landed in the garden and the blast blew the windows, complete with frames, into Goebbels' workroom: "Every one of us at least winced, the general quickly crawled under the desk, but the minister continued with his speech, undismayed as though nothing had happened. All he did was lift the page of the manuscript he was reading and shake off the powdered plaster. When we all listened to the recording, we could actually hear the explosion and the flow of Goebbels' voice, which had not changed, not even for a fraction of a second."[132]

Here we are presented with the heroic Goebbels, unmoved by the artillery bombardment, while the general crawls under the table.

In this speech, "In Case of Emergency," Goebbels appealed to Berliners to fight and make "War without mercy. . . . At the walls of our city the attack of the Mongols must and will be halted." Goebbels also tells the Berliners: "I and my staff shall remain in Berlin of course . . . also my wife and my children are here, and here we shall stay."[133]

Goebbels probably made this declaration with an eye on posterity.[134] No doubt he felt he should set an example for the people of Berlin. Too many cases were known where gauleiters had exhorted their populations to fight unto death, while they themselves had sought safety elsewhere. But when Goebbels said he and his family would stay on in the capital, the Berliners knew they could believe him. His personal courage had never been in doubt. In his euphoric speech the gauleiter promised his Berliners the "Reich of social justice in a happier future, sure to come." As time ran out Goebbels remembered his Catholic background: Be strong in your faith and the heavenly kingdom shall be yours. . . .

On the same day Hitler gave his permission for Goebbels and his family to move into the Fuehrer's bunker. It consisted of an ante-bunker, and a main bunker situated on the lower level; the two were connected by a spiral staircase. The antebunker was comprised of twelve rooms, four of which were put at the disposal of Magda and the children. Meals were taken in the broad corridor dividing the bunker in two. The main bunker housed Hitler and Eva Braun. It consisted of eighteen rooms, one of which was put at Goebbels' disposal.

In the evening Hitler gave orders for his military associates Keitel and Jodl to take over the command of what was left of the armies in South Germany. On April 20, Hitler had already appointed Admiral Doenitz as supreme commander for North Germany.[135] Separated from his most loyal military associates—particularly Keitel who, with his almost doglike devotion, was a typical example of a victim of Goebbels' Hitler myth—Hitler was left with only two important party members and close associates, Goebbels and Bormann. Bormann kept busy pretending that a turn of fortune was imminent, while Goebbels had resigned himself to waiting for the end.

Goebbels still kept up liaison with his ministry, received his state secretary, Naumann and took part in the conferences, but he no longer was in touch with reality. In the bunker everything turned around the Fuehrer. Everybody knew the end was near, yet Hitler's decisions were still sacrosanct. The concept of the Fuehrer state was kept alive for as long as the Fuehrer was still alive. Reduced to a physical wreck, Hitler seemed most of the time completely apathetic. There were moments when life seemed to flood back again; this was enough to terrify his entourage and start up again the machinery carrying out Hitler's orders, which had practically come to a standstill in the rest of the Reich.

Goebbels was no longer touched by events. He played with his children, read stories to them aloud, and kept his diary up to date. He patiently waited for the last hour, only too glad to have it all over with, the sooner the better.

But in the bunker the tragicomedy continued. Once more it became apparent what nonentities Hitler's close associates actually were and how he, a prisoner condemned to die, was still able to crush them completely. Goering sent Hitler a telegram from Bavaria seeking his approval to take over the general leadership of the Reich. Goering invoked the decree of June 29, 1941, which designated Goering as Hitler's successor in case the Fuehrer died or was incapacitated.

Speer describes Hitler's reaction to Goering's telegram. The Minister of Armaments had landed with a Fiesder-Storch on the East-West Axis, which was to be the center of the capital Hitler and Speer had planned to build for an estimated future population of ten million. Speer had come once more to see Hitler to confess that he had not obeyed the Fuehrer's orders to carry out a scorched-earth policy. Speer tells how he spoke to Hitler in a quiet voice and how Hitler had not "shown any reaction" except that "his eyes had filled with tears. . . ." Speer knew Hitler's hearing had deteriorated considerably, yet Speer spoke in a low voice. It is not impossible that Hitler could not understand clearly what Speer said to him. This seems more likely than that Hitler would often slip back into a state of complete

25. Reviewing troops in Rome, Italy, 1938. First row from left to right: Benito Mussolini, Adolf Hitler, King Victor Emmanuel, and Queen Elena. Second row from left to right: Herr von Ribbentrop, Nazi Foreign Minister; Count Ciano, Italian Foreign Minister; Goebbels; and Hitler's deputy Rudolf Hess.

26. Goebbels addresses the Berlin Home Guard from the balcony of his ministry after they had taken their service oath.

27. Goebbels.

apathy. Speer also witnessed the scene when Bormann handed the Fuehrer Goering's telegram with the comment that the Reich marshal was obviously planning a *coup d'état*.

At first Hitler reacted "apathetically." Neither Speer's confession nor Goering's telegram could shake him out of his lethargy. Only when Bormann continued poisoning him against Goering, and another radio telegram arrived in which Goering threatened to take over Hitler's powers if he did not hear from him by midnight of April 23, did Hitler at last wake up; he flew into a fit of rage. His face flushed and his eyes staring, oblivious of his surroundings, the words broke from his lips: "I've known it for a long time. I knew that Goering was rotten through and through. He let the Luftwaffe go to seed. He was corrupt. His bad example started the corruption in our state, and to make matters worse, he has been a morphinist for years. I've known it for a long time. I don't mind. Let Goering negotiate capitulation if he likes. The war is lost. It doesn't matter who does it."[136]

Yet Hitler sent a radio message to Goering depriving him of all rights of succession and demanding his resignation from all the posts he held. Only if he conformed would Hitler desist from taking stronger measures. Half an hour later Goering's answer arrived. Owing to a cardiac condition, the Reich marshal was resigning all his posts. After Goering it was Himmler's turn.

On the evening of April 28, the press service of the Propaganda Ministry monitored a news item broadcast from London by the BBC. Based on a Reuters message from Stockholm, it said that Himmler had offered to capitulate to the Western Allies.

The very day on which Goering had addressed his telegram to Hitler, Himmler had asked Count Folke von Bernadotte, at the Swedish consulate at Lübeck, to inform Eisenhower that Germany would capitulate in the West to continue the fight in the East until the Western powers joined them in their struggle against Russia.[137]

On the night of April 28, a sergeant of the Luftwaffe succeeded in landing a small training aircraft on the East-West Axis, although Russian tanks had penetrated into the center of Berlin. The sergeant had come to fetch Hannah Reitsch and the newly appointed supreme commander of the Luftwaffe, Greim, whom Hitler had promoted to the rank of field marshal at the same time. Both were prepared to die with their Fuehrer; but Hitler persuaded them to leave and ordered them to concentrate all available airplanes for raiding Berlin; they also were to arrest Himmler. Hitler's vindictiveness knew no bounds. Hannah Reitsch took with her also some letters, among them one Magda had addressed to her son, Harald Quandt.

The letter bears the date April 28, "written in the Fuehrer's bunker." Magda informs her son of her decision to die together with her husband and her other children, since the world after Hitler's death and the end of National Socialism would no longer be of any value to her and that also her children would be only wasted on such a world. Her letter was accompanied by a few lines from Goebbels, who told his stepson that he had decided to set "an example of loyalty." Harald could be proud to belong to such a family. The day would come when "we will once again stand before the world clean and unsullied. Just as clean and unsullied as our aims and our faith have always been."[138]

We also learn from Magda's letter that Hitler had the day before (April 27) taken his golden party badge off his lapel and fastened it on her dress. It was the only occasion when Magda was seen to cry. Had not Hitler meant to show by his action that he considered her to be the first among all German women?

It would take the spell of the Hitler myth as Magda had experienced it over the years, and her subtle erotic relationship to her "Fuehrer," to understand fully her feeling of immeasurable pride at this moment. Magda's demeanor in the bunker was, as so much else, described differently by different people. Young Captain Gerhardt Boldt, on service in the Fuehrer's bunker, wrote:

"Waiting for their end, Frau Goebbels gave no sign of fear to the last. Vivacious and elegant, she used to come up the spiral staircase taking two steps at a time. She had a friendly smile for everybody. . . . Her admirable strength of character was perhaps inspired by her fanatical faith in Hitler."[139]

Speer saw it rather differently. He visited Magda on April 24, 1945: "An SS doctor told me that Frau Goebbels was in bed, in a weak state suffering from heart attacks. I asked to be received. I would have preferred to speak to her alone, but Goebbels was already waiting in the antechamber and led me into the small bunker-chamber, where she lay in a simple bed. She looked pale and talked in a feeble voice about irrelevant matters; yet one could feel how she suffered at the idea of the hour approaching inevitably when her children would be put to death. Goebbels remained in the room; this limited our conversation to her state of health. Only toward the end she indicated what was really on her mind: 'How happy I am that at least Harald is still alive.' I, too, felt rather inhibited and did not know what to say—but what could one say in this situation? We took leave of one another silently and self-consciously. Her husband had not granted us even a minute on our own to say farewell."[140]

Speer tries to acquit Magda of any guilt for the death of her children. Speer recalls that already in mid-April 1945 Frau Goebbels had found "the idea insufferable . . . that her children should die, but had apparently accepted her husband's decision."[141]

Speer also maintains that Goebbels had coerced his wife to die with him and their children. This is contradicted by the statement of two of Goebbels' close associates, who say he had suggested to his wife that she should make her escape to the West, taking their children with her, as they had nothing to fear from the English.[142] It was Magda's own decision not only to share her husband's fate but also Hitler's. Her close attachment to the Fuehrer had never emerged more strongly than in those last days. With Hitler's end, history had lost all sense for her. She had become a victim of her husband's Hitler myth, and could not erase from her mind the Propaganda Minister's apocalyptic visions of what the future had in store for them. Hitler's death meant the end of the world, at least of a world in which it was worth living.

Like most wives of National Socialist leaders, Magda had only been allowed to have a veiled glimpse of the evil deeds perpetrated by the Nazi regime. But her intelligence told her that they were part and parcel of National Socialism and that none of the leaders could, therefore, hope to escape retribution.

She, no doubt, feared people would point to her as the wife of the man who acted as the mouthpiece and propagandist of the movement. In choosing death, Magda said "no" to a life of shame, which would await her whether she stood by her husband or denied him. She was also convinced that this was Germany's end, and that servitude and forced labor under the victor's heel would be the fate of the German people. Perhaps it was this last consideration, more than any other, that made her decide to take her children with them to their death. She no longer had any hope for Germany's future and consequently none for the future of her children. From her husband's criticisms of Germany's policy in the conquered eastern territories, she could draw only the conclusion that the victorious Slavs would not hesitate to take revenge on the Germans.

It is practically certain that Magda was not persuaded, let alone compelled, by Goebbels to die with him; rather, she had become the victim of her husband's propaganda. The various eyewitness accounts concerning Goebbels himself differ only in detail.

According to Boldt, Goebbels was always calm. At conferences Goebbels would hardly open his mouth.[143] Speer also was impressed, at least to a certain degree, by Goebbels' equanimity:

"Goebbels told me that his wife and his six children were now living in the bunker as Hitler's guests and would end their lives in this historical place, as he put it. Unlike Hitler, he never betrayed his emotions; no one could have guessed that he had actually finished with life."[144]

April 28, a Saturday, brought the final decision. At the same time as the news of Himmler's treasonable action reached the bunker, it became known that the Russians were near the Potsdamerplatz and that spearheads of Russian tanks were only a few blocks away from the Reich Chancellery.

All day long Hitler had been waiting to hear that the Twelfth Army under General Wenck had finally broken through to him. But Wenck and his army had been halted at Ferch near Potsdam. The moment had arrived for Hitler to tell his entourage of his decision to end his life by his own hand. After midnight, on April 29, Hitler married his mistress, Eva Braun. The marriage license was witnessed by Bormann and Goebbels. There followed a small reception, with champagne and refreshments. At three o'clock in the morning Hitler retired with his secretary, Gertrude Junge, and dictated to her his personal last will and political testament.[145]

Eva Braun never played a great part in Hitler's life. She was never allowed to play the hostess or come to the Fuehrer's headquarters. But now, as she had decided to stay with her Fuehrer and die with him, disregarding his advice to leave, and as National Socialism and the dream of the thousand-year Reich had come to an end, Hitler felt he should act like a gentleman and marry his mistress. The *petit bourgeois* Adolf Hitler did his duty after the genius Adolf Hitler had miserably failed.

Hitler's political testament consists of two parts: a general summing-up, and a statement concerning the appointment of his successor. In the summing-up Hitler emphasized that he had not wanted war but was forced into it by statesmen "who are Jews or who serve Jewish interests." He further declared that he would "remain in Berlin and die at my own free will at a moment when I realize that the residence of the Fuehrer and Chancellor can no longer be defended. . . . I die with a joyous heart, aware of the magnificent deeds and achievements of our soldiers at the front."

In the second part of his testament he appointed his successor, not before he had thoroughly abused his two most influential former associates:

"Before I die I expel the former Reich Marshal Hermann Goering from the party . . . in his stead I appoint Admiral Doenitz as Reich President and supreme commander of the Wehrmacht. Before I die I expel the former Reich Fuehrer SS and Reich Minister of the Interior Heinrich Himmler from the party and divest him of all official posts. . . ."

Then followed instructions concerning the future government. Its most important members were to be Dr. Goebbels as Reich Chancellor, Seyss-Inquart as Minister for Foreign Affairs, Bormann as Party Minister, and Hanke as Minister of the Interior. The testament finishes by ordering the future leaders of the nation "to strictly observe the racial laws and resist mercilessly the world poisoners of all nations, international Jewry."

At four o'clock in the morning the Fuehrer summoned Goebbels, Bormann, and the two generals, Krebs and Burgdorf, who had stayed behind in the bunker and had been present at the wedding ceremony, and asked them to witness his signature on the testament. Thereafter Goebbels retired to his room and wrote "Addenda to the Political Testament of the Fuehrer." Hitler had expressed the desire in his testament that Bormann and Goebbels, contrary to their wish to die with him, should obey his orders and continue as members of the new government. Goebbels commented in his addenda:

"The Fuehrer has ordered me to leave the Reich capital if it can no longer be defended, and to take part as a leading member in a government appointed by him.

"For the first time in my life I must refuse categorically to carry out the Fuehrer's orders. I am joined in this by my wife and my children. Quite apart from the fact that purely human considerations and our personal loyalty would never allow us to desert the Fuehrer in his most bitter hour, I would, if I obeyed the order, feel a deserter and scoundrel for the rest of my life who, having lost all self-respect, would also lose the respect of his people, without which no future service I might render the German nation and the German Reich is thinkable.

"In the delirium of treason that had engulfed the Fuehrer in these most critical days of the war, there must at least be some who stand by him unconditionally unto death, even if it be contradictory to his solemn and, in fact, justified orders, which he has laid down in his political testament.

"I believe that in acting as I do I shall render the German people the best service for the hard times to come, where good examples will be more important than men. There will always be men who will show the nation the way to freedom. But no revival of our *Völkisch* national life will be possible unless it can fall back on examples that are clear and easily understood. It is therefore that I and my wife, as well as our children, who are too young to express their own will but who, if they were adult, would fully agree with us, have irrevocably decided not to leave the capital, even if it falls into enemy hands,

and instead end our lives at the side of the Fuehrer, a life that will
have lost all meaning for me if I can no longer continue at the side of
the Fuehrer and in his service.

"Written in Berlin at 5:30 A.M., April 29, 1945.

"Dr. Goebbels."

The documents were handed to three couriers to take to Admiral
Doenitz; General Field Marshal Schörner, who was still fighting with
his army group in Bohemia (Hitler had appointed him supreme commander of the Army); and one to Munich. The couriers never reached
their destination, but the documents were later found.[146]

At 2:30 P.M. on April 30, Hitler took leave of his entourage and
shook hands with his associates for the last time. But he was still pro-
crastinating; he, who had never hesitated to send others to death,
found it very hard to end it all by his own hand. It simply defied his
imagination that everything should come to a conclusion the way it
did. He continued to walk the bunker like his own ghost, tormenting
his entourage, who were waiting for his death impatiently, either to
find freedom at long last, or to end it all themselves. The latter applied only to Goebbels and his family, particularly to Magda who,
thinking of her children, must have suffered more and more as the
hours slowly passed.

Magda did not appear—and very likely for this reason—when, after
luncheon, Hitler and his wife once again said goodbye to Dr. Goebbels, Bormann, generals Krebs and Burgdorf, the Fuehrer's two female secretaries, and his special-diet cook.

At last the couple retired and Goebbels and Bormann waited outside until they heard the shot. They entered Hitler's room. He and
his wife were dead. Hitler had fired a shot into his mouth. Eva Braun
had taken poison. The time was 3:30 P.M. Their corpses were carried
into the garden, soaked in gasoline, and set on fire.[147]

On the following day Goebbels sent a radio telegram to Admiral
Doenitz informing him of Hitler's death and that the Fuehrer had appointed him Reich President. The radio telegram contained a list of
the most important members of the new government. This was the
last official act of the last Chancellor of the Third Reich. Goebbels
joined his family and made the last entry in his notebook, which he
handed to Naumann for safekeeping; but Naumann burned it.[148]
Who on earth should be interested in what Goebbels had to say in his
last days and hours?

Toward evening the six children were put to death. How it was
done can be only surmised, since there are no witnesses. They were
probably given a sleeping potion with their last meal and then the

fatal injection. At 7:30 P.M. Goebbels gave his adjutant, Schwägermann orders to burn his and his wife's corpses, but not without firing
a shot first into each body so as to make sure they were really dead.
At 8:30 P.M. the couple made an appearance once more. Goebbels
was calm and collected; Magda, deathly pale, clung to her husband's
arm. They took leave of Schwägermann, their chauffeur, and an SS
man. Goebbels attempted a smile as he said they would go upstairs
and save their friends the trouble of carrying their corpses up into
the garden. Magda seemed incapable of uttering a word. After saying
goodbye, Goebbels put his gloves on, taking his time, as always, put
on his hat, offered his arm to his wife, and both proceeded upstairs.

Soon a shot was heard. The three men hurried upstairs and found
them in the garden, both dead: Goebbels shot through the temple,
Madga poisoned. Carrying out orders, the SS man fired a shot into
the minister's head. They poured gasoline over the two corpses and
set them on fire. Having done so, they hurried back into the bunker
in time for their getaway.[149]

The two bodies were burning in the midst of the burning Reich
capital, which Goebbels had conquered for Hitler and for the fate of
which Goebbels had felt responsible to the end of his life. Soon there
would be no Reich and no Reich capital. In this German tragedy
Goebbels certainly had played one of the leading roles.

As night descended the humidity of the air put out the flames. The
next day the Soviets found the corpses only partly burned. Fritzsche,
who had been taken prisoner, was asked to identify the badly disfigured bodies of Goebbels and his wife. Only then were they buried.
Joseph Goebbels rests in Berlin's soil, although nobody knows exactly where. He wanted his name to go down in history to be never
forgotten and forever linked to his beloved Berlin. In a sense he succeeded.

Longing for Greatness

In seeking death at Hitler's side, Goebbels saw his last chance to
escape oblivion, which to his mind would overtake all other of Hitler's
paladins, even the mightiest. Hence Goebbels' attempt to feed the
German people with inexhaustible variations of Hitler's greatness
and uniqueness, though Goebbels must have known better. May all
around him perish as long as his Hitler myth survived, because only
then would Joseph Goebbels survive. And the greater the gap between
the true Hitler and his myth became, the more deeply Goebbels
buried himself in the myth he had created. But to escape his own

schizophrenic state he constructed a historic figure, an ersatz Hitler, whose features he transferred to the living Hitler.

When Goebbels, who could sense danger from afar, discerned the first shadows of Germany's defeat, he created a new political idol for himself, Frederick II of Prussia. Frederick's portrait hung in his office at the ministry, and other portraits of the Prussian King were in his town palace. At a time when the party was still struggling for power, Goebbels had underlined the Prussian nature of National Socialism. He had claimed credit for having succeeded in pushing into the background the South German element, from which National Socialism had originally sprung.

When he saw catastrophe approaching—long before the others could—his relationship to Frederick II became more and more intense. He granted him not only his known historic epithet "the Great," but elevated him to "Frederick the Unique." Simultaneously, Goebbels tried to shepherd Hitler into the part of the Prussian King and link Hitler's fate in mystical context to that of Frederick II.

Goebbels immersed himself in the King's letters and studied Thomas Carlyle's book about the Prussian King. The Scotsman Carlyle, who was one of the creators of the zealous hero-cult, and who called himself "the Aurochs of the Teutonic forests," saw in Frederick the true founder of Prussianism, and he made this a mission of world historical importance. As other British who loved Germany, he was more German than the Germans—like Houston Stewart Chamberlain, who passionately admired Wagner and Goethe and saw in the Germans the coming people. Carlyle formed an image of Frederick II that persists to this day and that has been contested only recently. This highly idealized image Goebbels appropriated only too eagerly. He made the absurd attempt to extol Hitler, who was full of typically Austrian defects, as a kind of resurrected Frederick II.

On the occasion of the first showing of the film *The Great King* in April 1942, Goebbels made the theme of the film the leitmotiv of his broadcast on Hitler's birthday. In emphasizing the part Frederick the Great played during the Seven Years' War, Goebbels showed an uncanny foresight. Frederick appears to us, he said, "even greater and more overpowering in time of defeat than of victory . . . but never greater than when sitting in the chapel of the Castle of Charlottenburg, a toothless wreck of a man plagued by gout; he listened enraptured, relaxed at last—how long had he not dreamed of the moment to feel free of his immeasurable torments and oppressions—to the mighty sound of Graun's *Te Deum,* and broke into tears." Goebbels admired Frederick's strength "to rise triumphantly above vicissitudes and defeats." And this was April 1942 when, despite his setbacks during the previous winter, Hitler was still drunk with victory. And he ascribed to Hitler the very virtues that fascinated him in Frederick's personality; the same "sweeping force of his historical genius, the faith that could move mountains, his steadfastness in adversity, the unconditional devotion with which he served his secular mission and the heroic solitude and its somber shadow in which he followed his destiny. . . ." Goebbels perceived already in April 1942, when Hitler was still basking in the sun of his victories, the first portents of impending doom. And in this hour of supreme power, Goebbels talked of a King whose steadfastness in defeat was the finest jewel in his crown. Later, when defeat came for Hitler too and the blows of Fate followed one another in rapid succession, Goebbels read chapters of Carlyle's book and some of Frederick's letters to his Fuehrer, and more and more drew the parallel between Frederick's and Hitler's fate in his propaganda.

In trying to adjust himself to Hitler's mental world, he had copied his idol. He also tried to copy his other idol, Frederick II. He would take his afternoon nap in the chair at his desk, his chin pressed into his chest, a blanket covering his knees, like Frederick, who had been in the habit of taking his afternoon nap in the same uncomfortable way.

Goebbels' ability to absorb and live within another's personality was one of his outstanding characteristics. In the early days he had created the hero of his novel *Michael* in a dreamed-up image of himself. Such dreamed-up images of himself were also Hitler and Frederick II. Carlyle had created the myth around the Prussian King. It was left to Goebbels to create the myth around Adolf Hitler. Goebbels invested Hitler with every feature he himself would have liked to possess. That was why he took part so closely in Hitler's life, often at the price of complete self-denial and self-abasement. He would ascribe to Hitler all the characteristics inherent in greatness. And, in fact, the victorious Hitler seemed to possess them. But when in times of adversity Hitler showed no sign of greatness, Goebbels simply endowed him with the characteristics of Frederick II, as seen by Carlyle.

Hitler had little in common with the image Goebbels painted of him; but the more the image faded, the more Goebbels extolled its colors. He presented it as his greatest masterpiece, though he knew it was a fake. When it was destroyed, the faker destroyed himself so that no one would ever know the truth.

Goebbels expected Germany to sink into misery and servitude. Then, he hoped, his myth would be resurrected and he would pass into history as the most loyal friend and companion in death of "the greatest German of all time." But Goebbels had miscalculated. Hardly a generation later, most Germans have reached a standard of living superior to any they had ever enjoyed before, and misery on a national scale has become past history. But forgetting, as supreme wisdom shows, is the stuff history is made of.

Notes

Introduction

1. According to Wagener it was Reichsarbeitsfuehrer Hierl who suggested the use of "Fuehrer" for the first time in 1931. Tagebuch Wageners, Institut fuer Zeitgeschichte, Munich. ED 60/31

1 From National Bolshevik to Hitlerite

1. Helmut Heiber, Joseph Goebbels (Berlin, 1962), p. 3.
2. Ibid., pp. 7 f.
3. Ibid., pp. 11 f., and Curt Riess, Joseph Goebbels (Baden-Baden), 1950, p. 3.
4. Document Center, West Berlin, AH 3, party bureau correspondence.
5. Joseph Goebbels, Vom Kaiserhof zur Reichskanzlei: Eine Historische Darstellung in Tagebuchblaettern vom 1. Januar 1932 bis zum 1. Mai 1933 (Munich, 1934), diary note of April 25, 1933.
6. Heinrich Fraenkel and Roger Manvell, Doctor Goebbels, His Life and Death (Heinemann, 1960).
7. Heiber, Joseph Goebbels, p. 17, and Fraenkel and Manvell, Goebbels, p. 33.
8. Fraenkel and Manvell, Doctor Goebbels.
9. Ibid., p. 63.
10. Ibid., p. 41, and Heiber, Joseph Goebbels, pp. 25 f.
11. Joseph Goebbels, Michael: Ein Deutsches Schicksal in Tagebuchblaettern (Munich, 1929), diary note of November 2.
12. Gottfried Benn, Kunst und Macht (Berlin-Stuttgart, 1934), p. 92.
13. Heiber, Joseph Goebbels, pp. 24 f.
14. Fraenkel and Manvell, Doctor Goebbels.
15. Illustrierter Beobachter, Sec. Year, issue No. 22 (Nov. 30, 1927).
16. Friedrich Christian zu Schaumburg-Lippe, Dr. G. ein Portrait des Propagandaministers (Wiesbaden, 1963), p. 87.
17. Fraenkel and Manvell, Goebbels, pp. 64 f.
18. Ibid., pp. 71 f.
19. Adolf Hitler, Mein Kampf (Munich, 1942), p. 78.
20. Fraenkel and Manvell, Doctor Goebbels.
21. Ibid.

22. Alfred Rosenberg, *Letzte Aufzeichnungen: Ideale und Idole der Nationalsozialistischen Revolution* (Goettingen, 1955), p. 107.
23. Fraenkel and Manvell, *Doctor Goebbels*.
24. Ibid.
25. Rosenberg, *Letzte Aufzeichnungen*, pp. 214 f.
26. Albert Speer, *Erinnerungen* (Berlin, 1969), p. 470.
27. Hitler, *Mein Kampf*, p. 512.
28. Riess, *Joseph Goebbels*, p. 37.
29. Ibid., p. 38.
30. Fraenkel and Manvell, *Doctor Goebbels*.
    The divergencies between Fraenkel and Manvell, and Riess, who both refer themselves to Otto Strasser, are obviously due to the use of different versions of Strasser's memoirs. It only shows that "memoirs" should never be accepted as exact historical sources.
31. Hans Guenther Seraphim, *Das Politische Tagebuch Alfred Rosenbergs aus den Jahren 1934–35 und 1939–40* (Berlin-Frankfurt, 1956).
32. Hermann Esser, party membership card No. 2. He founded, during Hitler's incarceration, together with Julius Streicher and Arthur Dinter, his own party, the Grossdeutsche Volksgemeinschaft. In the Third Reich he was disposed of by being appointed state secretary for tourism.
33. 27 of the *Nationalsozialistische Briefe* (Nov. 1, 1926). The *N.S. Letters* (2.–42. Letter from May 15, 1925 to June 15, 1927, ed. Gregor Strasser) are kept at the Institute of Contemporary History, Munich. MA 171
34. Rosenberg, *Letzte Aufzeichnungen*, pp. 112 f. AZ/26/2/60
35. Helmuth Heiber (ed.), *Das Tagebuch von Joseph Goebbels 1925–26.* Stuttgart, *Schriftenreihe der Vierteljahrhefte fuer Zeitgeschichte*, Nr. 1. Date of diary note, Oct. 21, 1925.
36. Joseph Goebbels, *Lenin oder Hitler* (Zwickau, Sa. 1926).
37. Heiber, *Tagebuch*. Date of diary note, Jan. 13, 1926.
38. Rosenberg, *Letzte Aufzeichnungen*, pp. 112 f.
39. Fraenkel and Manvell, *Doctor Goebbels*.

2 The Conquest of Berlin

1. Joseph Goebbels, *Der Kampf um Berlin* (Munich, 1941), p. 23.
2. Ibid., pp. 25 f.
3. Ibid., p. 24.
4. Ibid., p. 26.
5. Ibid., pp. 52 f.
6. Ibid., p. 32.
7. Ibid., p. 44.
8. Ibid., p. 28.
9. Ibid., p. 61.

10. Ibid., p. 62, and following quotation.
11. Ibid., p. 63.
12. Boris von Borresholm (ed.), *Dr. Goebbels. Nach Aufzeichnungen aus Seiner Umgebung* (Berlin-Tempelhof, 1949), p. 50, and Wilfried Bade, *Joseph Goebbels* (Luebeck, 1938), p. 26.
13. Goebbels, *Berlin*, pp. 66 f. and following quotation.
14. Bade, *Joseph Goebbels*, p. 27.
15. Goebbels, *Berlin*, p. 66.
16. Ibid., p. 70, and the following quotation.
17. Ibid., p. 71.
18. Erich Ebermayer and Hans Roos, *Gefaehrtin des Teufels, Leben und Tod der Magda Goebbels* (Hamburg, 1952), p. 97.
19. Goebbels, *Berlin*, pp. 102 f.
20. Ibid., p. 85, and the following quotation.
21. Ibid., p. 86.
22. Ibid., p. 98.
23. Ibid., p. 104.
24. Ibid., p. 146.
25. Ibid.
26. The official church statement referred to a "judgment given by the Court (*Kammergericht*) on July 21, 1923, which deprived Fritz Stucke of the right to call himself vicar or wear the official clothes of a vicar of the *"evangelische Landeskirche."* The reason was, presumably, drunkenness. Goebbels, *Berlin*, p. 158.
27. Ibid., p. 152.
28. Ibid., pp. 203 f.
29. Ibid., p. 201.
30. Ibid., p. 202.
31. The letter is dated July 5, 1927, and is kept at the Document Center (West Berlin), AH3, party bureau correspondence. The underlined passage is underlined in red in the original.
32. Rosenberg, *Letzte Aufzeichnungen*, p. 189.
33. Document Center, AH3, party bureau correspondence.
34. Ibid.
35. Goebbels, *Berlin*, p. 136.
36. Ibid., p. 140. And the following quotation.
37. Mjoelnir-Dr. Goebbels, *Das Buch Isidor: Ein Zeitbild von Lachen und Hass* (Munich, 1929), pp. 26 ff.
38. Quoted from Heiber, *Goebbels*, p. 77.
39. *Das Buch Isidor*, p. 9.
40. Joseph Goebbels, *Wetterleuchten: Aufsaetze aus der Kampfzeit*, ed. Georg Wilhelm Mueller (Munich, 1939), pp. 33 f.
41. Goebbels, *Berlin*, pp. 176 f.
42. Goebbels, *Wetterleuchten*, p. 86.
43. Ibid.
44. Goebbels, *Berlin*, p. 178.

45. *Knorke! Ein Neues Buch Isidor fuer Zeitgenossen,* ed. Dr. Goebbels with the collaboration of Mjoelnir, Knipperdolling, Dax, Jaromir, and Orje (Munich, 1929), p. 17.
46. Goebbels, *Michael,* diary note of August 9.
47. *Knorke,* p. 18.
48. *Isidor,* pp. 85 f.
49. Ibid., p. 87.
50. *Knorke,* p. 12.
51. Ibid., pp. 21 ff.
52. Ibid.
53. *Isidor,* p. 50.
54. Goebbels, *Berlin,* p. 282.
55. Engelbrechten-Volz, *Wir Wandern Durch das Nationalsozialistische Berlin* (Munich, 1937), registered under 1928.
56. Ibid.
57. Bade, p. 48.
58. The exact date of this appointment is uncertain. Gregor Strasser held the post until 1927. In 1928 Hitler personally took over. His deputy was Himmler. The *NS-Jahrbuch* (NS Yearbook) of 1930 still cites Hitler and Himmler. The deadline for the printing was September 30, 1929, according to Heiber (p. 86). Corrections were still possible in October. Therefore Goebbels could not have been appointed before November. Actually Goebbels had been in charge of the propaganda campaign against the Young Plan for the whole Reich in May 1929.
59. Heiber, *Goebbels,* p. 82.
60. Ibid., and Bade, p. 52.
61. Bade, p. 55.
62. Goebbels, *Wetterleuchten,* pp. 29 f.
63. Ebermayer and Roos, pp. 113 f.
64. *Aufzeichnungen Wageners ueber Magda Quandt,* Institute for Contemporary History, Munich, ED/60/25, 1539–47.
65. Goebbels, *Wetterleuchten,* pp. 41 f.
66. Heiber, *Goebbels,* p. 97.
67. Rosenberg, p. 190.
68. Fraenkel and Manvell, *Doctor Goebbels.*
69. Borresholm, pp. 75 f.
70. Heiber, *Goebbels,* p. 100.
71. *Der Angriff* (Feb. 19, 1931).
72. *Der Angriff* (Sept. 14, 1931).
73. *Der Angriff* (Oct. 21, 1931).
74. Rosenberg, p. 189.
75. Goebbels, *Kaiserhof,* diary note (Jan. 7, 1932).
76. *Der Angriff* (Feb. 23, 1932).
77. Goebbels, *Kaiserhof,* diary note (Mar. 5, 1932).
78. *Der Angriff* (Mar. 5, 1932).
79. Goebbels, *Kaiserhof,* diary note (Mar. 15, 1932).

80. *Der Angriff* (Apr. 4, 1932).
81. William L. Shirer, *Aufstieg und Fall des Dritten Reiches* (Köln-Berlin, 1961), p. 154.
82. Joseph Goebbels, *Die Revolution der Deutschen* (Oldenburg an der Oder, 1933), p. 64.
83. Goebbels, *Kaiserhof,* diary note (June 4, 1932).
84. Ibid., diary note (Aug. 6, 1932), and following quotation.
85. Ibid. (Aug. 13, 1932), and following quotation.
86. Ibid. (Oct. 10, 1932).
87. Ibid. (Nov. 4, 1932), and following quotation.
88. Ibid. (Nov. 21, 1932).
89. Ibid. (Nov. 23, 1932).
90. Correspondence Meissner-Hitler, printed in the *Jahrbuch des Oeffentlichen Rechts,* Vol. 21 (1933–34).
91. Goebbels, *Kaiserhof,* diary note (Dec. 1, 1932).
92. Ibid. (Dec. 2, 1932).
93. Ibid. (Dec. 5, 1932).
94. Ibid. (Dec. 8, 1932).
95. Heiber, *Goebbels,* p. 120.
96. Rosenberg, pp. 112 f.
97. Goebbels, *Kaiserhof,* diary note (Dec. 22, 1932).
98. Riess, p. 124.
99. Shirer, p. 174.
100. Goebbels, *Kaiserhof,* diary note (Jan. 12, 1933).
101. Shirer, p. 177.

3. Propaganda Devours Culture

1. *Aufzeichnungen Wageners,* ED 60/31, 1827–36.
2. Goebbels, *Kaiserhof,* diary notes (Feb. 13 and 15, 1933).
3. The trial of war criminals before an international military court (*Nürnberger Process*), Nürnberg, *Sitzungsprotokolle,* Vol. XII, p. 277.
4. Series of articles in the weekly *Der Spiegel,* published between Oct. 21, 1959, and Jan. 6, 1960.
5. Goebbels, *Kaiserhof,* diary notes (Feb. 27 and 28, 1933).
6. Shirer, p. 192.
7. Goebbels, *Kaiserhof,* diary note (Mar. 4, 1933).
8. Rosenberg, p. 192.
9. *Weltkunst* (June 20, 1934), p. 300.
10. Rosenberg, p. 191.
11. *Aufzeichnungen Wageners,* ED 60/31.
12. Goebbels, *Michael,* diary note for Nov. 15.
13. Albert Speer, p. 40.
14. *Voelkischer Beobachter* (July 20, 1937).
15. Hildegard Brenner, *Die Kunstpolitik des Nationalsozialismus* (Hamburg, 1963), p. 68.
16. Goebbels, *Michael,* diary note for Dec. 18.

17. Goebbels, *Kaiserhof,* diary notes (Sept. 19, 1932).
18. *Die Musik,* periodical published by the NS Kulturgemeinde (Nov. 1934).
19. Wilfried von Oven, *Mit Goebbels bis zum Ende* (Buenos Aires, 1949), Vol. I., pp. 228 f.
20. Deutsches Zentralarchiv, Potsdam, Reichsministerium fuer Volksaufklaerung und Propaganda (RMVP), Dossier Knappertsbusch. All references to Knappertsbusch.
21. Quoted from Joseph Wulf, *Musik im Dritten Reich* (Gutersloh, 1963), pp. 180 f.
22. Ibid., p. 183.
23. Wili Schuh (ed.), *Richard Strauss-Stefan Zweig, Briefwechel* (Frankfurt a. Main, 1957), pp. 141 f.
24. Reported in the newspaper *Maasbode* (Jan. 1, 1935).
25. Wulf, *Musik,* p. 185.
26. *Voelkischer Beobachter* (July 14, 1935).
27. RMVP, Deutsche Zentralarchiv, Potsdam, Abteilung VI.
28. *Der Angriff* (May 12, 1933).
29. Joseph Wulf, *Literatur und Dichtung im Dritten Reich: Eine Dokumentation* (Gutersloh, 1963), p. 18.
30. Fraenkel and Manvell, *Doctor Goebbels.*
31. Speer, pp. 104 f.
32. Seraphim, *Rosenberg,* diary (Dec. 11, 1939).
33. Louis P. Lochner (ed.), *Goebbels Tagebuecher aus den Jahren 1942–43 mit Andern Dokumenten* (Zurich, 1948).
34. Periodical *Die Buehne* (1937), p. 274.
35. Joseph Wulf, *Theater und Film im Dritten Reich* (Gutersloh, 1964), p. 43.
36. *Deutsche Buehnenkorrespondenz* (June 15, 1935).
37. Viktor Reimann, *Die Adelsrepublik der Kuenstler, Schauspieler an der Burg* (Dusseldorf-Vienna, 1963), p. 241.
38. Otto Dietrich, *Zwoelf Jahre mit Hitler* (Munich, 1955), pp. 231 f.
39. Ibid., p. 157.
40. RMVP, Abt. VI, 44.
41. Ibid.
42. Ibid.
43. Ibid.
44. Ibid.
45. Speer, p. 182.
46. RMVP, Abt. VI.
47. Heiber, *Goebbels,* p. 139.
48. Ibid., p. 140.
49. *Nachrichtenblatt des RMVP,* DA 6901, AZ 2885/62, Institut fuer Zeitgeschichte, Munich.
50. *Nürnberger Process,* Vol. XII, pp. 103 f.
51. Oven, Vol. I, p. 222.
52. *Nürnberger Process,* Vol. XII, p. 112.

53. Ibid., Vol. XVII, pp. 173 f.
54. Ibid., Vol. XVII, pp. 275 ff.
55. *Film-Kurier* (July 8, 1933).
56. Speech to the heads of radio at Saarbruecken (Dec. 4, 1935), quoted from *Berliner Lokalanzeiger* (Dec. 5, 1935).
57. Dietrich, p. 251.
58. *Presse in Fesseln: Eine Schilderung des NS-Pressetrusts* (Berlin 1949), pp. 157 ff.
59. Ibid., p. 54.
60. Ibid., p. 111.

4. From Reich Minister to Reich Chancellor

1. Goebbels, *Kaiserhof*, diary note (Apr. 4, 1933).
2. Ibid. (Mar. 24, 1933).
3. Schaumburg-Lippe, *Dr. G.: Ein Portrait*, p. 33.
4. Ibid., pp. 51 f.
5. Ibid., pp. 55 f.
6. Ibid.
7. Report of the Deutsche Nachrichtenbureau, Institut fuer Zeitgeschichte, Munich, MA 4995.
8. *Rede des Vicekanzler Papen vor dem Universitaetsbund in Marburg,* Berlin.
9. Papen's statement at the Nuremberg trial, *Sitzungsprotokolle*, Vol. XVI, p. 326.
10. Ibid., Vol. XII, p. 526.
11. Seraphim, *Rosenberg*, diary note (July 7, 1934).
12. *Dokumente aus dem Kampf der Katholischen Kirche im Bistum Berlin Gegen den Nationalsozialismus,* ed. Bischoefliche Ordinariat (Berlin, 1946), p. 80.
13. Werner, Stephan, *Joseph Goebbels: Daemon einer Diktatur* (Stuttgart, 1949), p. 142.
14. *Dokumente*, pp. 51 f.
15. Ibid., pp. 52 f.
16. Ibid., p. 22.
17. Lochner, diary note (Feb. 19, 1942).
18. Speer, *Erinnerungen*, p. 40.
19. Heiber, *Goebbels*, p. 255.
20. Ibid., pp. 254 f.
21. Ibid., p. 259.
22. RMVP, No. 1033.
23. The final sum recorded in a document of November 1940 amounts to 2,663,052 marks and 58 pfennig, RMVP, No. 2221.
24. Fraenkel and Manvell, *Doctor Goebbels*.
25. RMVP, No. 759.
26. Ibid.; a letter from the ministry to architect Bartels (Jan. 14, 1942), No. 2221.
27. Schaumburg-Lippe, p. 15.

28. Ebermayer-Roos, as indicated.
29. Ibid., pp. 243 f.
30. Ibid., p. 268.
31. Ibid., p. 260.
32. Ibid., p. 278.
33. Ibid., pp. 266 ff.
34. Riess, *Joseph Goebbels*, p. 219.
35. Seraphim, *Rosenberg*, diary note (Feb. 6, 1939).
36. Ibid., dated "mid of May," p. 67.
37. Ibid. (Sept. 24, 1939).
38. Speer, *Erinnergungen*, p. 164.
39. Ibid., p. 126.
40. *Nürnberger Process*, Vol. XXI, p. 392.
41. Ibid., Vol. XIII, pp. 130 f.
42. Dietrich, *Zwoelf Jahre*, pp. 55 f.
43. Reinhard Bollmus, *Das amt Rosenberg und Seine Gegner* (Stuttgart, 1970), p. 61.
44. Institut fuer Zeitgeschichte, Munich, MA 8551.
45. Ibid., MA 5682, 5683, 5686, and 5691.
46. Note for Party member Tiessler, Berlin (Oct. 25, 1941), MA 5792. Institut fuer Zeitgeschichte, Munich.
47. *Nürnberger Process*, Vol. XVII, pp. 258 f. and 275 f.
48. Ibid., Vol. XVII, p. 161.
49. Report of DNB (Aug. 31, 1939).
50. *Sammlung Oberheitmann*, Bundesarchiv, Koblenz, ZSg. 109/5 (Sept. 30, 1939), VJ 197/39.
51. Newspaper reports from state documents, published by the British government (Jan. 1, 1971).
52. Schaumburg-Lippe, *Dr. G.: Ein Portrait*, pp. 237 f.
53. As 51.
54. Lochner, *Goebbels' Tagebuecher*, diary note (Jan. 28, 1942).
55. Ibid. (Jan. 30, 1942).
56. *Das Reich* (June 16, 1940).
57. Lochner, diary note (Jan. 28, 1942).
58. Shirer, *Aufstieg und Fall*, pp. 736 f.
59. Rudolf Semmler, *Goebbels: The Man Next to Hitler* (London, 1947), p. 32.
60. Ibid., p. 26.
61. Paul Merker, *Deutschland-Sein Oder Nichtsein*, as quoted by *Nationalzeitung* (Jan. 8, 1971).
62. Semmler, *Goebbels*, p. 26.
63. Ibid., pp. 32 f., diary note (May 14, 1941).
64. Shirer, *Aufstieg und Fall*, p. 769.
65. Dietrich, *Zwoelf Jahre*, p. 82.
66. Oven, *Mit Goebbels*, Vol. II, pp. 92 f.
67. Lochner, *Goebbels' Tagebuecher*, diary note (Mar. 6, 1942).
68. Ibid. (Mar. 2, 1943).

69. Remark made to Lida Baarova, according to her own statement.
70. Lochner, diary note (Mar. 20, 1942).
71. Shirer, *Aufstieg und Fall,* p. 837.
72. *SD Geheimbericht* (Oct. 26, 1942), No. 329, No. 788 to No. 891, Institut fuer Zeitgeschichte, Munich.
73. Shirer, p. 837.
74. Semmler, pp. 61 f.
75. Doubtful, according to recent historical research.
76. Tape recording, Deutsches Rundfunkarchiv, Frankfurt am Main.
77. *SD Geheimbericht* (June 10, 1943), No. 389, ref. to Speer's speech in the Sportpalast (June 5, 1943). Institut fuer Zeitgeschichte, Munich.
78. Speer, p. 270.
79. Lochner, diary note (Mar. 2, 1943).
80. Speer, p. 266.
81. Lochner, diary note (Nov. 27, 1943).
82. Johannes Popitz, financial expert of international repute, 1919 state secretary in the Reich Ministry of Finance, Prussian Minister of Finance from 1933 to 1944, joined the resistance; executed Feb. 2, 1944.
83. Dr. Joseph Wirth, member of the Reichstag 1920–21; Minister of Finance, 1929–30; Reich Chancellor, 1921–22. The Nazis branded him as *Erfuellungspolitiker* (fulfillment politician). His motto was: "The enemy stands on the right." He lived in Switzerland, 1933–48; he died in 1956.
84. Semmler, p. 18 f.
85. Speer, p. 207.
86. Semmler, pp. 199 ff.
87. Speer, p. 270.
88. Oven, Vol. II, p. 219.
89. MA 805/615, Institut for Contemporary History, Munich.
90. Ibid., MA 805/364.
91. Shirer, p. 859.
92. Lochner, diary note (Jan. 29, 1942).
93. Rosenberg, *Letzte Aufzeichnungen,* pp. 214 f.
94. Quoted from Alfred Fiedler, Generalinspector, *Der Werkdienst des Reichskommissars fuer die Ukraine.* Document Center, RF/SS 4842–4915.
95. *SD Geheimbericht* (Oct. 14, 1943), MA Varia 0979. Institut fuer Zeitgeschichte, Munich.
96. Lochner, diary note (Feb. 1, 1942 and July 28, 1943).
97. Ibid., note (Feb. 13, 1942).
98. Ibid., note (May 8, 1943), and the two following quotations.
99. Ibid., note (Apr. 2, 1942).
100. Ibid., note (Mar. 7, 1942).
101. Ibid., note (Apr. 26, 1942).
102. Ibid., note (Feb. 6, 1942).

103. Oven, Vol. II, pp. 68 f.

104. Lochner, diary note (Sept. 11, 1943).

105. Ibid., note (Sept. 12, 1943).

106. *SD Geheimbericht* (Aug. 2, 1943), MA 441/8, 0055–67, Institut fuer Zeitgeschichte, Munich.

107. Oven, Vol. II, pp. 91, 96.

108. Lochner, diary note (Sept. 23, 1943).

109. MA 314/3659–85. Institut fuer Zeitgeschichte, Munich.

110. Speer, p. 240.

111. Lochner, diary notes (Nov. 16 and 24, 1943).

112. *An die Arbeit,* broadcast by Goebbels (July 26, 1944). Special printing (Berlin, 1944).

113. Speer, pp. 390 f.

114. Ibid., p. 393.

115. Oven, Vol. II, p. 78.

116. Ibid., p. 79, and Speer, pp. 394 ff.

117. Oven, p. 87, and following quotation.

118. *Das Reich,* article *"Die Lage: Zentralinformationsdienst der Reichs-propagandaleitung der NSDAP und des Reichsministeriums fuer Volksaufklaerung und Propaganda,"* ed. Joseph Goebbels (Berlin, 1944).

119. Ibid.

120. *An die Arbeit.*

121. Oven, Vol. II, pp. 96 f.

122. Speer, p. 407.

123. *Die Lage.*

124. Oven, Vol. II, p. 236.

125. Semmler, pp. 178 f.

126. Ibid., p. 181.

127. Ibid., pp. 182–89; and *Nürnberger Process,* Vol. XVII, p. 282, statement of the official Franz Scharping.

128. Semmler, pp. 190 ff.

129. Oven, Vol. II, p. 303.

130. Tape recording, Deutsches Rundfunkarchiv, Frankfurt am Main.

131. Shirer, p. 1,017.

132. Oven, Vol. II, p. 305. The general in question is the commandant of Berlin, General Reymann.

133. *Voelkischer Beobachter* (Apr. 23, 1945).

134. Heiber, p. 395.

135. Shirer, pp. 1,017 f.

136. Speer, pp. 483 ff.

137. Shirer, p. 1,025.

138. Ebermayer-Roos, pp. 357 f.

139. Gerhardt Boldt, *Die Letzten Tage der Reichskanzlei* (Hamburg, 1947), p. 61.

140. Speer, pp. 484 f.

141. Ibid., p. 469.

142. Oven, p. 236, and Semmler, pp. 185 f.
143. Boldt, p. 61.
144. Speer, p. 484.
145. Shirer, p. 126, and *"Die Testamente,"* in J. Hohlfeld (ed.), *Dokumente der Deutschen Politik und Geschichte von 1848 bis zur Gegenwart,* Vol. 5, No. 210.
146. Hugh R. Trevor-Roper, *Hitlers Letzte Tage* (Zurich, 1948), pp. 176 f.
147. Shirer, pp. 1,036 f.
148. Fraenkel and Manvell, *Doctor Goebbels.*
149. Ibid., and Trevor-Roper, pp. 195 f.

Literature and Sources

No Nazi leader, except Hitler, stimulated writers and historians as much as Goebbels. Many books were written about him; some were written during the Nazi reign; their authors, collaborators of Berlin's gauleiter and Propaganda Minister, were mainly concerned with proving their chief's genius. Their accounts are of no literary or historical value; they are not even reliable records of events and data. Much more interesting are the books written by Goebbels' assistants after his death. There was no longer any need for flattery or adulation. On the contrary, the German catastrophe excluded any favorable evaluation of any of the Nazi leaders thought to be responsible for the tragedy that had overtaken Germany. Yet even in books hostile to their chief, Goebbels' collaborators are fascinated by his personality, his "demon." One of them, Stephan Werner, gave his Goebbels biography the subtitle *Daemon einer Diktatur* (The Demon of a Dictatorship). Boris von Borresholm is another author who in his book draws Goebbels as the incarnation of evil. But Goebbels' closest collaborators, his adjutant Friedrich Christian zu Schaumburg-Lippe, as well as his personal press officer Wilfried von Oven, show him as a man whose failure was brought about by the stupidity of the Nazi leaders and his personal loyalty to Hitler. Both authors make no attempt to hide their sympathy for their chief. Rudolf Semmler—he was Goebbels' second press officer—has some sharp criticism to offer in his diaries, published in London in 1947, but he cannot conceal the deep-down admiration he feels for his chief. These two points of view, the one depicting Goebbels as a demon, the other as a victim of Hitler's paladins, characterize the two factions of Goebbels' biographers from among those who had actually been working with him.

Then the biography by Curt Riess appeared. As a refugee he had no personal knowledge of Goebbels, yet he, too, appears to be fascinated by his personality. But feeling morally obliged to depict National Socialism as the essence of all evil, Riess was bound to characterize its chief propagandist accordingly as being the devil incarnate. Riess was the first to interview Goebbels' relations and collaborators. Their view colored the image Riess paints of Goebbels as the superdemon, the Mephistopheles of the movement; such views were held by some Nazi leaders even before Hitler came to power. In 1948 Louis Lochner, who had been a foreign correspondent in Berlin, edited the Goebbels diaries written between 1942 and 1943. They, and particularly the diaries from 1925 and 1926, edited by Helmut Heiber, brought about a change in the biographical evaluation of Goebbels' personality. A new picture was drawn of Hitler's Propaganda Minister by the two journalists Fraenkel and Manvell. The demoniacal Goebbels became a frustrated *petit bourgeois,* a sentimental romantic who, at the age of twenty-eight, still nurtured the spirit of an adolescent. Fraenkel too contacted members of Goebbels' family, but also interviewed some of Goebbels' schoolmates and girlfriends, as well as those collaborators who had known him in his early days in Elberfeld at the start of his political career, that is, Gauleiter Kaufmann and Dr. Otto Strasser, brother of Gregor Strasser, both of them Goebbels' archenemies. Helmut Heiber published in 1962 the most recent Goebbels biography. Heiber consulted the archives, and scientifically his work is, no doubt, superior to any published before. Heiber continued the process of Goebbels' de-demonization. (He attempted the same in his Hitler biography.) For Heiber, the men who led Germany into disaster were not demons but *petit bourgeois* run amok. In Heiber's view Goebbels became the main victim of his own propaganda. According to Heiber, Goebbels actually believed in what he must and should have known to be a shameless swindle. Heiber's thesis is contradicted by almost all views held by Goebbels' collaborators; it cannot be upheld. It can, however, be said that by creating the Hitler myth, Goebbels provided himself with an ersatz religion to which he adhered to the bitter end—and was bound to adhere as to a last and only protection against complete despair.

The sources I used were some of the files of the Propaganda Ministry (Reichsministerium fuer Volksaufklaerung und Propaganda) kept at the German Central Archives (Deutsches Zentral archiv), Potsdam, in particular those dealing with theater and music, as well as with the secret reports of the SD (Reichssicherheitsdienst), also kept there. In addition, I consulted the personal files, the party correspondence, and the records of the NSDAP court kept at the Document Center in West Berlin. There I also saw the list of court actions taken against Goebbels and the findings of the courts, as well as police reports about the gauleiter of Berlin. Some of the material has been transferred to the Federal Archives (Bundesarchiv) in Koblenz. The archives also keep the Collection Oberheitmann, which contains Goebbels' daily press instructions between July 1933 and September 1939.

I came upon a bulk of very important material at the Institute of Contemporary History (Institut fuer Zeitgeschichte) at Munich: a complete set of the *National Socialist Letters* (*Nationalsozialistische Briefe*), published by Gregor Strasser in the mid-twenties, which contain regular contributions by Goebbels; I also found the Goebbels diary of 1943 there. The institute also keeps the *Newsletters* (*Nachrichtenblaetter*) of the Propaganda Ministry, the NSDAP yearbooks, an important number of SD secret reports, as well as the correspondence between Rosenberg and Hess, revealing Rosenberg's hatred of Goebbels; also the diaries of Wagener, particularly interesting with regard to Magda Goebbels' relationship to Hitler. I was also able to listen to recordings of speeches by Goebbels and Hitler kept at the German Radio Archives (Deutsches Rundfunkarchiv) at Frankfurt am Main.

I should like to thank the directors of those archives and institutes, as well as their staffs, for their generous help and assistance.

Index

Index   345

Graf, Dr. Max, 176–77
Granzow (estate agent), 125
Graun, Karl Heinrich, 324
Great Fascist Council (Italy), 287–88
Great King, The (film), 324
Greece, 248, 249, 250, 275, 280
Greenwood, Arthur, 244
Greim, General Robert Ritter von, 317
Greindl, Josef, 193
Griesing, Otto, 203
Grimm, Hans, 182, 193
Groener, General Wilhelm, 138, 141
Grohmann, Will, 301
Grosz, George, 169
Grothe, Franz, 193
Grümmer, Paul, 193
Gründgens, Gustaf, 189–90, 193
Grynszpan, Herschel, 234–35
Guderian, General Heinz, 253, 294
Gundolf, Friedrich, 20–21, 98
Günthers, Hanns F. K., 10
Gutterer, Leopold, 198

Hadamovsky, Eugen, 204
Haeften, First Lieutenant Werner, 297
Hagen, Lieutenant Dr. Hans, 295, 296
Hague Convention, 242
Hahn, Otto, 291
Halbe, Max, 193
Halder, General Franz, 244, 262, 274
Halifax, Lord, 244
Hamburgische Dramaturgie (Lessing), 188
Hamburg Philharmonic Orchestra, 193
Hamilton, Duke of, 250
Handel-Mazzetti, Enrica von, 182
Hanfstaengl, Ernst "Putzi," 126, 162
Hanke, Karl, 128, 198, 199, 225, 229–30, 231, 232, 321
Hans Westmar (film), 187
Harden, Maximilian, 301
Harlan, Veit, 186
Hartmann, Paul, 189, 193
Harzburg Front, 130–31
Hase, General Paul von, 295, 297
Hauptmann, Gerhart, 67, 183, 186, 192
Hausmann, Manfred, 301
Hegel, Georg Wilhelm Friedrich, 9
Heger, Robert, 193
Heiber, Helmut, 62, 131
Heidegger, Martin, 192
Heidelberg University, 17, 22, 98
Heilmann, Fritz, 193
Heimkehr (film), 186
Heine, Heinrich, 18, 78, 98
Heineman, General, 92
Heinrich Kämpfert (Goebbels), 22
Heisenberg, Werner, 291
Helldorf, Count, 126, 297
Herrenklub, 142, 147
Herrenrasse, 9
Herrenvolk, 9, 282
Herrscher, Der (film), 185–86
Hess, Rudolf, 58, 91, 92, 231, 250, 256; flight to Scotland, 250
Heuss, Theodor, 301
Heydrich, Reinhard, 234, 235, 284–85; death of, 284
Hilpert, Heinz, 190, 191
Himmler, Heinrich, 5, 6, 11, 44, 126, 131–32, 154, 201, 216, 218, 228, 230, 231, 232, 233; expulsion from the party, 320; rapprochement with

Goebbels, 273–74; World War II, 254, 255, 269, 273–74, 296, 297, 307, 317, 321
Hindemith, Paul, 67, 173
Hindenburg, Oskar, 130, 157
Hindenburg, Paul von, 26, 96, 158, 159, 161, 164, 215; death of, 216–17; election of 1932 and, 132–37, 141, 142, 150, 151, 158; meetings with Hitler, 130, 158; senility of, 163
History of Rome (Mommsen), 15
Hitler, Adolf, 20, 29–30, 32, 33, 82, 89, 103, 106, 107, 109, 118, 119, 120, 121, 128 passim, 324, 325; anti-Semitism of, 9–10, 29, 99; appointed Chancellor of the Reich, 158–59; attempted assassination of, 289–99; Baarova affair and, 228, 230–31, 232; Bamberg meeting (1926), 53–55, 61; Berlin speech (1927), 80, 81; Catholic Church and, 35; death of, 322; education of, 16; elections of 1932, 132–59; foreign policy, 238, 275–81; Fuehrer myth, 3–11, 61, 109, 313, 316, 323, 325; Goebbels-Strasser relationship and, 34, 35, 36, 37–44; imprisoned, 28, 30; Kristall-nacht, 233–37; last meeting with Strasser, 152–53; Magda Goebbels and, 123–26; marriage of, 320; meetings with Hindenburg, 130, 158; Munich putsch (1923), 27, 28; oath of allegiance, 217; opinion of German generals, 254–55, 257; oratorical abilities, 82–86; political testament of, 320–22; popularity of, 270; reaction to Goering's telegram (1945), 316–17; Regierungsrat appointment, 134; Reichstag "peace" speech (1933), 214; religious affairs, 165; Sportpalast speech (1928), 112; statement on Goebbels (1927), 92–93; Stennes putsch, 127–29; will power of, 4–5, 41, 139. See also World War II
Hitler-Junge Quex (film), 187
Hitler Youth, 155
Hitz (painter), 169
Hoelscher, Ludwig, 193
Hoepner, Major General Erich, 253, 296, 298
Höfer, Werner, 301
Hoffman, Heinrich, 168
Hofmannsthal, Hugo von, 177
Höfner, Otto Philipp, 301
Hohenzollern family, 102
Höhler, Albrecht, 115, 116, 117
Holland, 243, 250
Höngen, Elisabeth, 193
Hoover, Herbert, 62
Hörbiger, Attilla, 186, 190
Hörbiger, Paul, 190
Horcher's (restaurant), 268
"Horst Wessel Lied," 116, 117, 159, 211
Hotter, Hans, 193
House of German Art, 168
House of the Soldiers' Association, 80
Hoyer, H. O., 82
Hubermann, Bronislaw, 68
Huch, Ricarda, 182, 183, 192
Hugenberg, Alfred, 113, 114, 128, 130, 161, 164, 204; resignation of, 222